SACRAMENTO PUBLIC LIBRARY
828 "I" Street
Sacramento, CA 95814
4/11

FIREBRAND
of LIBERTY

ALSO BY STEPHEN V. ASH

Middle Tennessee Society Transformed, 1860–1870:
War and Peace in the Upper South (1988, 2006)

Messages of the Governors of Tennessee [editor]:
vol. IX, 1907–1921; and vol. X, 1921–1933 (1990)

When the Yankees Came:
Conflict and Chaos in the Occupied South, 1861–1865 (1995, 1999)

Tennesseans and Their History
[with Paul H. Bergeron and Jeanette Keith] (1999)

Secessionists and Other Scoundrels:
Selections from Parson Brownlow's Book [editor] (1999)

A Year in the South: 1865:
The True Story of Four Ordinary People Who Lived Through the Most
Tumultuous Twelve Months in American History (2002, 2004)

Nineteenth-Century America: Essays in Honor of Paul H. Bergeron
[coeditor, with W. Todd Groce] (2005)

FIREBRAND

of LIBERTY

The Story of Two Black Regiments
That Changed the Course
of the Civil War

STEPHEN V. ASH

W. W. NORTON & COMPANY

NEW YORK · LONDON

Copyright © 2008 by Stephen V. Ash

All rights reserved

Printed in the United States of America

First Edition

For information about permission to reproduce selections from this book,
write to Permissions, W. W. Norton & Company, Inc.,
500 Fifth Avenue, New York, NY 10110

For information about special discounts for bulk purchases, please contact
W. W. Norton Special Sales at specialsales@wwnorton.com or 800-233-4830

Manufacturing by The Courier Companies, Inc.
Book design by M. Kristen Bearse
Production manager: Andrew Marasia

Library of Congress Cataloging-in-Publication Data

Ash, Stephen V.
Firebrand of liberty : the story of two Black regiments that changed
the course of the Civil War / Stephen V. Ash. — 1st ed.
p. cm.
Includes bibliographical references and index.
ISBN 978-0-393-06586-2 (hardcover)
1. United States—History—Civil War, 1861–1865—Participation,
African American. 2. United States. Army. South Carolina Volunteers,
1st (1862–1864) 3. United States. Army. South Carolina Volunteers,
2nd (1863–1864) 4. United States—History—Civil War, 1861–1865—
Regimental histories. 5. South Carolina—History—Civil War, 1861–1865—
Regimental histories. 6. Jacksonville (Fla.)—History, Military—
19th century. 7. Florida—History—Civil War, 1861–1865—Campaigns.
8. United States—History—Civil War, 1861–1865—Campaigns.
9. African American soldiers—History—19th century. 10. United States—
Army—African American troops—History—19th century. I. Title.
E540.N3A84 2008
973.7'4150975912—dc22
2008002503

W. W. Norton & Company, Inc.
500 Fifth Avenue, New York, N.Y. 10110
www.wwnorton.com

W. W. Norton & Company Ltd.
Castle House, 75/76 Wells Street, London W1T 3QT

1 2 3 4 5 6 7 8 9 0

TO

OMAR L. ASH, 1921–1980

LAWRENCE M. ASH, 1952–1972

CONTENTS

ACKNOWLEDGMENTS

IT IS A PLEASURE TO ACKNOWLEDGE HERE, however inadequately, the help and encouragement I have received in bringing this book to completion.

At or near the top of every historian's list of those who deserve thanks are librarians and archivists. I have called on many for assistance with this project, and they have invariably responded graciously. I am especially grateful to several at my own institution, the University of Tennessee: Aaron Purcell, Nick Wyman, and Bill Eigelsbach in Special Collections; Anne Bridges, library liaison for history; and the Documents and Microforms staff. I also thank my university for providing not only bountiful library resources but also a professional development leave that sped this book's completion.

I have benefited too from valuable research assistance from a number of other people, especially John Kvach and Cinnamon Brown, history graduate students at the University of Tennessee; Jennie Leland, history graduate student at the University of Maine; John Ulrich, a student at Harvard University; and Karen Needles, of Documents on Wheels, College Park, Maryland.

Several of my friends in the history profession gave generous help that made this a better book. Dan Crofts, Nelson Lankford, and Mark Wetherington read the manuscript and offered insightful suggestions; John Cimprich, Dan Sutherland, Dean Thomas, and Dan Schafer provided very useful leads on sources. My thanks go also to three people outside the history profession who have helped me greatly: Deborah Gershenowitz, adviser and friend; Maria Guarnaschelli, my editor at Norton; and David Miller of the Garamond Agency, who is not only a fine agent but also a fine editor. Among my past and present coworkers in the UT History Department, nine deserve special mention for their friendship and encouragement: Paul Bergeron, Todd Diacon, Dan Feller, Ernie Freeberg, Lorri Glover, Kim Harrison, Catherine Higgs, Sarah Krisko, and Bruce Wheeler.

My family has been an unfailing source of warm affection, strong support, and good company; my deepest thanks go once again to Jeanie, Mom, Ellen, Ginger, Landon, and my cousins. This book is dedicated to two of my kinfolk, my father and brother, who if they had lived long enough would have joined the others in celebrating its publication.

PREFACE

IT WAS, BY ANY RECKONING, a curious military expedition. There was no other like it during the American Civil War; perhaps there has never been another like it. Although shaped by strategy, it was born of idealism and redemptive fervor. Its mission evoked reactions ranging from exultation to horror. It ended in frustration, wrath, and flames.

It began in early March 1863, nine weeks after President Abraham Lincoln issued the Emancipation Proclamation, when two regiments of blue-uniformed black troops, some nine hundred men, boarded transport vessels at a Union-held island off the South Carolina mainland. From there they steamed southward along the Atlantic coast and then up the St. John's River into the heart of northeastern Florida, where they seized the town of Jacksonville. Most of these soldiers had been slaves just a few weeks or months earlier, men who had labored with hoe and plow on the cotton and rice plantations of coastal South Carolina, Georgia, and Florida to enrich their masters. Now, with a very different purpose, they wielded musket and bayonet. The officers commanding these regiments were prominent Northern abolitionists, men of passionate commitment who went to war not only to restore the Union but also to eradicate the scourge of slavery in America and transform the South.

The bold incursion into Confederate territory that these black soldiers and their white officers undertook was no mere raid. It was intended to establish a permanent post in Florida's interior. That post would have a very special mission, to serve as a beacon of freedom, a haven for black fugitives, and a firebrand of liberty that would help ignite the destruction of Southern slavery from within. Those who launched the expedition saw it also as an opportunity to confirm the value of black troops to the Union cause and add to their numbers. They perceived in it too strategic advantages that would help defeat the Rebel armies. Many people, both in and outside the Union military, hoped that the expedition would also secure a proving ground where the reformation of the rebellious and benighted South might begin. Great hopes were invested in this small expedition, and there were those who believed that if successful, it might change the course of the Civil War.

It is one of that war's more obscure episodes. Few historians have written anything substantial about it; there has until now been no book-length study. Many people quite knowledgeable about the war have never heard of the expedition. This neglect is not hard to explain. An operation of small scale in a secondary theater of war, it was dwarfed by the great campaigns in Virginia, Tennessee, and elsewhere in which huge armies clashed and men died by the thousands. But to dismiss it as unworthy of attention is a mistake. What happened along the St. John's River in March 1863 had important consequences that have not, until now, been recognized. It was in fact a pivotal episode of the war.

After three eventful weeks in Florida, during which the black troops fortified Jacksonville and repulsed Confederate counterattacks, fought side by side with white Union troops sent as reinforcements, and roamed up and down the river, liberating slaves, seizing provisions, and striking fear in the hearts of white Floridians while strictly avoiding any physical abuse of civilians, the expedition was abruptly and mysteriously terminated by the Union general commanding that theater of war. The troops returned to South Carolina deeply disappointed, their dream of fatally wounding slavery and redeeming Florida from the enemy frustrated.

What they did not know was that word of their achievements in Florida had already reached the North and had won strong praise among the public and in the Union government and army. This news came at a critical moment. Although emancipation was by now firmly established as Union policy, the use of black troops remained a very limited and highly controversial experiment. When the expeditionary force set out in early March 1863, few black regiments were in service, none had been well tested in combat or occupation duty, serious doubt prevailed that they would fight effectively, white troops regularly cursed them, and a great many Northern civilians opposed the very idea of blacks in uniform. President Lincoln and his advisers would not endorse full-scale recruitment of blacks unless it was certain that such troops would serve well and would be accepted by the Northern public and army. Strong evidence to the contrary at this decisive moment would very likely have swung the balance against black recruitment for good.

The events in Florida, and the reaction to those events among Northerners, told Lincoln what he needed to know. While the expeditionary force was still in Florida, the president gave the order that committed the U.S. Army to the massive enlistment of black troops. By the war's end in 1865 nearly two hundred thousand had served, providing a crucial addition of manpower without which the Union might very well have failed to conquer the Confederacy. Had the black troops suffered disgrace in Florida, had they crumbled in the face of Confederate counterattacks, or clashed with the white troops sent as reinforcements, or abused the civilian population, the whole movement to enlist blacks would very likely have been halted in its tracks, and the Civil War could have had a different outcome. This book explains how and why those two black regiments on the St. John's River in 1863 experienced not disgrace but triumph.

The expedition merits a close look not only because it had momentous consequences but also because it vividly exemplifies the complex web of motives and passions that shaped the events of the war. Idealism and courage were but two of those that brought forth the expedition and affected its course. Prejudice and fear were at work too, as were compassion, vengefulness, patriotism, partisanship, greed, faith, ambition, desire, devotion, and a host of other impulses, noble and ignoble. The expedition was a compelling human drama with a richly colorful cast of characters. Not all were soldiers, and not all were men.

The expedition was more, however, than the sum of its participants. It embodied the highest hopes of millions of Americans in the 1860s and the deepest fears of millions of others. People North and South, white and black, followed news of it intently and either cheered or mourned its outcome according to their vision of America's future. The story of the expedition is therefore not just a tale of what happened along a river in Florida in the spring of 1863 but also a revealing window through which to examine the clashing ideals and passions that sparked the Civil War and shaped its outcome.

The story told in this book is primarily from the Union point of view, particularly that of Colonel Thomas Wentworth Higginson, commander of one of the black regiments. His are by no means the only eyes that see herein, nor is his the only voice that speaks; still, this is far from a comprehensive account of the expedition. Telling the story from every perspective would, I fear, not only sacrifice thematic unity but also over-burden the narrative. Perhaps other historians will someday be inspired to recount the story from other perspectives, for it is surely intriguing and important enough to deserve multiple tellings. Until then I hope readers will be satisfied with this mostly one-sided tale of a remarkable moment of history, when black soldiers and their white officers journeyed deep into enemy country to make war on slavery.

NOTE ON USAGE

IN ORDER TO KEEP FROM JOLTING the reader out of the past and into the present, I have avoided using the neologism "African-American" in this book. Instead, I use terms current in the 1860s, "black" and occasionally "Negro." I use "colored" only when specifically referring to the United States Colored Troops, their official title during the Civil War.

Exaggerated black dialect of the sort that appears in some of the quotations in this book offends many modern-day readers, but it is an unavoidable part of the historical record. Very few Southern blacks in the 1860s were literate. When their speech was recorded, it was almost always by a white person who had his or her own idea of how it should be rendered, an idea shaped by factors besides the speaker's actual pronunciation, syntax, and diction. These factors included the writer's preconceptions and prejudices and the intended reading audience. Thus Southern black speech as rendered by Civil War–era writers varied widely. Here, for example, are three quotations of the spoken words of one black man, a South Carolina soldier named Prince Rivers, each recorded on a different occasion in 1862 or 1863 by a Northern white:

> This is our time. If our fathers had had such a chance as this, we should not have been slaves now. If we do not improve this chance, another one will not come, and our children will be slaves always.

> Every colored man will be a slave, & feel himself a slave until he can *raise him own bale of cotton* and *put him own mark upon it* and say *Dis is mine!*

> Yes, sah; I do call this a good chance, and I tell my people may be it's de *last* chance. Dat's de reason I jine de soldier. I was gettin' big wages in Beaufort, but I'd rather take less, and fight for de United States.

We cannot know for certain how Rivers and other Southern blacks actually spoke, only that they spoke differently in some ways from whites and that those who recorded such speech usually tried in their own way to convey that difference. Educated writers of that era also routinely transcribed the speech of uneducated whites in a distinctive, often grossly exaggerated form. In this book I remain faithful to the historian's creed by quoting the words of everyone, white as well as black, exactly as they are set down in the original source, with the hope that readers, when confronted with a distasteful passage, will appreciate its historical context and suspend their modern sensitivity.

FIREBRAND
of LIBERTY

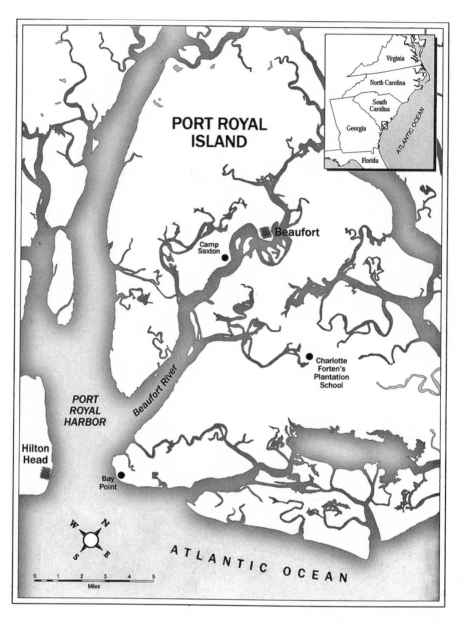

Port Royal area, 1863.
(COURTESY OF UNIVERSITY OF TENNESSEE CARTOGRAPHIC SERVICES LABORATORY)

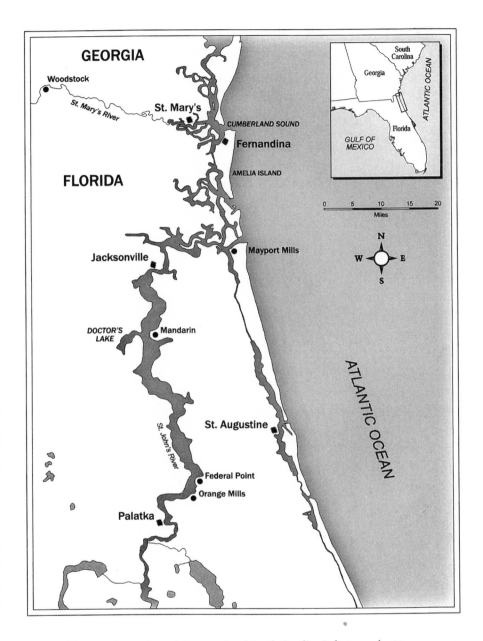

Theater of operations of the 1st and 2nd South Carolina Infantry, early 1863.

(COURTESY OF UNIVERSITY OF TENNESSEE CARTOGRAPHIC SERVICES LABORATORY)

PROLOGUE

THOMAS WENTWORTH HIGGINSON DECLARED WAR on slavery long before his government did. While politicians debated and compromised through the 1840s and 1850s, Higginson did battle. Slavery would not die a natural death, he predicted: "It is destined, as it began in blood, so to end." He welcomed that violent climax.[1]

The institution he waged war against held, by 1860, some four million black people in its grip. Throughout the southern United States they labored for their white masters and prayed for freedom. A lucky few escaped to the free states of the North, but the vast majority toiled away on the farms and plantations of the South with no hope of liberation. They resisted their exploitation in quiet ways, nurturing family and community and spirituality in the slave quarters, laughing at the foibles of their masters behind their backs, feigning illness and clumsiness and stupidity, but few dared challenge the institution openly. Southern whites nevertheless fretted constantly about the slaves, not always believing their own public avowals that slavery as practiced in the American South was benign and that the blacks were content in bondage—unless stirred up by outside agitators.[2]

Those agitators, Higginson among them, increasingly provoked white Southerners in the antebellum decades. Although never more than a small minority of the Northern public, the men and women of the abolitionist movement loudly and relentlessly proclaimed in their newspapers, books, petitions, speeches, and sermons that slavery was a sin and the nation must be cleansed of it. Among the abolitionists most disturbing to the white South were those who were themselves fugitives from slavery, most notably the brilliant and articulate Frederick Douglass of New York, who stood as a living rebuke to those who believed that the black race was inherently inferior and fit for nothing better than slavery.[3]

Whites who relegated the black race to eternal servitude were not to be found solely below the Mason-Dixon line. Many Northern whites scoffed at the abolitionists' insistence on the essential equality of blacks, and most were content to let slavery continue in the South. As the years went by, however, more and more Northerners came to oppose the spread of slavery into the western territories—not only from moral repugnance to human bondage but also from a desire to preserve the West for the free-labor system they believed would foster national greatness: Slaveholding, they thought, stifled progress and created inequality among whites. Too, many Northerners found their consciences pricked by the abolitionists' vivid depictions of the horrors of slavery, most memorably in the pages of Harriet Beecher Stowe's novel *Uncle Tom's Cabin*.[4]

White Southerners felt insulted and threatened by the vehement, often lurid denunciations of their "peculiar institution" that poured from the abolitionist presses and pulpits. Moreover, as their region increasingly lagged behind the North in population and economic power, they worried about slavery's long-term prospects for survival. Reacting forcefully through their representatives in Congress, they banned abolitionist literature from the mail in Southern states and wrung a concession from the North (as part of the Compromise of 1850) that provided federal assistance for slaveholders pursuing their escaped slaves in the North. Whenever the white South flexed its political muscles in congressional debates or national elections or threatened to secede from the Union, other concessions followed. So thoroughly were the interests of slaveholders protected by the federal government that many Northerners swore to the existence of a sinister "Slave Power," a cabal of powerful slaveholders that supposedly dominated the government and aimed to spread slavery throughout the nation.[5]

Higginson watched and contemplated these developments from his home in Massachusetts. Born in 1823 into a family with a proud lineage but no great wealth, he had graduated from Harvard and pursued a career as a Unitarian minister. The years of his youth and early adulthood found New England in a ferment of reformist impulses, and Higginson threw himself into a number of causes: temperance, women's rights, the condition of the industrial working class, and especially abolition. Although thoroughly self-controlled, with nothing of the wild-eyed radical in his demeanor, he championed his causes with a passion and impatience that only burned more hotly as he matured.[6]

From his pulpit Higginson proclaimed in 1848 that he would be "a recreant to humanity" if he "let one Sunday pass in the professed preaching of Christianity, and [left] the name of SLAVERY unmentioned." The next year, having had enough of such tirades, the more conservative of his congregants forced him to resign his post. Undeterred, he turned to writing and lecturing to help sustain himself, found a more congenial Unitarian church in which to preach his message of Christianity and social redemption, and discovered that he had an interested and growing audience for his sermons, essays, and speeches.[7]

Meanwhile he grappled with the problem of abolitionist strategy. The movement was divided. Some abolitionists insisted that only through politics could they accomplish anything. Others, led by William Lloyd Garrison of Boston, held that the compromises inevitable in politics would taint the movement: Abolitionists should renounce office seeking, refrain even from voting, and rely instead on "moral suasion" to convince Northerners and Southerners alike that slavery should be done away with. At one time or another Higginson embraced each of these approaches. He lauded the moral purity of Garrison, but he also ran for Congress (unsuccessfully) in 1850 under the banner of the short-lived Free Soil party. Increasingly, however, he gravitated toward a third alternative, one distasteful to Garrisonians and political abolitionists, disturbing to the Northern public at large, and thoroughly frightening to the white South.[8]

That alternative was violence. "Give me a convention of ten who have drawn the sword for right, and *thrown away the scabbard*," Higginson demanded in 1857, "and I will revolutionize the world." This call to reject both politics and persuasion in favor of violent upheaval increasingly dominated his pronouncements in the 1850s. "I tell you the conflict with Slavery is not a reform[;] it is Revolution." Most of his abolitionist colleagues protested that such militancy was too extreme. To them he replied, "I do not wish to *be* a fanatic—but I have no fear of being called so. There are times and places where . . . it seems that a man can only escape the charge of fanaticism by being a moral iceberg." His growing infatuation with violent change was fueled not only by his moral commitment to ending the enslavement of black people and his belief in a "higher law" than the Constitution but also by his insistence that men must undertake physical, "manly" feats to achieve their full potential.[9]

Higginson's lust to make war on slavery propelled him into a role in events of the 1850s that brought the nation several long steps closer to civil war. The first of these was resistance to the Fugitive Slave Act of 1850. Following its passage, slavery opponents in many Northern cities formed vigilance committees to prevent masters from retrieving their runaways. When the legal maneuvers of these resisters failed, some took the law into their own hands. Among them was Higginson, who in 1854 led a mob in an attack on the well-guarded Boston courthouse, where a fugitive named Anthony Burns was being held to await his return to the South. The attack failed, and Burns was sent back to slavery in Virginia. Higginson, who sustained a saber cut in the assault that left a lifelong scar on his face, was indicted for rioting. He defied the authorities, declaring from the pulpit: "Words are nothing—we have been surfeited with words for twenty years. I am thankful that this time there was action also. . . . Our souls and bodies are both God's and resistance to tyrants is obedience to Him . . . else we miss our proper manly life on earth." The indictment was eventually quashed on a technicality.[10]

Meanwhile a political crisis had erupted over the question of whether the Kansas Territory would be open or closed to slavery. Congress decided in 1854 to leave it up to the settlers. Proslavery Southerners and antislavery Northerners flocked to the territory to win it for their side, and before long they were killing one another. "Bleeding Kansas" now took center stage in the sectional conflict. Higginson, like many other abolitionists, joined an association to aid free-soil settlers. As its agent he purchased and forwarded crates full of revolvers and repeating rifles and ammunition for the settlers. Twice in 1856 he traveled to the territory to bring supplies and encouragement; on the second journey, for the first time in his life, he wore a gun.

Among the abolitionists doing battle in Kansas was a man named John Brown, a visionary whose devotion to the violent overthrow of slavery made Higginson seem moderate by comparison. One of Brown's favorite Bible verses was Hebrews 9:22: "[A]lmost all things are by the law purged with blood; and without shedding of blood is no remission." He quoted it often, invoking its mandate in 1856, when he murdered five unarmed proslavery settlers in cold blood. By the next year he was formulating a grander scheme to assault slavery, and he traveled east to enlist support and raise money. Higginson, drawn by Brown's fervent sense of mission and commitment to manly action, became one of his close allies, a member of the so-called Secret Six who funded Brown's new plan: to ignite a slave insurrection in the South.[11]

Spurred by Brown's audacity and informed by studying the history of slavery, Higginson now endorsed an amendment to abolitionist strategy: The slaves themselves should, indeed must, take a hand in their own liberation. "We white Anglo-Saxons are too apt to assume the whole work is ours," he said in 1858. "I see it otherwise now. Never in history was there an oppressed people who were set free by others." In the slave quarters of the South, he hoped, were "a dagger and a power to use it when the time comes."[12]

When Brown finally put his plan into action, Higginson was exultant. On an October night in 1859, Brown led twenty-one armed followers into the town of Harpers Ferry, Virginia. Their aim was to seize the federal armory there, recruit slaves from the surrounding area, put weapons in their hands, and thus spark a black uprising that would spread across the South and destroy slavery. But to Higginson's deep disappointment, the plot failed miserably. No slaves rose up, and Brown and his men were soon surrounded by Virginia militia and U.S. marines dispatched to the scene. Those conspirators who survived the ensuing shoot-out were captured, Brown among them. Convicted of insurrection by a Virginia court, Brown died on the gallows in December.[13]

White Southerners reacted to the events of the 1850s with alarm and ultimately with panic. The North, it seemed, was determined not just to abet slave runaways and block the South's expansion but to provoke a bloody servile uprising. Never mind that most Northerners condemned abolitionist extremism, especially Brown's plot; to white Southerners it seemed that abolitionists were calling the tune in the North. Many concluded that the South could not be safe in a Union that allowed abolitionism to flourish.[14]

The shock that finally shattered the Union was the 1860 presidential election. Abraham Lincoln of Illinois, a Republican who rejected abolitionism but vowed to halt the spread of slavery, won without a single electoral vote from the slave states. Many white Southerners, foreseeing a nightmarish future in which slavery was under increasing attack and the

South was politically impotent, now embraced secession as a preventive measure. In the weeks after Lincoln's election the seven states of the Deep South, led by South Carolina, left the Union and formed the Confederate States of America. In April 1861, following Lincoln's refusal to give up the U.S. Army's Fort Sumter in Charleston Harbor, Confederate artillery opened fire on the fort and forced its surrender. Lincoln immediately called on the Union states for troops to suppress the Southern "rebellion." Four states of the upper South then joined hands with the Deep South to repel the Northern invaders. And so the war began.[15]

Lincoln and most other Northerners went to war solely to reunite the nation and uphold the Constitution. Secession was illegal, they said, a rejection of democracy and the rule of law, a coup carried out by the Slave Power for its own nefarious purposes. But from the war's very beginning, abolitionists called on their government to make it a war against slavery, arguing that slavery was not only inherently evil but also the root cause of the Southern states' secession. The nation could never be truly united, they said, as long as the institution endured. Higginson himself had been making this argument for years. "Never, never, never," he proclaimed in 1854, "will there be peace in this nation, until Slavery be destroyed." But the Lincoln administration and a large majority of Congress resisted this call, insisting that the threat of emancipation would make reunification more difficult by provoking the Confederates to fight harder for independence. Orders went out to Union commanders in the invaded regions of the South early in the war not to interfere with the relation of master and slave.[16]

As the months passed, however, it became clear that the Rebels were determined to secure their independence no matter how conservative the policy of the U.S. government. Too, a series of stunning Confederate successes on the battlefield persuaded President Lincoln and others that Northern victory would not come easily and that all means must be employed to defeat the Rebels, including depriving them of their slave labor. One by one the Union government enacted measures that struck at slavery. But these measures were hedged about with qualifications that left the status of most of the enslaved people of the Confederate South uncertain.[17]

As the Union government moved hesitantly toward emancipation, Thomas Wentworth Higginson moved hesitantly toward enlistment in the Union cause. For him this was not a simple decision. In the prewar years he had publicly aligned himself with the disunion abolitionists, who favored letting the South leave the Union—indeed tried to provoke the South to leave—in order to free the U.S. government from the pernicious influence of the Slave Power. With the South out of the Union abolitionists could still wage war against slavery, the disunionists argued, and do so even more effectively. By 1861, however, Higginson understood that his nation could never be strong and secure unless the Rebel nation was destroyed.

Although critical of Lincoln's moderation on the slavery issue and skeptical of politics, Higginson had welcomed Lincoln's election, trusting that the radical wing of the Republican party would eventually prevail. The outbreak of war, which meant government-sanctioned violence against the South, cheered him. "I think the world is growing better all the time," was his insouciant response to the news of Fort Sumter. The question for Higginson now was whether he could do the cause of abolition more good by continuing his speaking and writing on the home front (he had given up the ministry in 1857) or by going into military service. Another consideration was his wife, Mary, crippled by rheumatism and incapable of caring for herself. Ultimately Higginson decided that abolitionism must make its presence felt in the Union army and that manly duty trumped family concerns. In 1862 he told an audience, "I will no longer say to you 'go,' but 'come,'" and subsequently enlisted.[18]

In September President Lincoln dispelled the uncertainty over his policy on slavery and confirmed the conflict's new dimension by issuing the preliminary Emancipation Proclamation. In it he announced that on January 1, 1863, he would—as a war measure, to help defeat the Confederacy—declare free all slaves in areas of the South then in rebellion.[19]

One other factor, no less crucial than the Confederacy's military successes and the failure of the conservative policy to coax the Rebels back to the Union, had pushed Lincoln to this culmination: the manifest desire of the South's enslaved men and women to be free and their determined efforts to free themselves. In every Southern region penetrated by the Union army and navy, even early in the war, when the conservative policy had prevailed, slaves slipped away from their masters and stealthily made their way to the Yankees. Their persistence in the face of danger and official discouragement, and their willingness to aid the Union cause, swayed many Northerners previously unsympathetic to the idea of emancipation. Many other Northerners, however, civilians and soldiers, remained fiercely opposed to emancipation. But even if Lincoln's constituents had unanimously endorsed his proclamation, it would not by itself free any slaves beyond the relative few who had come within Union lines. If slavery was to be extinguished, the war must be won, the Rebel nation conquered.[20]

Higginson, commissioned a captain, raised a company of volunteers and set about drilling them and learning the ways of the army at a training camp in Massachusetts. Then, in November 1862, a few weeks before his thirty-ninth birthday, he received a letter offering him command of a regiment of freed slaves being organized on the Union-held Sea Islands of South Carolina. Within days he was on a steamship headed south.

As colonel of the 1st South Carolina Infantry he assumed an enormous burden, as did his troops. Emancipation was controversial enough; the use of black soldiers was far more so. The eyes of the nation would be on Higginson and his men, and they must not falter. But in shouldering this heavy weight of command, Higginson also embraced a spectacular opportunity. Here, in the uniformed ranks of the 1st South Carolina, was the dagger he had envisioned years before. Deftly wielded, it might strike the very heart of slavery.

Chapter One

PORT ROYAL ISLAND, SOUTH CAROLINA

JANUARY 1, 1863

T HEY BEGAN ARRIVING EARLY, not long after daybreak. Some rode on horseback or in buggies, but many more came on foot, trudging along the sandy paths that converged on the camp of the 1st South Carolina Infantry Regiment. Most were black people, the women and girls with their heads wrapped in brightly colored kerchiefs, the men and boys more sedately clothed, but all in their Sunday finest, although it was a Thursday. Many of the women carried infants; some carried baskets of food.[1]

The sun rose in a perfectly cloudless sky. By midmorning it was dazzlingly ablaze, taking the edge off the cold and reflecting brightly off the blue water of the Beaufort River, which flowed southward along the island's east side. Periodically throughout the morning boats, small and large, propelled by oar or sail or steam, pulled up to the landing a quarter mile east of the camp and disgorged passengers. They too were mostly blacks. Three hundred arrived on the steamer *Boston* from Hilton Head, which was twelve miles south at the entrance to Port Royal harbor. The steamer *Flora* brought a thousand from Beaufort and other points upriver. Because there was no wharf and the tide was low, these two big transports had to remain a good distance offshore; rowboats ferried their passengers to the landing. The *Flora* also brought a military band, the fifers and horn players and drummers of the 8th Maine Infantry. They took position near the landing and began playing, spiritedly, if not expertly, to welcome the later arrivals. The soldiers of the 1st South Carolina took position there too, standing quietly in formation as the boats came and went.[2]

By eleven it was nearly time to begin. The band struck up a tune and moved inland from the landing. Behind it came the seven hundred sol-

diers of the 1st South Carolina, marching smartly with shouldered muskets in a column four abreast, clad in their distinctive uniforms of dark
blue coats and scarlet trousers. Their officers marched with them, con-
spicuous not only by their swords and epaulets and sky blue trousers but
also by their white skin. The soldiers were followed by the three thousand
or more civilians who had gathered at the landing.[3]

The procession made its way to a large grove between the landing and
the camp. It covered several acres and had once been the recreation ground
of the wealthy Smith family, whose abandoned plantation manor and slave
cabins were visible nearby. In the middle of the grove stood a platform
constructed for the occasion, on which sat a number of chairs. A large
American flag was on display nearby, stretched between two trees. The
bandsmen mounted the platform. Some of the others in the procession did
so too and took seats. Everyone else assembled before the platform, the soldiers grouped by companies but sitting or standing informally, the civilians filling in the spaces among them, likewise sitting or standing as they
preferred. Around the periphery of the crowd stood some of the junior
officers of the regiment and a few mounted officers from other units who
had ridden over to see the ceremony.[4]

The grove consisted of live oaks, massive, shiny-leafed evergreens
laden with long strands of wispy Spanish moss. Here and there the sun
penetrated the foliage, dappling the ground. The smell of barbecued beef
pervaded the air, wafting from charcoal-lined pits nearby, where ten spit-
ted ox carcasses were roasting. The scene struck some of those present as
more summery than wintry.[5]

Those gathered on the ground looked expectantly toward the platform.
Seated there were not only the speakers for today's event but also a number of specially invited guests, most of them women. A newspaper correspondent in the crowd noted that there was not one black person on the
platform.[6]

Among those seated, gazing back at the crowd, was Thomas Wentworth Higginson, the 1st South Carolina's commander. He was a relative
newcomer to the Sea Islands, having arrived near the end of November.
The insignia on his dress coat announced his military rank, but as many
of those present in the grove were aware, his colonelcy was only a faint
indication of his stature in the wider world. His appointment as regimental commander had been much talked about on the islands and in the

Col. Thos. Wentworth Higginson
1st S.C.Vols
1862

Thomas Wentworth Higginson.
(FROM *THE OUTLOOK*, 59 [1898])

North. That appointment would by itself have guaranteed him a place among today's speakers, but his prominence in the abolitionist movement made his appearance on the platform especially meaningful.[7]

Although he had been here less than six weeks, Higginson was well informed about the events in this theater of war leading up to this moment. In the fall of 1861, when the war was still young, a huge Union amphibious force of naval warships, transports, and army troops had sailed south along the Atlantic coast and dropped anchor off Hilton Head. Its mission was to seize Port Royal Harbor, the finest deepwater port in the region, to use as a coaling and supply station for the Union naval vessels blockading the Confederacy's south Atlantic coast. The Confederate defense proved feeble. On November 7 the warships blasted into submission the forts guarding the entrance to the harbor, and the soldiers quickly occupied the forts and points on the neighboring islands. In time the Union army extended its control to a number of the other Sea Islands, which hugged the mainland of South Carolina, Georgia, and northeastern Florida. Now, as 1863 began, the Union troops in this region (denominated the army's Department of the South) numbered some fourteen thousand, and the navy posted dozens of warships there as part of its South Atlantic Blockading Squadron. As a theater of war the region was overshadowed by Virginia and Tennessee and the Mississippi River, but it was not unimportant. The Union forces there maintained the blockade and threatened the key Confederate cities of Charleston and Savannah, which were, respectively, fewer than sixty miles northeast and thirty miles southwest of Port Royal Harbor.[8]

Although Union strategists regarded the south Atlantic coast as a secondary theater, right now they would have rejoiced at any new military success there, for nearly everywhere else the war was going badly. In northern Virginia the Rebel army of Robert E. Lee had in mid-December soundly defeated the Union Army of the Potomac; Fredericksburg was thus added to the lengthy list of Virginia battlefields on which the Yankees had been whipped. Along the Mississippi River, Union General Ulysses S. Grant's attempt to capture the Confederate citadel of Vicksburg had been thwarted in late December by Rebel cavalry raids on his supply lines. In Middle Tennessee, a Northern army and a Southern army were at this moment mauling each other in a bloody battle along Stones River whose outcome was uncertain; a Rebel victory would deny the Yankees control of that strategically crucial region. The Confederates had suffered reverses in this war, to be sure, but so far they were defending their independence quite convincingly. Across the North, as Christmas 1862 came and went and the new year dawned, there was frustration, anxiety, and war-weariness.[9]

The seizure of the Sea Islands was gratifying to the Union high command, but further successes along the south Atlantic coast seemed unlikely anytime soon. The warships of the navy's blockading squadron managed to seal off most of the coastline of South Carolina, Georgia, and northeastern Florida, but blockade-runners continued to slip in and out of Savannah and Charleston, bringing in vital foreign supplies for the Rebel war effort and carrying away cotton in payment. The squadron's commander argued that he needed more ships to enforce the blockade thoroughly, as was true; but blockade-running through the two cities would never be completely eliminated until they were captured by the Union army. The Department of the South was, however, in no shape for offensive operations. For one thing, it was plagued by a chronic shortage of troops, for the high command generally forwarded available reinforcements to theaters deemed more important. No immediate movement against Charleston or Savannah was contemplated at this time; the army was content simply to hold the Sea Islands and protect the navy's bases there. The frequent turnover in departmental command was another problem. The last commander, the fourth since the department was created, had died of yellow fever in the fall, and his successor had not yet arrived. In any event, no matter who commanded the Department of the South it seemed that his strategic vision never amounted to anything more than ensuring the success of the navy's blockade. But some who pondered strategy, Higginson among them, wondered if something more might be accomplished along the south Atlantic coast, some daring and imaginative stroke that would deal the Rebels a truly grievous blow.[10]

The inertia in the Department of the South was aggravated by the distracting issue of contrabands. No sooner had the army and navy secured this enclave in 1861 than they encountered an unforeseen problem. The Sea Islands and the adjoining stretches of mainland were among the richest agricultural areas of the South. There, on large plantations, slaves labored in great numbers producing rice and long-staple cotton. At every point seized or threatened by the Yankee ships and troops, plantation owners abandoned their homes and fled inland, taking what possessions they could. They did not succeed in removing all their slaves, many of whom took advantage of the confusion to slip away and hide, reemerging only after their masters had departed. Thousands were on hand to greet the Union soldiers and sailors as they occupied the Sea Islands. As time passed, many more, runaways from the mainland, came in. Some had slogged for days or even weeks through swamps, famished and thirsty, barely outpacing pursuers with bloodhounds, narrowly dodging Confederate army patrols and pickets, frantically paddling stolen canoes or makeshift rafts to reach Union gunboats or cross over to the occupied islands.[11]

By the end of 1862 the Department of the South harbored some eighteen thousand black people. What to do about them had perplexed the Union authorities from the first day of occupation as much as any military problem they faced. In fact black fugitives confronted the Yankee occupiers with this question in every invaded section of the Confederacy. Puzzling over how to deal with these anomalous masterless slaves, an issue unprecedented in American history, Northerners had had to invent a name for them. They settled on "contrabands," derived from "contraband of war," which is what one Union general had labeled them in 1861 to justify not returning them to their Rebel masters. As of today their legal status was no longer in doubt, but other questions about them remained unresolved. "Contrabands" would stick as a handy name for the Southern blacks who came within Union lines, a term employed by whites and blacks alike.[12]

Higginson glanced at his pocket watch as the ceremony began. It was eleven-thirty. Chaplain James H. Fowler of the 1st South Carolina rose from his chair and opened the proceedings with a prayer, which was followed by a few moments of solemn music from the band. Higginson then stood up to introduce the first speaker, William Henry Brisbane.[13]

In his cultured Boston voice, Higginson lauded Brisbane as a remarkable man of conscience. He was a native South Carolinian, a former planter who had owned thirty-three slaves. Preparing to move to the North in 1835, he had sold them. Later, having converted to abolitionism while living in the North, he was overwhelmed with guilt. He traveled back to South Carolina, repurchased those of his former slaves he could locate, and freed them. Now he was again in his native state as an agent of the U.S. Treasury Department. He was here on the platform to read the preliminary Emancipation Proclamation, a final version of which President Abraham Lincoln was to sign today in Washington. Higginson remarked on the appropriateness of having the proclamation read "by a South Carolinian to South Carolinians." The crowd cheered.[14]

While the meaning of the proclamation was revolutionary, its text was disappointing. It was a stilted, passionless, necessarily legalistic document that betrayed nothing of the president's profound hatred of slavery or his rhetorical brilliance: "I, Abraham Lincoln, . . . do hereby proclaim and declare. . . . And I do hereby enjoin upon and order. . . . In witness whereof, I have hereunto set my hand," and so forth. Nevertheless, Brisbane was nearly overcome by emotion as he read it. At several points he was interrupted by more hurrahs, especially when he spoke the words "shall be then, thenceforward, and forever, free." When he concluded, a young lieutenant of the 1st South Carolina, Quartermaster Luther Bingham, called for three cheers for the president, which were delivered enthusiastically.[15]

Higginson cheered with the rest. None of the whites in attendance was more gratified than he by the president's action, and none had fought harder in the long struggle to eradicate slavery. This day being honored in Smith's grove was for him a truly glorious moment. It was far more glorious, of course, for the black men and women assembled before the platform; their cheers celebrated their personal deliverance from bondage. Yet their elation was tempered, as was that of the cheering whites, by their recognition that the struggle to end slavery was far from over. Within the Rebel lines millions of other black people still labored for their masters, suffered under the lash, and dreamed of freedom.

On the platform in the grove, William Brisbane was not yet finished. His other task was to read the proclamation of Military Governor Rufus Saxton that had heralded the grand ceremony now under way. Issued six days earlier and headed "A Happy New Year's Greeting to the Colored

People in the Department of the South," it was a stirring pronouncement better suited to the occasion than the one just read:

> In accordance, as I believe, with the will of our Heavenly Father, and by direction of your great and good friend, whose name you are all familiar with, Abraham Lincoln, President of the United States, and Commander-in-chief of the Army and Navy, on the first day of January, 1863, you will be declared "forever free."
>
> When in the course of human events there comes a day which is destined to be an everlasting beacon-light, marking a joyful era in the progress of a nation and the hopes of a people, it seems to be fitting the occasion that it should not pass unnoticed by those whose hopes it comes to brighten and to bless. Such a day to you is January 1st, 1863. I, therefore, call upon all the colored people in this Department to assemble on that day at the head quarters of the First Regiment of South Carolina Volunteers, there to hear the President's Proclamation read, and to indulge in such other manifestations of joy as may be called forth by the occasion.
>
> It is your duty to carry this good news to your brethren who are still in slavery. Let all your voices, like merry bells, join loud and clear in the grand chorus of liberty—"We are free," "We are free,"—until, listening, you shall hear its echoes coming back from every cabin in the land—"We are free," "We are free."

The audience responded with twelve deafening hurrahs.[16]

The next speaker evoked a less exuberant response. John C. Zachos stepped forward to read an ode he had composed for this occasion. It began

> *Ye sons of burning Afric's soil,*
> *Lift up your hands of hardened toil;*
> *Your shouts from every hill recoil—*
> *To-day you are free!*

and went on in a similar vein for nine more stanzas. Following the reading, the ode was sung (to the tune of "Scots wha' ha' wi' Wallace bled") by those seated on the platform, who had been provided with printed copies.[17]

Higginson perhaps suspected that the blacks' muted response to Zachos

Contrabands in the former Smith plantation slave quarters, 1862.
(COURTESY OF LIBRARY OF CONGRESS)

had to do not only with the stiffness of his verse but also with his position
as a plantation superintendent. From the earliest days of occupation on
the Sea Islands, the contrabands and the federal authorities had engaged
in a tug-of-war over the question of labor. The authorities sought to put
the blacks to work on the abandoned plantations, paying them wages to
grow cotton while instructing them in the ways of free labor and laissez-
faire capitalism. The blacks, or most of them, were willing to work on the
plantations—many in fact had continued working on their home plantations after their masters fled—but they insisted on certain prerogatives
that they had been accustomed to all their lives and that were intrinsic to
the distinctive system of slave labor that prevailed on the islands and the
adjoining stretches of mainland. They wanted to work at assigned daily
tasks on their own rather than labor in gangs from sunup to sundown
under the eye of an overseer, and they wanted free time to cultivate their
own gardens and raise their own livestock and poultry. Moreover, they
now balked at cotton cultivation, which in their view only enriched oth-

ers. Had they been able to choose their livelihood without coercion, it would have been a kind of peasant self-sufficiency, raising corn and sweet potatoes and green vegetables and animals on small plots of land they could call their own. By early 1863 a rough compromise had been worked out on the occupied islands, giving the blacks a measure of independence and self-sufficiency while still requiring them to work for wages growing cotton on the plantations, which were managed by Northern civilian superintendents under War Department aegis. But the tug-of-war went on, with laborers and superintendents frequently exasperating each other.[18]

Nor was this the only source of racial friction on the occupied Sea Islands. As early as March 1862 Northern missionary preachers and teachers had begun arriving there to work among the contrabands. Sponsored by philanthropic societies and drawn south by the opportunity to give substance to their humanitarian impulse and abolitionist fervor, they were more or less welcomed by the federal authorities, who were struggling with the contraband problem. They were dubbed Gideon's Band, or Gideonites, and many were women; these were the women seated on the platform in the grove this day.[19]

The Gideonites' sincere sympathy for the victims of slavery had a strong streak of paternalism. To them the blacks seemed childlike, uncouth, licentious, superstitious, and badly in need of the guiding hand of respectable middle-class Northerners like themselves. In the schools and churches they conducted on the plantations they taught not only the three Rs and Bible lessons but also Yankee morality and comportment. The blacks, for their part, embraced the Gideonites with one arm and repelled them with the other. They were eager to learn to read and write, and children and adults alike flocked to the teachers' classrooms. But they were skeptical of the didactic instruction. Among other things, the blacks resented attempts to tame their emotional, uninhibited style of worship, which was marked by fervent singing and shouting and rhythmic movement; they wanted no lectures on how to praise God.[20]

The behavior of some of the Union troops in the department was a source of friction too. The political division in the North over the Emancipation Proclamation was replicated in the army. Officers and men ran the gamut from radical Republican to conservative Democrat; almost all were racist to some extent, but the Democrats were vehemently Negrophobic and opposed to abolishing slavery. Blacks came in contact with white soldiers all the time, not only on the plantations but also at Hilton Head, Beaufort, and other locations where thousands labored for the army as teamsters, dockworkers, cooks, and the like. Wherever contrabands encountered soldiers, they frequently endured insult and humiliation and at times robbery and physical assault. Most bore it quietly, but all resented it. The contempt of the more conservative soldiers extended to those who came south to help the blacks—the "Gids," as they derisively called them.[21]

There was ill feeling among the blacks too over the attempt by the department commander some months earlier to conscript all the able-bodied men into a militia unit. When some resisted, the army resorted to arresting them at gunpoint or trapping them by ruses, such as luring them to a Fourth of July celebration where they were forcibly detained. The conscription was eventually halted and the unit disbanded, but fear of another such attempt, and a general distrust of the army, lingered among many blacks. These concerns kept attendance down on this day in Smith's grove. General Saxton and others had gone around in the preceding days encouraging blacks to come to the ceremony, assuring them they would not be molested and offering free boat transportation. Saxton anticipated that five thousand would attend; a little more than half that number actually did so. As Colonel Higginson looked around the crowd in front of the platform, he noticed that almost all the black civilians were women or children or older men.[22]

Race relations on the occupied islands were not, however, all rancor and conflict. Many of the contrabands felt grateful to the Yankees, especially now that their freedom was ensured. Even those—and there were many—who ascribed their deliverance to God were ready to acknowledge the Yankees as His agent. Most had a kind of abstract gratitude to the U.S. government and a more definite gratitude to certain representatives of that government whom they encountered on the islands. While some white soldiers detested and abused them, others extended a hand in friendship. Some of these were lifelong abolitionists; others were men whose sympathy had been sparked by what they had seen and heard of slavery since coming to the islands: the whipping posts on the plantations; the hideous scars on black backs; the heartrending stories of slave families separated by sale. Many of the blacks were grateful as well to the

Gideonites, whose selflessness and compassion they appreciated despite their patronizing and moralizing; relations between the two were in many cases warm, even affectionate.[23]

What the future held for the black people on the occupied islands neither they nor anyone else could predict with certainty. Even if their freedom was now assured, that of their loved ones still within Confederate lines was not. The war must be won. And even with the Union victorious and slavery destroyed there would remain not only the issue of labor but also that of racial equality, an issue starkly underscored by the dearth of black faces on the platform in Smith's grove.

Next to step forward on the platform was the Reverend Mansfield French, a missionary from New York who had been laboring in the vineyard of the Sea Islands for many months. He bore a large, elegant silk flag on a staff, a gift to Higginson's regiment from a New York City church. Gold-colored tassels fringed the flag, which bore the words "To the First Regiment of South Carolina Volunteers. The Year of Jubilee Has Come."[24]

French gave an impassioned speech, to which Higginson listened politely although he detested the minister's pomposity and his tendency to draw attention to himself whatever the occasion. French then formally presented the standard to Higginson, who took hold of it, waved it before the crowd, then stood it beside him and started to give the acceptance address he had prepared. He had not yet uttered the first word, however, when a voice rose in song from amid the multitude before him. He could not pick out the singer, but the voice seemed to be that of an older black man:

> My Country, 'tis of thee,
> Sweet land of liberty,
> Of thee I sing.

Instantly the voice was joined by those of two black women and then more and more black voices. Higginson abruptly fell silent and stood staring at the crowd, perplexed. This was not part of the program. It was altogether spontaneous and all the more astonishing to the whites in attendance because few had ever before heard blacks on the Sea Islands sing the anthem.[25]

With each line of the song, more black voices joined the chorus, which swelled in volume and emotional intensity. Soon hundreds were singing. The scene was one of the most moving Higginson had ever witnessed. "It made all other words cheap," he thought; "it seemed the choked voice of a race at last unloosed." Behind him he heard some of those seated on the platform start to join in; quickly he turned and motioned to them to stop, saying, "Leave it to them."[26]

As the singers' voices faded at the end of the last stanza, thunderous applause erupted from the crowd. Many people were in tears. When Higginson resumed speaking, he began by saying that what they had just heard was far more effective than any speech he might make. Until this day, he noted, the black people here assembled "never could have truly sung 'my country.'" Inspired by what he had just experienced, he went on to speak for half an hour. Many of his listeners were spellbound.[27]

His speech concluded, Higginson summoned to the platform two of his soldiers, the regiment's color-bearers, Sergeant Prince Rivers and Corporal Robert Sutton. Turning to Rivers, Higginson handed him the new silk flag and solemnly charged him with defending it to the death. Looking him directly in the eye, he said, "Do you understand?"; the sergeant replied emphatically, "Yes, sir!" Turning to Sutton, Higginson handed him the regiment's bunting flag and elicited the same pledge. Then he stepped back, folded his arms, and listened as the two men addressed the crowd.[28]

To repeated cheers and applause, especially from his fellow soldiers, Rivers reiterated his vow to die rather than surrender the flag and expressed his desire to "show it to all the old masters." Sutton too evoked a fervent response, urging his comrades to march the flag all the way to Richmond and show it to the Rebel president Jefferson Davis, to persevere until all those still in bondage were freed, and to serve above all their "Great Captain, Jesus, who never was defeated."[29]

When Rivers and Sutton had finished, Higginson called on Quartermaster Bingham, who had the best singing voice among the officers, to lead the regiment in a chorus of "Marching Along." By now it was one-thirty, but still the ceremony went on. Rufus Saxton came forward. He was much loved by the blacks, who fondly dubbed him General Saxby. He spoke briefly and simply, alluding to the regimental flags and expressing hope that a day would come when there were so many black Union regiments in the field that their flags would overshadow the whole South.[30]

His listeners, especially the men of the 1st South Carolina, clapped and cheered. No one present had done more than he to create this unit, which consisted of volunteers from among the contrabands in the department; the regiment's post was named Camp Saxton in his honor. The blue- and red-uniformed men hurrahing before him were testimony of his perseverance in the face of strong opposition. But the notion of raising and employing black troops in the Union cause remained controversial, the number of such troops remained very small, and their value remained unproved. Saxton was determined that this great experiment would succeed, and so were the men who cheered him.[31]

As he resumed his seat on the platform, a woman rose from another chair and stood before the crowd. Her name was Frances D. Gage, and she was one of the Gideonites. Her presence undoubtedly struck most of those in attendance as remarkable; it was highly unusual for a woman to address a public gathering. Many would have been further surprised to learn that besides teaching she was employed as a newspaper correspondent. Her reports on affairs in the Department of the South appeared regularly in the New York *Tribune*, signed "F. D. G."[32]

Even more extraordinary were the words she proceeded to speak on the platform, for she issued a summons to insurrection that made the previous speakers' rhetoric seem reserved by comparison. Indeed, she echoed the startling call to arms that John Brown and Higginson had addressed to the South's slaves before the war. She had once visited the Danish West Indies, she said, and had come away deeply impressed by the story of how the plantation slaves there had risen up en masse in 1848, confronted the ruling class, and won their freedom. Those still enslaved on Southern plantations could do the same, she declared. They could liberate themselves and bring down the Confederacy in a single day if only they realized their power. Her own sons were in the Union army, and she was willing to sacrifice them for the cause of freedom if necessary; she hoped that the black people gathered before her were just as willing to sacrifice for that cause.[33]

A man in civilian clothes succeeded Gage on the platform. He was unfamiliar to most of those in attendance, including Higginson; "Judge somebody" was all the colonel knew. He turned out to be another Treasury agent, one Lyman D. Stickney, but why he had been invited to address the crowd was something of a mystery. He was well spoken, however; he had clearly spent some time preparing his remarks, and the sentiments he expressed were certainly in harmony with the spirit of the occasion. He directed them especially to the soldiers in the audience: "Liberty, though of slow growth, is a plant indigenous to all climes, and like the gospel which redeems us from the primal curse of man's first disobedience, is adapted to every class and condition of men. Education, however, is indispensable to the enjoyment of rational liberty. You, of the First regiment of South Carolina volunteers, are now in a school, the best suited of all others to prepare you for the high destiny of your future. . . . Here, beneath the folds of that flag . . . you begin your career as citizens of the United States."[34]

There were but two more items on the program. Henry G. Judd, a general superintendent of plantations, joined three other men in singing an ode he had composed for the ceremony. Entitled "January 1, 1863," it began:

> This day is the birth-time of millions!
> The dawn of the year sixty-three
> Will be marked on the dial of ages,
> The hour when a RACE became free![35]

The finale was a rousing one. Audience and speakers and platform guests joined in singing a song they all knew by heart. Everyone called it simply the John Brown song:

> John Brown's body lies a-mouldering in the grave . . .
> But his soul goes marching on!

Higginson then brought the proceedings to a close with a few remarks. It was two-thirty. The ceremony had lasted three hours.[36]

The blacks, both civilians and soldiers, proceeded to a site nearby where rough tables had been constructed. For the next hour and a half they feasted on the ten roast oxen, mountains of hard bread covered with molasses, and three hundred gallons of a specially prepared beverage that they liked, consisting of water sweetened with molasses and flavored with ginger and vinegar. To this food and drink, provided at government expense by order of General Saxton, were added the contents of the

Dress parade of a black infantry regiment (not the 1st South Carolina) on the Camp Saxton parade ground, 1864; Smith plantation buildings visible in the right background.
(COURTESY OF LIBRARY OF CONGRESS)

baskets that many of the attendees had brought. The dinner was for the blacks only; the whites were not invited.[37]

Around four o'clock people began departing, some tramping home on the sandy paths they had followed that morning, others heading down to the landing where the *Flora* and *Boston* and smaller vessels waited to return them to Beaufort or Hilton Head or other points on the islands. The soldiers of the 1st South Carolina then donned their accoutrements, straightened their caps and clothing, took up their bayoneted muskets, and assembled in a long double line in preparation for their dress parade, which some of the civilians stayed to watch. Higginson positioned himself before his men and began shouting orders in a crisp, clear voice, putting the regiment through the routine evolutions and manual of arms. He watched the men perform, as always, with a sense of pride. They were superb on the parade ground.[38]

As the sun neared the horizon, he halted the troops and then dismissed them. They broke ranks and ambled back to their camp. Higginson headed in the same direction. He had been invited to a reception that General Saxton was hosting at his headquarters in Beaufort that evening but had declined. He preferred to stay close to camp as much as possible;

he had not in fact visited Beaufort since the day of his arrival on Port Royal Island, though it was only a few miles away.[39]

He walked to the camp and entered his tent. It was roomy as military accommodations went, consisting of two nine-by-nine-foot wall tents joined together, one side serving as an office and the other as a bedroom. But the furnishings were meager. In the office, which he shared during the day with his adjutant, were a secretary and chair, a crude settee taken from an abandoned church nearby, and a stool cobbled together from scraps of wood and cane. In the bedroom were a couch made of empty wooden boxes covered with worn army blankets, another settee from the church, and a narrow bed. But the place was as homelike as he could make it: The floor was boarded; a wreath of orange boughs hung on one canvas wall; a copy of Les Misérables lay on the secretary. There was also a little makeshift wood-burning stove for heat. It was nothing more than a long tin flue, widened at the bottom and resting on a box of sand, its top poking out of the tent. He had nicknamed it Fever & Ague, for it seemed to keep the place always either too hot or too cold.[40]

He sat in his tent through the evening, reading some mail that had just arrived. He carried on a voluminous correspondence, not all of it military or familial, for he remained as active as he could in his reformist causes and his literary career. While he had earned a reputation as a reformer as early as the 1840s, only in the late 1850s had he emerged as a respected man of letters. Inspired by the Transcendentalists' call for a truly original American literature, independent of English models, he had begun in his early adult years by writing poetry but eventually recognized that he had no great gift for that. His forte proved to be the essay. He published in Putnam's Monthly Magazine and the North American Review and became a regular contributor to the Atlantic Monthly after its founding in 1857. He had not reached the top rank of American writers, but now, at age thirty-nine, he was well established in the second rank, known and respected among the North's serious reading public. His many friends in literary circles included some of the exalted elders: Henry Wadsworth Longfellow, John Greenleaf Whittier, Ralph Waldo Emerson.[41]

Among his numerous literary correspondents was an unusual woman some years younger than he who lived in Amherst, Massachusetts. She had first written to him in April 1862 in response to his recent article in the Atlantic Monthly proffering advice to aspiring writers. She approached him timidly in her letter, asking his opinion of some poems she enclosed: "Mr. Higginson,—Are you too deeply occupied to say if my verse is alive?" He was immediately struck by their freshness and profundity and became intrigued by this unknown talent who had created them. He wrote her back, she sent more poems, and they continued to exchange letters after his enlistment. Her name was Emily Dickinson.[42]

Like the one that prompted Dickinson to write him, most of Higginson's essays were unconnected to his reformist passions; he wrote of literature, history, nature, travel, and so forth, for these popular topics were his bread and butter. But he did devote a good number of essays to his causes: abolitionism, primarily, but also women's rights. He was far in advance of most male reformers in advocating women's legal and political equality. In an 1859 essay sardonically titled "Ought Women to Learn the Alphabet?" he drew the line as uncompromisingly as he did on the issue of black rights: "Woman must be a subject or an equal: there is no middle ground." Another of his passions, promoted in such essays as "Saints and Their Bodies," was physical fitness, a cause in which he found himself practically alone and well ahead of his time. He feared that the North's rapid urbanization was producing a generation of men and women unused to strenuous labor and thus increasingly weak and sickly. Men in particular, he believed, should cultivate "solid strength" through exercise—he recommended hiking, swimming, ice skating, and gymnastics—the better to accomplish the manly deeds demanded of them.[43]

Higginson also took time this evening, after reading his mail, to write a long entry in his journal describing the day's events. Once the sun disappeared the air grew chilly, and periodically he stoked his little heating stove. Sometime after dark he took a break and walked over to the tent of Chaplain Fowler. He found that the chaplain had visitors. Among them was a very pretty young woman named Charlotte Forten, whom Higginson had met that morning. A genteel and well-educated Philadelphian, she was one of Gideon's Band. She taught school at a plantation on St. Helena Island and had been among the invited guests on the platform during the ceremony. Her skin was so light that some who saw her did not realize she was a Negro; she was, in the common parlance, a "quadroon." Also in the chaplain's tent was the regiment's chief surgeon, Dr. Seth Rogers, who had known Charlotte Forten since before the war and with whom she had had a joyful reunion today.[44]

The group sat talking for a while, warming themselves around the chaplain's homemade fireplace. Higginson was, as usual, good company, genial and witty, although at times he just sat quietly, looking tired and careworn. At one point he remarked with dry humor that army service gave one a new perspective: He had, the day before, ordered the ten whole oxen prepared as blithely as he might have ordered a couple of pounds of beef from the butcher for his family dinner back home. Charlotte Forten said little; she was normally at ease in company but found herself abashed in the presence of Thomas Wentworth Higginson.[45]

The colonel left after a time and again settled into his tent by himself. From nearby came the voices of his soldiers and the smell of tobacco smoke. He had given the men permission, on this great occasion, to stay up as late as they liked in celebration, so tonight there would be no taps. And he had issued a special ration of tobacco, which the men regarded as a great treat. Campfires blazed here and there among the soldiers' tents. The men huddled around them, many of them engaged in fervent prayer meetings. The sky remained clear, and the moonlight was strong enough to keep the darkness at bay even without the fires.[46]

Higginson loved being around his men when they were off duty like this. He was fascinated by the stories they told and the songs they sang and the prayers they offered and by their accents and expressions, so earthy and exotic to his cultured New England ear. As he listened tonight, he reflected on what this day meant to them. He thought of the greeting he had had from one of them early that morning. The soldier had sought him out to say, "I tink myself happy, dis New Year's Day, for salute my own Cunnel. Dis day las year I was servant to a Cunnel of Secesh; but now I hab de privilege for salute my own Cunnel."[47]

Higginson finished his reading and writing and retired to his bed. As he fell asleep, he could still hear the prayers, songs, shouts, and laughter of his men. The voices grew hoarse as the night wore on, but the camp was still alive with their sound when the morning sun illuminated the white canvas of the tents.[48]

Chapter Two

PORT ROYAL ISLAND AND THE
ST. MARY'S RIVER

JANUARY 2–FEBRUARY 15

C AMP SAXTON AND ITS adjoining parade ground lay on a flat, tree-less expanse of land within sight of the river. A year and a half ear-lier this land had been lush with ripening cotton cultivated by the Smith family's slaves. Among the few reminders of the once-mighty Smiths vis-ible now, besides their abandoned manor, were the plantation hogs that rooted through the live oak grove and the nearby pine thickets and cypress swamps. These hogs, now as free as the Smiths' slaves, were notorious for occasionally wandering onto the parade ground during the 1st South Car-olina's dress parades, which to Colonel Higginson's mind rather spoiled the dignity of the occasion. The other inconvenience of the parade ground was the dust. Unless settled by a rain shower, it rose in clouds during drill and parade, choking men and officers and obscuring Higginson's view of the assembled regiment.[1]

Whatever the drawbacks of the parade ground, the camp was attrac-tive—not only by military standards but also in the opinion of its many civilian visitors. It was laid out with strict regularity, the men's tents lined up in neat parallel rows forming a succession of company streets, the offi-cers' tents in a row at one end of the camp, perpendicular to the streets. By Higginson's order, the camp was swept clean every day.[2]

The officers lived in wall tents. The privates and noncommissioned officers lived in simple A-tents, each covering a space about seven by eight feet; four were assigned to each tent, making for snug sleeping arrange-ments. The men had been supplied with planed lumber for flooring their tents, and they had gathered moss to place on the floors as a sort of mat-tress, over which they laid their rubber blankets. On this they slept, cov-ered by their wool blankets. In cold weather they closed up the ends of the tents with canvas flies. Although they had no fireplaces or stoves as their officers did, they could sleep warmly even on the coldest Sea Island nights.[3]

A well dug by the men provided water for the regiment; they also dug pits for latrines. Each of the regiment's ten companies had a wooden cookhouse, where food was prepared over an open fire. Another wooden structure was used as the guardhouse. The upper floor of the Smiths' ginhouse was now the regiment's hospital. Certain other features of the camp struck visitors as picturesque. Some of the companies had built dining halls next to their cookhouses; these consisted of a wooden frame covered with palmetto fronds. Most remarkable was the great circular tent dubbed the Pagoda, built under Chaplain Fowler's direction to serve as both church and school. It was thirty feet in diameter, with ten-foot poles supporting it around the circumference and a taller one in the center that raised the roof to a point. The roof consisted of discarded tents and sails stitched together. The Pagoda could shelter two hundred men; it reminded Higginson of a circus tent. It never sat empty for very long, for the soldiers of the 1st South Carolina were nearly as enthusiastic about learning to read and write as they were about worshiping the Lord.[4]

Higginson spent much of January 2 in his tent, writing. The paperwork required to maintain the regiment was enormous. Whenever he was immersed in it, he thought of his former commanding officer in Massachusetts, who had joked that for every regiment the Union army enlisted to fight the Rebels it ought to enlist another just to fill out the necessary forms and write reports. But Higginson's writing today was not all official. He composed a long letter to his wife, Mary, describing yesterday's grand ceremony. He wrote Mary as often as he could, still troubled by guilt about leaving her to go to war. Crippled by rheumatism, she was unable to care for herself, and he had had to entrust her to a relative. After finishing the letter to Mary, he wrote a shorter one to his mother.[5]

In his letters home, Higginson regularly recounted his progress in organizing and recruiting and drilling the regiment. He was proud of what he had accomplished since assuming command on November 24.

Among the first things he had done after arriving was learn something of the regiment's history. The genesis of the 1st South Carolina predated his arrival by many months. In early April 1862 the commander of the Department of the South, Major General David Hunter, had boldly requested permission from the War Department to strengthen his weak force by raising fifty thousand troops from among the blacks in his jurisdiction. Hunter, one of the very few high-ranking Union officers who was an abolitionist, was well aware that this would be regarded as a radical proposition; although the U.S. Navy enlisted blacks as sailors, no black man was permitted to wear an army uniform. He knew too that his proposal had serious political as well as military implications, for at that point the Lincoln administration was still proceeding cautiously in the matter of slavery.[6]

Receiving no reply from the War Department, Hunter went ahead on his own. In May he dispatched squads of white troops throughout the occupied Sea Islands with orders to bring in all able-bodied male contrabands between the ages of eighteen and forty-five. Hundreds were rounded up, told they were going to be enrolled in a regiment officered by whites, and then transported to Hunter's headquarters at Hilton Head. Faced, however, with resistance from the blacks and protests from free-labor plantation superintendents deprived of workers, Hunter released all the conscripts unwilling to serve. But he kept the unit intact. The men who volunteered to stay in it remained at Hilton Head for training, armed with muskets and uniformed in distinctive red pants.[7]

Word of the "Hunter regiment" soon reached Washington and raised a ruckus. Conservatives in Congress demanded to know if Secretary of War Edwin M. Stanton had authorized the unit. The secretary replied that he had not and ordered Hunter to explain. The general defended himself forcefully, but to no avail. The Lincoln administration refused to sanction his black regiment, and on August 9 Hunter ordered it to disband. The men subsequently went home except those of one company, commanded by a white sergeant named Charles T. Trowbridge; they had just been posted to St. Simon's Island on the Georgia coast and did not receive the order to disband.[8]

In late August Hunter relinquished command of the department and returned to the North. But by then a tidal shift had occurred in Washington regarding policy on slavery. Sensing opportunity, Brigadier General Rufus Saxton, military governor of the Department of the South and, like Hunter, a devout abolitionist, petitioned the War Department for permission to enlist and arm a force of black men. Recognizing that the subject was still sensitive, he carefully avoided referring to this force as soldiers.

SERGEANT HARRY WILKINS

SERGEANT WILLIAM BRONSON

SERGEANT HENRY M'INTYRE

Three soldiers of the
1st South Carolina Infantry.
(FROM *THE OUTLOOK*, 59 [1898])

He also limited his request to five thousand men and specified that they would be used defensively, to guard the Sea Island free-labor plantations against Confederate raids. A letter from Stanton dated August 25 gave him what he asked, adding that the enlistees would be treated as full-fledged U.S. Army troops, albeit with a circumscribed mission. Apprised of the continued existence of Trowbridge's company, Saxton decided to keep it in service and use it as the nucleus of his first regiment. It became Company A of the 1st South Carolina Infantry.[9]

Saxton then set about energetically to fill the regiment's ranks. He traveled from one occupied island to the next, giving recruiting speeches, assisted by Chaplain Fowler and others. At the same time, he considered the question of a commander for the regiment. Higginson was earnestly recommended by Fowler, a fellow Harvard graduate, Unitarian minister, and Massachusetts abolitionist who had known him since before the war. Captain Higginson received Saxton's letter offering the command and a colonelcy in mid-November. He immediately booked passage to Beaufort but without committing himself to the position. His first meeting with Saxton and his first encounter with the regiment convinced him that this was where he should be, and he did not return to Massachusetts.[10]

When Higginson took command, the regiment numbered about five hundred men. By January it numbered about seven hundred, still below the minimum necessary for official mustering in. Meanwhile three black Union regiments had been organized in occupied Louisiana and another in Kansas, and they were formally mustered into service before Higginson's regiment was. But given the 1st South Carolina's history, Saxton and Higginson rightfully claimed that it was the very first black unit to serve the Union cause in this war.[11]

All the men of the 1st South Carolina were volunteers. Their new colonel was curious about their motives for enlisting, as well as their backgrounds and personal traits, and he took every opportunity to get to know them. Almost all had until recently been slaves, of course, although a few had been born free or had been emancipated by their owners before the war. Most hailed from the South Carolina or Georgia Sea Islands or the adjoining sections of mainland—the Main, as the men called it. A good number, however, especially in Company G, were from northeastern Florida. Men in their late teens or twenties predominated in all ten companies, but there were many in their thirties, quite a few in their forties, and a handful even older. On the enlistment forms, the great majority identified their previous occupation as laborer; they had toiled with hoe and plow on the long-staple cotton plantations of the islands or the rice plantations on the Main. But there were also former house servants in the regiment and many artisans, including carpenters, coopers, masons, and shoemakers.[12]

Comparatively few enlistees had been on the islands under Union aegis for very long. The men who were here when the Yankees arrived in late 1861 had soon settled into jobs as free-labor plantation hands or government laborers, many of them living with their families; when the call went out to volunteer for the black regiment, most refused, for they had no desire to uproot themselves. A lot of them also carried a grudge over the rough treatment dealt out by Hunter's conscription squads in May

1862, and they remained suspicious of the army. Most of the regiment's enlistees were, instead, men from the Main who had escaped from slavery within the last few months by slipping away from their masters and making their way to Union navy patrol boats on the coast or to army posts on the islands or by taking advantage of the sudden appearance of an army raiding party in a transport vessel at their plantations.[13]

Nearly all such men had left loved ones behind, and in talking with them, Higginson learned that this was a powerful motive for volunteering. Over and over the soldiers spoke of their desire to return to the Main in force and rescue their wives, children, parents, brothers, and sisters. "I hab leff my wife in de land ob bondage," he heard one of them lament; "my little ones dey say ebry night, where is my fader?"[14]

Perhaps the worst of slavery's many wrongs was the damage it inflicted on the black family. Maintaining a stable family life in the slave quarters of the South, given the master's power over every aspect of the slave's existence, was an enormous challenge. Most devastating was the forced separation by sale of husbands and wives, parents and children, an evil far more common than Southern whites, who boasted of slavery's benevolence, liked to admit. But even in servitude black families endured. The bonds of devotion that they nurtured, although strained by slavery, were strong. Strained even more by the disruptions and opportunities of war, these bonds nevertheless remained intact. They stretched across the miles that separated those who had gained freedom within Yankee lines from those who still toiled under their owners' watchful eyes. All understood that without further successful assaults on Rebeldom their dream of reuniting would likely never come to pass.[15]

Higginson also perceived among many of his soldiers less personal motives for enlisting. Some voiced a desire to help free their race as a whole; some talked of gratitude toward, and identification with, the Union. "I believe de United States is fightin' for me," said one, "and for my people." Despite the enforced illiteracy and ignorance that had been their lot as slaves, the men knew what the war was about. "They fully understand the importance of the contest," Higginson noted in his journal, "& their part in it." He transcribed the words of one soldier who had summed things up particularly well: "Our mas'rs dey hab lib under de [U.S.] flag, dey got dere wealth under it, & ebry ting beautiful for dere chil'en & under it dey hab *grind us into money & put us in dere pocket*; &

dat minute dey tink dat ole flag mean freedom for us dey pull it down & run up de rag ob dere own; but we'll nebber desert it boys, nebber."[16]

The men were inspired also by a sense of pride in soldiering, exemplified by some members of the Hunter regiment who had told a contraband who asked what their uniforms meant: "[W]e's Uncle Sam's chil'n now; we's none of your fiel' hans." Unit pride in what the men always referred to as "de Fus' Souf" was strong too. For some the regiment was actually a family affair; there were a number of soldiers related by blood or marriage: brothers, cousins, uncles, and nephews.[17]

Few had joined up for the money, as far as Higginson could judge. Unlike many white troops, they received no enlistment bounty. Pay was promised, of course, but it was long in coming and in any event was only thirteen dollars a month for privates; many could have done that well as laborers or officers' servants.[18]

Nor, as Higginson discovered, was revenge much of a motive. Many of the men were victims of brutal masters, yet hardly any expressed a desire to retaliate personally. Their feelings in this regard were exemplified by a soldier of the Hunter regiment who had offered a prayer in which he recounted the sins of his old master but asked the Lord to forgive him: "Oh, God, shake him over the brink of hell but don't let go of him."[19]

Certain men of the 1st South Carolina particularly impressed and intrigued their colonel. One was Sergeant Prince Rivers of Company A, who held the honored post of color-bearer and had spoken on the platform on Emancipation Day. The forty-year-old Rivers was distinguished not only by his arresting physical presence and gift for oratory but also by his literacy and command ability. Large, strong, very black, and graceful in movement—Higginson described him as pantherlike—he had been owned by an aristocratic family in Beaufort who employed him as their carriage driver. He had stayed behind when they and all the other local slaveowners fled to the mainland in November 1861, and he was in Beaufort working for good wages when the Hunter regiment was formed. Unlike many of his fellow contrabands, he joined it willingly despite the financial sacrifice that entailed, and he stayed on gladly when his company was absorbed into the 1st South Carolina. Higginson relied on him not only to make recruiting speeches around the islands and to write daily reports but also (as provost sergeant) to police the camp and help discipline the men, who held him in great respect. The colonel remarked in all seriousness that with some formal education Sergeant Rivers would be qualified to command an army.[20]

Much more articulate and refined in manner than most in the regiment, Rivers was often called on by newspaper correspondents, missionaries, and other interested whites to express the black soldier's viewpoint. The New York *Independent* of November 27 had quoted him on the significance of the creation of the 1st South Carolina: "This is our time. If our fathers had had such a chance as this, we should not have been slaves now. If we do not improve this chance, another one will not come, and our children will be slaves always." He had a vision of the future as well as the present. The black men and women of the South not only must gain freedom during this war, Rivers insisted, but must also secure it afterward. Only by obtaining land of their own, he thought, could his people remain truly free.[21]

Private Cato Wareing of Company F interested Higginson in a different way. He was in his sixties, probably the oldest man in the regiment, and he had been a driver, or slave foreman, on a plantation in the South Carolina lowcountry. Now he was detailed as a nurse in the regimental hospital and as such excused from drill and guard duty and other soldierly chores. A superb raconteur, he entertained his comrades with suspenseful storytelling, colorful diction, hilarious mimicry, and exaggerated facial expressions. Higginson had passed by one night in November while Wareing was holding forth beside a campfire and had found himself instantly captivated. Sitting down by the fire, the colonel accepted an offering of roasted sweet potatoes and peanuts and then listened as the narrator continued the tale of his escape from "de Seceshkey," which for sheer dramatic power rivaled anything Higginson had ever seen on the stage.[22]

Private Wareing amused his audiences, but there was a hard edge to some of his stories. He had seen horror and known terror in his life as a slave, and these he described candidly and vividly. He told of the punishments on his plantation. His master was cruel, his mistress crueler. Each morning she inspected her house furniture for dust with a white handkerchief; if any servant had not cleaned to her satisfaction, as was the case more often than not, beatings were ordered. As driver Wareing was required to wield the whip. If the offender was a man, he was taken outside and stripped naked. His hands were tied to a high horizontal pole,

with his toes just touching the ground. Wareing would deal out the specified number of lashes, sometimes several hundred, while his master stood
behind him with a paddle ready to punish the driver himself if he failed
to inflict sufficient pain. The penalty for a woman was the same except
that she was not stripped; instead, her skirt and chemise were pulled up
over her head. On days when the master and mistress were entertaining
company, a stick wrapped with cloth would be rammed down the throat
of the slaves condemned to punishment, thus stifling their screams and
leaving the guests undisturbed.[23]

After the war began, Wareing's master began demanding harder and
harder labor from his field hands. When they could take it no longer,
Wareing dared to intervene. He went to his master and begged him to
relax his demands; the man cursed and told him he would be whipped the
next morning. Before the sun came up, Wareing ran off. He did not even
tell his wife he was leaving, knowing she would try to talk him out of it. In
a dugout canoe he paddled through flooded rice fields toward the coast.
For weeks he pressed on, by boat and on foot, navigating by the sun and
stars, frequently lost, surviving by his wits while barely avoiding pursuers,
vicious dogs, starvation, Confederate army patrols, and even betrayal at
the hands of a fellow slave. Finally he stumbled on a Yankee gunboat and
was taken aboard. "Wen I git on de boat," he recounted, "I thought I was
in hebben."[24]

By January Higginson had gotten to know a lot about his men, but
the most important question could not be answered just by listening in
on their campfire chats and observing them on the parade ground: How
would they behave under fire? The little evidence available was encouraging but hardly conclusive.

General Saxton had managed to get some of the men into action in the
fall of 1862. He did so by interpreting loosely the secretary of war's August
25 letter permitting him to raise black troops. While the letter specified
that the troops' mission was to defend the occupied islands, it also directed
Saxton to use "every means in your power to withdraw from the enemy
their laboring force and population, and to spare no effort consistent with
civilized warfare to weaken, harass, and annoy them."[25]

Relying on this ambiguous clause, Saxton deemed himself authorized
to carry out raids on the mainland with the 1st South Carolina, and by
early November he had decided to do so. This was risky, however, for at

A detachment of the 1st South Carolina under attack by Confederates along the
Doboy River in Georgia, November 1862.
(FROM *OFFICIAL PORTFOLIO OF WAR AND NATION* [WASHINGTON, 1907])

that point the men were not fully trained. They had not mastered the
intricacies of marching order, combat formations, and the manual of
arms, nor did they obey commands in the instantaneous, unthinking way
that marks a battle-ready unit. They did, however, know how to load and
fire their weapons efficiently. Learning that was relatively simple, for there
was nothing complicated about the single-shot, muzzle-loading muskets
they were armed with; besides, most of them had had as much experience
with guns before their enlistment as the typical white soldier had had, for
masters commonly allowed their slave men to hunt wild game now and
then to supplement their food allowance.[26]

Determined to demonstrate to skeptics the value of black troops, Saxton accepted the risk of putting his raw regiment into action. On November 3 sixty-two men of the company under Charles T. Trowbridge (now
a captain) boarded the transport *Darlington* with orders to prowl the
Main and harass the Rebels. There being no regimental commander yet
appointed, Lieutenant Colonel Oliver T. Beard of the 48th New York was
detailed to command the mission. For eight days the vessel steamed along
the coast and up the rivers of Georgia and northeastern Florida. At more
than a dozen points it landed to allow the troops to go ashore and wreck
Rebel saltworks, seize or destroy useful supplies, and bring away any

slaves who wanted to come. On three occasions the boat was ambushed by Confederate troops hidden along the shore, and each time the men of the 1st responded like veterans, taking cover on deck and coolly returning fire. By the time the *Darlington* headed back to port the boat had been hit by no fewer than 150 bullets, and four black soldiers had been wounded. Lieutenant Colonel Beard, theretofore opposed to the idea of black troops, was much impressed by the men of the 1st and said so in his report on the mission: "They behaved bravely, gloriously, and deserve all praise."[27]

On November 13 three companies of the 1st, comprising some 160 men, set forth from Beaufort on another such amphibious expedition, again aboard the *Darlington* and under Lieutenant Colonel Beard's command. These companies were quite green, and had received their muskets only four days earlier. On November 18 they landed at a point on the Doboy River in Georgia. Beard led a detachment of thirty-four men inland to reconnoiter. On emerging from a wooded area, these few dozen were suddenly attacked from front and flanks by a sizable force of dismounted Confederate cavalrymen hidden in thickets. The black soldiers were seized by fright. Some broke and ran, but they quickly rallied and joined their comrades in a well-executed fighting retreat. Four black soldiers were wounded on this raid too, and again Beard officially commended the troops.[28]

The men of the 1st South Carolina likewise thought they had done well on the raids, and a noticeable surge of morale in the regiment resulted. "We have grown three inches," one participant declared, while another was heard to say, "I feel a heap more of a man." When Higginson arrived at Camp Saxton later that month, the first soldier he spoke to was one who had been wounded in the skirmish on the eighteenth. "Did you think that was more than you bargained for?" Higginson asked him. "*Dat's just what I went for, Massa,*" was the prompt reply.[29]

Higginson was encouraged by such esprit and by reports of the men's bravery under fire, but he knew that the November raids were not a full test of the regiment. He believed, although he could not be sure, that his men would do as well in combat as white troops—perhaps better. He knew that they had one incentive to stand fast in the hour of battle that white soldiers did not: If captured, they would be reenslaved or worse.[30]

No one understood this better than the men themselves, of course, although they did not know that the Confederate government had

recently formulated an official policy in response to the North's recruitment of blacks. President Jefferson Davis decreed in December that any
slave captured in Yankee uniform would not be treated as a prisoner of
war but would instead be turned over to state authorities to be dealt with
under the laws on slave insurrection. These laws prescribed, for the most
serious offenders, execution. At the very least any soldier of the 1st South
Carolina who fell into Rebel hands could expect to be returned to his old
master or auctioned off to a new one. Hanging was a real possibility.[31]

Whether black soldiers would fight as well as white soldiers was a question now being argued by many people, and not just in the Department
of the South. It was one aspect of a larger issue that was provoking fierce
debate among Northerners: Should Negro troops be used at all? There
were but a handful of such regiments in service at this time and few more
being created. None had been formed at the War Department's initiative;
Secretary Stanton had merely approved the creation of some black units
here and there after being petitioned by local commanders such as Rufus
Saxton. President Lincoln refused to commit the government fully to the
recruitment of blacks, for there were too many unresolved military and
political questions about it.[32]

The November raids of the 1st South had received some favorable newspaper coverage in the North. The New York *Daily Tribune* proclaimed
that "the negro troops have been tested, and . . . they have triumphed."
The abolitionist press, including William Lloyd Garrison's *Liberator* and
the New York *Independent*, was especially laudatory. The *Independent*'s
correspondent in the Department of the South asserted that the raids
not only demonstrated the courage of the men of the 1st South but also
provided striking evidence "of the capacity of the negro race for warlike
exploits."[33]

Most Northerners, however, remained skeptical of the value of black
troops. The racism that permeated Northern white society led many to
believe that blacks simply lacked the moral fiber to make good soldiers.
Many feared especially that black soldiers would commit acts of savagery
on defenseless white civilians in the invaded regions of the South. The
most conservative Northerners—especially Democrats, most of whom
were unreconciled even to freeing the slaves, much less making soldiers
of them—dismissed altogether the question of blacks' self-restraint and
combat proficiency, for they rejected the very notion that their country

should call on blacks for help. Enlisting them, declared a New York newspaper, is a "humiliating admission that this great people [are] compelled to ask the aid of slaves and draw from the South an element of strength to enable us to maintain and preserve our liberties." Another Northern paper fumed at "the idea of calling on *him* [i.e., the black man] ... to fight our battles," denouncing it as "a confession of our own weakness and cowardice" and a species of "insanity." Many other Northerners worried that putting blacks in the army would demoralize white soldiers. A letter to the editor of the New York *Times* insisted that "there is not one man in ten but would feel himself degraded as a volunteer if negro equality is to be the order in the field of battle. . . . One negro regiment, in the present temper of things, put on equality with those who have the past year fought and suffered, will withdraw an amount of life and energy in our army equal to disbanding ten of the best regiments we can now raise."[34]

The Department of the South provided a good deal of evidence that the white soldiers of the Union would not willingly serve alongside blacks. The 1st South Carolina regiment was reviled by many of the officers and men of the white units on the islands. A Gideonite noted that the white troops at Beaufort "exhibit a degree of hatred really fiendish towards the black regiment." One of those white soldiers, a member of the 6th Connecticut Infantry who sent regular reports to his hometown newspaper, had this to say about the 1st South: "Their Colonel is the Rev. Mr. Higginson of Worcester, who has had nigger on the brain from the time of his conception. . . . There exists a most thorough contempt on the part of the white officers and soldiers towards this Regiment, and no opportunity is allowed to pass but that they vent their feelings in actions and words." By isolating the 1st South in its camp four miles from the nearest white troops, General Saxton reduced the risk of racial altercations, but when men of the regiment got passes to go to Beaufort, they usually took the precaution of traveling in groups and carrying their weapons.[35]

Opposition to enlisting blacks was not unanimous, of course, either in the army or among the Northern citizenry. The radical wing of the Republican party was favorable, as were abolitionists. But nearly all Democrats were aghast at the idea, and even the moderate Republicans, whom President Lincoln regarded as the vital center of public opinion, were unsupportive. The New York *Times* exemplified the moderate viewpoint. Black troops might fight well, one of its editorials conceded, "though we somewhat doubt it." But whatever military advantage might be gained by enlisting them en masse would be more than offset by the protests that would explode in the army and among the general public. "As we can hardly afford just now to accumulate causes of dissension and controversy among ourselves, it may be wise to avoid questions certain to give rise to them."[36]

In this, as in all the other issues he confronted, President Lincoln was acutely sensitive to the temper of his constituents and the momentum of events. Strong evidence that further enlistment of blacks would hurt more than help the Union cause would likely persuade him to end the experiment; he might even disband the black units already recruited. Given strong evidence of the opposite sort, however, he might well declare the experiment a success and move forward with it. For now the president would watch, listen, and wait.

Higginson followed this national debate closely, particularly the question of the battle-worthiness of black troops. As he did so, he could not help wondering how he himself would act in the moment of crisis. Although he had faced armed opponents in desperate and even violent circumstances, in both Boston and Kansas, he had never been engaged in military combat. In fact, for a regimental commander, he had little military experience of any sort. His previous service, as a company commander in the 51st Massachusetts, had lasted less than three months, and his unit had not left its home state during that time. There was muttering from some of the more seasoned soldiers in the Department of the South that he was a dilettante unfit to command.[37]

Higginson had no doubts about his ability to drill and discipline his troops and provide for their health and comfort. He had picked up that sort of skill and knowledge quickly in the training camp in Massachusetts, finding it easy to master. Nor did he doubt his ability to navigate the bewildering sea of army regulations and procedures. In these respects he had already, in his first weeks on the Sea Islands, proved a capable, even superior regimental commander. But he admitted to himself that his true mettle as a leader had yet to be tested. It could be proved only under fire.[38]

Of his commitment to his task there could be no doubt. A fervent sense of mission drove him. Not only was he helping bring about the destruction of slavery, the overthrow of the Southern Slave Power, and the restoration of the Union, but he was also, he firmly believed, helping prepare blacks for their future role as full citizens of the Republic. He worried over every sign of Democratic resurgence in the North and every rumor of an armistice between the Union and Confederacy, for like Sergeant Rivers, he believed that this war represented a unique opportunity that must be seized, and from his reading of history he knew that revolutions are sometimes reversed. While he struck no one who met him as a fanatic, all who conversed with him at any length sensed his earnestness and devotion to this cause and his aversion to self-indulgence while in its service. He deemed his assignment to the 1st South Carolina, as he told his mother in a letter four days after taking command, "the best fortune of my life."[39]

Rarely, if ever, did he admit openly the daunting sense of responsibility he felt. The 1st South Carolina and the few other black units now serving were, Higginson knew, under the microscope of public and official scrutiny. Any serious trouble in these regiments—excessive desertion, mutiny, cowardice on the battlefield, a decisive defeat at the hands of the Rebel army—could be catastrophic, derailing the whole movement to enlist blacks. Nothing less than the outcome of the war and the fate of the black race were at stake in this experiment, Higginson believed, and his actions and decisions could do enormous good or enormous harm.[40]

On assuming this great responsibility and surveying his new domain, Higginson decided that the unique nature of his regiment required some adjustment of his command style; the soldiers of the 1st South Carolina could not be dealt with exactly like those of the 51st Massachusetts. He was far in advance of most of his contemporaries in insisting that blacks deserved not just freedom but also full legal and political equality; this principled egalitarianism, however, sometimes grated against his visceral elitism. Higginson was well-to-do, educated, and refined, and these qualities, he believed, were attributes of the ideal citizen. Nearly all the black people he had met or heard of in his life were poor, ignorant, and unpolished. From this he concluded that the black race was backward and needed the aid and guidance of whites such as himself to be fully prepared for the civic equality that was its due. But it was not just charity and lessons on the three Rs, aesthetics, and deportment that the black race needed, in Higginson's view: Blacks also had certain defects of character that needed correction. To what extent these defects were innate and to what extent learned, he had not fully resolved in his own mind. Like most others of his era, he believed that the races of humankind each had an inherent and unique character, yet he understood that centuries of slavery and discrimination in America had also shaped the Negro race. Whatever its origin, Higginson was convinced that the black character was distinctive and in some ways inferior and thus in need of reforming. In dealing with the men of the 1st South, he put his assumptions and beliefs into practice.[41]

In his view, slavery (and perhaps nature) had kept these men child-like. They were "simple, docile, and affectionate," he wrote in his journal, and they exhibited greater "extremes of jollity & sobriety" than whites. When off duty, they often seemed to play like rowdy youngsters, and they were given to fibbing and other juvenile vices. When he first arrived at Camp Saxton, he was struck also by the extreme blackness of the men— "hardly even a *mulatto*," he wrote, "about all as black as printer's ink"— and by their strange language. They all looked alike to him, and he could barely understand many of them. As he got to know them, however, their distinctive visages and personalities became apparent to him, and their language intelligible. But he continued to regard them paternalistically (with exceptions such as Prince Rivers). Feeling like a parent with a home full of lovable but boisterous children, he laughingly dubbed them "my young barbarians." But like any good parent, he saw it his duty to encourage them to leave behind their childish ways in due time and grow into mature adults.[42]

Slavery had denied his soldiers not only manhood, Higginson believed, but also a sense of dignity, and he was determined to remedy that. He quickly put a stop to their habit of doffing their caps to their officers and addressing them as "Massa." A true soldier, he instructed them, while deferential and obedient to authority, is not servile or obsequious; he addresses his officers as "sir" or by their rank, and he greets them with a proper military salute, standing erect with cap on. Furthermore, the colonel told them, they should expect to have that salute returned, for in the army even the lowliest private is accorded respect. Their habitual use of "nigger" in referring to themselves and their people Higginson saw as further evidence of a lack of dignity and self-respect, and he forbade it.[43]

Self-reliance was another casualty of slavery, in Higginson's view. His troops were more dependent on their officers than were white troops, he judged, and would be more influenced by their behavior on the battle-field. Under firm leadership the men would undoubtedly fight well, but under poor leadership they would be more likely than whites to break and run. This weakness must be overcome to make them not only better soldiers, he thought, but also better citizens.[44]

Another deficiency he perceived in them was their pathetic ignorance. While many were enthusiastically studying the three Rs in Chaplain Fowler's Pagoda, hardly any were even minimally literate or numerate (here again Prince Rivers stood as an exception). Nor could they tell time, and some did not even know the months of the year. All this imposed an extra burden on Higginson and the other officers. In white regiments it was common practice to detail well-educated enlisted men as clerks to handle the most tedious paperwork, and it could be assumed that every soldier was familiar with the clock and the calendar. Illiteracy limited the men's effectiveness as soldiers in substantial ways. For instance, when on guard duty they could not read the passes that granted people permission to leave or enter the camp, thus requiring them to summon Prince Rivers or some officer. But the men of the 1st South lacked more than just basic schooling. While they understood the meaning of the war, many had no sense at all of what the world was like outside the plantation regime of the south Atlantic coast. Higginson was concerned about the impact of his men's ignorance not only on their military effectiveness but also on their prospects as future citizens of the Republic.[45]

As he came to know his "young barbarians," the colonel was pleased to find some of the most negative stereotypes about slaves contradicted. For one thing, he observed, although they were undeniably ignorant, the men of the 1st were not on the whole mentally dull. Nor were they lazy or sluggish. One moonlit night not long after his arrival he had watched in fascination for two hours as the troops energetically and even mer-rily unloaded a late-arriving supply boat at the landing—this after a hard day's work. Later he came upon one of them sitting by a campfire and suggested that he ought to be in bed after that arduous extra duty. "O no, Cunnel," the man replied, "dat no work at all, Cunnel; dat only jess enough to *stretch we*."[46]

Nor did he find the men of the 1st South Carolina hard to manage. When he first arrived, discipline was lax; there was a great deal of over-staying of leaves and a good many outright desertions. He quickly cut these problems down to manageable proportions through the judicious use of mild punishments, such as forfeiture of a month's pay or a week or two of extra fatigue duty on a bread and water diet. These correctives he preferred to the harsher ones that officers were permitted to inflict— including tying offenders up by their thumbs or shackling them with ball and chain—for he presumed that the brutality of slavery had inured blacks to such treatment. That the men as a whole followed orders acquiescently, some observers ascribed to the habit of obedience they had learned as slaves, although Higginson was not so sure of that. Many of the vices that plagued the bivouacs of white soldiers he found virtually absent at Camp Saxton. There was little theft, no drinking or gambling to speak of, hardly any swearing, and not much feigning of illness to avoid duty.[47]

Although he was a rigorous disciplinarian, Higginson's competence, commitment, and concern for his men quickly won him their respect and before long their devotion. He was gratified by their response to his leadership, and as the weeks went by, he grew confident that in the heat of battle they would do their duty—as long as he and their other officers did not fail them.[48]

By January the regiment had a full complement of officers: three field officers (colonel, lieutenant colonel, major), thirty company officers (a captain, first lieutenant, and second lieutenant for each company), and the various staff officers (adjutant, quartermaster, surgeon, assistant surgeon, chaplain). Higginson took a particular interest in the company officers, who had direct control of the men. They were, for the most part, former sergeants in Maine and Pennsylvania and New York regiments in the Department of the South, the 8th Maine Infantry contributing a particularly large share. About half had served with the Hunter regiment, while most of the rest had been recruited by General Saxton since August. All had volunteered to lead black troops, though few could be called fervent abolitionists; most were attracted by the opportunity for promotion. Racial egalitarians they surely were not, but at least they were uninfected by the virulent Negrophobia that characterized so many other white troops, and they were enthusiastic about the ability of their men to make good soldiers. Hunter and Saxton would not have commissioned them in the 1st South otherwise.[49]

Higginson had sized up the company officers quickly after his arrival and was for the most part pleased. Although by his standards they were uncultivated and only half educated, and few were as proficient in drill as he, the colonel judged them "truly good & reliable," "thoroughly manly," "earnest, well meaning young fellows, who understand what they have attempted & mean to do it." In his relations with them he sought to strike a proper balance. They soon learned that their commander was unfailingly polite and approachable but neither chummy nor paternalistic; he kept a distance that fell just short of aloofness.[50]

Charles Trowbridge.
(FROM *THE OUTLOOK*, 59 [1898])

What these officers needed, Higginson had immediately decided, was better drilling and bookkeeping skills and some lessons on how to treat the men. This last was particularly important. As he instructed his men to expect a return salute as a mark of respect, so he instructed his officers to give it. Likewise, he banished "nigger" from the officers' vocabulary as firmly as he did from the men's. Nor did he tolerate cursing or abusive language toward the troops. While he found the officers generally "patient & kind" in dealing with the men, there were occasional exceptions. The first time he caught an officer swearing at a soldier, he called him immediately to his tent; the captain emerged a little later in tears, vowing (profanely) that he would never swear again.[51]

Saxton granted Higginson free rein in staffing the regiment's officer corps, but for the most part the colonel kept the officers he had found when he arrived. There were two exceptions. He got rid of the captain of Company D, whose health was so poor that he was neglecting his duty, and he got rid of the first lieutenant in the same company, to whom, Higginson reported, he had "moral objections"—perhaps a drunkard. He also brought in a few new officers of his own choosing.[52]

The most capable and experienced of the company commanders was twenty-eight-year-old Charles Trowbridge of Company A. Higginson relied on him greatly, although the two could hardly have been more dissimilar. Raised in a working-class Brooklyn neighborhood and a bricklayer by trade, Trowbridge was poorly educated and had never lost the manners and accent that marked the raucous culture of Bowery Boys, volunteer firemen, and ward heelers. Brawny and tough, he reminded Higginson of a prize-fighter. After the war broke out, he joined the 1st New York Engineer Regiment, earned a sergeant's stripes, and learned such skills as bridge building. The regiment came to the Sea Islands in November 1861 with the invasion force, and it was undoubtedly here that Trowbridge acquired his abolitionist sentiments and sympathy for the black race, for these were anathemas where he grew up. He was the very first Union soldier to lead black troops, having been appointed recruiter and company commander by General Hunter back in May. He had handled his company ably while posted independently on St. Simon's Island and during the raid of early November; on the deck of the *Darlington* he had unflinchingly exposed himself to enemy bullets while directing the return fire of his troops. Higginson was a bit troubled by what he regarded as a certain lack of respect on Trowbridge's part toward his men—he habitually addressed them as "boy" and mimicked their accents mockingly—but this troubled the men themselves not at all, for they recognized it as good-natured kidding. In fact they delighted in it, and they adored their captain, not just for his geniality but also for his bravery and command ability and earnest concern for their welfare. They welcomed him by their campfires when he joined them, as he often did, to sing hymns. His name baffled them, however, and they never learned to pronounce it properly; to them he was always "Cappen Scroby."[53]

The only real disappointments among the officer corps, to Higginson's mind, were the field officers, John D. Strong and Liberty Billings. He was sorry to find that neither had any military experience, nor did they seem to have any capacity for learning on the job. "They will never be soldiers," he said. Both had been appointed by Saxton just a few weeks before Higginson's arrival, apparently on the strength of their abolitionist principles alone. Major Strong impressed the colonel as not only unmilitary but also unamiable. Lieutenant Colonel Billings, a Unitarian minister and former chaplain of a New Hampshire regiment, was likable but somewhat vain. Although the two were worthless for drill, discipline, and paperwork, Higginson eventually found a use for them as recruiters—Billings, in particular, could give a rousing stump speech—and so they spent much of their time traveling to the various occupied islands in the department, drumming up enlistments. Because they were serviceable in this capacity and committed no grievous offenses, Higginson kept them on, but it was obvious that if he were to be disabled in combat, one of the captains would have to take command of the regiment.[54]

Higginson worried about how his officers would behave in combat but took ironic comfort from the fact that the same Rebel threat that steeled the determination of his soldiers also loomed over the officers. Jefferson Davis's December proclamation denied prisoner of war status to captured Yankee officers commanding black troops; they too would be turned over to state authorities, in whose hands they could expect to meet the same fate as John Brown. The image of the gallows was never far from the minds of the officers of the 1st South Carolina, and Higginson believed that it would help brace them in battle.[55]

Higginson's problem with the morally objectionable lieutenant required him to go see General Saxton. On January 6 he mounted a horse and headed northward along the sandy road to Beaufort. It was the first time he had left the area of the camp since arriving in November. The weather had warmed considerably since Emancipation Day, and his ride would have been very pleasant except for the rain. The pretty Beaufort River bent westward in a graceful curve as it flowed south between the town and the camp, and it was visible from nearly every point along the road. The town was four miles away but came into view long before that, across the expanse of blue water.[56]

When he reached Beaufort, Higginson made his way toward Saxton's headquarters on Bay Street, which ran along the river's edge by the wharf. Fourteen months of Yankee occupation had taken a heavy toll on the little town, as he could see. Before the war many of the great planter families of the South Carolina coast had had their summer homes here. Their houses, imposing two-story mansions with wide piazzas, white fences, ornamental gardens—and slave huts in the rear—still stood along the tree-shaded streets. But now these houses sheltered people very different from the Rhetts and Barnwells and served purposes other than gracious living. Seven were in use as military hospitals, including one for contrabands. Others were commissary or quartermaster or provost marshal offices, troop barracks, officers' billets or headquarters, or missionaries' residences. All had been pillaged and vandalized by soldiers and contrabands. The elegant parlors had been stripped of furniture, and the stately libraries of books; the family portraits had been torn from the walls or slashed by bayonets; the pianos had been demolished and their ivory keys

Rufus Saxton.
(COURTESY OF LIBRARY OF CONGRESS)

pilfered. Gardens sat neglected and weed-ridden. The town's abandoned churches, likewise looted and mutilated, now served as schools for blacks. The former public library housed homeless freed people.[57]

Although this was Higginson's first visit to Saxton's headquarters since reporting there on the day he arrived, he had seen the general frequently in the interim, for Saxton visited the camp that bore his name several times a week to observe dress parade and talk with the colonel. The two no doubt greeted each other warmly on this rainy Tuesday, for they greatly admired each other. Saxton had already decided that Higginson deserved a general's star and command of a brigade of black troops as soon as several more regiments could be recruited. Higginson was grateful to Saxton for his wholehearted cooperation in everything concerning the 1st South Carolina, and he was touched by the general's sincere commitment to the welfare of the black race.[58]

Saxton was one of the rare abolitionists in the regular army officer corps. A Massachusetts native, now thirty-eight years old, he had graduated from West Point in 1849 and had served capably in the prewar army at various posts. Arriving on the Sea Islands with the invasion force in 1861, he was assigned first as quartermaster. Now he was the department's military governor, overseeing not only the recruitment of black troops but also the operation of the free-labor plantations, the work of the missionaries, and all other matters involving blacks and white civilians. Somewhat shorter than Higginson, bearded, and prematurely bald, Saxton had the erect posture of the professional soldier and was a superb horseman. He was a bachelor, but not for much longer; he had fallen in love with eighteen-year-old Matilda Thompson of Philadelphia, one of the Gideonites, and they were to be married in March.[59]

Saxton had absorbed his abolitionism as a boy from his father, who was now in Beaufort serving as his secretary. What the general had seen in his months on the Sea Islands only confirmed his conviction that slavery was, as he put it, "the foulest wrong which has disgraced humanity in the nineteenth century." His abolitionism was inextricable from his deep religious faith. "You have as good a right to freedom as I have, or any other living man," he had proclaimed to a gathering of black soldiers and contrabands in November; "GOD NEVER MADE A MAN TO BE A SLAVE." That God was at work in the Emancipation Proclamation he believed with all his heart. He was confident, moreover, that the freed slaves would, with assistance from right-thinking whites, prove capable of self-support and progress. Once, when asked by a group of Northerners to characterize the Sea Island blacks, Saxton had summed them up in two simple and heartfelt words, intending thereby to rebuke both those whites who dismissed the blacks as hopelessly inferior and those who had faith in them but regarded them as wildly exotic. They were, he said, "intensely human."[60]

Higginson stayed to dine with Saxton, and the two undoubtedly discussed various matters besides the errant lieutenant. The 1st South Carolina was, as Higginson had learned at his first meeting with him, one of the general's passions. Saxton invested fervent hopes in the regiment and, like the colonel, foresaw disastrous consequences if it proved a disappointment. He worried especially that the regiment's ranks were filling too slowly, for he feared that the government might renege on emancipation if it appeared that the black men of the South were unwilling to fight for their own freedom.[61]

Saxton had other frustrations that he may have discussed while the two ate dinner, none of them news to Higginson. The general had to struggle ceaselessly to get the unit properly equipped and keep it supplied, for certain men with power in the department were disinclined to do anything for the "nigger regiment." He had had trouble getting tents even though they were abundant in the supply depot at Hilton Head. Medical supplies were likewise dispensed meagerly and grudgingly to the 1st South Carolina, and the muskets it was issued were mostly second-rate. Many of Saxton's requisition letters were simply ignored. The imminent return of General Hunter to departmental command might improve matters, but Saxton could not count on it. And he had headaches besides those involving the regiment. For one thing, he had to fight constantly to see that the contrabands on the free-labor plantations got a fair shake from the government, and he was often stymied. Back in the fall he had gone so far as to request reassignment. His sense of duty and the hope that he could still accomplish some good for the blacks eventually persuaded him to stay at his post, but he longed to leave the Department of the South and take a field command in a more active theater.[62]

Higginson sympathized with Saxton's predicament and admired his persistence, but privately he thought that some of the general's problems were his own doing. Saxton was exceedingly good-natured and honest and trusting, incapable of meanness or deviousness and slow to recognize those faults in others—in all, a curiously gentle and ingenuous man for one so long a soldier. He was too reluctant to complain and demand, thought Higginson, too blind to deceitfulness and fecklessness, too easily imposed on by self-seekers and incompetents; witness the colonel's two field officers, not to mention any number of headquarters attachés, Gideonites, and plantation superintendents whom Higginson regarded as equally worthless.[63]

When Higginson returned to camp that evening, he met surgeon Seth Rogers and joked that his little trip today had reassured him that there was a world beyond Camp Saxton. Rogers was the only man in the regiment to whom Higginson was close. The two had been friends and fellow antislavery activists in Massachusetts before the war; Higginson had recommended Rogers's appointment as regimental surgeon.[64]

Two days after his meeting with Saxton, Higginson again visited Beaufort on business, and while there he took time to watch some white regiments drill. Nothing he saw made him in any way ashamed of his own men; the white troops were generally no better on the parade ground than the blacks even though they had served much longer, and in some respects they were inferior. Under his tutelage the 1st South Carolina had rapidly acquired the mechanical precision and automatic obedience in marching, changing formation, and handling weapons that every drillmaster sought—and that could spell the difference between victory and disaster in battle. Thinking it over, the colonel concluded that it was now time to really show off the regiment. He would march his troops to Beaufort and flaunt their skills.[65]

At one in the afternoon of Saturday, January 17, the men, fully uniformed and bearing their brightly polished muskets with fixed bayonets, assembled on the parade ground at Camp Saxton. To General Saxton's immense satisfaction, the regiment now had sufficient enrollment for official mustering in. With the arrival four days earlier of a large contingent of recruits enlisted by Lieutenant Colonel Billings at the posts of Fernandina and St. Augustine in Florida, the 1st South Carolina numbered 850, all black save for the thirty-eight officers. These newest recruits, however, being wholly untrained, would not accompany the regiment today.[66]

Higginson surveyed his men on the parade ground and saw that all was ready. They were eager and expectant. The colonel's only regret this day was that they still wore the red pants that General Hunter had requisitioned back in April in order to distinguish his black unit. Higginson detested these pants, for he objected to any official distinction between his men and other troops; he was trying to get replacements in light blue, the same color he and the other officers (and almost all officers and men of white units) wore. The men likewise hated the red pants, but for a different reason: "[T]he rebels see us, miles away," as one put it.[67]

It was one-fifteen when Higginson gave the order that put the men on the march to Beaufort. At the head of the column Sergeant Rivers and Corporal Sutton bore aloft the flags. The troops proceeded in the casual, unsynchronized route step, singing all the way. The sounds of the John Brown song and "Marching Along" and other martial airs rolled across the sandy plain until the regiment halted on the outskirts of town. There, by prearrangement, it was met by the band of the 8th Maine, which struck up a tune and led the column into town. Down Bay Street the regiment went, past General Saxton's headquarters, the men now marching briskly in step, their eyes riveted to the front. Curious whites and blacks watched from doorways, windows, and sidewalks. At the far end of town the regiment reversed course and marched back up Bay Street to the nearby parade ground of the white regiments posted in Beaufort. There for an hour it drilled to Higginson's crisply shouted commands before a crowd of contrabands and white soldiers and civilians. Some of the white soldiers jeered, but the men of the 1st South Carolina ignored them. The contrabands were jubilant; one was heard to say, "Yah! Yah! de secesh 'll have to look out now!" When the drill ended, Higginson led his men southward to Camp Saxton. They sang all the way back.[68]

Officers and men alike agreed that this had been a red-letter day for the regiment. Its performance had been all that the colonel had hoped for, and it had received, amid the sneers and taunts of the white soldiers, compliments not only from the contrabands but also from some of the officers of the white units. The men talked excitedly about the day's events around their campfires until taps. "We didn't see a ting in Beaufort," one said proudly; "every man hold he head straight up to de front; every step was worth a half-a-dollar." Prince Rivers was ecstatic: "When dat band begin for play in front of us," he told Higginson, "Good Heaven, *I left dis world altogether*."[69]

Another notable event occurred four days later, on January 21, when Major General Hunter visited the camp to review the regiment. He had arrived on the islands only three days earlier to resume command of the department. Higginson was looking forward to meeting him. This was the man who had issued his own emancipation proclamation in May 1862, declaring free all slaves in the three states constituting the Department of the South. His bold act had won him acclaim in abolitionist circles and a rebuke from President Lincoln, who quickly countermanded the decree. Nothing daunted, Hunter had proceeded to enlist black troops without authorization and, when called to account, had defended himself with spirit and wit in a well-publicized letter. "No regiment of 'Fugitive Slaves' has been, or is being organized in this Department," he wrote in response to the secretary of war's inquiry. "There is however, a fine regiment of persons whose late masters are 'Fugitive Rebels.'" Arming blacks had earned him not only the displeasure of his government but also special attention from the enemy: The Confederate War Department declared him an outlaw, to be treated as a capital felon rather than a soldier if captured. Too radical and brash to suit his superiors in Washington, Hunter eventually grew frustrated and asked for a leave of absence, which was granted in August 1862. Much had changed since then, however, and now he returned to the Sea Islands a vindicated man.[70]

Higginson had been warned of Hunter's visit and was flattered that he had chosen the 1st South Carolina for his first official review of troops since coming back to the department. Surely, the colonel thought, Hunter would come in the late afternoon for dress parade. To his dismay, however, the general showed up earlier, during battalion drill, when the men were dressed down. He was accompanied by several staff officers, two newspaper correspondents, and General Saxton. Higginson dutifully ordered the regiment to perform the manual of arms, pass in review by compa-

nies, and carry out various maneuvers while
Hunter looked on, but he was disappointed
to see that his men were not at their sharpest
today. Hunter seemed pleased, however, and
when Higginson formed the regiment into a
large, hollow square facing inward and invited
the general to speak, he strode readily to the
center of the square. He was greeted with spontaneous cheers from the troops, who knew that
he was the father of their regiment.[71]

Hunter was not what Higginson had
expected. A mild-mannered sixty-year-old man
with a drooping dyed mustache and a brown
wig, he seemed, as the colonel confided in his
journal that night, more "like a kindly elderly
gentleman in uniform" than the audacious
radical who had so provoked his own government and the Rebels; there was about him no
"air of concentrated purpose." Moreover, his
speech to the men, while heartily delivered and
well received, struck Higginson as awkward

David Hunter.
(COURTESY OF LIBRARY OF
CONGRESS)

and stiff. He began by complimenting them on their proficiency in drill,
adding that he saw "no reason why you should not make as good soldiers
as any in the world." He wished he had a hundred thousand such troops,
he said; he was certain that they would fight well, for they were fighting
for the liberty of their people. He concluded with a promise to see that
they got everything they were entitled to from the army. The troops gave
him three more cheers, along with three for his staff and three for liberty.
General Saxton then stepped into the square to announce that Hunter
had promised to have the regiment armed with good new Springfield
rifles. The men cheered wildly.[72]

Before Hunter departed for his headquarters at Hilton Head, Higginson and Saxton consulted with him. The colonel wanted Hunter's
approval to requisition light blue pants for the men, which he got. But
he had something else in mind too. Ever since taking command, he had
contemplated an amphibious raid like those Lieutenant Colonel Beard
had led in November, but he had put the matter off until he thought the

regiment was ready. Now the time had come, he believed. Saxton agreed wholeheartedly, and the two laid the proposal before General Hunter. Permission was granted.[73]

Higginson and Saxton moved quickly to organize the raid. On January 23, just two days after Hunter's visit, three steamers pulled up to the camp landing and began taking aboard men and supplies. The largest, but most lightly armed, was the *Ben De Ford*. The *John Adams*, a converted ferryboat, carried four powerful pieces of artillery. The smallest of the vessels was the *Planter*, a former Rebel tugboat that had been spirited away from Charleston and delivered to the Yankees in May 1862 by fugitive slaves. Higginson designated six companies—A, B, C, F, G, and H—to go on this expedition, but when some of the men of companies E and I begged to be included, he allowed thirty-four of them to come along.[74]

When making his case to General Hunter, Higginson had emphasized the useful supplies that could be gathered from the Main, especially lumber. This argument was disingenuous, however. As far as the colonel was concerned, he and his regiment were raiding Rebeldom "to win our spurs." Their precise destination was the St. Mary's River, which flowed eastward into the Atlantic along the Georgia-Florida border. Higginson had decided this after talking with a number of his men about the various points along the Main they were familiar with. The St. Mary's could be navigated for at least forty miles up from its mouth, and there were known to be lumber mills along it. But the primary reason Higginson chose this target was that one of his most trusted men, color-bearer Robert Sutton, had been raised on that river and could serve as guide. Corporal Sutton had long been urging his colonel to lead an expedition up the St. Mary's. Many others in the regiment were likewise eager for such an adventure and confident that they were prepared. "Ought to go to work, Sa," one said to Higginson; "don't believe in we lyin' in camp eatin' up de perwisions."[75]

The three steamers departed separately on the twenty-third, the *Ben De Ford* carrying Higginson and four companies and the other two vessels one company apiece—altogether, 462 officers and men. Among the supplies aboard was a stack of printed copies of the Emancipation Proclamation to be distributed in Rebel territory. The *John Adams* was slow, and the *Planter* was plagued by engine problems, and it was not until the twenty-sixth that they finally rendezvoused with the *Ben De Ford* in Fernandina

Harbor, the jumping-off point for the upriver voyage. In the meantime Higginson had learned from some naval officers that a Union gunboat had ascended the St. Mary's nine months earlier and had been fired on by Confederate batteries and riflemen along the shore. He declined to alter his plan, however, hoping that the Rebels would no longer be vigilantly defending the river after such a long lapse of time with no Yankee incursions and figuring that no matter where he chose to go, there would be a risk of enemy attack.[76]

Leaving behind the *Ben De Ford* because it was too big to go far upstream and the *Planter* because its engine was undependable, Higginson proceeded up the St. Mary's on the *John Adams*. On deck was a detachment assigned to man the big guns; below were two hundred more men, all that could be crammed into the space available. Higginson had learned from Robert Sutton that a company of Confederate cavalry was bivouacked near Township Landing, a point on the Florida bank of the river ten miles up. He intended to land there and lead a force inland to surprise the Rebels in their camp.[77]

Night had fallen, but the moon shone brightly as the *John Adams* steamed upriver. Just below Township, Higginson put ashore by rowboat a detachment of troops, among them Sutton, with orders to proceed quietly to the landing, secure control of it, and allow no one found there to leave. There was no village at the landing, only a plantation house and outbuildings, known to be used occasionally as a Rebel picket post. After an interval the *John Adams* continued on to the landing. Finding it safely secured, Higginson disembarked with the rest of his troops. Robert Sutton had by now found a local black who could guide them right to the Rebel camp, which was five miles away; it had been the corporal's pleasure to inform this man that he was, by virtue of the president's proclamation, free. After weeding out those with coughs and posting sufficient guards to protect the landing and the boat, Higginson led a force of about a hundred officers and men inland, admonishing them to move as silently as possible along the narrow path through the pine woods. It was a little after midnight on January 27.[78]

Higginson never knew who actually surprised whom, but some two miles from the landing his advance guard suddenly encountered mounted men to their front. Rifle and pistol shots rang out in the dark. A private of Company G standing next to Higginson fell dead with a bullet through his heart. Higginson called out to his men to take cover and fix bayonets. Those near him responded immediately and began to return fire, although there were no real targets to be seen. But the men to rear of the column became confused and almost panicked. From the sounds and muzzle flashes it appeared that the enemy troopers were spreading out around them, now firing from both flanks as well as the front. The men held their ground, however, with the fierce encouragement of their officers, and the Rebels' fire eventually slackened. Higginson then ordered his soldiers to cease firing. The ensuing silence indicated that the enemy cavalrymen had withdrawn. Higginson realized that he had lost all sense of time; whether this skirmish had lasted an hour or just a few minutes, he could not tell.[79]

Convinced that the Rebels had fled in defeat, Higginson's men were eager to press on to their camp. But the colonel was cautious. He had lost the element of surprise, he knew nothing of the enemy's numbers or intentions, and the mounted Confederates had the advantage of mobility. Too, General Saxton had warned him to take no big risks, for fear of a disaster that would set back the cause of black recruitment. The troops had stood up well in this little encounter, and the enemy had left them in possession of the field; this seemed enough of a victory for now—"a good beginning," Higginson decided. He gave the order to return to the landing.[80]

After improvising stretchers for the seven wounded and one dead soldier, they made their way back through the dark woods. Higginson posted a small force ashore as pickets and sent the rest of the men aboard the *John Adams*. After the sun rose, Robert Sutton appeared at Dr. Rogers's makeshift infirmary on the boat; he had been wounded in three places in the skirmish but had kept it secret to avoid being pulled out of action. As the surgeon treated his wounds, Sutton calmly recounted the night's events. Before the vessel took on board the pickets and pulled away from the landing to head back down the river, Higginson gave the order to burn the plantation house and outbuildings to the ground so they could no longer be used by the enemy.[81]

By noon that day the *John Adams* was tied up at the wharf of the ghost town of St. Mary's, situated at the mouth of the river on the Georgia side. On the way up, Higginson had spotted some lumber on the wharf, and he now intended to take it. Once a bustling little entrepôt, St. Mary's was these days so frequently visited by Yankee gunboats that its inhabitants, except for three elderly white women, had abandoned it. Higginson had been told by naval officers that the place was regularly used by the Rebels as a picket or an observation post. The officers had informed him furthermore that if he stopped at the town, the three women would tell him lies, insisting that they were good Unionists and that they had seen no Rebel soldiers in a long time; moreover, his vessel would in all likelihood be fired on by Confederates hidden in the woods behind the town as it pulled away from the wharf. Higginson had already made up his mind that if this latter prediction came true, he would burn the town.[82]

Dispatching some troops into the woods as pickets, he set others to work loading the lumber. He then spoke with the women, who responded exactly as predicted. He ordered their house searched for evidence of consorting with the enemy, but nothing incriminating was found. The lumber loaded and the pickets back aboard, the *John Adams* was just pulling away from the wharf when it was struck by a volley of gunfire from the woods—"a regular little hail-storm of bullets," in Higginson's words. Fortunately, no one was hit. The colonel directed the deck crews to fire their big guns into the woods, then ordered the boat back to the wharf and sent a company ashore to clear out the Rebel snipers, who promptly disappeared. Meanwhile he prepared to destroy the town. After frantic pleading by the women he agreed to spare their house but commanded that every other building downwind from it be torched, which amounted to all but three or four of the town's fifty or so standing structures. St. Mary's was furiously aflame as the *John Adams* pulled away and headed back to Fernandina Harbor.[83]

Higginson was not yet ready to bring the raid to a close. While the *John Adams* recoaled and the wounded men and lumber were transferred to the *Ben De Ford*, he went ashore at Fernandina. There he met an army officer who told him of a large stockpile of bricks near the village of Woodstock, Florida, forty miles up the St. Mary's River. These, the officer said, would be useful in strengthening a fort near Fernandina held by the army. At the same time, a navy officer told him of a rumor that a Rebel blockade-runner was anchored in the river near Woodstock, waiting for a chance to slip downstream and through the blockade; he was anxious to know if this was true. Higginson listened to both with interest and recalled that Robert Sutton's erstwhile owner lived in Woodstock. A visit to the village, he decided, might prove rewarding.[84]

On the evening of January 29 Higginson set out with a couple of hundred men aboard the *John Adams*, again leaving behind the oversize *Ben De Ford* and the unreliable *Planter*. Robert Sutton's knowledge proved crucial as the *John Adams* made its way up the river, which in its farther reaches was narrow, tortuous, choked with driftwood, and overhung with tree branches. Even with his skilled piloting, the boat ran aground eight times during the night. Each time, however, its captain and crew managed to free it. This moonlit voyage deep into enemy territory up a twisting, tapering river with steep, wooded banks impressed Higginson profoundly. Never before had he felt such a sense of exotic mystery and danger. The spell was broken only by the boat's arrival at Woodstock an hour or so before dawn on the thirtieth. Higginson immediately sent Major Strong and two companies ashore with orders to surround the village quietly and let no one leave. He himself disembarked after daybreak with the rest of the officers and men.[85]

Looking around, he regretted having promised in Fernandina to secure bricks, for there was a lumber mill here with boards stacked in huge piles, ripe for the plucking. The mill was the property of Mrs. Alberti, who also owned the biggest house in town and had once claimed Robert Sutton as her slave. Sutton had made his escape months before in a dugout canoe and had returned surreptitiously sometime later to bring away his wife and child. Higginson decided to call on Mrs. Alberti and invited her former bondsman to come along. The colonel found her to be a woman of aristocratic bearing and irritating hauteur. "To what am I indebted for the honor of this visit, Sir?" she asked him. He directed her attention to Corporal Robert Sutton, remarking that he believed she knew him. "Ah," she replied with icy contempt, "*we* called him *Bob*."[86]

Sutton's only response was to turn to his colonel and offer to give him a tour of the Alberti slave jail, to which he had secured the key. It was a small building near the house. When Sutton opened the door, Higginson was sickened. Here were chains and large iron staples for securing slaves for punishment and three sets of stocks, two of which had holes so small that Higginson surmised they were used to hold women or even children. In another building nearby he was shown an even more appalling sight, a peculiar device meant to bind offending slaves in an unnatural and painful position, neither standing nor sitting nor lying; it was nothing less than an instrument of torture. Higginson ordered that the stocks, chains, staples, and key be taken aboard the *John Adams*; he would present them as trophies to General Saxton. He regretted that the size of the torture device prevented bringing it back. He refrained from burning down the slave jail only because he feared the flames would spread to the lumber, which he hoped might eventually be seized for army use.[87]

Higginson then ordered his troops back aboard the *John Adams*, which steamed downriver a mile or two to the landing of the brickyard he had been told of. Several hours later the vessel pulled away loaded with bricks. Questioning of local blacks and whites had revealed that the rumored blockade-runner did exist and was anchored upriver but was too broken down to pose any threat to the federal blockade. As the *John Adams* headed downstream, Higginson, satisfied now with what the raid had accomplished and ready to return to Camp Saxton, went below to rest.[88]

The adventure was not yet over, however. Gunfire suddenly erupted from the Georgia bank of the river. Higginson heard and felt bullets smacking into the boat's hull. He ran up onto the gun deck along with some of his men, who immediately began shooting at the enemy. The gun crews opened up with their cannons. The deck was quickly enveloped in white smoke. Most of the men remained confined below deck by Higginson's order, jostling with one another for access to the few portholes, from which they could return fire. They pleaded to be put ashore so they could go after the Rebels and fight "*in de clar field*," but Higginson rejected that as pointless and potentially disastrous. For a time the enemy riflemen moved downstream along the bank, keeping up their fire, but eventually they quit. Only one person on the boat was hit in this encounter: its captain, killed by a bullet through the brain as he stood on the upper deck beside the pilothouse. Higginson feared that his loss would jeopardize the vessel's downriver voyage, but the crew and pilot Sutton brought the boat away safely and with no further casualties, although it was fired on again from the Florida side near Township Landing.[89]

At Fernandina, Higginson had the bricks unloaded from the *John Adams*, moved his headquarters to the *Ben De Ford*, and ordered the whole raiding force to head home. On the way back, he wrote a lengthy report of the operation for Saxton, praising the behavior of the regiment. On board also were some white soldiers and their officers being transferred from Fernandina to Hilton Head. The white soldiers were disgusted at the situation they found themselves in; they refused to sleep below with the men of the 1st South Carolina, preferring to expose themselves to the elements on deck. One of their officers, a lieutenant, remarked snidely to one of Higginson's captains that "these niggers" could never be relied on to fight. The captain's fierce reply quickly silenced him: "You d—d fool; these soldiers have already fought more bravely than you ever will."[90]

Higginson had the *Ben De Ford* dock at Beaufort before returning to camp so the wounded could be hospitalized there and he could see General Saxton. At dawn on February 2 he stepped onto the wharf and walked with Dr. Rogers to Saxton's headquarters to present his report and the slave jail trophies—as Rogers put it, "a message from heaven & one from hell." The general was not yet up, but Higginson was ushered into his bedroom. Saxton was elated by his account of the raid. They talked over breakfast, and then the colonel returned to camp.[91]

The material results of the raid were few. By Higginson's order the troops had brought away from the various points where they had landed, besides the lumber and bricks, some railroad iron, a small flock of sheep, a few horses and steers, some rice and corn, bedding for the regimental hospital, and a modest assortment of other useful supplies. They had also distributed copies of the Emancipation Proclamation, although to what effect they could not know. They had not encountered many slaves and had brought back only a few. Nevertheless, Higginson was much pleased by the raid, for it had accomplished just what he had hoped. The troops had gained experience in combat, demonstrated their mettle, and suffered no reverse. Moreover, in obedience to the colonel's stern command, they had indulged in no pillaging and had mistreated no Rebel citizens. "The men have been repeatedly under fire," he boasted in his report, ". . . and have in every instance come off not only with unblemished honor, but with undisputed triumph. . . . There is a fiery energy about them beyond anything of which I have ever read, except it be the French Zouaves." Robert Sutton he lauded as "the real conductor of the whole expedition"; Sutton received sergeant's stripes as his reward. Higginson also praised his officers—not least Major Strong, who had carried out his duties with surprising ability and had bravely exposed himself to enemy fire on the deck of the *John Adams*. The colonel was ready now to admit that he had misjudged the man.[92]

Higginson was also satisfied with his own performance, although he did not discuss this with others. Under fire he had not flinched, and he had kept his head. Thinking it over, he decided that facing enemy fire required less bravery than, say, rushing into a burning building or plunging into raging waters to rescue someone; bullets were invisible, and thus the danger was less apparent. He had found too that the exigencies of command distracted him from the physical danger and the horrible sights and sounds of combat. When the soldier fell dead at his side in the Township Landing skirmish, he later wrote, he was so busy assessing the situation and giving orders that he "felt it no more than if a tree had fallen."[93]

The men themselves were jubilant over what they called "de expeditious," and in the days following their return to Camp Saxton they told and retold stories about it around their campfires. Robert Sutton, who recovered quickly from his wounds, particularly enjoyed recounting his return to his former place of servitude. Listening to these increasingly exaggerated tales, Higginson realized that the raid had already begun to assume mythic status in the men's minds. He saw too that it had strengthened the regiment by solidifying the men's confidence in themselves and in their officers and likewise the officers' confidence in them. The men were eager now for another taste of victory. When, they asked, would the colonel again lead them to the Main and into battle against "de Secesh"?[94]

Tales of the St. Mary's raid spread not only through Camp Saxton but through the whole department, often in distorted form. The white soldiery heard some derogatory rumors: The men of the 1st South Carolina had panicked, thrown down their muskets, and scattered as soon as they encountered Rebel troops, or they had stood their ground, but only because they had been told that their own artillery would mow them down if they ran. Those who heard and believed these rumors were more than ever convinced that the experiment of arming blacks was worse than useless. But some white soldiers heard stories of the raid closer to the truth. A few began to manifest a grudging respect for the men of the 1st South Carolina; "they fight like deamons," wrote one.[95]

The weather on the Sea Islands turned warm and springlike in the second week of February, a remarkable phenomenon to a New Englander such as Higginson. The colonel recorded with near astonishment that mockingbirds were singing during the day, and tree frogs at night, and that robins were much in evidence. Flowers bloomed, and the foliage turned green; even the long-neglected ornamental shrubbery around the Smith manor struggled back to life. Higginson noted also that the flock of two dozen or so sheep that grazed nearby, another trophy of the expedition, lent an incongruously pastoral aspect to the camp. They would not graze for much longer, however. He intended that as soon as they were fattened, they would become mutton for the men, to replace the "impenetrable beef" routinely issued.[96]

On Sunday, the fifteenth, a clear, still day, the regiment assembled for a special occasion, a wedding in camp. The groom was Lieutenant George Dewhurst, Higginson's twenty-four-year-old adjutant. His bride was Hattie Somerby, a Bostonian to whom he had been engaged for some time and who had just arrived by steamship. She had made up her mind to set up housekeeping in camp, unlike most of the officers' wives. Immediately following dress parade, Higginson had the regiment form a hollow square. The men were clad in blue pants, at last. For some reason, however, they had been issued pants of dark blue rather than the standard light blue, but they were happy enough with them, and so was their colonel, who noted that they showed dirt less readily than light blue pants. Into the center of the square stepped the bride and groom, he in his dress uniform and she in a gown of green silk. The male and female attendants were Gideonites who had come down from Beaufort along with the 8th Maine band. Chaplain Fowler performed the rites. The men of the 1st South Carolina watched quietly and attentively. After husband and wife exited the square together, the colonel dismissed the regiment.[97]

In his tent that evening Higginson wrote a lengthier than usual journal entry. He had much on his mind. Tomorrow he and Saxton would go to Hilton Head to meet with General Hunter. Higginson had a proposal to make that he had been mulling over since the St. Mary's expedition. Always concerned that his journal might get into the wrong hands, he did not detail the proposal in its pages. But he did allude to it in the last paragraph he wrote this night; twice his pen spelled out the word "Florida."[98]

Chapter Three

HILTON HEAD

FEBRUARY 16

THE STEAMER THAT HIGGINSON AND SAXTON boarded in Beaufort on the morning of February 16 for the fifteen-mile trip to Hilton
Head took them down the Beaufort River and into Port Royal Harbor.
The scene in the harbor was impressive even to those who had seen it
many times; this was but Higginson's second experience of it. Anyone who
doubted the immense power of the Union navy had only to look upon
this sight to be persuaded. Here were vessels in great numbers, some at
anchor, others under way, ranging from small tugs and courier boats to
great transports and gunboats and ironclad monitors and tall-masted frig-
ates. Chief among them was the wind- and steam-powered frigate *Wabash*,
flagship of Rear Admiral Samuel F. Du Pont's South Atlantic Blockading
Squadron, manned by a crew of 523 and equipped with forty-six guns.
From the admiral's quarters aboard the *Wabash* flowed a steady stream of
dispatches to the dozens of armed vessels that enforced the blockade along
the coasts of South Carolina, Georgia, and Florida.[1]

As Higginson and Saxton gazed around admiringly, the steamer
threaded its way through the fleet and made for Hilton Head, on the far
side of the harbor. It was the easternmost point of Hilton Head Island
and, along with Bay Point, which was two and a half miles across the
water to the northeast, it marked the entrance to the harbor. Yankee
engineers had built an immense wharf at Hilton Head that projected a
good quarter mile out into the harbor, where the water was deep enough
to accommodate even the biggest ships. Here the steamer docked. Higginson and Saxton disembarked and made their way to Major General
Hunter's headquarters.[2]

Before the war there had been little at this site besides the summer

General Hunter's headquarters at Hilton Head.
(COURTESY OF LIBRARY OF CONGRESS)

home of a planter family named Drayton. The Confederates had built a fort here to defend the harbor, and after it fell in November 1861, the place was designated a Union army post and headquarters of the Department of the South. As the army constructed barracks, offices, warehouses, hospitals, and other facilities, it became a populous settlement, spreading over a hundred acres. Contrabands were hired to do the heavy labor. Sutlers and other civilian entrepreneurs came down from the North and established stores and restaurants and hotels along what was soon dubbed Robber's Row. Gideonites took up residence at the post and at some of the plantations in the island's interior to minister to the blacks. Four regiments of infantry and one of engineers were quartered at or around the post, along with two artillery batteries and a company of cavalry—nearly six thousand troops in all.[3]

Even with the sizable population, the continual coming and going of ships, and the never-ending loading and unloading and construction, Hilton Head seemed to Higginson anything but a bustling Yankee post. It was, rather, "like some foreign military station in the tropics," he thought. "The general impression of heat and lassitude . . . ; the sandy, almost impassable streets; and the firm, level beach . . . : all these suggested Jamaica or the East Indies." The atmosphere at Hunter's headquarters reinforced the sense of tropical languor. The building was the former

Drayton summer house, a wide one-story many-windowed structure with a veranda, painted white and overlooking the beach. A sentinel stood guard indifferently at the entrance, waving through pretty much anybody who asked to be admitted. Inside, as the caller was ushered through a succession of rooms into Major General Hunter's presence, he or she might catch a glimpse of the headquarters cat drowsing in the sunlight by a window and staff officers lounging around playing cards. The scene was "rather picturesque," Higginson decided, "but perhaps not altogether bracing."[4]

The general commanding the department received Higginson and Saxton affably and informally. He was anything but the spit-and-polish sort. Today his uniform vest was unbuttoned; some days he did not wear a uniform at all around headquarters, just a simple black suit. His wig was in place, however, as always. Higginson was struck again, as he had been when Hunter visited Camp Saxton a few weeks earlier, by his easygoing demeanor, so oddly devoid of urgency or "concentrated purpose." The man could be stirred to decisive action, as he had proved back in May 1862, when he began recruiting black troops on the Sea Islands without the War Department's permission; he could even act provocatively, as when he issued his own emancipation proclamation that same month—promptly overruled by the president, who at that point was still undecided about freeing the slaves. But Higginson was beginning to suspect that Hunter was basically indolent and indecisive until galvanized by some unpredictable impulse.[5]

Today Hunter seemed to be in no hurry at all to settle down to business. He chatted amiably with his callers and at one point summoned his adjutant, Lieutenant Colonel Charles Halpine, to entertain. Halpine, an Irish-born journalist and politician, had achieved some minor literary recognition publishing light verse and humorous essays under the pen name Private Miles O'Reilly, and Hunter asked him to read his latest composition. It was some time before Higginson and Saxton were able to present their case.[6]

What they proposed was to send the black troops back to the Main, not on a mere raid this time but to seize and hold some point permanently. No such expedition had heretofore been successfully undertaken in the Department of the South; the only Confederate territory now occupied by Hunter's forces was a few of the Sea Islands and Key West. This was a bold proposition, and Higginson and Saxton feared that Hunter might be unreceptive. They had therefore come well armed with arguments to sway him.[7]

Chief among these arguments was that a permanent foothold on the mainland would greatly aid in recruiting black troops. Saxton in particular was unhappy with the rate of enlistment, a matter he had worried about ever since he got the War Department's approval to recruit a military force of blacks on the islands back in August. It had taken until mid-January to bring the 1st South Carolina to full strength, and a second black regiment that Saxton was now organizing was filling very slowly. The problem of course was that the men most likely to volunteer were incoming fugitives from the Main. The difficulties of getting from the mainland to the Yankees, requiring either a hazardous journey through Rebel-controlled territory and across the water to an occupied island or the serendipitous appearance of a Union naval vessel or army amphibious force, kept the numbers of such fugitives down to a comparative trickle. A fortified post on the Main, Higginson and Saxton argued, would amount to an open floodgate, especially if it was held by black troops, whom the mainland slaves would embrace without suspicion. The expeditionary force, the two officers suggested to Hunter, should take along at least two thousand extra muskets and uniforms so that the slave men who would surely come pouring in could immediately be put into the ranks.[8]

The brigadier and the colonel certainly did not have to expend any effort persuading Hunter of the desirability of recruiting blacks. They did, however, have to convince him that black troops should invade the Main. For all his enthusiasm about black soldiers, Hunter believed that they were best employed in garrison duty, for they seemed to be more resistant than whites to the diseases such as malaria that afflicted troops in this theater of war, diseases particularly prevalent among stationary forces. Assigning the blacks to the essential garrison duties in the department, Hunter thought, would relieve white troops of that responsibility and free them for offensive operations without subjecting the blacks to any added health risks.[9]

Higginson and Saxton were prepared for this objection. Their answer was that the blacks were wasted on garrison duty, for their peculiarly fervent motivation generated a lust to engage the enemy and a zeal in battle that white troops could not match. Higginson had seen this at first hand,

and he was adamant that blacks belonged on the front line. A few weeks earlier he had written a letter to the governor of Massachusetts, subsequently published in Northern newspapers, that stated the case pointedly. The men of the 1st South Carolina were driven by a "fiery energy," he declared. "To use them for garrison duty only would be like reserving cavalry to defend a fortress, or making a reconnaissance with heavy artillery."[10]

Higginson and Saxton also shared the belief that black troops were the key to winning this war and that the U.S. government should proceed with full-scale enlistment of blacks in every theater. As they well knew, however, the government was still unwilling. At this moment Congress was considering a bill, sponsored by the radical Republican representative Thaddeus Stevens of Pennsylvania, to authorize the War Department to undertake massive black recruitment, some 150 or more regiments, but it had sparked fierce opposition, and its passage was doubtful. To Stevens, the issue was simple. "Of what use [will] be the Proclamation of Emancipation," he asked during debate on the House floor, "unless followed up by an army of negroes [?]" But moderate Republican members were unenthusiastic, and the Democrats were hostile. "Blacks [are] not necessary to put down the rebellion," claimed one Democrat; moreover, "they [are] not worthy to aspire to the position of freemen. . . . To so employ them would be a crime against the ages, [and] a violation of the Constitution." Another declared that "the white Anglo-Saxon race [is] capable of taking care of itself." Moreover, even in the unlikely event that the Stevens bill passed, it would merely authorize, not require, the president and secretary of war to enlist blacks en masse. All indications from the White House and the War Department at this point suggested that such authorization would not be acted on.[11]

Behind the reluctance of the Lincoln administration and the opposition in Congress was the continued unwillingness of the Northern public. Saxton, Higginson, and a few other officers commanding black troops had been vigorously promoting their cause by writing laudatory reports on their regiments intended for publication and by cultivating friendly newspaper correspondents. These efforts had paid off to some extent. Favorable comment on the 1st South Carolina, for example, and especially on the St. Mary's River raid, had appeared in the last three weeks in such newspapers as the New York *Tribune*, the New York *Evening Post*, the New

York *Times*, and the Boston *Daily Advertiser*. The more radical papers had by now endorsed massive recruitment of blacks; among them was the *Tribune*, whose editor affirmed that "the negro is indeed the key to our success." But as yet no tidal shift had occurred in press or public opinion that might encourage the government to push forward with black enlistment. Democrats remained bitterly opposed, as exemplified by a recent editorial in the Hartford, Connecticut, *Daily Times* that raged at the notion that "white and black soldiers are to march together under the banners of the Union, upon equal terms" and repeated the familiar arguments that enlisting blacks was "demoralizing to the army, as well as humiliating to the Union." This editor was certain that the "whole scheme of negro soldiers will fall, as the emancipation proclamation must inevitably fall, after doing much more harm than good."[12]

More important, the moderate Republican press, regarded by President Lincoln as the voice of the vital center of public sentiment, remained unconvinced. An editorial in the February 13 issue of the Boston *Daily Advertiser* had this to say:

> Wherever troops can be obtained, who are trustworthy and amenable to discipline, and who can be held in check and restrained from disorder and excess, . . . the government [should] call them into service. . . . Colonel Higginson's evidence is valuable, for the purpose of showing that such troops can be recruited to some extent among the slave population, and that they can be used with safety. . . . It is a very long step, however, to conclude from the success of this limited experiment that it is possible to raise an army of [blacks]. . . . Those who propose schemes of this sort forget the ignorance and mental darkness, which generations of oppression have fastened upon the mass of the slave population. . . . Those who . . . hope that we are to finish this war by black levies, are falling into a dangerous error.

While this editor seemed unlikely to change his mind no matter what the 1st South and the few other black units in service accomplished, the tenor of articles and editorials in other moderate newspapers seemed to leave open the possibility that they might in the future endorse the mass enlistment of blacks—but only if truly convincing evidence of the effectiveness of black troops was forthcoming.[13]

As Saxton and Higginson undoubtedly believed and perhaps reminded Hunter this day, a successful and well-publicized invasion of Rebeldom by the 1st South Carolina might tip the balance in the press, the public, the Congress, and the administration. But there would be little benefit to the cause of black recruitment if the regiment frittered away its time and energy guarding the Sea Islands.

Higginson and Saxton had come prepared today not only to justify an expedition but also to argue for a specific objective: Jacksonville, on the St. John's River in northeastern Florida. There was much to be said for this choice, and they proceeded to discuss its merits with General Hunter. The St. John's flowed northward from deep inside the state to a point below Jacksonville where it turned eastward, eventually emptying into the Atlantic. It had been a major artery of commerce before the war, being navigable to large vessels for at least fifty miles above Jacksonville. The town itself, some twenty-five miles by water from the river's mouth, was one of the largest in Florida, and it had good wharves. Once it was seized and fortified, the expeditionary force could use it as a base from which to launch further incursions up the river or inland. And there would be no shortage of guides for such incursions, for a number of men in the 1st South Carolina had been raised along the St. John's.[14]

The U.S. Navy had unchallenged control of the river. In the spring of 1862, Du Pont's squadron had established an "inner blockade" of the St. John's—that is, instead of merely sealing off the river at its mouth by patrolling outside the bar, blockade vessels were posted well within the bar, on the river itself. At any given time, from two to five steam-powered navy gunboats were on the St. John's, and at least one of them patrolled regularly as far as Jacksonville or even beyond. These blockaders coaled at Fernandina, on the occupied Sea Island of Amelia, about twenty miles north of the river's mouth.[15]

Although the Florida mainland was under Confederate control, the Rebels were helpless to prevent this routine Yankee penetration up the St. John's. There was not a single Confederate naval vessel there, and Confederate army troops could do nothing but snipe at the Union gunboats from the banks of that very wide river, an annoyance to the boat crews but not a threat. In the fall of 1862 the Rebels had tried to block the river by placing powerful artillery in a fortified position on St. John's Bluff, on the south bank below Jacksonville. This held the gunboats at bay for a time, but the Yankees soon responded with an amphibious operation that put troops ashore at a point on the river below the bluff. These troops marched inland, outflanking the fortification and forcing the Confederates to abandon it. Union naval control of the St. John's was thus secure, and that meant an army force in Jacksonville or anywhere else on the river could be readily supplied by transports and protected by gunboats.[16]

Another point in favor of sending the expedition up the St. John's was that the Rebel forces in northeastern Florida were known to be weak. Confederate Brigadier General Joseph Finegan commanded in the region. His District of East Florida, comprising all of the state east of the Suwannee River, was part of a Confederate army department whose commander, General P. G. T. Beauregard, had his headquarters in Charleston. Beauregard's primary mission was to defend Charleston and Savannah, and it was there that he concentrated the bulk of his forces. It was hardly a secret that he regarded defending Florida as a secondary concern and refused to commit many troops to it. Reports from the U.S. naval officers on the St. John's, who regularly went ashore to scout around and question local citizens, indicated that the Rebel troops in the region were stretched very thin. Finegan probably had at most a few thousand men and perhaps only a few hundred. With this minuscule force he had not only to keep an eye on the St. John's River and the Union garrisons at Fernandina and St. Augustine but also to maintain a cordon on both the Atlantic and Gulf coasts to try to keep slaves from escaping to the enemy.[17]

Higginson and Saxton thus had no doubt that Jacksonville could be taken and held by Union troops. In fact, as they well knew, it already had been—not once but twice. In March 1862, when the Union navy secured control of the St. John's River, two army regiments had occupied the town by order of Brigadier General Thomas W. Sherman, then commanding the department. It appeared at the time that this occupation, which was uncontested by the Rebels, would be permanent. But then Sherman was replaced by Hunter, who in early April ordered that Jacksonville be abandoned, claiming that the limited forces available to him were overextended. A small Union amphibious force had again occupied the town without significant opposition in October 1862, following the capture of the Rebel fortification on St. John's Bluff; again, however, it was withdrawn after a short time.[18]

Although Jacksonville was a strategically desirable point to hold, the decision on both occasions to relinquish the town was defensible, for the Department of the South was chronically short of troops. Regarded as something of a stepchild by the high command in Washington, it was generally among the last departments to be reinforced and the first to be called on to send reinforcements to other theaters deemed more important. Recently, however, the situation had changed. Not only did Hunter now have at his disposal one black regiment at full strength and another aborning, but he also had just received from another department reinforcements totaling no fewer than ten thousand troops, sent by order of the War Department to take part in the major offensive against Charleston that Hunter was planning in concert with Admiral Du Pont. The Department of the South was at this moment stronger than it had ever been, giving Higginson and Saxton hope that Hunter would now be willing to spare troops to hold Jacksonville.[19]

The colonel and the brigadier had little trouble demonstrating that an expedition up the St. John's was feasible, but it remained to be proved that it would actually be profitable. Just how many black recruits could be expected to come in was uncertain. Unlike coastal South Carolina and Georgia, northeastern Florida had few great plantations, and its slave population was comparatively small. On the eve of the war, according to the census report, there had been fewer than five thousand black people—young and old, male and female—in the four Florida counties that lay along the St. John's. It was known, moreover, that since the navy seized control of the river, some slaveowners living near it had removed their slaves to safer areas. It was known also that the Rebel army had ordered all free blacks living along the river to move inland, fearing they would aid the enemy.[20]

Furthermore, the Confederate troops in the region, though few, were under orders to guard vigilantly against escaping slaves. According to reports the Yankees had received, Finegan's units and the Rebel guerrillas or vigilantes who also patrolled northeastern Florida had succeeded in catching a number of slaves making their way to the enemy; some of these they had hanged as an example to others. Unquestionably, many potential black fugitives in the region were deterred by the threat of capture by Rebel troops.[21]

Some slaves were deterred from fleeing too by rumors that they would be mistreated by the Union army. Masters deliberately spread such stories among their bondsmen. The Yankees intended to ship all the blacks they took into Cuba and sell them, they claimed, or hitch them to carts and force them to work like mules. But some slaves needed no such discouragement to keep them from running to the Yankees because they were content with their lot—or at least content enough to reject the notion of abruptly uprooting themselves and heading off into the unknown. This sort of attitude had been manifested during the St. Mary's raid, when a number of the slaves whom Higginson and his men encountered expressed no interest in leaving their masters for a promised life of freedom on the occupied islands. Too, there were a few slaves who identified so closely with their masters that they not only would refuse to flee but would inform on those who tried to do so. Higginson's soldiers spoke bitterly of such people as "secesh negroes."[22]

These facts certainly cast doubt on the likelihood of recruiting many black men along the St. John's. But Higginson and Saxton could answer with another undeniable fact: Even with all the hindrances and discouragements and dangers, slaves in the region continued to flee from their masters in considerable numbers to seek sanctuary with the Yankees. The blockade vessels on the St. John's frequently took aboard fugitives, sometimes gathering in dozens on a single sweep up and down the river. During the last occupation of Jacksonville several hundred black runaways had come in and subsequently left with the occupation force. These escapees came not just from the counties along the St. John's but in many cases from farther away. A permanent occupation force of black troops on the river, insisted the colonel and the brigadier, would enormously improve a slave's chances of successful flight and would encourage more to flee.[23]

Higginson and Saxton had still more bolts in their quiver of arguments for the expedition. Florida was an important source of the corn and cattle that fed the Confederate army. A Union force on the St. John's could seize the provisions within its grasp and disrupt the Rebels' procurement system throughout a wider area, thus not only helping to feed itself but also forcing the already hungry soldiers of the Confederacy to pull their belts a notch tighter. Furthermore, there were reports of substantial amounts of cotton and turpentine in the St. John's area, which U.S. Treasury Department agents would be eager to confiscate and sell for the benefit of the government.[24]

A St. John's expedition would yield not only military and economic profit, Higginson and Saxton argued, but also political profit. President Lincoln hoped that as the Rebel states were subjugated militarily, they could be reconstructed politically. He was convinced that many citizens in the Confederacy were fundamentally loyal to the Union but had been either stampeded into supporting secession or forcibly suppressed by the Rebels and that many others who truly believed in the Confederate cause could be wooed back to the Union once they understood that the cause was hopeless and that the U.S. government was forgiving. In several Rebel states where the Northern army had a significant foothold, notably Tennessee and Louisiana, Lincoln had appointed an official to rally support for the Union and establish a loyal state government. A successful invasion of the Florida mainland could open up a new field for political reconstruction, which the president would surely find very gratifying.[25]

Northeastern Florida seemed especially fertile ground for reconstruction. The existence of strong Union sentiment in the region was not just a supposition but a demonstrable fact. Before the war Northerners had settled there in considerable numbers for reasons of health or business, and when secession came, they generally remained true to the Union. Many native white Southerners in northeastern Florida, influenced by their region's marginal relationship with the plantation South, where lay the heart of secession, likewise stood fast against the tide of secession. But voicing Union sentiments publicly became dangerous once Florida seceded. The secessionist majority demanded unanimity, and vigilantes and Rebel authorities cracked down hard on dissent. Some Unionists fled their homes and refugeed to the North. Those who did not had to deny their faith in order to live in peace.[26]

Unionism in northeastern Florida may have been silenced, but it was by no means extinguished. When Union forces seized Jacksonville in March 1862, the town's many Unionists celebrated joyously, openly welcoming the invaders and declaring their loyalty to the old flag. The unexpected order to withdraw the occupation force in April left them stunned and bitterly disappointed. Rather than face the wrath of the returning Rebels, most made the agonizing decision to abandon their homes and livelihoods and leave with the U.S. troops. But Unionism on the St. John's did not disappear with the departure of the Jacksonville contingent. A permanent federal occupation force on the mainland could liberate the silent Unionists who remained, providing a solid base of loyalty on which to build a new Florida government.[27]

Hope of reconstructing the state was bolstered too by reports of disaffection among citizens who had originally supported the Confederacy. Economic hardship, for one thing, was eroding civilian morale. The embattled and blockaded Rebel nation was ravaged by shortages and inflation. Its government seemed unable to cope with this crisis, and many citizens, particularly the hard-hit plain folk, were growing angry and disillusioned. During the occupation of Jacksonville in October, U.S. soldiers had encountered ragged women who spoke plaintively of the high price of goods and their desperate struggles to feed their families. Even more corrosive to morale was resentment over military conscription. Enacted in 1862, the Confederate draft provoked fierce opposition, especially among nonslaveholding families with farms or artisan shops, who could ill afford to lose the labor of their menfolk and who deeply resented the exemption of certain favored men, including large slaveholders. Rumors reached the federals that guerrilla bands had been formed on the Main to resist conscription, and that desertion was increasing among Finegan's troops. With protection and encouragement by Union forces, the disenchanted, hungry, war-weary Rebel citizens of northeastern Florida might be persuaded to rally around the Stars and Stripes and help reconstruct their state.[28]

Along with disaffected Rebels and liberated Unionists, there was a third potential constituency of a reconstructed Florida government, Northern colonists. Recently there had been much talk in the North of redeeming Florida by settling loyal people there. The least populous of the Rebel states, it was regarded by many Northerners as a kind of frontier, offering ample room for settlement. The foremost advocate of the colonization idea was a Massachusetts man named Eli Thayer, who in the 1850s had been prominent in the movement to plant Yankee free-soilers in the Kansas territory (a movement that Higginson had also taken part in). What Thayer now proposed was to organize and arm twenty thousand Northern volunteers and send them into Florida to establish free-labor farming communities. These settlers would initially be enrolled as soldiers and supplied by the U.S. Army, but after a time, having staked out their homesteads, they would revert to civilian status and be free to pursue agriculture and community building while remaining armed and vigilant against Rebel attack. Once the safety of their settlements was assured, women and children could join them. Thayer envisioned these colonies not as permanently isolated enclaves but as seedbeds;

from there the principles of Unionism, free labor, and democracy could spread, eventually liberating all Florida from the tyranny of the Slave Power.[29]

The Thayer plan won considerable support among the Northern public and in the government. Those endorsing it included the Unionist refugees from Florida living in the North, who by this time had emerged as a vocal lobby for the reconquest of their state. Favorable editorials and letters had appeared in newspapers. A delegation of German-Americans had recently called on President Lincoln to inform him that five thousand of their fellows were ready to go to Florida as colonists. A petition to Lincoln to appoint Thayer military governor of Florida with authority to carry out his proposal, drawn up by some of the Florida refugees, had been endorsed by 131 congressmen. Several of Lincoln's cabinet members had declared their support, and the president himself had hinted that he was favorable.[30]

Other Northerners argued for a variant of Thayer's proposal that would colonize Florida not with Yankees but with freed slaves. Some who backed this idea were white abolitionists who hoped to establish black emancipation on a firm foundation; others were white conservatives who feared that unless the freed people were provided for in the South, they would flock to the North. But the idea also won the support of the most prominent black person in America, the former slave Frederick Douglass of Rochester, New York. Douglass scorned the notion of deporting the emancipated slaves to some foreign land, a notion endorsed by Abraham Lincoln, among many others, for he insisted that blacks had just as much claim to America as whites. Opening Florida to colonization by the freed people, on the other hand, seemed to Douglass just and beneficial, a way to insulate them from white oppression while confirming their stake in America. "Let the freed slaves be sent into that state," he urged in the November 1862 issue of *Douglass' Monthly*, "with implements to till the soil, and with arms to protect themselves."[31]

Whatever plan might be adopted to people Florida with loyal settlers, it would require that they secure title to the land. On this matter a third visitor present today in General Hunter's headquarters spoke up. A civilian in his early forties, he was Lyman D. Stickney, the Treasury Department employee who had addressed the crowd in Smith's grove on Emancipation Day. He had accompanied Higginson and Saxton on the steamer from Beaufort this morning, and he was eager to offer the commanding general his thoughts on the proposed St. John's expedition.[32]

Stickney's official title was direct tax commissioner for Florida. Congress had passed the Direct Tax Law in June 1862. Its ostensible aim was to enable the government to collect directly in Rebel territory a federal tax levied on the states in August 1861; in fact it was a device to confiscate secessionists' land. Under this act, the secretary of the treasury appointed a three-man commission for each seceded state that Union forces had entered. The commissioners would assess all real properties in areas under federal control and announce the tax due on each. If the tax was not paid in sixty days, as was probable, for the owner was likely to be a fugitive Rebel or someone else unable or unwilling to render unto the federal Caesar, the commissioners would condemn the property in the government's name and then sell or lease it.[33]

Right now the territory in which Stickney and his two fellow Florida commissioners could actually seize property amounted to the two small Sea Islands where Fernandina and St. Augustine sat. Stickney was anxious for an invasion of the Florida mainland to expand his sphere of operation, and he told General Hunter so. In arguing his case, however, he was not acting simply as a Treasury Department functionary disinterestedly carrying out the law. As far as Stickney was concerned, the Florida Direct Tax Commission was the spearhead of Thayer's colonization movement. Stickney was in fact closely allied with Thayer and had spent much time with him in Washington in the last few months working to win government support of his plan.[34]

Stickney probably told Hunter of his connection with Thayer, but there were certain other matters that he assuredly did not share with Hunter or anyone else present this day. Stickney was a man with secrets. A New England–born attorney who had lived also in the Midwest and South, he was a rootless and unprincipled opportunist and a political chameleon, changing color to suit whatever situation he found himself in. Living in New Orleans in 1860, he had been a good Southern rights man, joining in the general denunciation of the vile Republicans. Visiting Tallahassee in the winter of 1860–61, he had hobnobbed on the best of terms with the secessionist politicians who were at that moment taking Florida out of the Union. After spending only a few months in Florida, during which time he engaged in some highly suspect and probably fraudulent business dealings and ran up a sizable hotel bill that he never paid, he left the South voluntarily to seek his fortune back in the North. There he promptly reincarnated himself as a devoted Republican, an ardent opponent of slavery and friend of the black race, and a longtime Florida Unionist dispossessed by the Rebels and driven from the state for his loyalty.[35]

The desire to ingratiate himself with men in power drew Stickney to Washington. There he wrote to President Lincoln, speaking on behalf of the Florida refugees and signing his letters "With high regard" and "Devotedly your friend." Eventually he worked his way into the good graces of the secretary of the treasury, Salmon P. Chase, by convincing him that he could help get Florida back into the Union. In October 1862 he was rewarded with the position of direct tax commissioner. He talked one of his fellow commissioners into going his bond, claiming falsely that he was worth fifteen thousand dollars but that the Rebels had seized his property.[36]

Stickney had not a whit of interest in the actual work of the Direct Tax Commission and spent almost no time on it. He simply collected his salary and left matters to the other commissioners. What did interest him was using his position to enrich himself. He devoted most of his time to procuring goods in Beaufort and Hilton Head and in the North for sale in a general store in Fernandina in which he was a secret partner, shipping the stuff at government expense with the claim that it was for the commission's use. He planned to establish another store on the Main as soon as the army gained a foothold. Should the Thayer plan succeed, he calculated, business opportunities in Florida would be boundless and he would be well positioned to exploit them. He dreamed of turpentine and cotton.[37]

So glib and engaging a character was Stickney, and so artful a confidence man, that no one in the Department of the South had yet caught on to him. To Higginson he was "our devoted civic ally." Saxton, inclined to see only the best in someone anyway, thought him a fine fellow and took him along on his rounds among the islands to address the contrabands. Dr. Seth Rogers, who met him on a ship on the way to Fernandina, came away convinced that "Judge" Stickney was "an able defender of the oppressed and a gentleman."[38]

As Stickney and the others set forth their arguments, Hunter listened. He raised objections here and there, but he was really not as skeptical of their proposal as Higginson and Saxton feared. Such an expedition would in fact complement many of his own desires. An early proponent of no-holds-barred warfare against the Slave Power, he had long insisted that one of the surest ways to weaken and punish the Rebels was to free their slaves. "They would rather lose one of their children," he quipped, "than a good negro." In December 1861, while he was stationed in Kansas and well before Union policy had turned emancipationist, Hunter had advocated sending a military force deep into Rebeldom with orders to liberate and arm slaves as it went: "The Great God of the Universe has determined that this is the only way in which this war is to be ended, and the sooner it is done the better."[39]

Moreover, although one of his first decisions as commander of the Department of the South had been to withdraw the occupation force from Jacksonville, Hunter had no objection in principle to holding points on the Main; it was simply a question of disposing wisely his limited resources. In late May 1862, just two months after assuming command, he had told Secretary of War Stanton that if sufficiently reinforced, he would not only capture Charleston and Savannah but also seize other positions on the mainland—he specifically mentioned Jacksonville—to create havens for runaway slaves. Now, with the recently arrived reinforcements, Hunter was at last confident that he could successfully carry the war to the Rebel Main.[40]

Furthermore, as far as Hunter was concerned, the black troops in particular could be spared for an expedition into Florida because he did not intend to use them in the upcoming campaign against Charleston. He was willing to put them into action, despite his belief that they were better employed as garrison troops, but he worried about how his white troops would react to fighting alongside them. Given the intense racial hostility of so many white soldiers, Hunter had concluded that it was best not to send white and black troops into battle side by side.[41]

On the matter of speeding up black recruitment, so important to Rufus Saxton, Hunter agreed fully. The commanding general had noted with displeasure that the 1st South Carolina and the new regiment being raised depended heavily for recruits on incoming fugitives from the Main. The refusal of so many able-bodied contrabands living on the occupied islands to volunteer perturbed him; they should be willing to fight for the government that had freed them, he thought, and for the liberty of their still-enslaved brethren. Although he had not yet issued the order, he had recently made up his mind to conscript every military-age black man on the islands who could wield a musket, exempting only those employed as army laborers or officers' servants. (This was yet another instance of his brashness, for he had no such authority; the War Department order permitting Saxton to enlist blacks specified that they be volunteers. In fact the U.S. government, unlike the Confederate government, had no power at this time to draft anyone into the army, black or white.) The unwilling contrabands and the plantation superintendents would howl, Hunter knew, as they had when he had done the same thing last May, but be damned to them. Even with this draconian measure in force, however, the problem of recruiting would remain unresolved; fully tapping the reservoir of black military strength in the department required opening conduits on the Main.[42]

In one other respect did Hunter's aims and those of his visitors converge. As Stickney certainly knew and doubtless reminded him today, Hunter had publicly endorsed the Thayer plan. In September 1862 the famous Kentucky abolitionist Cassius M. Clay had written to Thayer, at Thayer's solicitation, heartily approving his plan. Thayer forwarded this letter to President Lincoln but only after securing on it—under the words "Earnestly approved"—the signature of Hunter, who was in Washington at the time. In December, after it had become known that Hunter was to resume command of the Department of the South, his endorsement was again sought, and he gladly added it to the petition sent to the president by the Florida refugees with the signatures of many congressmen. The public too knew that Hunter stood behind the Thayer plan, for newspapers had reported so.[43]

Another matter was undoubtedly on Hunter's mind today, although it did not come up in the discussion. The commanding general was under pressure to prove himself. There was muttering on the islands, among soldiers and civilians, that he was not up to the job. In part this stemmed from his appearance and demeanor; he struck many of those who met him (including Higginson) as less than forceful and decisive, despite his occasional provocativeness. In part too it stemmed from resentment of his radicalism on the part of conservative officers and men; many were disgusted by his solicitude for blacks. But more than anything else, it was the lack of military activity in the department that raised doubts about

Hunter's competence. Fifteen months had passed since Union forces arrived in this theater, yet not a single Union soldier now stood on the mainland. Charleston and Savannah remained securely in Rebel hands; the conquered territory in the department amounted to a few islands. What had Hunter done as departmental commander to defeat the Southern rebellion, either last spring and summer or since he had returned in January?[44]

Hunter insisted of course that his hands had been tied by inadequate troop strength. Now reinforced, he was ready to take the offensive. However, as he had had to admit in a letter to the War Department just nine days ago, the movement against Charleston would be delayed for weeks. It was the navy's fault, he said; his troops were "ready to embark at six hours' notice," but three indispensable ironclads that Admiral Du Pont had promised him were not yet available. No matter where the blame lay, however, the postponement could only strengthen Hunter's critics in the department and perhaps raise questions in Washington as well. A successful occupation of the Main by his black troops might disarm the critics or at least stifle their grumbling until he could get his major offensive under way. Such a bold stroke would attract particular notice at this time, for there was no dramatic activity on any other front. In Virginia and Tennessee the opposing armies were huddled in their winter quarters, unlikely to move until mid-spring; along the Mississippi River, Grant's army was still bogged down in its effort to capture Vicksburg.[45]

Hunter made up his mind. He would approve the St. John's expedition. He announced his decision abruptly—"before half our logical ammunition was exhausted," as Higginson noted. Their purpose achieved, the colonel and the brigadier and the tax commissioner left the commanding general's headquarters, returned to the steamer at the wharf, and headed back to Beaufort.[46]

The expedition that Saxton and Higginson now turned their attention to organizing would be unlike any before seen in this war. For all their marshaling of facts to prove its military advantages, neither man thought of this as first and foremost a military mission. A permanent lodging on the Florida Main would certainly discomfit the Rebel army, as the two had pointed out to Hunter, but they regarded that as an incidental benefit of their primary aim. The potential political reward of the expedition—getting Florida back into the Union by rallying oppressed Unionists, disaffected Rebels, and perhaps Northern colonists—was likewise, in Saxton's and Higginson's minds, a desirable but no more than incidental benefit, which would in any event take a long time to bring to fruition.

Saxton intended the expedition to be, more than anything else, an assault on slavery. However much he had talked to Hunter of filling the ranks of black regiments, he saw this as something far grander than a mere recruiting mission. A post on the Main, fortified and held by his black troops, would, in Saxton's vision, be a great beacon of freedom, a magnet of liberty, drawing fugitive slaves by the thousands and perhaps tens of thousands from all over the Southeast. Florida would become a vast haven for the oppressed. There the blacks could establish homesteads, be equipped and taught to defend themselves, and thus remain secure against reenslavement whatever the war's outcome. Florida was especially suited to such an enterprise, Saxton thought, for its peculiar terrain lent itself to defensive warfare. Witness the success of the Seminole Indians in fending off white invaders for so many years. The Seminoles had ulti-mately been defeated and removed, of course, but they had been few and scattered and poorly armed. The black men and women who flocked to Florida in the wake of the St. John's expedition could, Saxton believed, if provided with a solid foothold and the means to defend it, maintain their freedom forever.[47]

Higginson was thinking along similar lines, but on an even grander scale. He hoped that the expedition would be the first of many. As more black regiments were raised, they could also be sent into the Confederate interior to seize and fortify positions and raise high the banner of free-dom. "A chain of such posts," he thought, "would completely alter the whole aspect of the war in the sea-board slave States."[48]

In conceiving this audacious strategy, Higginson unquestionably had in mind John Brown's raid on Harpers Ferry, with which he had been so intimately involved. Brown had envisioned igniting the destruction of slavery by invading the South with an armed force and securing in the Appalachian Mountains strongholds to which slaves would flee by the thousands. There, organized and armed, they would defeat all attempts to subdue them. Higginson, possessed by the idea that slavery could be extinguished only by violence and that the slaves must take a hand in their liberation, had applauded Brown's mission and helped finance it. To his deep disappointment the raid had been quickly crushed, and Brown's

scheme had been widely viewed as quixotic or downright insane. But that
was in Virginia in 1859. Florida in 1863 was another matter. The expedition to the Main might redeem Brown's failure. It could be the blade tip of
the dagger that Higginson had long dreamed of, the dagger of black revolt
that would deal the fatal blow to slavery.[49]

Higginson had in mind a more personal object too, which he had confided to his journal the night before the meeting with Hunter. He was
deeply concerned about the fate of his men. He worried constantly that
a war-weary North might give up the fight, withdraw its armies from
the South, and agree to an armistice granting the Rebels independence.
Should this happen, the men of the 1st South Carolina would be in peril.
They would not wish to flee to the North, Higginson knew, nor could they
look forward to much of a future if they did. They wanted to remain in
their native South, and they were willing to fight to preserve their freedom. But Higginson doubted that they could hold out for long on the Sea
Islands against an offensive by a victorious Confederacy; they would be
overwhelmed and reenslaved or slaughtered. They must occupy a more
defensible site. Florida, the colonel thought, was better. In considering
the expedition's precise target, he had noted in particular Jacksonville's
proximity to the Okefenokee Swamp. He was thinking not only of the
Seminoles, like Saxton, but also of the fugitive slaves of earlier times
known as Maroons, who had held out defiantly against reenslavement
in the island interiors of the Caribbean and the swamps of southeastern
North America. Higginson seriously considered the possibility that in
leading his regiment into Florida, he might be taking an irrevocable step.
He wondered "whether I might not end my days as an outlaw—a leader
of Maroons."[50]

Higginson's and Saxton's conceptions of the expedition's purpose differed only in detail and emphasis. Fundamentally the colonel and the
brigadier agreed: The 1st South Carolina Infantry would invade Florida
to make war on slavery.

Chapter Four

FROM PORT ROYAL ISLAND TO JACKSONVILLE

FEBRUARY 17–MARCH 10

HARDLY HAD HIGGINSON AND SAXTON left General Hunter's headquarters with approval for the St. John's expedition when rumors about it began circulating through the department. On February 19, just three days after the meeting, a newspaper correspondent at Hilton Head dispatched a distorted account that was printed in the New York *Tribune* on February 27:

> For some weeks preparations for a foray upon an extensive scale, into some of the most thickly populated districts of one of the three States comprised in the Department of the South, have been in progress with the greatest possible secre[c]y.... The plan is to surprise the Rebels, not with the phantom, but the reality of servile insurrection, by the sudden appearance in arms, in the region selected, of a body of no less than 5,000 negroes, properly led by whites and supported by regular troops. Communication has been opened and kept up for some time by trustworthy contrabands with the bondmen of the chosen field of operations, and they know when the liberating host will appear, and are ready to rise in thousands and swell it to a wave so mighty that it will sweep both Rebellion and Slavery out of existence wherever it may roll. ... The question of fighting Rebels with their slaves [will thus be] placed beyond the control of politicians.

The next day the *Tribune* published an editorial defending the purpose of the expedition (the precise destination of which the newspaper did not name) against the protests already being voiced by outraged Northern Democrats.[1]

Given the location of the *Tribune* correspondent, the source of the leak was undoubtedly Hunter or one of his staff. Many officers in the department were careless about such things, and journalists on the occupied islands frequently reported information about Union army and navy movements and strength that was of great interest to Rebel commanders on the Main, who regularly read Yankee newspapers. Higginson fretted about such breaches of security and was always tight-lipped about his own plans. In the days following the Hilton Head meeting he did not commit to paper any details of the St. John's expedition, even in his private journal or letters, and he spoke of it only to those he thought really needed to know. Fearing leaks from his headquarters in Beaufort, he even asked General Saxton not to issue written orders for the expedition until the troops were aboard the transport vessels. The colonel's efforts were pretty much wasted, however. Before long the expedition's mission and destination were known and talked about all over the department. No other report appeared in print, however, until after the troops had sailed.[2]

The St. John's expedition was not the only spicy meat that gossipmongers in the Department of the South battened on in the latter part of February. Another lively topic of conversation was a high-ranking officer who had gotten himself into trouble by saying out loud that he would rather see the North lose the war than rely on black troops to help win it. He was Brigadier General Thomas G. Stevenson, a brigade commander in the force that had recently arrived in the department to strengthen Hunter in anticipation of the Charleston campaign. This force was (in the words of a newspaperman on the islands) "tinctured—no, *permeated*" by proslavery sentiment, and Stevenson was not shy about airing his opinions. Word of his indiscretion got to Hunter, who immediately relieved him of duty and put him under arrest. He would remain under arrest, said the commanding general, until President Lincoln decided what to do with him. Opinion in the department about this incident divided sharply and predictably along partisan lines. Conservatives came to Stevenson's defense. Others, including Higginson, applauded Hunter; officers like Stevenson, the colonel believed, "need discipline." The episode was further evidence that however easygoing Hunter might seem, he had some raw nerves and could be provoked to decisive action. It was also a pointed reminder that the 1st South Carolina was far from winning full acceptance in the army of the Union.[3]

Meanwhile Higginson and Saxton worked out details of the expedition, stockpiled supplies, and arranged transportation. This was a much bigger undertaking than the St. Mary's raid, for the St. John's expedition involved not only more troops but also a permanent change of base. Everything the soldiers required, down to their company cooking kettles and laundry tubs, would have to be shipped to Florida. Arms and ammunition would of course command priority. Higginson's men would be better armed on this expedition than on the raid; on February 20 they received new muskets to replace the inferior ones most of them carried. These replacement weapons were not the Springfields that General Hunter had promised; but they were good imported Austrian rifles, and Higginson was pleased with them. On the day these arrived, so did two additional howitzers (small smoothbore cannons) for the *John Adams*, which would transport part of the regiment to Jacksonville.[4]

While Higginson and Saxton made their preparations, the familiar routine at Camp Saxton continued. The men's day began with reveille at six-thirty, breakfast at seven, and surgeon's call at seven-thirty. Then came drill for all those not detailed to guard or fatigue duty, followed by a rest period and then more drill until dinner at noon. At two drill resumed, after which the men had an hour's break to prepare for dress parade at four-thirty. Supper was at five, roll call and tattoo at eight. The day ended with taps at eight-thirty, when the men were expected to be bedded down in their tents with campfires extinguished. The fading of the winter's chill, the lengthening of the days, and the luxuriant ripening of the island flora made all these duties seem less onerous to the men and officers, and they grew more lighthearted as the spring advanced. Higginson was amused to see soldiers who were detailed to gather firewood returning to camp with the logs balanced on their heads and their calloused hands full of daffodils and narcissi. He and his men were cheered too by the many new birdcalls now emanating from the live oak grove and the cypress swamps, although in nearly every case they turned out to be the work of some sly mockingbird. Turtles, frogs, and snakes were now stirring about too, but thankfully it was still too early in the season for the dreaded invasion of flies, mosquitoes, and fleas.[5]

Each evening between supper and tattoo, as long as it was not raining, the men gathered around campfires in the company streets. Some sat quietly smoking or cleaning their rifles, some practiced drill or reading and writing, but most came together in what Higginson called "strange concerts, half powwow, half prayer meeting." He never lost his fascination with these nightly rituals, and he filled his journal and letters with transcriptions and descriptions of the vivid prayers, heartfelt speeches, rich songs, and rhythmic movement he witnessed. "Let me lib wid de musket in one hand and de Bible in de oder," he heard one soldier pray, "—dat if I die at de muzzle of de musket, die in de water, die in de land, I may know I hab de blessed Jesus in my hand, and hab no fear." The livelier songs were accompanied by a percussive stamping of feet and a rapid castanet-like clapping of hands. Sometimes the singer would be surrounded by a circling, chanting, shuffling, whirling ring of men, in what was known as a shout. Many of the songs, however, were slow, plaintive spirituals in a doleful minor key, often with a responsive refrain sung by a chorus of soldiers. Some of these struck Higginson as true poetry, among them:

> *I know moon-rise, I know star-rise,*
> > *Lay dis body down.*
> *I walk in de moonlight, I walk in de starlight,*
> > *To lay dis body down.*
> *I'll walk in de graveyard, I'll walk through de graveyard,*
> > *To lay dis body down.*
> *I'll lie in de grave and stretch out my arms;*
> > *Lay dis body down.*
> *I go to de judgment in de evenin' of de day,*
> > *When I lay dis body down;*
> *And my soul and your soul will meet in de day*
> > *When I lay dis body down.*

The men thought of themselves as a "gospel army," the colonel wrote, and to him the deep religiosity that pervaded Camp Saxton made "all the white camps seem very rough & secular."[6]

Encouraged by the warming weather, the visits of curious civilians to the black soldiers' camp continued too. Higginson generally ignored these interlopers if he could, but on Saturday, February 21, he welcomed one and invited her to dine with him. She was Charlotte Forten, the pretty young quadroon Gideonite and friend of Dr. Rogers. The colonel had not seen her since the Emancipation Day ceremony, but two days ago he had sent her a message. This note—conveyed by Rogers, who had gone to see her at the plantation on St. Helena Island where she taught school—asked

Forten to join the expedition to Florida and serve there as a teacher for the men of the 1st South Carolina. It also begged her to keep the matter secret for now. Today she came to speak with Higginson about his proposal.[7]

The twenty-five-year-old Forten had been born and raised in Philadelphia, the daughter of prominent and well-to-do parents whose forebears for several generations back had been free. Educated at home and in private schools in New England, she played the piano, read Latin, French, and German, and had developed a talent for writing prose and poetry. She had published some of her work while still in her teens and had continued to write and publish while teaching school in the Northeast. Recently the *Liberator*, the journal of radical abolitionist William Lloyd Garrison, had printed several long, descriptive letters from her about her experiences among the contrabands on the Sea Islands, where she had arrived in October 1862. The plantation school where she taught with several other female Gideonites had been drawing some 200 black youngsters daily; but now, with the advent of planting season, the older children were called to the fields, and attendance had declined to 125 or so.[8]

In some ways Forten felt herself a misfit in the world she inhabited. Nearly all the people of her social class were white—she had been the only black student at the girls' grammar school she attended in Massachusetts, and she was now the only black teacher on St. Helena Island—and she felt keenly the many slights she received on account of her race. Few whites, even among the most broad-minded, such as the Gideonites, fully accepted her as an equal, and many were grossly hostile. On the other hand, she did not accept as equals most of the people of her own race, especially those of the Sea Islands, whom she viewed (in common with the other Gideonites) as semisavages who must be lovingly but firmly remolded in the image of middle-class Northerners. The contrabands, for their part, looked askance at Forten. The children came to love her, but many of the adults regarded her as just a "nigger" acting white.[9]

Her relationship with Seth Rogers brought her much joy, although tinged by wistfulness. She was in fact involved in a passionate affair with the doctor, who was not only white but also married and fifteen years her senior. She had known him since 1860, when he treated her at his water cure clinic in Massachusetts. From the moment of their reunion at the Emancipation Day ceremony they had rarely been out of each other's thoughts. Rogers had gone to see her on St. Helena Island no fewer than three times since then, although this required not only taking leave from duty but also traveling four miles to Beaufort, across the river by ferry, and another five miles to Forten's plantation. Two of these were overnight stays. Between visits they sent notes to each other, and she also sent some ginger cakes that the doctor only reluctantly shared with his fellow officers, as Colonel Higginson remarked wryly, along with other comments about Rogers's closeness to his "little friend."[10]

Whether their mutual infatuation had progressed to a physical relationship, only they knew. Both were discreet about the affair. But its romantic intensity was evident in the pages of her private journal. "I w[ou]ld like him to know how constantly I think of him," she wrote on January 26 and, after he visited her two weeks later, this: "He said he wished he lived nearer that he might come in and read to me sometimes. Ah! w[ou]ldn't *I* enjoy that, unspeakably." When he came to see her on February 19, bearing Higginson's message, they rode alone on horseback at twilight through woods adorned with fragrant, flowering jasmine vines. "Dr. R. broke off long sprays and twined them around me. I felt grand as a queen. . . . I shall never forget how that rosy light, and the moon and stars looked to us as we caught them in glimpses, riding through the dark pines. How wild and unreal it all seemed and what happiness it was. . . . There is a magnetism about him impossible to resist."[11]

Their romance had no future, given their circumstances and the realities of the world they lived in. Surely both expected that it would soon end. For now, however, they would continue, circumspectly but hungrily. It was undoubtedly at Rogers's urging that Higginson invited Forten to go to Florida. She, for her part, decided that she would go.[12]

On February 23, two days after Forten's visit, the 2nd South Carolina Infantry arrived at Camp Saxton. Rufus Saxton had begun organizing this regiment in January, as soon as the ranks of the 1st were filled. Its commander was Colonel James Montgomery, who had won fame in the 1850s as a warrior in the free-soil cause on the Kansas plains. Montgomery had come to the Department of the South in late January and had set about enlisting men on the Sea Islands—or had tried to, until he saw that the well was dry. In early February he headed to Key West, the remotest post of the department and the only one not yet scoured for black recruits. Orders from General Hunter authorized him to seize every able-bodied male contraband on the Key, whether willing to be a soldier or

James Montgomery.
(FROM WILLIAM G. CUTLER,
HISTORY OF THE STATE OF KANSAS
[CHICAGO, 1883])

not, but Montgomery found that volunteers came forth readily. He enlisted more than a hundred, brought them aboard the transport vessel he had arrived on, and asked its captain to set a course for Port Royal Island, where a campsite for the new regiment had been laid out next to the 1st South Carolina's.[13]

As the boat entered the Beaufort River late in the day on the twenty-third, nearing the end of its long voyage, Montgomery asked the captain to put in at the camp landing. The captain, thoroughly disgusted at being required to transport black recruits for the army, took this opportunity to get even. He ignored Montgomery, continued upriver to Beaufort, and docked at the wharf. The colonel and his tired men now faced a four-mile march to camp. At that moment General Saxton came to their rescue. He had gone to the camp that day, hoping to greet Montgomery and his men on their arrival, only to see the transport pass right by. Immediately he mounted up, rode back to Beaufort, and ordered the captain to obey Montgomery. It was well after dark when the colonel and his men finally came ashore at the camp.[14]

Saxton intended to send the 2nd South Carolina on the St. John's expedition, but whether it could contribute much was questionable. Right now it amounted to just a couple of companies, with no prospect of adding to its numbers until a foothold was secured on the Main. The men were of course as raw as they could be, wholly untrained; it would take time to make them anything like soldiers. Nor could they be fully equipped right away. Montgomery had secured uniforms from the department's supply depots, but for now weapons were unavailable. He would have no difficulty finding officers to lead the men, however. There were many applications from soldiers of white units in this and other departments for any available position in the new regiment.[15]

No tent was ready for Montgomery when he arrived, so Dr. Rogers offered his own and slept that night in the tent of his nephew, the company commander James Rogers. In a letter he wrote the next day, the surgeon described the forty-nine-year-old Ohio-born Montgomery: "A compact head on slightly rounded shoulders, a tall form of slender build, dark, bronzed face, deep brown and slightly curling hair, a Roman nose, heavy beard and moustache." The colonel's manners belied his reputation as a rough Westerner. Gentlemanly, soft-spoken, and straitlaced, he had a pleasant smile that he displayed often, and he abstained strictly from liquor, tobacco, and vulgar language. His speech was fluent, and his grammar flawless. He reminded people of a schoolmaster and indeed had been one for a time. But just beneath his soft surface was iron determination. He generally got his way in confrontations. Had he had any armed soldiers with him on the transport returning from Key West, the captain and crew would surely have found themselves obeying his commands at gunpoint.[16]

Montgomery had also been, in his younger days, an itinerant Campbellite preacher, and even now he was driven by a fierce biblical faith. Never troubled by doubts about his own righteousness or ability, he viewed his work in the cause of freedom as service in a holy crusade. Now and then his pleasant expression abruptly gave way to a fearsome glare as he spoke of doing the Lord's will by crushing the rebellious South and castigating the traitorous slaveholders. In the late 1850s, after staking claim to a homestead in the strife-ridden Kansas Territory, he had led a band of free-soil jayhawkers that left in its wake dead bodies and plundered homes of proslavery Kansas settlers and Missouri "border ruffians." The Civil War offered a wider field for his work of violent retribution. His government had so far been shamefully lenient toward the secessionists, he thought; it must loose fire and sword to scourge and purify the South.[17]

Montgomery was one of those abolitionists who hated slavery without caring much about the slaves. He worried far more about what the poisonous, reactionary "peculiar institution" did to the divinely sanctioned American Republic than what it did to the enslaved. To abolitionists of the benevolent sort he acknowledged the essential humanity of the black race, and he no doubt believed in it, in a theoretical way; but in his gut he considered blacks disgustingly uncivilized, intellectually inferior, repulsively ugly, and many generations away from being ready to assume civil or political or social equality with whites—if indeed they would ever be ready. He was skeptical even of his own troops, whom he habitually called "niggers." Convinced that they would be less brave and less dependable than white troops because of what slavery and their very nature had made them, he was satisfied simply to get whatever he could out of them in his crusade to humble and despoil their former masters.[18]

Higginson, who had known Montgomery slightly before the war and admired his work in the cause of freedom, had eagerly anticipated his arrival in the Department of the South. A man with his experience in warfare would be very useful in Florida. Higginson had a feeling, however, one that was confirmed as he came to know him better, that Montgomery was contemptuous of army regulations and paperwork and uninterested in really drilling and disciplining his men. He seemed to regard the 2nd South Carolina as a kind of freebooting guerrilla band, like the one he had led in Kansas, rather than as a trained body of soldiers schooled to face the enemy in stand-up battle. Higginson worried too that Montgomery's lust to punish the rebellious South would propel him beyond the bounds of civilized warfare.[19]

With February's end the pace of events began to quicken in anticipation of the St. John's expedition. On the first of the new month Montgomery led his two companies to a campsite at Beaufort. They would board their transport at the town's wharf and thus relieve the pressure on Camp Saxton's landing. The next day Dr. Rogers summoned all the newer recruits of the 1st South Carolina he had not yet examined. About 100 reported to him; he regretfully discharged 30 for physical or mental incapacity. With 8 men now in the general hospital at Beaufort and 17 in the regimental hospital (who were to remain behind in the care of the assistant surgeon J. Milton Hawks), the 1st South Carolina would sail to Jacksonville with about 775 officers and men. The two companies of the 2nd would bring the total expeditionary force to around 900.[20]

March 3 proved to be a notable day. An army paymaster showed up to give the men of the 1st South Carolina their long-overdue pay. Higginson spent a good part of the day counseling men who came to him with questions about how to bank the money, send it to their wives, and so forth. He also spent time with an agent of the U.S. Sanitary Commission, a private benevolent association that provided for the wants of soldiers and had authority from the government to inspect army camps and recommend improvements. During the course of the day, agent M. M. Marsh nosed around Camp Saxton, peering into tents, cookhouses, latrines, and the hospital and questioning Higginson and Dr. Rogers and others. He carried an eleven-page printed reporting form that required answers to nearly two hundred questions about the regiment's campsite, rations, water supply, refuse disposal, tents, bedding, health, and so on. In this case his report was quite favorable, a credit to Higginson's attention to regulations and discipline and his concern for his men. Marsh's only recommendations were to allow more space between tents and to require the men to bathe daily. Rogers was particularly pleased with the results of the agent's visit. Apprised of the doctor's frustrations in dealing with the departmental bureaucracy, Marsh gave him permission to draw on the well-stocked Sanitary Commission office in Beaufort for any medical supplies he needed. Rogers immediately dispatched an assistant to Beaufort with a requisition.[21]

March 3 was also the day that Higginson's men began loading the transport steamers that would take them to Florida. One of these, the *John Adams*, was familiar to the men of the 1st South Carolina, having been their mainstay on the St. Mary's raid. The others were the *Boston* and the *Burnside*. All were army vessels, and only the *John Adams* was armed; but Higginson was counting on support from navy gunboats once he reached the St. John's. The three transports anchored off Camp Saxton's landing, where a huge accumulation of supplies sat: not only ammunition, rations, camp equipment, and medical stores but also supply wagons, draft horses, and hundreds of muskets to arm the current and future recruits of the 2nd South Carolina. All this had to be laboriously loaded onto flatboats, ferried out to the transports, hauled aboard, and stowed away. Quartermaster Luther Bingham supervised the process, which took a good twenty-four hours. The light of the nearly full moon allowed the men to work around the clock.[22]

On the fifth the *Burnside* weighed anchor and steamed up to the Beaufort wharf, where it took aboard the men and officers of the 2nd South Carolina (Colonel Montgomery had by now recruited a major, two captains, and two lieutenants for his regiment). The vessel then returned to the landing. That afternoon Higginson's men struck their tents, bade farewell to Camp Saxton, and trooped down to the landing laden with their rifles, cartridge boxes, rubber and wool blankets, folded tents, knapsacks, haversacks, and canteens. Ferrying the men out to the transports boatload by boatload was another lengthy process, and it was well after dark before all were aboard. Fortunately the weather was good, so they did not have to stand around in rain. Company A under Captain Trow-bridge joined the 2nd South Carolina on the *Burnside*, companies B and C and Lieutenant Colonel Billings boarded the *John Adams*, while Colonel Higginson, Major Strong, Dr. Rogers, and the other seven companies climbed aboard the *Boston*.[23]

Higginson, the senior officer on the expedition, was in overall command. Late on the fifth he received his formal written orders from Saxton. The general carefully spelled out the objectives of the mission in order of priority, adding a fervent but most unmilitary benediction:

> Head-quarters, Beaufort, S.C.
>
> March 5, 1863
>
> Colonel,—You will please proceed with your command, the First and Second Regiments South Carolina Volunteers, which are now embarked upon the steamers John Adams, Boston, and Burnside, to Fernandina, Florida.
>
> Relying upon your military skill and judgment, I shall give you no special directions as to your procedure after you leave Fernandina. I expect, however, that you will occupy Jacksonville, Florida, and intrench yourselves there.
>
> The main objects of your expedition are to carry the proclamation of freedom to the enslaved; to call all loyal men into the service of the United States; to occupy as much of the State of Florida as possible with the forces under your command; and to neglect no means consistent with the usages of civilized warfare to weaken, harass, and annoy those who are in rebellion against the Government of the United States.
>
> Trusting that the blessing of our Heavenly Father will rest upon your noble enterprise,
>
> > I am yours, sincerely,
> >
> > R. Saxton,
> >
> > Brig.-Gen., Mil. Gov. Dept. of the South.[24]

By now the men and officers all knew they were headed for the Main to make war on slavery. The atmosphere on the three crowded transports crackled with excitement and anticipation; this would be an "expeditious" like no other. For those men who had left behind loved ones on the Main, the mission would have particularly special meaning. None was more eager to go than Private John Quincy, the cook of Company G of the 1st South, who was aboard the *Boston*. His wife and two children were still held in bondage in Palatka, a town on the St. John's above Jacksonville. Quincy seemed like an old man among his mostly young comrades in the regiment, although he was only in his mid-forties. His flight to freedom in 1862 must have shocked his master, for he had been among the most favored of slaves, one of those permitted to hire his own time—that is, to labor independently, expected only to turn over a portion of his earnings to his owner. He had worked as a hostler, living apart from his master and paying him twenty dollars a month. A man of deep and abiding Christian faith, Quincy had once told Dr. Rogers that he had been "trabblin by dis truth sometin' like twenty-five year." He had learned to read a little too, although recently he had lost his glasses. Three days ago he had asked the doctor to "send up North" for a new pair so he could resume his study of the Bible. Quincy also served as a sort of lay preacher in the 1st South and was often called on to offer a prayer or speech when some important event was at hand. He believed in his heart that his regiment was an instrument in the hands of a righteous God. Describing the firing of one of the big guns of the *John Adams* during the St. Mary's raid, he had told a congregation of soldiers that "when de shell went out it was de scream ob de great Jehovah to de rebels." He also believed, and repeatedly told his comrades, that a soldier who was truly brave and trusting in the Lord would be impervious to Rebel bullets.[25]

Among the many others aboard the transports who were eagerly anticipating the expedition was a man not in uniform. It was Lyman Stickney, direct tax commissioner for Florida. He had remained in Beaufort since the February 16 meeting with General Hunter, devoting not one minute to the work of the Tax Commission but instead procuring goods for his store in Fernandina and the one he hoped to set up in Jacksonville. Stickney was fairly salivating with hunger for the profits he expected to reap once the expedition had secured a foothold. On February 18 he had sent one of his business partners a letter in which while saying nothing specific about the St. John's expedition, he predicted gleefully: "There is a good time coming."[26]

Several women, black soldiers' wives who earned money doing laundry for the officers and men of the 1st South, were also on the transports. One was fourteen-year-old Susie King, who was married to Ned King, a twenty-five-year-old private in Company E. Born a slave on one of the Georgia Sea Islands and raised in Savannah, she had learned surreptitiously from free blacks and friendly whites how to read and write. Along with several of her kinfolk she had gained freedom in 1862 by fleeing to a Yankee gunboat on the Georgia coast. When not busy at her washtub, she gave reading and writing lessons to the men of the 1st.[27]

Charlotte Forten was not aboard a transport. She planned to go with two of the officers' wives, who intended to wait several weeks before joining their husbands in Florida. Three nights ago she had received a note from Dr. Rogers, his last before departing. He urged her to join him soon in Jacksonville. With the note he sent a little gift of some sort, one so personal that she would not name it even in her journal; all she would say was that it was "beautiful and true." Perhaps innocently, or perhaps as a pointed reminder of the ties that bound him, Rogers also enclosed an affectionate note he had recently received from his wife in Massachusetts. "It somehow brings me nearer to him," Forten wrote.[28]

The *Burnside* set out for Fernandina as soon as its complement of troops was on board. The *Boston* and *John Adams* lay anchored near the landing until the next morning, March 6, when they steamed down the river and across the harbor and tied up at the long wharf at Hilton Head. Here Higginson had one last matter of business. From General Hunter he procured a letter addressed to Admiral Du Pont, requesting the navy's cooperation in Higginson's "important mission" without identifying its purpose or exact destination. While arranging this, Higginson no doubt learned of the two significant general orders Hunter had just issued. One instructed the troops of the Department of the South to be prepared for imminent action in a major offensive; the objective was not named in the order, but it was widely understood to be Charleston. The other order put into effect Hunter's earlier decision to conscript every able-bodied male military-age contraband on the occupied islands. No exceptions would be made for hands on the free-labor plantations or anyone else, unless employed by the army. The draft would begin immediately. General Saxton strongly opposed this measure, as Hunter and Higginson knew, for he had long assured the contrabands that military service would be strictly voluntary. This was not how Saxton wanted to fill his black regiments, but Hunter was adamant.[29]

Hunter's letter to Du Pont was dispatched to the admiral's flagship in the harbor. Du Pont immediately sent back a letter for Higginson to show to the captains of navy vessels wherever he went, authorizing them to render assistance. With this, Higginson's preparations were complete. That afternoon he gave the order that put the *Boston* and *John Adams* on a southward course to Florida.[30]

As the expedition set forth, Saxton sent a letter to Secretary of War Stanton telling him of it. The general was determined that the exploits of his black troops in Florida would not pass unnoticed by the nation's leaders or by the public at large. "I feel great hopes that we shall strike a heavy blow," he told Stanton. "I have reliable information that there are large numbers of able-bodied negroes in that vicinity who are watching for an opportunity to join us." If weapons and ammunition sufficient to arm all these potential black recruits could be provided, "it is my opinion that the entire State of Florida can be rescued from the enemy, and an asylum established for persons from other States who are freed from bondage by the proclamation of freedom, from which they can never be driven. The history of the Florida Indian war shows how strong this peculiar country is for a defensive warfare." He promised to send more reports as the mission progressed.[31]

This dispatch to the War Department exuded unalloyed optimism; privately, however, Saxton, no less than Higginson and the others who had set the expedition in motion, was acutely mindful that it might well end in disaster. Once the Rebels recognized the revolutionary nature of the mission, they were sure to rally desperately against it and do all in their power to crush it. And failure could be catastrophic, as Saxton and others saw it, not only for the men of the expedition but also, by casting doubt on the efficacy of colored troops, for the entire black race and for the Union. The potential rewards of a successful mission, however, justified the awful risk. Victory in Florida would not only bolster the cause of black recruitment but might also inspire a wholly new strategy by which to defeat the Southern rebellion and destroy slavery.[32]

An hour or so before noon on Saturday, March 7, the *Boston* and *John Adams* steamed into Cumberland Sound, having traveled a little more than a hundred miles from Hilton Head. The guns of Fort Clinch, on the northern tip of Amelia Island, guarded the sound, into which the St. Mary's River emptied. The fort, and with it all of the island, including the town of Fernandina, had been evacuated by Rebel forces in March 1862 and occupied since by Union troops. Passing the fort, the two ships proceeded southward through the channel separating the island from the mainland. A passage of a few miles brought them to Fernandina's harbor. There they rendezvoused with the *Burnside*, which had arrived twenty-four hours earlier.[33]

Fernandina was a pretty town of some three or four hundred houses and other buildings—or it had been, before the Yankee garrison troops began pillaging, dismantling, and burning it. Among the once-attractive houses lining its sandy, shell-covered streets was that of Joseph Finegan, formerly a prominent lawyer and businessman and now the commander of Confederate forces in eastern Florida. Like Beaufort, Fernandina was now full of contrabands, predominantly refugees from the Main. Only a few dozen white residents of the town, most of them Northern-born, had remained when the Rebels pulled out. Quite a number of the contrabands were wives, children, or parents of soldiers of the 1st South Carolina. No more than a hundred of the thousand or so blacks in Fernandina were able-bodied men, and all of them were employed as army laborers. Gideonites conducted two schools for black children in church buildings, but no free-labor plantation had been organized on the island for lack of agricultural tools and draft animals. The great majority of the contrabands thus sat idle day after day, crammed into run-down buildings and subsisting on army rations. Many were sick and not likely to get better, for the only doctor on hand was the post surgeon, who was overworked and not much interested in the blacks. Spring was farther advanced here than at Port Royal, and the hot weather and clouds of mosquitoes and flies rendered the crowded town ripe for an epidemic.[34]

After reaching Fernandina, Higginson met with some of his officers and decided that the little convoy would sail for the St. John's River at sunrise. That afternoon or evening Lyman Stickney approached Higginson with a request. He sought permission for Calvin Robinson and William Morrill, who operated a general store in Fernandina, to open a branch in Jacksonville once its possession was secure. Robinson, a thirty-four-year-old Vermont native, had moved to Jacksonville in 1857 and prospered as a merchant. He was one of the Unionists who had joyously welcomed the Yankee occupiers in the spring of 1862 and then frantically departed with them when they suddenly abandoned the town. He had thereafter spent time in the North lobbying for the reoccupation of the Florida mainland and the adoption of the Thayer plan. There he met Stickney, who persuaded him to move to Fernandina with the promise of a job with the

Tax Commission. Arriving in January 1863, Robinson worked for a time as an assistant assessor but soon quit to go into partnership with Morrill, a young, recently discharged Union army musician who was running a government-licensed store in town.[35]

What Stickney did not tell Higginson was that he himself was a partner in the Fernandina store and would likewise share the profits of the Jacksonville venture. It was to Robinson he had written on February 18 that there was "a good time coming." Nor was this Stickney's only deception in his quest to get rich from the expedition. With him aboard ship was a young man named Herbert Stoddard, for whom Stickney had secured an official pass by implying that he was a clerk employed by the Tax Commission. He was actually no such thing, but rather Stickney's private assistant. Moreover, while in Fernandina, Stickney made no effort to do any Tax Commission business, nor had he since last visiting the town in late January; he likely did not even bother to stop by the office where the other two commissioners dutifully carried out whatever business was being done. He may have had a hand, however, in arranging for one of those commissioners, John S. Sammis, to accompany the expedition to Jacksonville. If the commission did anything there, it would be Sammis's work, for Stickney intended to devote his whole effort to making money.[36]

Higginson, suspecting nothing and regarding Stickney's request as a trifle amid all the concerns he had right now, approved it without much thought. He saw no reason not to. Robinson and Morrill were duly licensed to do business in the Department of the South, Stickney vouched for them, and the store would impose no burden on the military, for Stickney promised to get it up and running himself as a favor to the partners until they could take charge. The colonel stipulated only that Stickney arrange matters agreeably with the 1st South Carolina's sutler, who would be setting up a store in Jacksonville catering to the troops.[37]

The three transports steamed out of Fernandina Harbor at sunrise on the eighth as Higginson had directed, following the channel north toward Cumberland Sound. The *John Adams*, a lumbering converted ferryboat, had fallen behind and out of sight of the other two vessels by the time they reached the sound. The *Boston* and *Burnside* proceeded together around the tip of Amelia Island and headed south toward the mouth of the St. John's, twenty miles away. They reached it at nine-thirty and hove to outside the bar. This was a tricky bar, even when the tide was high as it was now, and they could go no farther without a guide. Visible in the distance to the west were the two navy gunboats that currently constituted the blockading force on the St. John's, the *Norwich* and *Uncas*, lying at anchor inside the bar. After a time the *Uncas* steamed over the bar, then reversed course and led the two transports safely across.[38]

The transports anchored near the gunboats, and Higginson arranged a meeting with the naval officers in command, Lieutenant William Watson of the *Uncas* and Commander James Duncan of the *Norwich*. When he showed them the letter from Admiral Du Pont and explained his mission, they responded enthusiastically. They and their crews, like most other sailors on blockade duty, were bored with the humdrum routine and eager for some excitement. They agreed to escort the convoy to Jacksonville and remain there, if needed, to provide artillery support for the occupation force. Higginson consulted with the two officers quite a while, drawing on their knowledge of the river, of Jacksonville, and of the Rebel forces in the region. Eventually it was agreed that the expeditionary force would weigh anchor at two the next morning and proceed as quietly as possible up the river. If all went well, it would arrive at Jacksonville at sunrise and they hoped would surprise any Rebel troops who might be in the town.[39]

One remaining bit of preparation was accomplished later that day, when Montgomery's 120 men aboard the *Burnside* were at last issued muskets and ammunition. Montgomery ordered that they be given some quick instruction in handling and loading the weapons and then allowed them to fire a few practice rounds from the ship's deck. This might be all the musketry training they would have before going up against the enemy on the Main.[40]

The wide St. John's narrowed a bit at this point before flowing into the sea. The current here was thus comparatively swift; but the river's surface was as smooth as a mirror, and the four ships, anchored facing upstream, lay nearly motionless. The water was amber-colored but clear. Separated from the water's edge by a strip of stark white sand, dense woods lined most of the riverbank on each side. The St. John's had been an important artery of commerce before the war, and the scene here at its mouth had been lively; but now it was quiet, almost lifeless save for the splashing of the abundant fish and the calls of innumerable birds. The constant presence of the Yankee gunboats had driven away not only the maritime trade but also the secessionist inhabitants. On the south bank sat the village of Mayport Mills, consisting of some houses, a church, a store, a lumber mill, and two lighthouses, one a ruin from the days of Spanish rule, all deserted now, with sand drifts creeping up their walls. Hugging the north bank was a tiny island where there sat another village known as Pilot Town, home to the river pilots whose skills every ship that plied the St. John's had depended on. Some of those pilots still resided there, working now for the U.S. Navy. Higginson went ashore with a few of the naval officers to have a look at Pilot Town. There they proudly pointed out to him the scraggly little vegetable garden that they cultivated in the sandy soil.[41]

All the while Higginson and his officers kept a lookout for the *John Adams*. Morning passed into afternoon, and still the ship did not arrive. Higginson became concerned not only for the safety of the vessel, which he feared was unseaworthy, but also for the fate of the expedition. It was known that Rebel scouts periodically prowled the riverbanks here. The longer the *Boston* and *Burnside* sat, the more likely that they would be spotted. Should the expedition thus lose the element of surprise, it could prove disastrous. Higginson had heard that the Rebels had vowed to burn Jacksonville to the ground if the Yankees tried again to occupy it. There was another disturbing possibility: Rather than destroy the town, the enemy might take advantage of forewarning to concentrate troops there and try to repulse the landing.[42]

"Waiting, waiting, waiting," wrote Seth Rogers as the sun neared the horizon. He was aboard the *Boston* with Higginson, who, the doctor noted, was now wearing "a steady frown." Rogers had concerns besides those that troubled his commander. He worried about the health of the men, cooped up as they were in the packed, stuffy holds of the transports. "I dread confinement in close air for them," he wrote, "much more than I do rebel bullets." He had worked hard to see that the ships were kept clean and the men comfortable, but there was a limit to what he could do. Already today he had found a soldier on the *Boston* "in a collapsed state" that appeared fatal, and when inspecting conditions on the *Burnside*, he had found several men ill, including Colonel Montgomery. Fortunately the weather was mild today, the temperature no higher than eighty degrees. A really bad spell of heat, the doctor knew, could be deadly.[43]

By the time the sun set, a little before 6:00, there was still no sign of the *John Adams*. Higginson faced a quandary. If the missing vessel did not arrive by 2:00 A.M., he could proceed without it, but that would deprive him of not only two companies but also his only armed transport. Of course Watson and Duncan had promised the support of the gunboats, which would certainly provide substantial firepower: The *Uncas* carried three guns, two of them thirty-two-pounders, while the *Norwich* carried six, including a thirty-pounder rifled cannon. But the two naval officers had also warned Higginson that the *Uncas* was in bad shape, its engine unreliable, and the *Norwich* was low on coal. The latter vessel also leaked badly, some days having to be pumped out two or three times. Higginson concluded that he could not risk going into action without an armed vessel and therefore must await the arrival of the *John Adams*, at least for one more day.[44]

The sun rose in a clear sky over the blue Atlantic on the morning of the ninth, but it brought no sighting of the *John Adams*. Higginson was by now consumed with worry. He ordered the captains of the two transports to raise steam, weigh anchor, and head out beyond the bar in order to get a better view to the north and be in position to guide the *John Adams* across the bar should it appear. Hours passed, the tide went out, and the water level over the bar fell. Finally, just before the bar became impassable, the missing ship came into view, making its way slowly from the north. The other two transports led it across the bar, and all three anchored near the gunboats. It was almost noon.[45]

Higginson soon learned the cause of the ship's long delay. When it reached Cumberland Sound yesterday morning, it had encountered a thick fog and had to heave to. By the time the fog disappeared the tide had gone out, and the ship could not make it over the St. Mary's bar, requiring another long wait until the next high tide.[46]

While he rejoiced to see the ship safe and again with the convoy, Higginson now had another hard decision to make. Should he assume that the expeditionary force had been spotted and that the news was on its way to the Rebel commander and therefore start up the river immediately to try to take Jacksonville before the enemy could react? Or should he assume that the expedition was still undiscovered and therefore stick to his original plan, going up the river by night and thus greatly increasing the likelihood of taking the town by surprise? The latter course of action, he decided, was worth the risk. The expedition would sail at two tomorrow morning. Throughout the rest of the day, however, he kept an anxious watch on the horizon on the mainland side. Whenever he spotted smoke, he checked its direction, using compass and map to see if it might be rising from Jacksonville. He never saw any from that direction, but still he could not rest easy. He feared what might await him and his men at the town.[47]

He moved from the *Boston* to the *John Adams* so that he could direct the artillery fire if it was needed. The rest of the day was spent making final preparations aboard the transports and gunboats. Higginson issued an order forbidding the firing of muskets from his vessels without the express permission of the senior officer aboard. Some of the soldiers had been taking potshots at pelicans, to Higginson's amusement, but now he thought it best to avoid anything that might alert unfriendly persons in the vicinity to the presence of the transports. Dr. Rogers continued to worry about the troops, who by now had spent four days in their cramped quarters. The man who had collapsed yesterday had since died, his cause of death listed by Rogers as "debility." However, there were no new cases of sickness today, and the soldiers on the *Burnside* who had been unwell were now better. Health was good on all three transports, and so was morale; the men, wrote the doctor, were eagerly "anticipating a fight."[48]

At two in the morning of Tuesday, March 10, the five vessels weighed anchor, formed into line, and headed upriver at a speed of under six knots, the gunboats in the lead. The big side wheels of the *John Adams* revolved slowly, creaking and splashing. The other ships, all propeller-driven, betrayed their presence only by the muted throbbing of their engines and the swishing of their backwash. The moon was just five days past full. It gleamed brilliantly in a starry, cloudless sky, reflecting off the smooth water and providing light to navigate by. On the decks of the gunboats and the *John Adams* sailors and soldiers manned the cannons, and on the decks of all three transports infantrymen stood ready, muskets in hand. Although the river was wide—well over a mile in some stretches—it was shallow in many places; the channel was deep enough to accommodate all the vessels, even the *Norwich* with its ten-foot draft, but it was narrow and shifting and at some points ran close to the bank. There was a real danger of ambush, and Higginson and the naval officers had to be prepared. There was also a threat of "torpedoes," underwater mines, which the Rebels had been known to place in rivers patrolled by the Yankee navy.[49]

Jacksonville was only fifteen miles from the mouth of the St. John's as the crow flies, but following the meanders of the river, the vessels had a twenty-five-mile journey ahead of them. As they chugged slowly upstream, past low marshes and high bluffs, Higginson watched with fascination from the deck of the *John Adams*, experiencing the same deeply affecting sensation that had seized him on that moonlit night on the St. Mary's River six weeks before, a feeling of exotic enchantment and mysterious danger. "Again," he wrote, "there was the dreamy delight of ascending an unknown stream, beneath a sinking moon, into a region where peril made fascination. . . . Had I been some Aladdin, convoyed by genii or giants, I could hardly have felt more wholly a denizen of some world of romance."[50]

Another officer aboard one of the transports was at that moment thinking quite different thoughts. Lieutenant Luther Bingham, the 1st South's quartermaster, was writing a letter to his family in New York. Mortality was on his mind, as it often was—perhaps an excusable obsession in his case, for in his twenty-six years on earth he had endured the deaths of his mother, stepmother, and younger brother. His was not a gloomy personality, however. He was cheerful and very popular in the regiment, not only among his fellow officers but also among the men, whom he often joined in singing around their campfires and at Sunday services. Higginson had called on him to lead a chorus of "Marching Along" at the Emancipation Day ceremony. Now, as he and his comrades headed toward an unknown fate, Bingham wrote to confess his fear of facing combat for the first time but also to reassure his family: "I know not what may happen to me in a few short hours. I shall try and do my duty. I do hope I shall not be a coward. I know not that I shall ever see you again. Such may be the case—that I may never—though I do not expect it, for I feel that I am to go home to spend a happy, useful life."[51]

The first sign of trouble in the convoy was not gunfire or an explosion but the scraping of keels on the sandy bottom. The St. John's was a capricious river, and even the most experienced pilot could never be sure of its depth at a given point; what was deep one week might be silted up the next. Running aground was not uncommon for big vessels, especially when the tide was less than full. Now it began to happen to one after another of the five ships. Each incident brought the whole convoy to a halt, to await the freeing of the stranded vessel by a laborious process of poling and reversing engines. Before long it became obvious that the expedition would not reach Jacksonville on schedule. The town was still miles away at six, when the sun's first light became visible in the east. That was also about the time that the *Norwich* ran fast aground. It could not be budged until the incoming tide raised it, a matter of several hours. The convoy was forced to proceed without it.[52]

Those final sunlit miles offered picturesque scenery but stirred growing apprehension among officers and men as Jacksonville got nearer. No more bluffs were now to be seen, just a flat landscape, most of it dense with pines and palmettos and Spanish moss right up to the river's edge. Here and there pastures and cultivated fields appeared. Some of them were large, sprawling tracts surrounding a plantation manor and a cluster of slave cabins; many more of them were modest, neatly tended plots surrounding cozy-looking cottages and sturdy barns that reminded Higginson of New England more than anything he had heretofore seen in the South. But there were signs of war along the river too, including the charred remains of a number of sawmills destroyed by the Rebels because they were owned by Unionists.[53]

The last bend in the river brought the convoy from a southerly to a westerly course. As the vessels rounded the point, Jacksonville came into view two miles ahead on the starboard, or northern, bank. There was a burst of excitement on the transports, quickly succeeded by quiet as the men prepared themselves, their stomachs knotted with anticipation. As they steamed nearer, those on deck could make out the wharves jutting out from the town's riverfront, the whitewashed houses and stores and red-brick warehouses that lined the streets, and the great shade trees that towered over the streets and buildings.[54]

The *Uncas* heaved to and anchored in the stream opposite the town, its officers and gunners watching intently for any sign of Rebel troops. The three transports, by prearrangement, each headed to a different section of the town, the *John Adams* to the upper wharf, the *Burnside* to the lower, the *Boston* to one between. It was 8:00 A.M. Children were playing on the wharves. On the street behind them, men in civilian clothes lounged about. Women came to the doorways of the houses to watch as they became aware of the approaching ships.[55]

The *John Adams* reached its destination first. A man came forward from the street and grabbed the line that was tossed from the deck. Higginson jumped over the ship's side and onto the wharf, the first member of the expedition ashore. Behind him the men of Companies B and C also leaped over the side, without waiting for a gangplank. Their officers immediately got them into marching order and led them at the double-quick into the town.[56]

Within minutes the *Boston* and *Burnside* had docked and disgorged their companies, which likewise marched rapidly to their assigned positions. The stunned townspeople, by now aware that this was not one of the usual brief, benign visits from a Yankee gunboat and that the hundreds of armed and uniformed men they saw were almost all Negroes, began scurrying to their homes.[57]

Higginson watched as his soldiers efficiently seized possession of the town just as he had planned. Sentinels took position at street corners. A strong cordon of pickets formed around the town's periphery. No Rebel troops were to be seen. Not a shot had been fired. The officers and men of the 1st and 2nd South Carolina were exultant. Jacksonville was theirs.[58]

Chapter Five

JACKSONVILLE

MARCH 10–20

T HE TOWN HAD BEEN CAPTURED with breathtaking speed. Now the work of liberation and conquest could begin. Higginson had two immediate tasks to deal with, however, before anything else. One was to ensure that the post of Jacksonville was secure and orderly. The other was to gather information about the Rebel forces in the vicinity: where they were; how strong; what they were capable of doing.

Within hours of the landing he issued a formal order notifying both soldiers and civilians how the town would be governed under his rule:

> In taking possession of Jacksonville for the U.S. Government, protection is promised to all loyal inhabitants, and freedom to the enslaved.
>
> Personal property will be respected, and all officers will be held responsible for restraining their commands from all violence, & all plunder. Where judged necessary, for public uses, provisions & forage may in some cases be taken, but great caution will be used by officers. . . .
>
> All white male citizens are ordered to report themselves before sunset at Headquarters, that their names may be registered.
>
> No soldiers will be allowed to stray about the town, except under the direction of their officers, and all officers will be held responsible for the discipline of their men.

The order also designated Captain James Rogers of Company F as post provost marshal, responsible for maintaining order and dealing with the townspeople. Rogers's company would serve as provost guard, the military police.[1]

Questioned by Higginson, the white townspeople professed no knowledge of Rebel troops in the area. But some of the blacks provided helpful information. It turned out that as the convoy approached, there had been enemy soldiers in town, a small detachment doing picket duty. On sighting the ships, they had withdrawn—apparently in haste, for the lieutenant in command had left behind his sword. This detachment was part of a Rebel force encamped eight miles west of Jacksonville.[2]

Higginson could assume that the commander of this enemy force knew of the expedition within hours of its landing. He ordered that his pickets take position well beyond the town. He also sent Montgomery with his two companies and Company A of the 1st, commanded by the tough Brooklynite Charles Trowbridge, on a reconnaissance westward. Montgomery returned later in the day, having led the scouting party out beyond the picket line, although not nearly as far as the Rebel camp. They had been observed along the way by mounted men who remained at a distance, but they had encountered nothing else of interest.[3]

As the sun set on that first day of the occupation of Jacksonville, Higginson worried. His black informants had described the Rebel force to the west as small, but he could not be sure. It might be strong enough to challenge his own, and its commander might already be preparing to attack. Darkness would allow the enemy to approach the town unobserved. A night attack was possible. There had been no time for the 1st and 2nd South Carolina to prepare defensive works. Higginson now ordered that the picket line be pulled back close to town. He could not, however, simply post pickets for the night, send the rest of the men to their billets, and hope for the best. All must stay positioned around the town's periphery until morning, sleeping as best they could. Higginson himself lay down in a grove of lindens on the outskirts of town. This would be his headquarters tonight.[4]

It was "the most terribly anxious night I ever passed," he later confided in his journal; "we were all perfectly exhausted, the companies were posted in various parts of the town, all momentarily expecting attack." Several times during the night nervous pickets fired into the darkness, but whether their targets were real or imagined no one knew. The gunfire disturbed the sleep of the soldiers who were managing to get any, but it did not silence the mockingbirds that inhabited Higginson's little grove. They "sang all night like nightingales," he recorded with wonderment, "in the sweet air & among the blossoming trees."[5]

The red dawn of March 11 was a welcome sight to the tense, groggy soldiers. The threat of surprise attack dissipated as the sun rose. Higginson ordered that the picket line again be extended well beyond the town, then turned his attention to fortifying the place.[6]

Jacksonville stretched for nearly a mile along the river and extended about half a mile back from the waterfront on gently rising ground. The town was laid out in orderly, rectangular blocks. Trees tall and broad, mostly live oaks, shaded the streets and buildings and rustled pleasingly in the breeze. The look of prosperity and tidiness that the town had once enjoyed, and that invariably struck visitors as New England–like, had been badly eroded but not altogether erased by the rigors of life on the Confederate home front and two previous Union occupations. There were handsome houses, stores, hotels, and warehouses in abundance, many of them brick; but now several of these lay in ashes, and most were abandoned and run-down. The town had also boasted gas lighting for streets and homes and businesses, but the gasworks was now defunct. Sidewalks, an uncommon sight in small Southern towns, graced the streets of Jacksonville, but the streets were not paved or cobblestoned; feet, hooves, and wheels sank deep into the sandy soil and raised clouds of dust on rainless days.[7]

Some twenty-one hundred people, nearly half of them black, had lived here on the eve of the war. Many of the whites had been Northern immigrants, though few of them now remained. In fact, no more than five hundred people of any sort lived here now, as best Higginson could judge. Of these, only a handful were black, and fewer than seventy were white men. The blockade had strangled the economy of this once-vibrant river port, Yankee army and navy incursions had opened paths of escape for slaves and Unionist whites, and Confederate volunteering and conscription had taken or driven away many others. It was a wonder that anyone remained.[8]

On the west end of town a ruined depot marked the eastern terminus of the Florida Atlantic & Gulf Central Railroad. The track survived, however, running to the Rebel camp and far beyond. Any enemy attack would likely come from this direction. The swampy creek along the northern and eastern edges of the town would hinder, although not prevent, attack from those directions. Higginson decided that the whole periphery of the town except the riverfront would have to be fortified. Moreover, the numerous trees beyond the town must be felled for a great distance to deprive attackers of cover. Likewise, the scattered houses and sheds and fences in the suburbs would have to be burned down. The *John Adams*, the *Uncas*, and the *Norwich* (the last had arrived a few hours after the landing yesterday, having finally been floated free by the tide) gave Jacksonville's defenders a great advantage, as did the flat terrain surrounding the town. The ships' powerful cannons could sweep the ground over which attackers must advance.[9]

Around midmorning, while most of Higginson's men were at work clearing fields of fire or constructing defenses, gunfire erupted a mile or so west of town, on the picket line of the 2nd South Carolina. Some two hundred mounted Rebel troops had suddenly appeared from the west and were moving forward in battle formation. Heavily outnumbered, the pickets retreated eastward. Posted just west of town straddling the railroad were both companies of the 2nd. At their captains' command—Colonel Montgomery was in town at the time, consulting with Higginson— the two companies formed into line of battle. Soon the enemy cavalrymen appeared on their front, and a sharp exchange of gunfire ensued, the resounding cracks of the black soldiers' muskets mingling with the weaker reports of the enemy's carbines and pistols. As the line of cavalrymen spread out across their front and threatened their flanks, the men of the 2nd fell back in some disorder to another position a short distance to the rear, but there they stood firm. After a few minutes the Rebel horsemen broke off the fight and withdrew.[10]

The enemy were punished in this little encounter—several men had been seen to fall from their horses—but they were undeterred. Minutes later Confederate infantrymen emerged from the trees into which the cavalry had just disappeared. They numbered more than two hundred, twice the strength of the 2nd South Carolina. Forward they came in line of battle preceded by skirmishers, firing their muskets and overlapping the black troops' line south of the railroad. The left-flank company of the 2nd made a brief stand, firing a few volleys, but then broke and ran toward town. The other company followed. The Rebel foot soldiers continued to advance[11]

With disaster looming, Montgomery suddenly appeared. He had heard the gunfire and come out to investigate. He called to the fleeing men of the 2nd. They rallied around him and once more began to return the enemy's fire, resolutely, if not expertly, loading, aiming, and firing as they had been taught to do just three days ago. Montgomery's presence stead-

Brick warehouse on Bay Street, Jacksonville, 1864.
(COURTESY OF NATIONAL ARCHIVES AND RECORDS ADMINISTRATION)

ied them, even when at one point he dropped flat on the ground to take cover as the Rebels loosed a heavy volley.[12]

This line held. The Rebel infantrymen halted, exchanged fire for a time, and then began to fall back. Now came the bone-rattling boom of large cannons; the *Norwich* and *Uncas* had opened fire from their positions on the river. As big shells screeched overhead and burst terrifyingly among the retreating Confederates, they ran for cover and disappeared into the trees.[13]

The skirmish had been brief, a half hour's work, but intense. Two men of the 2nd had been wounded, and one, Private Bristol Walker of Company A, had been killed. The smoke and confusion during the fighting had made it hard to judge how many Rebels had fallen, and their retreating comrades had carried them all off, but the soldiers of the 2nd were sure they had inflicted more than a dozen casualties. Colonel Montgomery proclaimed it the hottest fire he had ever been under, and he praised his troops.[14]

The men of the 2nd had indeed done well considering how green they were, but their lack of training and discipline had been disturbingly obvious. The other lesson to be learned from this fight was that the Rebels did not intend to allow the occupation of Jacksonville to go uncontested. Whether they could drive the 1st and 2nd South Carolina from the town was another matter, however. If they had no more strength than they had manifested in this encounter, the nine-hundred-man expeditionary force had little to worry about once the town was properly fortified. But perhaps this had been only a reconnaissance detachment.

During that day and those that immediately followed Higginson was content with defensive measures and devoted most of his attention to securing the town from attack. He did not intend to move against the Rebel camp to the west. Not only was he unsure of the enemy's strength, but by moving inland, he would sacrifice the advantages of controlling the river and being under the gunboats' protection. When it came time to strike beyond Jacksonville, the river would provide the path.[15]

At daybreak each morning the picket line was extended well beyond town. Each evening before dark it was pulled back close to town, but disposed differently from one night to the next to keep the enemy guessing. During the first few days, patrols were dispatched beyond the picket line to scout for Rebels and learn the lay of the land. Meanwhile, barricades were erected around the town, and fields of fire were cleared. Higginson also adopted stratagems to keep the enemy—and the townspeople, who might communicate with the enemy—ignorant of the strength of the Union force holding the town. There would be no dress parades, for one thing, or any other assemblage of the whole force in one place. Moreover he had the men set up numerous tents just inside the barricades; these would be uninhabited but would, he hoped, fool enemy scouts.[16]

Once the defenses were stout enough, Higginson allowed the troops not on picket duty to retire to their billets at night. These were in the brick warehouses that lined Bay Street, the town's commercial center, which paralleled the river by the wharves. Still worried about a Rebel incursion, however, the colonel directed the men and their company officers to sleep on the second floors and bolt the ground-level doors. Another reason for billeting the troops in these buildings was protection from fire. Higginson feared that the Rebels might still carry out their reported threat to burn Jacksonville to deny it to the Yankees. It was not impossible that an enemy could slip into town at night with kerosene and matches and wreak havoc.[17]

The townspeople demanded a share of Higginson's attention too. The great majority were white women and children, their husbands and fathers for the most part absent, serving in the Confederate army or employed elsewhere in Rebeldom. Many of the women claimed to be Unionists, but Higginson was skeptical, as were his troops, a number of whom had lived here as slaves. Even if they were secessionists, however, the women were no threat as far as Higginson was concerned. Curiously, although he had long been among the most radical and outspoken proponents of women's rights, he did not regard women as fully responsible agents in public affairs, and in some respects he viewed them as paternalistically as he did his black troops. He therefore demanded nothing of those in Jacksonville except that they surrender any weapons they might have in their homes, and he benignly allowed them and their children to move around freely and even pass in and out of town as they wished during daylight hours. Some were so desperately poor and hungry that it stirred his sympathy; he gave orders allowing them to draw rations from the post commissary. Dr. Rogers likewise took pity on them and offered to treat any civilian who asked for his help. He set up a post hospital in an abandoned hotel, after Higginson and Montgomery assured him that the town was secure enough to allow the sick and wounded soldiers to be brought ashore from the temporary infirmary on the *John Adams*.[18]

From the first day of occupation Higginson and Provost Marshal Rogers had to deal with complaints from the women in town, mostly about the soldiers' behavior. Not surprisingly, white Jacksonvillians were utterly appalled to find themselves policed by black troops. As far as anybody knew, no other civilians had had to endure such a fate in this war. "To bring these horrid niggers . . . is insufferable," one was heard to exclaim. "They will surely murder us—you cannot restrain them." Women pleaded with the officers for protection. A few, however, accepted the situation gracefully once they began recognizing men they knew among the soldiers. Higginson took note of one in particular, an "intelligent and lady-like woman" whose husband was a Confederate officer. She "rather surprised me," the colonel admitted, "by saying that it seemed pleasanter to have these men stationed there, whom they had known all their lives, and who had generally borne a good character, than to be in the power of entire strangers."[19]

Hoping to avoid clashes, Higginson sternly ordered his men to leave the townspeople alone—especially the women—except when duty demanded and an officer approved. But practically every day there were complaints that some black soldier had insulted a white woman. Higginson had each duly investigated, but it almost always turned out that the soldier had merely responded in kind to some contemptuous remark. Many complaints were frivolous; one woman protested that a soldier had had the temerity to sit down to rest on her front doorstep. Others, however, were legitimate. For one thing, people's chickens and pigs were disappearing despite Higginson's strict orders against pillaging. On the whole, though, the colonel thought his troops were behaving well in the face of considerable provocation, including racial slurs of the grossest sort. "When I found out what the old sinner had said to the soldiers," he wrote in his journal after one particularly outrageous incident, "I wondered at their self control in not throttling her." There was in fact not a single credible report of physical abuse of a citizen. One of the gunboat captains told Higginson that the white troops who had occupied Jacksonville last year had been considerably rougher on the townspeople. The colonel especially admired the restraint manifested by those of his men who had been slaves here, one of them a sergeant whose brother had been hanged in town after he was caught trying to lead a party of fellow slaves to the Yankees.[20]

The white men in Jacksonville were a very different matter from the women, as Higginson saw it. Although there were only a few dozen and hardly any were of military age, the colonel regarded them as a potential threat. Those who failed to report to him as ordered on the day of the landing were subsequently rounded up and brought to his headquarters. Higginson took down the names of all who came before him and informed them that if they refused to take an oath of allegiance to the Union, they would be locked up. Most took the oath; a few refused. But even those who took it were subsequently required to carry passes from headquarters permitting them to move around town. If they went beyond the town limits, they could not return without special permission from Higginson.[21]

The men who were thus humbled, restricted, and ordered about like slaves were aghast at the humiliation of it all. Among them was a fifty-three-year-old tailor named Thomas Andrews, who later that month penned an account of his tribulations that seethed with rage:

> I was amongst the last who were sent for, and had gone home and shut myself up, determined to see as little of the enemy as possible. From this, however, I was summoned by a negro corporal and four black soldiers,

armed with muskets and bayonets, who ordered me to march to the Colonel and take the oath. One walked on each side and two behind—the corporal by the side. At every turning of the street he ordered, "file right," or "file left," as the case might be. To be so ordered by negroes was the most mortifying trial that I had ever undergone, but this was not all. Reaching the Colonel's quarters I was ordered to take the oath.

I remonstrated that I was an old man, unable to bear arms and scarcely able to cut a piece of wood for my family. He replied that [even] if I could not bear arms, I could aid others, and I could take the oath or walk up stairs to prison. Having a large and distressed family I was compelled to yield, and then received a pass. Thereafter, when I went into the streets I was compelled to show it to a negro sentinel posted at every corner. Being permitted to pass, I was forbidden to walk on the side walk and was obliged to go in the street around these sable gentlemen.[22]

Higginson had several men held in custody. One was not a civilian but an unlucky Confederate army officer who happened to be in town recuperating from illness when the expedition arrived. The others were citizens who refused the oath or who seemed to Higginson too dangerous to let loose. A rumor circulated among the townspeople that these prisoners were being held as hostages to ensure good treatment of any of Higginson's soldiers who might fall into Rebel hands.[23]

That was not the only talk around town. The citizens were shocked to learn of the presence of James Montgomery, notorious throughout the South since his days as a ruthless guerrilla leader in the free-soil cause in Kansas. Moreover, the townspeople quickly began to pick up disturbing hints of the expedition's purpose. Before long it was understood by them that these black troops and their abolitionist leaders had come to Florida to make war on slavery. There was speculation too that the expedition was the spearhead of Eli Thayer's colonization scheme, which had been widely reported in the Southern press. News of the Direct Tax Commission had also filtered into Florida. One story now going around Jacksonville was that property along the St. John's would be confiscated by the United States government and auctioned off to German colonists. Because residents of the town passed beyond the picket lines all the time, it could be assumed that whatever facts and rumors they picked up would become known to the Rebel force to the west and to General Finegan.[24]

As the days passed, Higginson's fear of a Rebel assault on the town

Sanderson house, Jacksonville, c. 1864.
(COURTESY OF NATIONAL ARCHIVES AND RECORDS ADMINISTRATION)

abated, but his fear of an incendiary raid did not. Some nights, depending
on how the wind blew, he slept with his clothes on. Moreover, he began to
agonize over the responsibilities of command. This was something he had
not anticipated but that was perhaps inevitable. Whether as a company
commander in Massachusetts or a regimental commander on Port Royal
Island, he had never exercised independent military authority; there was
always a superior officer near at hand with ultimate responsibility. But
now the fate of a momentous undertaking rested wholly on his shoulders.
The strain of constantly worrying that he might have failed to take sufficient precautions or make the best use of his resources, and might even be
leading his men into disaster, began to tell on him emotionally and physically. "There sometimes steals into my mind, like a chill," he confided in
his journal, "that most sickening of all sensations the anxiety of a commander." He found that it helped to retire alone to his quarters for a while
in the afternoons; there he would read a chapter or two of a translation of
John Paul's *Titan* that he had recently received from the North. The brief
distraction from his duties calmed and refreshed him.[25]

After that first night when he slept in the linden grove, his quarters were in the finest house in Jacksonville, a two-story ten-room brick mansion with a front piazza on each floor and a cupola from which the Stars and Stripes now waved. It stood on the corner of Forsythe and Ocean, a block up from Bay, and was the abandoned home of a very wealthy lawyer named John P. Sanderson. A New York native, Sanderson was one of the few Northern-born Jacksonvillians who had sided with the Rebels. As a delegate to the Florida secession convention in January 1861 he had helped write the ordinance that took the state out of the Union. After the war broke out, he contributed a thousand dollars to help build a gunboat to be donated to the Confederate navy to guard the St. John's River. The boat was never finished, however, and when the Yankees occupied Jacksonville in March 1862, Sanderson fled the town and refugeed into the interior. His house had served as headquarters for that occupation force and the subsequent one in the fall and thus had been spared the destruction visited on many other buildings in town.[26]

Higginson took one room for his own; Dr. Rogers, Lieutenant Colonel Billings, Major Strong, and adjutant Dewhurst took others. It was one of the biggest and finest residences the colonel had ever seen—"a sort of palace," as he described it in a letter to his mother. Black labor had built it; one of Higginson's men, in fact, Sergeant Thomas Hodges of Company C, had been among the carpenters. It was very new and had the most modern conveniences. These included running water and gas lighting, but of course they were not working now. Higginson particularly admired the marble fireplaces, the billiard table that occupied one of the first-floor rooms, and the finely crafted bookshelves that lined Sanderson's office. The ivory billiard balls were missing now, however, and almost all the books were gone. Most of Sanderson's elegant furniture was gone too, perhaps carted off by less affluent neighbors but more likely by Yankee officers when the earlier occupation forces pulled out. Thanks, however, to the efforts of Provost Marshal Rogers, who, mounted on a confiscated pony, was leading a squad of soldiers around town each day to remove furniture from abandoned buildings and store it for safekeeping, Higginson and his housemates were gathering enough to make the place comfortable.[27]

It was perhaps in Sanderson's office that Lieutenant Dewhurst came across and appropriated what he deemed an apt trophy of the expedition, a copy of the municipal blue book, which included among other useful information Jacksonville's slave code. He thumbed through it with ironic delight, savoring each regulation that would never again confine or subjugate or chastise the black men and women of the town:

> *Be it ordained* . . . That every slave, free negro, or mulatto, found in the streets of the town of Jacksonville, or in any yard, kitchen, or other place, not being the residence of said slave, free negro, or mulatto, after bell ring, or nine o'clock in the evening, without a written pass from his or her owner, master, employer, agent, or guardian, shall be liable to be taken to the town jail, by the town patrol or marshal.
>
> . . . That it shall be the duty of the marshal to notify the owner, master, employer, agent, or guardian, of every such slave, free negro, or mulatto so imprisoned, of such imprisonment; and on such notification, if a penalty of one dollar is not paid by such owner, master, employer, agent, or guardian, within one hour after such notice, said marshal shall punish said slave, free negro, or mulatto, by whipping, not less than ten nor more than thirty-nine stripes. . . .
>
> . . . That no slave or free person of color shall, in the streets, or elsewhere in the town of Jacksonville, fight, quarrel, riot, or otherwise act in a disorderly manner, or be impudent [or] use any insulting language to any white person, under the penalty of chastisement . . . not exceeding twenty-five lashes.[28]

Dewhurst no doubt shared the blue book with Higginson, who surely found it interesting too. At the same time, however, it was a subtle reminder that the expedition had actually freed very few slaves so far and none who could be added to the ranks of the black regiments. It was apparent that almost all the slaves in and around Jacksonville, especially the able-bodied males, had either escaped to the Yankees previously or been removed by their owners to safer areas upriver or inland. If the expedition's primary aim was to be achieved, Higginson must lead his men deeper into Florida.[29]

Within two days of the landing, however, he was beginning to doubt that he could do so with the force he had. Jacksonville could not be abandoned, of course; it must be held as the expedition's base. Moreover, it must be held by more than a token garrison, as the Rebel attack on the eleventh had made clear. Also, until Higginson knew the full strength of the enemy force he faced, he must assume that it was considerable. As far as he could tell at this point, securely defending Jacksonville would require the great majority of his troops, leaving few to spare for an upriver movement. He now realized that in his eagerness to get his black soldiers into Florida he had underestimated their task; the nine hundred men of the 1st and 2nd South Carolina were simply not an adequate force.[30]

It was probably on the twelfth that Lyman Stickney approached Higginson with a suggestion. He told the colonel that when the expeditionary force was laying over in Fernandina, he had talked with Colonel Joseph Hawley, commander of the garrison there, who had told him that if the expedition ever needed reinforcements, he could provide up to four companies of infantry and a battery of field artillery. Was Higginson now interested? Stickney asked. If so, he would be glad to return to Fernandina with one of the transports and see if Hawley would keep his word.[31]

Higginson was torn: The Fernandina troops would be a welcome addition to his strength—he could post them in town, thus freeing that many of his own men for an upriver venture—but Hawley's troops were of course white. Higginson had always opposed having his regiment serve alongside whites, fearing racial friction, and he had especially opposed including any white troops on this expedition, for he did not want his black men to have to share the glory. Now, however, it was apparent that the expedition would get nowhere without reinforcements and that the only ones to be had were white. Reluctantly he authorized Stickney to take a transport to Fernandina and appeal to Hawley for help. On the morning of the thirteenth Stickney headed downriver aboard the *Boston*.[32]

Stickney may have been lying to Higginson. That Hawley would have made such an offer through the direct tax commissioner alone rather than to Higginson or any of the expedition's other officers, including Montgomery, who had spent much time with Hawley while waiting for the rest of the convoy to reach Fernandina, was unlikely, yet no one but Stickney seemed to know of it. Even if the tax commissioner was telling the truth, however, his willingness to return to Fernandina had less to do with procuring reinforcements than with procuring merchandise for his store in Jacksonville. The store was already up and running; soon after the landing Stickney had gotten Higginson's permission to occupy the abandoned building on Bay Street that had once been the mercantile establishment of his current business partner, Calvin Robinson. This, said Stickney, could serve as both the office of the Direct Tax Commission and the store that Stickney had promised to help Robinson set up. The colonel, still unaware that Stickney was splitting profits with Robinson, gave this store little thought. He merely told Provost Marshal Rogers to keep an eye on it and in particular to make sure no liquor was sold there. Stickney put his assistant, Herbert Stoddard, in charge of the place for now, until Robinson could come from Fernandina. There was hardly any merchandise to put out on the shelves, however, just whatever odds and ends Stickney had been able to bring with him or acquire in Jacksonville since the landing. But that would change. Whether or not the *Boston* returned with troop reinforcements, Stickney was determined that it would return with his business partner and a sizable load of goods for the store. If anybody asked, he would claim that the goods were for the Tax Commission's use. He had no intention of reimbursing the government for transportation costs.[33]

In the days following the stand of Montgomery's troops west of town there were no more Rebel attacks except occasional sorties by small bodies of cavalrymen, which were easily repulsed. Higginson sent the picket line out a little farther each morning. Squads of soldiers, carrying axes and combustibles, followed the pickets; one by one they cut down every tree and burned every structure that could provide cover for a good two miles from town. Rebel pickets sometimes contested this inching forward, but they were always driven off sooner or later. The Union picket line eventually stabilized a mile and a half or so out; the Confederate picket line stabilized where the uncleared terrain began. In between was what Higginson dubbed the Debatable Land, rarely crossed by either side in the daytime. The colonel continued to pull the pickets back close to town at sunset.[34]

An unlikely hero emerged in these little brushes with the enemy: the 1st South Carolina's chaplain, James H. Fowler, a fervent Massachusetts abolitionist who found the excitement of skirmishing irresistible. Mounted on a confiscated horse and carrying two revolvers at his waist and a rifle slung across his back, he galloped out to the picket line each day "like a wild man," in Higginson's words, and put himself in the forefront of every encounter with the Rebels. "What for Mr. Chapl[a]in done preach[?]," one of the men was heard to ask; ". . . he's the fightenest man in de Reg[imen]t and he swear like de berry debble." Once he tasted combat, the Reverend Fowler demoted his clerical duties to secondary importance. It was all Dr. Rogers could do to persuade him to leave the picket line long enough to officiate at the funeral of the 2nd South Carolina soldier killed on the eleventh. When the expedition's first Sunday in Jacksonville arrived and Fowler gave no indication that he intended to hold a service, some officer prodded him gently with a question: Was this not the Sabbath? "Nay," proclaimed the chaplain like some Old Testament prophet, "it is the Day of Judgment!"[35]

Fowler also took on himself the tasks of evicting the people outside town whose houses were marked for destruction and seizing their useful possessions. Like those in town, they were mostly women and children, their menfolk in the Rebel army, and they were mostly poor, their homes rude cabins. Fowler devised a simple rule of property confiscation, one that struck Dr. Rogers as "rather scriptural." "What seems to belong to the woman," declared the chaplain, "I yield to her, but what seems to belong to the man, I have brought into camp." Those evicted must make a choice, Fowler announced sternly: They could move into town and live under Union rule or go in the opposite direction and live with the Rebels. For those who manifested any loyalty to the Confederacy, he had a grim warning, as Dr. Rogers recorded: "Their friends in arms were to be killed soon unless they came in and surrendered."[36]

The surgeon had more sympathy than the chaplain for these wretched, displaced Southerners. "Some . . . are very pitiful and call out my deepest commiseration," Rogers wrote on March 14. "Today I visited a poor widow who has a son in the rebel service. Her house was burned and she, with her children, was brought into town. She has not been able to walk a step during the last five months. On examination I found that her prostration was due entirely to privations and hardships resulting from the war. For more than a year her food has been 'dry hominy' with now and then a little fish. . . . [I]t must be difficult for her to understand the justice of our coming here to invade the homes of those who had always earned their bread by the sweat of their brows."[37]

Fowler the warrior-chaplain was not the only one who distinguished himself in the little firefights along the picket line; some of the black troops did too. Higginson took note especially of Company K of the 1st, which had never won any plaudits for discipline or drill and had no previous combat experience. Going into action on March 18 to clear out a nest of enemy pickets, these men displayed great "coolness and courage," in their colonel's estimation; it was "the best skirmishing we have ever done."

Ironically, however, in this shining moment of valor there occurred an incident so absurdly hilarious that it immediately earned a place among the regiment's legends. Higginson related it in his journal: "It was noticed that one of [the men of] the advancing line appeared to move with difficulty. . . . It soon appeared that he had come up with & captured a fine *goose* & not wishing to lose it, could find no way to hold it but *between his legs*, so he went on, deliberately loading & firing & occasionally advancing, with the goose writhing & struggling & hissing in this natural pair of stocks. Both came off unwounded & finally retired in good order, when the affair was over."[38]

The navy gunboats anchored in the river continued to provide strong support to Higginson's infantrymen, firing on any pesky Rebel force that showed itself long enough to be targeted. The soldiers' ruthless scalping of the suburban landscape rendered the ships' big cannons that much more lethal, for now there was virtually no place within two miles of town to hide from the naval artillerists. Moreover, there were not just two gunboats now but three. On March 12 the *Paul Jones* steamed up the river to join the *Uncas* and *Norwich*. This was an 863-ton side-wheeler, recently commissioned, built especially for riverine warfare, and very powerful; on its gun deck sat two twenty-four-pounder howitzers, two fifty-pounder rifles, two nine-inch smoothbores, an eleven-inch smoothbore, and a truly fearsome hundred-pounder rifle with a range of several miles.[39]

The *Paul Jones*'s captain was Commander Charles Steedman. Outranking the other gunboat captains, he assumed command of the little squadron. Higginson took a liking to this native South Carolinian who had remained true to the old flag. Steedman impressed him as not only capable and courteous but also "manly"—the highest praise Higginson could bestow.[40]

He would no doubt have judged Steedman very differently had he been able to penetrate the naval commander's gracious Southern manner and read his thoughts. Steedman was in fact utterly contemptuous of Higginson from the moment they met. While siding with the Union, he remained in other respects very much a South Carolina gentleman, appalled by the idea of freeing and arming blacks and revolted by Yankee abolitionists. After dealing politely with the officers of the 1st and 2nd South Carolina for a week, Steedman vented his disgust in a letter to his wife. The army expeditionary force, he wrote, "[is] composed entirely of niggers & the fanatical set of nigger worshippers. You can have no idea how annoying it has been to me in being obliged to act with these people."[41]

With the reinforcement of the St. John's naval squadron, the clearing of fields of fire, and the fortification of the town's periphery, Higginson was satisfied that the post of Jacksonville was secure from attack by a force even much larger than his own. This third matter, the town's defensive works, was pretty much completed within a week of the landing. Employing the military engineering expertise of Captain Trowbridge along with the muscle and sweat of the men, Higginson turned Jacksonville into a fortress. The easiest part was fortifying the northern and eastern edges of town, where the swampy creek provided considerable protection already. Here the men felled trees by the dozens, using some to construct barricades along the creek, especially at the bridge and the ford where roads leading into town crossed it, using others as abatis, laying them side by side just outside the barricades with their tops pointing outward to create a thicket impenetrable to attackers. The western side of town, the likeliest target of a Rebel assault, was a more difficult problem. No creek protected it, while no fewer than three roads and the railroad led to it. Here the spade as well as the ax was put to use. In addition to barricades and abatis, the troops built two formidable earthworks, one on each side of the railroad, each a full two hundred yards long on its front face with flanks running back at an angle for fifty or sixty yards. Montgomery's men dug the one south of the tracks and christened it Fort Higginson; men of the 1st South Carolina dug the other and returned the courtesy by naming it Fort Montgomery. These works, behind which a man could stand and fire while exposing only his head and shoulders to the enemy, provided protection not only for the infantrymen but also for gun crews. Higginson had several howitzers brought ashore from the *John Adams* and mounted in the forts so as to be able to sweep the ground in front.[42]

By the fourteenth, with defensive measures progressing well, Higginson was ready to extend the expedition's reach a bit. Anxious to open up avenues of escape for slaves in the interior and to learn what lay deeper in Florida, he decided to send some raiding parties up the river aboard the two transports still on hand. He did not feel secure enough yet to dispatch many troops for this purpose, but he could spare Montgomery's two companies. They were of doubtful value in defending Jacksonville anyway, and Montgomery was getting restless cooped up in town with his men

West end of Forsythe Street, Jacksonville, c. 1864, looking toward the
fortifications built just beyond the western edge of town.
(COURTESY OF NATIONAL ARCHIVES AND RECORDS ADMINISTRATION)

doing picket and fatigue duty; he was itching to reenact his Kansas triumphs and smite the secessionist Floridians with the sword of righteous
retribution. Higginson thought he could also spare perhaps one company
of the 1st South Carolina. He would not let these raiding parties roam far,
however, for he wanted them safely back inside the post by nightfall.[43]

At 5:00 A.M. on the fourteenth, an hour before sunrise, the *John Adams*
pulled away from its wharf and headed southward, up the river, with
Montgomery and his troops aboard. Nine hours later they were back, having put some of their number ashore at one or more points along the river
to scout around. Although they failed to bring in any slaves, they could
boast a good catch of another sort. Higginson, who watched from the
wharf as the *John Adams* approached, described the scene: "The steamer
seemed an animated hen-coop. Live poultry hung from the foremast
shrouds, dead ones from the mainmast, geese hissed from the binnacle, a
pig paced the quarter-deck, and a duck's wings were seen fluttering from
a line which was wont to sustain duck trousers." There was nothing here

to indicate that Montgomery and his officers and men had exercised any restraint in foraging, as Higginson's order on the day of the landing had demanded. But as he observed the parade of poultry, Higginson found himself more amused than angry; five days among the Rebel citizenry were enough to begin eroding his insistence on strict propriety.[44]

The *Burnside* likewise raised steam, cast off, and sailed upriver on the morning of the fourteenth. On board were Company C of the 1st South Carolina and its captain, William Randolph. Gray-bearded and fussy, Randolph (age forty-eight) was the oldest of the regiment's company commanders. Higginson thought he acted more like a grandmother than a father to his troops, but he knew how to carry out a military assignment: He and his company returned about six that evening with a bigger haul than the 2nd South Carolina's, including not only chickens but also horses, hogs, and some Rebel citizens they had taken prisoner, one of them a slave owner they had caught returning home after removing his human property to a hiding place inland. They also reported seeing many cattle upriver that they had been unable to bring back and quantities of baled cotton.[45]

In the succeeding days the 2nd South Carolina and detachments of the 1st carried out more such river raids. On the sixteenth the *John Adams* returned with the best haul yet: not only horses, mules, cattle, hogs, corn, cotton, and a wagon but also thirty blacks who had waked up that morning on their plantation as slaves and would go to bed that night in Jacksonville as free people. On the seventeenth Montgomery and his men boarded the *Burnside*, steamed upriver, and went ashore at a place called Mandarin. From there they scouted four miles inland and came back accompanied by seventeen newly freed black men, women, and children. The four able-bodied males among them immediately enlisted in the 2nd. Higginson and his officers and men were gratified by the liberation of these few dozen slaves and the addition of a handful to the ranks. Now, Dr. Rogers exulted, "we are fairly at work at our legitimate business." Whatever else happened or did not happen in Florida, the expedition could never be dismissed as utterly profitless.[46]

On one of the river raids a soldier of Higginson's regiment had the opportunity to visit the place where he had labored as a slave until October 1862, when he escaped to a Yankee gunboat. It was a plantation called Mulberry Grove, situated on the river some miles south of Jacksonville.

There he had been known as "long-legged Jake," and there he had lived with his wife, Etta. His master, A. M. Reed, had at some point abruptly sold Etta off to Georgia, leaving Jake alone and devastated. Now, coming ashore from the steamer with his musket in his hand and long-festering anger in his heart, Jake marched up to the big house and demanded to see Reed "face to face" so he could "teach him what it is to part man and wife." Reed was not there, but his daughter was. Jake frightened her badly, but he eventually left without doing violence.[47]

Higginson acquired a personal prize from one the raids, a fine sorrel horse, probably part of the bounty that Company C brought back on the fourteenth. Struck by this sleek, fast, well-trained animal, the colonel exercised his prerogative to buy it from the U.S. government for the set price of $125 and make it his own. He called it Rinaldo. No sooner had he claimed it than it was recognized by one of his soldiers, nineteen-year-old Albert Sammis of Company C, who was detailed as Higginson's orderly. Private Sammis, it turned out, had raised the horse on the plantation south of Jacksonville where he grew up. The plantation and the horse had been owned by John S. Sammis, Lyman Stickney's fellow direct tax commissioner, who had accompanied the expedition from Fernandina to Jacksonville. He had sold the horse early in the war to a Confederate officer for $275.[48]

John Sammis was a tall, blue-eyed, amiable man in his early fifties. A New Yorker by birth and upbringing, he had moved to Florida in 1830. Not sharing the distaste for slaveowning that characterized many transplanted Yankees, he had acquired a plantation and slaves and made a fortune growing cotton; on the eve of the war he was one of the richest men in Florida, worth $120,000. His sympathies nevertheless remained with the Union after the state seceded. He did not flee north, however, but stayed, submitting to Rebel rule to protect his property.[49]

Sammis was far more prescient than most slaveholders in the months preceding the breakup of the Union. Alarmed by the increasing sectional antagonism and convinced that his human property was endangered, he decided to convert his slaves into cash. A year or so before the war broke out he had nearly all of them shipped to New Orleans and sold on the auction block. He then took up residence in Jacksonville. After Florida left the Union, he made his peace with the Rebels; along with John P. Sanderson, he donated money in July 1861 to build the Confederate gunboat that never sailed. But when federal forces occupied the town in March 1862, he was among the first citizens to step forward and publicly declare for the Union. Like all his fellow townsmen who did likewise, he was stunned by the Northern liberators' abrupt abandonment of Jacksonville and had to make an agonizing decision. Recognizing that he was now a marked man in Rebeldom and that his property would surely be confiscated, he departed with the Yankees. He thereafter lived in New York and Washington and became a leading voice of the Florida refugee lobby. This brought him into contact with Stickney, who recommended him for the post of tax commissioner.[50]

By that point Sammis was in difficult financial straits. Glad to have the job, grateful to Stickney for helping him get it, and deceived by Stickney's lies about his past, Sammis willingly pledged much of the little property he had left to provide Stickney's bond as well as his own. After relocating to Fernandina in early January 1863 he labored dutifully on Tax Commission business, never complaining about Stickney's absence. Now he was doing the same in the store on Bay Street in Jacksonville. He remained innocently unaware of his fellow commissioner's duplicity; "friend Stickney," he called him.[51]

Higginson liked Sammis, whom he had first met at Camp Saxton in December, when Sammis was in transit to Fernandina. But he did not know him well, and he wondered about him. There were some curious things about the man. For one, he took an unusual interest in Private Albert Sammis, who Higginson assumed was his former slave. The colonel suspected that the light-skinned young soldier was John Sammis's son.[52]

Had he been inclined to pursue the matter, Higginson not only would have confirmed his suspicion about Albert's parentage but would also have become aware of one of the odd realities of this particular part of the South. Albert Sammis was in fact John Sammis's son. He had never been a slave, however; his mother was a mixed-race free woman named Mary, who was John Sammis's wedded wife. Although state law declined to recognize such unions between white men and free black women, northeastern Florida's long history of Spanish rule fostered a relatively tolerant racial climate that quietly accepted them. Elsewhere in the South, save perhaps Creole Louisiana, publicly avowed biracial marriages were virtually unthinkable. John Sammis did not flaunt his, but neither did he deny it. He and Mary lived together as husband and wife, and he openly acknowledged Albert and the other sons and daughters she bore him. All who knew him well were aware of his peculiar domestic situation; but no one expressed outrage, and he rose to prominence in local affairs. The federal census taker who came around in the summer of 1860 obligingly listed Mary and the children as white to avoid trouble. When John refugeed from Jacksonville, he brought Albert north. In December 1862 he delivered the young man to Camp Saxton, where he enlisted in the 1st South Carolina. Had Higginson known more about John Sammis's private life, he would surely have found himself perplexed by this genial, loyal planter who gathered some people of color to his bosom with a husbandly and fatherly embrace while disposing of others like cattle.[53]

Higginson had little time to spare for such ruminations, however, for each day in Jacksonville added to the burden of command that oppressed him so. On the morning of the eighteenth there came a surprising report from the picket line: The enemy had delivered a message under flag of truce for the commander of the Union force occupying Jacksonville. Signed by a Rebel lieutenant colonel, it warned Higginson to remove all women and children from the town within twenty-four hours: "After that time they will remain in the town on your responsibility." It went on to say that the Confederates were willing to provide transportation for any citizens who desired to refugee into Rebel territory. The clear implication was that the enemy intended to attack, burn, or shell the town.[54]

Higginson dispatched a reply by flag of truce, pointing out that he had never prevented women and children from leaving Jacksonville; now, however, given the Rebels' proposal, he would cooperate in removing any who chose to go. Then he announced in a formal, written order that he would provide wagon transportation out of town for those who wanted to go to the enemy. The wagons would convey them to the church near the brickyard some distance west of town, which the Rebels had proposed as a rendezvous point. He would not allow any black people to go, however.[55]

Higginson was sure the Confederates were bluffing. His written order urged civilians loyal to the Union to stay, "as no danger is apprehended to the city, or to the inhabitants." Others were not so sure, however. Dr. Rogers, for one, worried that Rebel artillery shells would soon come crashing into Jacksonville, and he made plans to remove the sick and wounded from his hotel-hospital to one of the transports should that happen. The majority of the citizens were apparently unruffled by the Rebels' threat or at least were willing to accept the risk in order to stay and preserve their property and livelihoods, for they declined to evacuate. Some 150 decided to accept the Confederates' offer, however, and on the nineteenth they were transported to the Rebel wagons waiting at the church, escorted by Major Strong and Provost Marshal Rogers. Among them was the tailor Thomas Andrews, who had received permission to accompany his wife and children. By Higginson's order Andrews headed off to Rebel territory taking nothing but the clothes he wore. Although distraught about abandoning his worldly possessions, the tailor was relieved beyond measure to escape the degrading domination of Yankees and Negroes. He was forced to endure one last indignity, however: As the evacuees were transferred from Union to Confederate custody, Captain Rogers sat on his pony, impishly whistling the John Brown song loudly enough for all to hear.[56]

Sunset that evening ushered in a good deal of anxiety for those in Jacksonville who feared that the enemy intended to assault or bombard the town. Higginson continued to dismiss that threat, but by now he had something else to worry about. Six days had passed since Lyman Stickney sailed off to Fernandina on the *Boston* to seek reinforcements. The colonel had assumed that he would return in a day or two, but nothing had been heard from him. That very night, however, to Higginson's relief, the tax commissioner reappeared, albeit in an unexpected fashion. The navy gunboat *Uncas*, which had set out on a downriver patrol that afternoon, returned an hour or so before midnight and deposited Stickney on the wharf. The tax commissioner promptly reported to Higginson, with quite a story to tell.[57]

After arriving at Fernandina on the thirteenth, he had failed to get any reinforcements from Colonel Hawley. Undaunted, he decided to go to Hilton Head and appeal to General Hunter. The *Boston* steamed out of Fernandina Harbor carrying not only Stickney but also Calvin Robinson, who intended to return to Jacksonville with the tax commissioner to assume management of the store on Bay Street. On the fourteenth the transport tied up at the long wharf at Hilton Head, and the two men proceeded to the commanding general's headquarters. Stickney's account of the situation on the St. John's River and his earnest pleading for reinforcements impressed Hunter. The general promptly dispatched a message to Hawley, ordering him to send to Jacksonville any troops he could spare without endangering his own post. Furthermore, Hunter told Stickney that he could take back to Jacksonville aboard the *Boston* one of Rufus Saxton's white regiments.[58]

The steamer then took Stickney and Robinson to Beaufort. General Saxton designated the 6th Connecticut Infantry, commanded by Major Lorenzo Meeker, to go to Jacksonville. It took time for this regiment to collect supplies, round up men on detached duty, break camp, and board the transport, but all had been accomplished by the eighteenth. Just before the *Boston* set sail that day, Stickney procured from Saxton an appointment as superintendent of freedmen in Florida. His duties would be to take charge of all the black people who came under Union control in the state, provide for those unable to care for themselves, turn over for conscription all males fit for military service, put the rest to work at agriculture or other useful occupations so that they would be self-sufficient and not burden the government, and see to the moral well-being of all. Stickney volunteered to serve in this position and to do so without pay.[59]

On the nineteenth the *Boston* docked once more at Fernandina, staying only three hours. Stickney again failed to get reinforcements from Hawley, whose orders from Hunter gave him some discretion in the matter; perhaps the tax commissioner did not even bother this time to ask for the four companies that Hawley had allegedly promised, having now a whole regiment to take back to Higginson. The steamer pulled away from Fernandina at two that afternoon. Some hours later it crossed the St. John's bar and proceeded up the river. About a dozen miles below Jacksonville, however, it ran fast aground; it would have to sit there until floated free by the morning tide. The appearance of the *Uncas* that evening gave Stickney the opportunity to get off the stranded transport and go immediately to Higginson.[60]

There were, as usual, some things that the tax commissioner was not telling. For one, he had not been idle during those several days in Beaufort when the 6th Connecticut was preparing to depart. He and Calvin Robinson had busied themselves procuring goods for their store in Jacksonville. Likewise, during those three hours in Fernandina on the return trip, the two men transferred merchandise from their store there to the transport. Nor did Stickney admit to Higginson that his pro bono service as superintendent of freedmen in Florida was purely self-serving. He had no more intention of caring for the contrabands than he had of doing the work of the Tax Commission; as far as he was concerned, the appointment was merely another pretext for shipping merchandise to the Jacksonville store at government expense—an even better pretext than Tax Commission business, for there was hardly any limit to the amount and variety of goods that he might claim to be procuring for the welfare of the freed slaves.[61]

Higginson listened to Stickney's report with relief and excitement tempered by trepidation. An entire regiment of reinforcements, rather than just the four companies he had been hoping for, would free up that many more of his black troops to move deeper into Florida on their mission of redemption and liberation. But at the same time, as soon as the 6th Connecticut landed in Jacksonville, he would face the unprecedented challenge of getting black and white units to serve side by side in harmony. Given the intense bigotry manifested by many of the white soldiers in the Department of the South and the black troops' fierce pride in themselves, such harmony could not be taken for granted.[62]

After Stickney left, Higginson stayed up to write a journal entry and a letter to his mother. It was well after midnight when he finally retired. For many in Jacksonville it was a restless night, but no Rebel attack or bombardment materialized. Dawn brought a measure of comfort as well as a new day, the twentieth of March. A few hours after sunrise a transport rounded the point downriver and hove into view.[63]

Chapter Six

JACKSONVILLE, THE EAST BANK, AND PALATKA

MARCH 20–27

T HE TRANSPORT THAT STEAMED UP TO Jacksonville in midmorning on the twentieth was not the *Boston* but the *Burnside*, which had been sent downriver a couple of hours after midnight to assist the grounded vessel. It took aboard several companies of the 6th Connecticut and then returned. The *Boston* eventually got unstuck and resumed its upriver journey, depositing the rest of the regiment on one of the town's wharves just before noon. Whether because there was no room left in the brick warehouses on Bay Street or because Higginson was no longer so worried about the safety of the men at night, these Connecticut Yankees were quartered in vacant houses.[1]

Their first night in Jacksonville was miserable. Around eleven-thirty musket fire erupted along the picket line west of town, signaling a possible Rebel attack. The howitzers in the fortifications and the big cannons on the *Paul Jones* then opened up, the gunners firing blindly into the dark to try to scare off the enemy. Everyone in town was jolted awake. Major Meeker, commanding the 6th, ordered his men out of their quarters and into the streets so they could be ready to man the defensive works. They stood there in formation, getting drenched in a windblown rain, until it was decided that there was no emergency and they were sent back to bed. Just three hours later, however, another alarm was raised, more naval artillery shells screeched through the darkness, and the Connecticut men were again roused from their sleep and assembled in the streets. Although no Rebels appeared, some of the men of the 6th were not allowed to return to their billets this time but were instead marched off to reinforce the picket line. One Yankee thus discomfited wrote grumpily in his diary that he and his comrades "lay in the swamp all night."[2]

As far as Higginson could tell at this point, these Connecticut troops would be a good addition to his force—provided they got along with the 1st and 2nd South Carolina. They were eight hundred strong, all were seasoned soldiers (having been in service since September 1861), and they had as much combat experience as any troops in the Department of the South could boast. The regiment had taken part in the capture of Port Royal in November 1861 and since then had participated in two of the very few pitched battles fought thus far in this theater. Two of its companies were among the force that had engaged the Rebels at Secessionville in June 1862 in an attempt to oust them from one of the Sea Islands near Charleston, and most of the regiment had seen action in October at Pocotaligo, where the enemy parried a Union thrust inland from Port Royal that was intended to cut the rail link between Charleston and Savannah. In the latter engagement the 6th lost five killed and twenty-nine wounded. Among the wounded were the colonel and lieutenant colonel, both cut down by Rebel artillery fire and still absent recuperating. The other officers of the 6th were even now wearing black ribbons in honor of another comrade wounded at Pocotaligo. He had not lived to assume the lieutenancy awarded for his gallantry there; after suffering in the hospital for four months, he had succumbed to his wound on February 22.[3]

Opinions differed on the state of the 6th Connecticut's discipline and training. It had behaved well enough in battle, although one of its men had been discharged in November for cowardice at Pocotaligo, ritually drummed out of the service in front of the whole regiment with his head shaved. At a brigade review in January the acting department commander and other observers had commended the 6th. But the Sanitary Commission agent who inspected the regiment four days before it embarked for Jacksonville judged its "Drill not as thorough as among neighboring Regiments; and discipline less perfect than when the Col. was in command." At the same time, however, he noted the men's "Gentlemanly bearing."[4]

It appeared that the 6th Connecticut, although more experienced than the 1st South Carolina, was not as finely honed. But Higginson was pleased to see that these Yankees were eager for action. Since October they had sat at Beaufort doing nothing more exciting than picket duty. To relieve their boredom and homesickness, some had formed a glee club, others a literary society. Some entertained themselves and their comrades by organizing a minstrel group and giving performances; wearing black-

face, sporting outlandish costumes, and declaiming in absurdly exaggerated Negro dialect, they enlivened the regiment's evenings with singing
and dancing and comedy.[5]

Had Higginson known of the minstrelsy in the 6th Connecticut, he
would not have deemed it a particularly troubling portent. Nor would he
have found it worrisome that among the events the regiment had staged
for its own amusement last New Year's Day—along with a wheelbarrow
race, a greased pig chase, and the like—had been a competition featuring
male contrabands who had been enticed to kneel around a large tubful of
flour with their arms tied and root through it hoglike with their noses to
find the quarter dollar hidden therein. The troops roared with delight at
this spectacle, as they did at the minstrel shows. But such racial conde-
scension was so common among Northern whites as to be unremarkable;
what Higginson had to worry about was racial hostility. Some of the men
of the 6th were manifesting displeasure at being posted with black units—
the "woolly heads," one called them; the "Nig's," sneered another.[6]

Serious trouble between the white and black troops in Jacksonville
could be disastrous—and not just to the expedition. This was now the
first racially integrated military operation of the war, as far as Higginson
knew. Any racial conflict here would be widely reported in the North and
would be seized on by opponents of black enlistment, wounding that cause
perhaps fatally. Trouble could be touched off easily. A racial slur hurled at
a black soldier on the streets of Jacksonville or on the picket line, followed
by a sharp retort, a shove, a threatening fist, a blow, a hurried assembling
of friends of the combatants, more angry words, more blows: Thus were
race riots ignited. And all these men were of course heavily armed.[7]

As the 6th Connecticut settled into its new assignment, Higginson
watched anxiously for any hint of friction between black and white. He
felt more than ever the awful burden of responsibility, the sense that the
eyes of the nation were on him and that his success or failure might well
affect the outcome of the war. "Now," he wrote grimly in his journal, "I
have to show not only that blacks can fight, but that they & white soldiers
can work in harmony together."[8]

The day of the Connecticut regiment's arrival passed without incident,
as did the next. On the twenty-second, a Sunday, there came a welcome
sign. A service, the first religious service in town since the expedition
arrived, was held that morning in Jacksonville's Episcopal church. Offi-

ciating was the Reverend Mansfield French, a Methodist who had come
from Beaufort aboard the *Boston* with the reinforcements. He was the
Gideonite who had presented the new flag to the 1st South at the Emancipation Day ceremony in Smith's grove. As he gazed from the pulpit this
morning, French saw a crowded church. There were a number of army
and navy officers, a few Jacksonville citizens and contrabands, and many
common soldiers—black and white soldiers, sharing the pews in peace
and Christian fellowship. The minister delivered a sermon on "the sword
of the Lord and of Gideon." The organ, still working despite the church's
long abandonment, was played by a member of the 6th Connecticut; other
men of that regiment served as the choir.[9]

Higginson was not there. Evangelical sermons were not to his taste.
More to the point, the minister was not to his taste; the colonel in fact
detested the Reverend French. While there was no denying that the man
was devoted to helping the freed slaves, he had always struck Higginson
as pompous, egotistical, and disgustingly ingratiating toward people with
influence in the Department of the South. He was a favorite of the secretary of the treasury and of General Saxton. Higginson was especially
resentful about the flag. It was not enough for French that he had secured
it as a gift from a Northern church and presented it to the 1st South; he
had also had that fact emblazoned on the banner itself—in lettering bigger than the regiment's name.[10]

During the service French announced that Quartermaster Luther Bingham was establishing a Sunday school for the children in Jacksonville. It
met that afternoon for the first time, in the Presbyterian church on Ocean
Street. Bingham had spread word of the school among the townspeople,
and he was now pleased to see a good number of youngsters there—girls
and boys, black and white—along with several soldiers of the 6th Connecticut who had volunteered to assist as teachers.[11]

Bingham was the young lieutenant who had written anxiously to his
parents as the expeditionary force neared Jacksonville. He had served
with the 1st South Carolina for more than four months now. While he
found the work fulfilling and was well liked, in some respects he felt himself an outsider. He messed with the field officers and the other staff officers but did not feel close to them. Not only was he younger than most of
them and very junior in rank, but he was also an evangelical while they
were mostly Unitarians; to him their faith seemed bloodless and sterile, a

product of cold intellect rather than fervent spirit. He was, moreover, less politically and socially radical than they, and less educated. They often teased him, or at least he took their bantering that way. "I have to breast quite a current, to stand up for my side of the question," he wrote his parents. "I could be quiet and say and do nothing for Christ, and all would go well. But *that*, the grace of God helping me, *I will not do*." He was convinced that Colonel Higginson in particular regarded his Sunday school idea condescendingly and skeptically. Bingham was determined to be not only a good Christian but also a good soldier. Since penning the somber letter on the transport headed up the St. John's on March 10, he still had not faced the test of combat. "Pray for me that I may be true to duty, and always ready," he wrote from Jacksonville, "—that I may never fear to face danger when it is my duty to face it."[12]

The quartermaster opened his school this Sabbath afternoon with hymns and prayers and then proceeded to read from the Bible. But before finishing the lesson, he was called away. A message from Colonel Higginson announced that a transport vessel had arrived and Bingham was needed to supervise its unloading. Turning the class over to his assistants, he left the church, saddled his horse, and rode down to the wharf.[13]

What he found there came as a stunning surprise. It was the army transport *General Meigs*, and on board were three companies belonging to the 8th Maine Infantry, another of General Saxton's white regiments. They had been dispatched from Beaufort the day after the 6th Connecticut, with orders to report to Jacksonville. The other seven companies of the regiment had left Beaufort at the same time aboard the *Delaware* with identical orders; they would be arriving soon. All told, the Maine regiment numbered nearly 850 officers and men. Along with 1st and 2nd South Carolina and the 800 Connecticut troops, the Union soldiers in Jacksonville would now number more than 2,500.[14]

Bingham got the Maine troops off the ship and found quarters for them in vacant houses. They were grateful to be ashore, for they had had a very rough, stormy ocean voyage. Most had been seasick, and some were still wobbly and dizzy and weak.[15]

As the Maine men trudged off to their billets, Colonel Higginson pondered this new development. It was not just unexpected: it was, as he confessed in his journal, "bewildering," "a puzzle." Lyman Stickney had gotten no indication at Hilton Head or Beaufort that any unit other than the Connecticut regiment would be sent to Higginson's aid. Moreover, these Maine troops brought with them only ten days' rations, by Saxton's order. Would a supply ship bring more provisions, or was Higginson simply expected to make use of this regiment for a few days and then send it back? The major in charge of these three companies had no answers. Perhaps the 8th's commander had some, but he was on the *Delaware*.[16]

The 8th Maine was no stranger to Higginson. Nearly half his company officers had belonged to it before transferring to the 1st South Carolina. Moreover, the regiment had been posted on Port Royal Island as long as he had been there, and its band had played at the Emancipation Day ceremony and had accompanied the 1st on its triumphant march to Beaufort a couple of weeks later. But how good an addition it would be to the expeditionary force was uncertain. Its men were seasoned soldiers, to be sure; like those of the 6th Connecticut, they had been in service since September 1861 and in the Department of the South since November 1861. They were also well drilled and disciplined, frequently complimented in that regard by official observers. Drunkenness was very rare in the regiment, there being a good deal of temperance sentiment among these Maine men. But unlike the 6th Connecticut and the 1st South Carolina, the 8th Maine had never seen combat, not even the slightest skirmish. Its service had so far consisted entirely of picket, provost, and fatigue duty at Beaufort, Hilton Head, and the Georgia Sea Islands. This did not mean, however, that it had suffered no losses. It had in fact experienced an appalling number of deaths in its ranks, by comparison with which the fatalities in the 6th Connecticut and the 1st South were slight. Nearly all these deaths were a consequence of the weeks in 1862 that the men of the 8th had spent slogging through tidal water and mud to construct fortifications on Tybee Island, Georgia. Malaria and other diseases had decimated them; more than a third fell sick, and ultimately some 150 died. The soldiers of the 8th Maine were acutely aware that they had not yet tested their manhood on the field of battle, and most were anxious to do so; but few regiments could claim to have sacrificed more for the Union cause.[17]

There was reason to believe that the 8th was uninfected by the racial hostility that marked so many white regiments, or at least not virulently infected. That so many of its members had volunteered for service in the 1st South was certainly a good sign. These Maine men were no racial egalitarians, by any means; last Christmas Day they had staged the same sort of demeaning spectacle featuring contrabands rooting through a tub of flour that the 6th Connecticut had howled over a week later. Nevertheless, some of the 8th's soldiers professed admiration for the accomplishments of the black troops. "I say bully for them," wrote Private Daniel Sawtelle of Company E, after hearing of the 1st South's raid up the St. Mary's River. Corporal Henry Burnell of Company I, who arrived in Jacksonville on the *General Meigs*, wrote a letter to his family soon after disembarking in which he noted: "The negroe reg[iments] are here. They have been giving the rebels fits."[18]

There was, however, an undercurrent of hostility of another sort in the regiment, one that might prove troublesome in Jacksonville. It was perhaps a consequence of the 8th's frustrating lack of opportunities to grapple with the enemy on the battlefield. Whatever the cause, some of the Maine men were itching to make war on Southern citizens' property and were contemptuous of the army's orders against pillaging and vandalism. Andrew Newman of Company G was among them. "We hav been Here on this island Now About six month Agarden [i.e, a-guarding] rebbles propty," he had written his father from Beaufort in December. "I think if tha wold Take and burn it [it] wold Bee the best thing that We cold do[,] for this garden Rebbles popety I don't think Much off it."[19]

A little after one on Monday afternoon, the twenty-third, the quiet in and around Jacksonville was abruptly shattered by the sound of an artillery projectile whooshing through the air and exploding on the ground. This was not the work of the gunners in the fortifications or on the gunboats. It was what many had feared ever since the citizens were invited to come into the Rebel lines: The enemy had brought up artillery to shell the town. The projectile came from the west, apparently fired from some point behind the Rebel picket line, and it was clearly a large one, perhaps thirty pounds or more, not the ten- or twelve-pound variety commonly used in the Confederate field artillery. The two gunboats on hand, the *Norwich* and *Uncas* (the *Paul Jones* had gone upriver that morning), went immediately into action, firing rounds from their big guns toward the west. The Rebels lobbed a few more shells in the direction of the town, none of which did any damage, and then ceased fire. The lengthy pause between each round suggested that there was only one artillery piece, and the fact that it was well out of sight beyond the Rebel picket line indicated that it could not have been precisely aimed. The gunboats continued firing for a while, then quit. The excitement was over in less than an hour, and quiet returned to Jacksonville.[20]

At almost the same moment that the first enemy shell exploded, Higginson received word that the *Delaware* had arrived with the rest of the 8th Maine and its commander, Colonel John D. Rust. He dispatched a message to Rust, explaining that he could not greet him until this new emergency was over. After the artillery fire ended, the two colonels met.[21]

Rust was a tall, stout man with a booming voice, big front teeth that showed even when he was not smiling, and a dark, frizzy beard that nearly covered his chest. Higginson had first met him in January in Beaufort and was unimpressed. "[V]ery inferior," he decided, "a mere bar room politician from Maine." Although by now he had eighteen months' experience as an officer, Rust had "smelt no powder," as Higginson remarked disdainfully in his journal. Moreover, he was despised by many of his soldiers as a martinet, a bully, and a fanatic. While none could deny that he kept the 8th Maine sharp and orderly, most thought his discipline inexcusably harsh and his disposition tyrannical. The officers were appalled by his lack of respect for them; he habitually denounced them as scoundrels and fools and belittled them in front of the men. Even worse in the eyes of some of the 8th's soldiers were Rust's politics. A rabid abolitionist who liked to lecture his troops on the wisdom and necessity of emancipating and enlisting Southern blacks, he infuriated those of a more conservative bent. He was a favorite of General Saxton's.[22]

With all of Rust's flaws, Higginson nevertheless welcomed his arrival in Jacksonville, for Rust was his senior and would therefore assume command. While this would put the fate of the expedition at least temporarily in the hands of someone with mediocre talent, an abrasive personality, and no combat experience, Higginson was more relieved than perturbed. He felt as if an immense weight had been lifted from his shoulders; now he could simply carry out orders and leave the agonizing decisions to someone else.[23]

Higginson's sense of relief was very quickly tempered by the discovery that Rust did not want to take command. Although he agreed to do so formally, he told Higginson that he felt like a mere visitor, would not presume to dictate, and would not take up quarters in the town but instead stay aboard the *Delaware*. Moreover, he confessed that he had no idea why his regiment had been ordered to this place, except simply to reinforce the black troops and allow them to operate more freely, and he could not explain why he was provided with only ten days' rations. As Higginson talked with him, he realized that Rust had no intention of exercising real leadership.[24]

Within a couple of days, however, the 8th's commander seemed to abandon his reticence, to Higginson's gratification. "Col. Rust is in command," he wrote on March 27. "We get on perfectly." What Higginson did not know was that Rust had been persuaded to truly take charge by the earnest pleading of two men. One was Lyman Stickney. The other was Charles Steedman, commander of the *Paul Jones*, which returned from its upriver voyage on the evening of the twenty-fourth. Perhaps they thought Higginson too inexperienced or downright incompetent or suspected that he was buckling under the strain of command. Steedman may have been motivated by his distaste for Higginson's radicalism, unaware that Rust was no less fervent an abolitionist. Stickney perhaps saw some personal advantage in having someone besides Higginson in charge in Jacksonville. Whatever the reason, these two men, both of them liked and trusted by Higginson, went privately to Rust (whom they could not have known well and probably knew not at all) and convinced him not to let Higginson remain in de facto command.[25]

Steedman's overnight mission on the *Paul Jones* was a reconnaissance intended to gather information on what lay upriver as far as Palatka, information that would be of value when the expedition moved farther into the interior. The reconnaissance proved unexciting but by no means fruitless. Leaving Jacksonville a little before ten on the morning of the twenty-third, the side-wheeler paddled southward. Steedman and his officers scanned the river and its banks for anything of interest. Before long they spotted a small boat with a single occupant; it turned out to be a runaway slave, whom they took aboard. Around midafternoon they saw someone on the riverbank waving a white flag. They sent ashore a boat, which brought back another black fugitive. Late that afternoon the *Paul Jones* reached Palatka, fifty miles from Jacksonville. It was known that a detachment of Rebel troops was posted nearby, so the vessel did not dock but rather anchored in the stream. Steedman wanted to let the enemy know he was here, however, and so at his command the ship's guns fired four shells over the town in the supposed direction of the Confederate camp. After a time the *Paul Jones* weighed anchor and steamed back down the river. By now the sun was setting. A little after dark the vessel anchored at a point on the east bank known as Orange Mills. There Steedman sent ashore a foraging party, which brought back five sheep. All on board then settled in for the night.[26]

The next morning Steedman sent more foragers ashore. They came back with a steer, a blacksmith's bellows, and a black man named John, who was no longer the property of a slaveowner named Frank Hernandez. Weighing anchor in the early afternoon, the *Paul Jones* headed back to Jacksonville. In the late afternoon the lookouts spotted a small boat coming toward them from the shore. Steedman ordered it to be taken alongside, and its sole occupant, a white man, was brought aboard. He identified himself as a Unionist seeking refuge from the Rebels. After resuming its downriver journey, the *Paul Jones* reached Jacksonville a little before eight that evening.[27]

Three black runaways and a white Unionist: That was the human harvest of Steedman's reconnaissance. The naval commander's impression, which he communicated to Higginson, was that almost all the slaves along the river between Jacksonville and Palatka had in recent days been moved inland by their masters, at least temporarily, for safekeeping. This was undoubtedly the case everywhere along the river, for news of the expedition had surely spread far and fast in the St. John's region. Only five fugitive slaves had come into Jacksonville since the *John Adams* and *Burnside* brought several dozen from upriver on the sixteenth and seventeenth: the three Steedman had just delivered and two from Mandarin (ten miles upriver) who slipped away in a stolen boat and were taken aboard the *Norwich* just before dawn on March 19. In fact, since the seventeenth more white than black fugitives had come in; among them was a deserter from the Confederate army.[28]

Frustrated by the minimal progress in liberating slaves during the last week, Higginson began to reconsider strategy. It was becoming apparent that the expeditionary force could not achieve its primary goal if it simply hugged the river. No matter how far up the St. John's it penetrated, it would have to strike inland to make war on slavery.[29]

The three blacks who arrived on the *Paul Jones* were presumably turned over to the nominal superintendent of freedmen, Lyman Stickney, although it is unlikely he bothered to do much for them. They joined the seventy or so blacks currently in the town, some of whom had been living there with their masters when the expedition arrived. The white Unionist refugee fell under the jurisdiction of the post provost marshal. Captain Rogers of the 1st South no longer held that position. At Colonel Rust's suggestion, Captain Henry Boynton of the 8th Maine took over as provost marshal on the twenty-fourth, and his company replaced Rogers's as provost guard. Higginson readily agreed to this. The provost guard was the military police force, and Higginson worried that white soldiers might get unruly if they were challenged, ordered about, or arrested by blacks on provost duty. He did not think the black troops would react that way to white provost guards.[30]

Assigning white troops to provost duty also smoothed some ruffled feathers among the white townsfolk. With the departure on March 19 of those who preferred to live in Rebel territory, the general temper of the town's citizens grew less hostile, and with the arrival of the 6th Connecticut and 8th Maine some soldiers and citizens even began to fraternize. Among them was Private Martin Emmons of the 6th, who started going out "sparking" in the evenings when off duty, joined by some of his comrades. A number of the local girls were happy to receive these Yankee boys, and Emmons soon concluded that duty in Jacksonville was not at all unpleasant. Several of the younger army and navy officers found a congenial place of resort at the home of some cultured females of Spanish descent on Adams Street. There they were entertained with singing, piano playing, and flirtation. Higginson, whose headquarters was directly behind the women's house, thought the young officers should be more discriminating, for the women struck him as rather repulsive; "sallow singing . . . spinsters," he called them, "semi-ladies," "entirely without charms"—and secessionists to boot.[31]

Higginson had become concerned about the safety of both civilians and soldiers in light of the enemy's long-distance artillery barrage on the twenty-third, brief and ineffective though it was. The next day—he was still in de facto command at that point—he took steps to prevent another such attack. By now it was known, no doubt from reports of civilians passing between the lines, that the shells had been fired by a very large rifled cannon that the Rebels had mounted on a flatcar and moved up within range of town on the railroad track that ran west from Jacksonville. If the track could be destroyed at some point far enough from town to keep the cannon out of range, the threat would be ended. Higginson assigned this task to the white troops. On the twenty-fourth several companies, including at least one from the 8th Maine and two from the 6th Connecticut, marched westward along the railroad track beyond the Union picket line. They encountered no Rebels; apparently the enemy pickets had been pulled back to the west. At a point that their officers deemed sufficiently distant from town, the Yankee troops halted, pried up a stretch of rails, gathered the crossties into a pile, set fire to them, and heated and bent the rails to render them useless. Satisfied that the Rebels would cause no more trouble with their railroad gun, they then marched back to town.[32]

At three-forty the next morning came sudden, terrifying evidence that someone—either the Connecticut and Maine officers or Higginson—had badly misjudged the range of the Rebel gun. From a point on the railroad less than two miles west of Jacksonville an object rose abruptly into the dark sky. Visible by the sparks it emitted, it traced a long, graceful arc before crashing into an abandoned house on the west side of town and exploding with a blinding white flash and a deafening bang. A redhot iron fragment penetrated the next-door building that served as the 8th Maine's hospital, narrowly missing the regiment's chief surgeon as he slept on his cot. Some minutes later a second shell burst in the air nearby. A third soon followed; it crashed through the roof of a house owned by a citizen named Paran Moody, continued into the bedroom where he and his wife were asleep, ripped through the mosquito netting surrounding their bed, smashed into a rocking chair over which they had draped their clothes, shattered the bedroom mirrors and window glass by sheer concussive power, exited through the east wall of the house, and buried itself several feet deep in the Moodys' garden without exploding. The couple bolted awake to find themselves covered with plaster and splinters but unharmed.[33]

By this time the startled officers and men of the expeditionary force were shaking off their grogginess and swinging into action. In Forts Higginson and Montgomery and aboard the *Norwich*, which was anchored near the west end of town, gunners ran to their posts, charged and primed their cannons, and began firing in the direction of the enemy gun, as best they could judge it. Meanwhile the long roll of drums summoned the infantrymen from their billets and into the streets, where they formed up and waited for further orders. "We fell in on the double quick," wrote Private Daniel Sawtelle of the 8th Maine, "thinking that the Johnnies [i.e.,

Rebels] were coming." A few moments later one of his comrades called out, "There comes one." "We looked to the west," wrote Sawtelle, "and saw what at first appeared to be a very bright star, but it rose rapidly and came in our direction. It struck a little before it reached us, bounded several times, and stopped." Like the third shell, this was luckily a dud.[34]

At the Sanderson house, headquarters of the 1st South Carolina, Dr. Rogers was sound asleep when the first shell exploded. It woke him instantly, interrupting a dream. When he regained his senses enough to recognize what was going on, he was deeply alarmed: "It seemed as if we were at last fairly in for it." His assistant surgeon soon appeared, asking whether they should evacuate the patients from the regimental hospital or "trust Providence." Rogers told him to go to the hospital "and assure them all that the Lord was on the side of our big guns." But he was worried about the patients, fearing that even if the enemy shells missed them, the awful strain of lying helpless during a bombardment might exacerbate their ailments and play havoc with their nervous systems.[35]

As his assistant hurried off to the hospital, Rogers climbed up into the cupola atop the Sanderson house for a better view of the action. He did not stay long. Within minutes an enemy shell "burst in the air and sent a fragment whistling above my head with a note so shrill that I began to think of Gabriel's trumpet and crawled down again." Another piece of that round hit in front of the headquarters only a few feet from where Colonel Higginson and Major Strong were standing. The colonel had observed the shell with fascination along most of its trajectory, "showing a light as it rose, and moving slowly towards us like a comet, then exploding and scattering its formidable fragments."[36]

After firing seven rounds, all of which landed in town, the enemy gun fell silent and was presumably hauled back to the west by its locomotive. Perhaps its ammunition was depleted; more likely, the return fire from the *Norwich* and the forts had forced its withdrawal. Given the accuracy of the Rebel cannonade on this occasion, it seemed a miracle that no one in Jacksonville had been killed or injured. Some in town were convinced that the bombardment was too precisely concentrated in the vicinity of Higginson's headquarters to have been aimed randomly, and they wondered if an informer might have passed information to the Rebels to help direct the fire. One who suspected so was Susie King. A laundress of the 1st South and the wife of one of its soldiers, she fled to a safer part of town when rounds began bursting near her quarters, which were close to Higginson's. As she hurriedly exited her room and ran into the street, she later wrote, "I expected every moment to be killed by a shell."[37]

The 8th Maine stayed in formation until dawn, ready for battle, but no Rebel infantry appeared. After the firing stopped, some men dug up the dud round in the Moodys' garden. It was identified as the ammunition of a Blakely rifled cannon, a thirty-two-pounder of English manufacture commonly used by the Confederates to defend fortified cities such as Savannah. The shell was taken aboard the *Norwich* as a souvenir.[38]

The bombardment gave Higginson another reason to go forward with an operation he had been contemplating for several days, a reconnaissance in force west toward the Rebel camp. He had long been anxious to learn more about the strength and position of the enemy force opposing him; now he wanted also to destroy the railroad track a good distance from town to keep the Blakely at bay. By late morning on the twenty-fifth he understood, to his relief, that Colonel Rust had assumed real command of the expedition, and he got Rust's permission to proceed with the reconnaissance. Now free of command responsibility, he decided to lead it himself. Since the expedition arrived in Jacksonville, he had been eager to get into action but had kept himself out of harm's way as a commander was supposed to do. Now he could go forth and lead in battle.[39]

The units he assembled on the morning of March 25 would constitute, as far as he knew, the first racially integrated U.S. Army force to go into action in this war. There were four companies of the 6th Connecticut, four of the 8th Maine, and five of the 1st South, a good two-fifths of the expeditionary force. The troops were ordered to take one day's rations, full canteens of water, and sixty rounds of ammunition. A handcar on which was mounted a ten-pounder rifled cannon would go with them, pushed and pulled along the railroad track by human power behind the advancing infantry. This little flatcar was big enough to hold the gun, its crew, some ammunition, and Colonel Higginson, but small enough to be manhandled past the stretch of track destroyed yesterday by the white troops. Higginson's mission was to advance four miles west from Jacksonville, gather intelligence, tear up track, and return. Colonel Rust forbade him to go farther for fear that the Rebels might attack Jacksonville from another direction while it was lightly defended.[40]

An hour or two before noon Higginson gave the command that put the troops in motion westward in three columns separated by several hundred yards. The Maine men were on the right, the Connecticut men on the left, the black men in the center close to the track. When they passed the Union picket line a mile and a half out, Higginson ordered skirmishers to go ahead of the columns; they would give warning if the enemy appeared. Three companies, one from each column, went forward as skirmishers. These men advanced in a long line, each separated from the next by a distance of five paces but with no wider gap between companies. Higginson, perched atop the little flatcar with his spyglass to his eye, was moved by the sight. "[W]hite-black-white, forming one harmonious line," he wrote. "For the first time I saw the two colors fairly alternate on the military chessboard; it had been the object of much labor and many dreams, and I liked [seeing] the pattern at last."[41]

Once they passed beyond the zone that Higginson had had thoroughly cleared, the troops found themselves in a flat pine barren, mostly open rather than dense. Here and there were marshes, copses of hardwood, and houses surrounded by plots of cultivated land. Before long there appeared in the distance some mounted Rebel pickets. The skirmishers fired a few rounds at them, but they withdrew westward as the reconnaissance force advanced, staying for the most part out of musket range.[42]

At the four-mile point Higginson halted the columns and recalled the skirmishers. He did so reluctantly, bowing to his superior's directive but wishing he could push on until he encountered something of interest. He let the troops rest awhile and then put them in motion eastward. In the meantime they had partially dismantled a nearby railroad trestle spanning a creek.[43]

As they headed back to Jacksonville, Higginson kept his glass pointed westward. Soon he saw puffs of black smoke rising beyond some trees a couple of miles away. The smoke continued to rise as his troops marched on, but its point of origin seemed to progress eastward at about the same pace as Higginson's force. The likeliest explanation was that the Rebels had brought up a locomotive. But that would be senseless—unless the locomotive was pushing the dreaded Blakely on its flatcar.[44]

All doubt was removed minutes later, when Higginson spotted the big enemy gun through a break in the trees, "raised high in the air," he wrote, "like the threatening head of some great gliding serpent." As he watched, white smoke billowed abruptly from its barrel and a black projectile arced across the intervening terrain. It exploded in the air some distance north of him, near where the Maine troops were marching along a plank road.[45]

Higginson did not observe the effect of the shell, for some trees blocked his view; only later did he learn of the havoc it wreaked. It burst over the heads of the men of the 8th, hot fragments whirring in all directions at lethal speed. Those nearest the explosion ran for their lives, discipline momentarily forgotten amid the awful noise and terror and smoke and confusion—all except three men, privates in Company I. These three were not braver than the rest; they were casualties, struck down by a single big piece of the projectile. William Willis, a twenty-year-old, blue-eyed farm boy, was crippled for life, his right heel nearly cut off and the rest of the foot mangled and shattered. Joseph Goodwin, likewise a farm boy but a year younger than Willis, was even more horribly maimed: The entire right side of his body from shoulder to hip was sliced off, leaving vital organs exposed; he was still alive but surely could not last long. Most shocking was the fate of Thomas Hoole, a twenty-seven-year-old house painter and the sole support of his widowed mother in Brunswick; the shell fragment decapitated him, blasting his head to pieces.[46]

As the deadly chunk of iron sped from Hoole's head through Goodwin's body and then through Willis's foot, it splattered brains and blood and flesh all over the men marching near the unfortunate three, a sickening introduction to combat for these untested Maine troops and one that was never erased from their memories. "It was a terrible sight," wrote Daniel Sawtelle of Company E, "and was my first near view of death in that manner. The man that had his head taken off there was nothing left but the whiskers under the chin. The other one [Goodwin] lay on his left side, the stump of arm . . . the flesh having been stripped off, the white bone was sticking out and up waving about. The blood was pouring from their wounds."[47]

Sawtelle and another soldier carried Goodwin several hundred yards to a mule-drawn cart driven by a black man; it had been brought along to serve as an ambulance. They deposited poor Goodwin in the cart and then accompanied him back to the 8th's hospital in town. "He suffered terribly," Sawtelle recorded, "and was unconscious a great part of the time. When he was conscious, he would curse us as if he thought he could anger us and get us to put him out of his misery. He would ask us to shoot him and then curse us because we did not." Other Maine soldiers carried Willis to the hospital and brought away Hoole's body.[48]

As soon as Higginson spotted the Blakely, he ordered the crew of his ten-pounder to open up on it. They kept up their fire as their little flatcar was pushed and pulled eastward by some of the men of the 1st South. Meanwhile the Blakely continued to fire as its locomotive pushed it forward at the same pace, keeping a distance of two miles or so from the withdrawing Union troops. Surely, thought Higginson, this must be the strangest artillery duel of the war. He resisted the temptation to turn his troops around and make a rush for the Rebel cannon and locomotive. Although the only enemy soldiers visible were a thin line of cavalry pickets, there was probably a more substantial force near at hand to defend the big gun, or else the Rebels would not have risked bringing it up. In any event, the locomotive could quickly pull the Blakely westward to safety if the Union troops threatened it.[49]

The Blakely came to a halt and grew silent after firing for about forty-five minutes. It had done no harm to the reconnaissance force after the first shot. Its fire had apparently been directed at the ten-pounder on the handcar, thus threatening the men of the 1st South more than the white troops, but Higginson kept his eye on it and called out to his black soldiers each time he saw it discharge a round. The railroad track was flanked on each side by a ditch several feet deep, providing excellent shelter, and their colonel's warning gave the men enough time to scurry into the ditches and take cover before the slow-moving thirty-two-pound shells arrived. Some of those shells were, moreover, duds.[50]

This was the first time the black soldiers had been under artillery fire aimed squarely at them, and Higginson feared they might panic. But as the rounds harmlessly burst in the air or plowed into the ground, the men lost their fear of them. They even began to make sport of them, shouting derisively at each futile shot. Like Higginson, they were unaware of the grisly toll that the first shell had exacted on the 8th Maine.[51]

As soon as he realized that the Blakely had stopped firing, Higginson directed the black troops to begin prying up rails; he had not done so until now because it would slow the withdrawal. The men removed rails from a long stretch of track and lugged them back to town. Higginson also ordered that some houses along the way that might be useful to Rebel pickets be put to the torch. Dr. Rogers, who had ridden out from town on horseback about noon to join Higginson's force, volunteered to take charge of destroying one of them. He had never before sought vengeance against the Rebel citizenry; no doubt, like Higginson, he found his sympathy wearing thin after dealing with the people of Jacksonville. In any event, the surgeon took pleasure in this task and boasted cheerfully of it in a letter home: "I chose a very new, good [house], and kindled my fire in a costly mahogany sideboard."[52]

By three that afternoon the reconnaissance force was back within the Jacksonville fortifications. Higginson could hardly deny that this day's work was less than fully satisfying. The destruction of the railroad would certainly keep the Blakely at a safe distance from town for a good long while—perhaps permanently, for replacement rails were in very short supply in Rebeldom. On the other hand, Higginson had lost three men without inflicting any enemy casualties as far as he could tell. And he had learned nothing of value about the strength and disposition of General Finegan's force.[53]

At the same time he launched the reconnaissance, however, Higginson had given his blessing to another operation that might prove more rewarding. At eleven-thirty that morning the *General Meigs* set off upriver with Colonel Montgomery and both companies of the 2nd South Carolina. This would not be a one-day excursion like the river raids of March 14 to 17, for Montgomery intended to take his men far up the St. John's and then penetrate a good distance inland. Colonel Rust gladly approved this plan, for he had brought his own regiment to Jacksonville with the understanding that its presence there would allow the black troops to extend the expedition's reach.[54]

Ravenous for another chance to strike boldly and suddenly into enemy territory, gather up slaves, add to the ranks of his regiment, and make the Rebel citizens feel the hard hand of war, Montgomery had been straining at the leash for days now. He boasted that he would take along no provisions other than a little hardtack, for he intended to live off the land. His only fear, he told Higginson, was that his men would blister their feet on the march inland, for they all were raised on Key West and had never had to walk farther than the length of that little island.[55]

Also aboard the *General Meigs* were some members of the 1st South who had gotten permission to go along on this adventure. One was Chaplain Fowler, who had decided that the exhilarating peril of combat was more to his liking than the quiet satisfaction of ministry and who was no doubt bored by the routine into which the Jacksonville post had settled. Another was Lieutenant Colonel Liberty Billings, who likewise craved excitement. Higginson readily agreed to let Billings go, for he was still worthless as a field officer, while his proved ability as a recruiter of black troops might make him useful to Montgomery. These two officers were joined by a middle-aged private, Company G's cook, John Quincy. He had begged to be allowed to come along in the hope that Montgomery's raiding party would make it to Palatka, where Quincy's wife and children were held in bondage.[56]

Since arriving in Jacksonville with the expedition, Quincy had continued his fervent lay preaching to the men of the 1st South, reminding them that they were warriors in a holy cause and that the Lord watched them with special interest. Any soldier of the 1st who fell while bravely facing the enemy on the battlefield, he said, could be "pretty sure of stepping directly into heaven." Furthermore, he declared, those who not only stood firm in combat but also trusted God with all their heart would never be touched by enemy bullets or shells. Private Quincy himself trusted wholly in the Lord, and he was determined to do his duty if summoned to meet the enemy face-to-face.[57]

Before this day was through, Higginson gave his approval to an adventure of another sort that might benefit the expedition. Not long after he settled back into his headquarters following the return of the reconnaissance force, he was informed that a sergeant of Company G wanted to speak with him. Ushered in, the sergeant told him that his friend Thomas Long, a corporal in the same company, had conceived a plan and wished to submit it for Higginson's consideration. It was as daring a thing as one could imagine. Long, a tall twenty-three-year-old native of northeastern Florida, who knew the region well, proposed to make his way surreptitiously into the interior and burn down a long railroad trestle that crossed a swamp several miles beyond the Rebel troops' camp, which was eight miles west of Jacksonville. If he succeeded, the Rebels, who depended on the rail line for supplies, would have to pull farther back into the interior, leaving Jacksonville that much more secure.[58]

Higginson gave his assent, and Long set out that evening. Before departing, the corporal exchanged his blue uniform for civilian clothes. But neither he nor anyone else who knew of his mission believed that he could pass himself off as an innocent slave if the Rebels caught him, for he carried two Colt revolvers, a knapsack containing three days' rations, a box of matches, and a container of turpentine. Should he fall into the enemy's hands, the only question was whether he would be executed at once or whipped first to extract information.[59]

Dr. Rogers, who knew Long, was deeply moved by this courageous act. That night, just after Long set out westward, alone and on foot, the doctor told of him in a letter home, describing him as "a thin, spiritual-looking, unassuming black man, who trusts God" and praising him as a true hero. Like John Quincy, Thomas Long believed that fearlessness and faith would keep him from harm. Rogers was less sanguine: "My expectation of seeing him again is very small."[60]

The *General Meigs* steamed southward all day and well into the evening. Just above Jacksonville the St. John's abruptly widened, and for a long distance beyond that its width ranged from three to five miles and its current was barely detectable. Here it seemed more a lake than a river, a great, dark lake, for the rich alluvium it carried made the water brown and murky. The farther south the steamer went, the more tropical was the scene. There were orange and lemon trees in profusion, mainly cultivated but some wild, and even a variety of banana. Most of the trees, however, were the familiar pines and palmettos and moss-laden live oaks; they crowded along the riverbanks except where tilled fields and pastures intervened. There were no bluffs here and hardly any high banks; even the tallest elevations were no more than a few feet above the waterline. At several locations along the shore sat large hotels, an incongruous sight in this remote and rural section of the South. Before the war these had been the winter resorts of wealthy invalids, mostly Northerners, but now they stood empty.[61]

Thirty-five miles or so from Jacksonville the *General Meigs* hove to and anchored for the night. The next morning, the twenty-sixth, it proceeded a short distance to a place on the east bank known as Federal Point. Here was a plantation with a wharf, owned by a man named Cornelius Dupont. Montgomery disembarked along with seventy-five of his soldiers. To their disappointment, they found no slaves to liberate. Nor did they find the plantation owner, who had galloped away minutes before to avoid Montgomery's clutches and to spread the alarm among his neighbors. Montgomery did seize prizes of another sort, however, all of Dupont's horses except the one he had ridden off on. The colonel then led the seventy-five soldiers inland, hoping that their untested feet would withstand a real march.[62]

The steamer went on upriver with the fifty or so men who remained on board under command of one of Montgomery's officers. They would rendezvous with the others that evening at a predesignated point. Later in the morning the boat tied up at another wharf on the east bank, about ten miles downstream from Palatka. This place was called Orange Mills, even though there was only one mill here, a steam-powered sawmill that had been burned to the ground a few months before by the crew of a navy gunboat. It was not a town, hardly even a hamlet; besides the ruined mill, there was nothing but a post office, a few houses, and a large orange grove, covering fifteen acres or more. The troops went ashore and pillaged the houses, taking furniture and sugar and other valuables. They then reboarded the *General Meigs* and continued upriver to a point opposite Palatka, which sat on the west bank. Here was where Montgomery and his detachment were to rejoin them.[63]

By now it was about 4:00 P.M. Again the troops went ashore on the east bank, this time in the steamer's small boats, for there was no wharf here. There were two farms in the vicinity, but the men who owned them were nowhere to be found. Their families were here, however, and so were three slaves, whom the soldiers took into custody. Before pitching their tents and settling in for the night, the troops stripped both places of everything useful, including horses, chickens, hogs, potatoes, salt, and cooking pots. Then they butchered two beeves for supper.[64]

After leaving the Dupont place at Federal Point, Montgomery and his little force marched inland a few miles to another plantation. It was owned by a prominent fifty-six-year-old Rebel citizen named Francis L. Dancy, a onetime U.S. Army officer and a personal friend of Jefferson Davis's. Two black men were here, but the other slaves and the Dancy family were gone, having fled after being warned by Cornelius Dupont. In the slave quarters the soldiers found the slaves' noon meal, freshly prepared but uneaten. They helped themselves to it and then continued their march, taking with them the two slave men, a mule, and all the poultry and hogs they could catch. Before they had gone far, one of the slaves slipped away and disappeared. The mule, old and decrepit, proved unable to keep up with the troops, so they shot it and left its body by the road.[65]

They marched to a point on the river about a mile south of Orange Mills, where they ransacked another place owned by Dancy. About this time they also captured a white man who lived nearby, forty-six-old Thomas T. Russell, a farmer of modest means but also a state senator. Montgomery saw this as a good opportunity to spread terror among the Rebel populace. He spoke harshly to Russell, then let him go. Within days Russell wrote two reports of this encounter, sending one to a Tallahassee newspaper and the other to General Finegan. Montgomery "informed me that he had come up for the purpose of permanently occupying Palatka," Russell told Finegan, "and that they intended restoring Florida to the Union at all hazards; that he would have a force of some 5,000 men at Palatka in a few days; that they had been acting in a mild way all along, but that they intended now to let us feel what war actually was; . . . that all the negroes were declared free and he intended to take all he could find."[66]

Russell's alarming report on the expedition was not the first to appear in the Confederate press. Word of the invasion of Florida by black troops led by radical Yankee abolitionists had already been conveyed through the lines by citizens of Jacksonville and was spreading rapidly through Rebeldom, confirming white Southerners' worst fears about the North's intentions. On March 17 the Tallahassee *Florida Sentinel* had reported the arrival of an enemy force on the St. John's that included "A black Brigade [*sic*], commanded by the notorious Montgomery, of Kansas memory." Eight days later the editor of the Augusta, Georgia, *Daily Chronicle and Sentinel* expressed alarm at the invasion and called on General Finegan to "adopt a vigorous policy towards these black scoundrels, and either capture or drive them from the State. Their white leaders should be forthwith hung whenever they may fall into our hands." The Savannah *Daily Morning News* told its readers of "the negro-Yankee horde of murderers, thieves and incendiaries, who are attempting to establish themselves at Jacksonville." This was, the Savannah editor warned, undoubtedly the commencement of "Eli Thayer's scheme for the negro colonization of Florida." But he assured his readers that the enemy would ultimately be repulsed: "It is not probable that [the black troops] will be allowed to remain in possession of Jacksonville very long—certainly they will not be permitted to penetrate the interior." Such editorial bluster could not, however, assuage the fears of the white South. An armed force of fugitive slaves and white abolitionists was on the loose inside the Confederacy, and it was clear that it would not be as easily suppressed as John Brown and his band.[67]

Montgomery and his detachment continued south toward their rendezvous point, the men by now surely tired and footsore. Before long they spotted the *General Meigs* lying at anchor and the other men of the 2nd camped onshore. They pitched their tents alongside those of their comrades and bedded down for the night. The river narrowed here to just a mile and a half, and a quarter moon shone overhead. Palatka could be seen across the water. Tomorrow the *General Meigs* would go there.[68]

Montgomery was pleased by this day's work. While he had not liberated many slaves, he had unquestionably made some Rebel citizens feel his righteous wrath. This was the kind of warfare he craved: not wholly unrestrained, not savage, but certainly hard and vengeful and unbound by gentlemanly rules—and not closely monitored by superiors or fettered by army regulations. His soldiers too seemed to revel in being unleashed in enemy territory.[69]

To the officers and men back in Jacksonville, on the other hand, this was a day of grieving and frustration. The remains of two soldiers of the 8th Maine were laid to rest in Jacksonville's cemetery. The dead men were Thomas Hoole and Joseph Goodwin, who had been struck down west of town the day before by the deadly Blakely shell. Hoole went headless to his grave, but at least he had died instantly and painlessly. Poor Goodwin had lived for two agonizing hours with his right arm and much of his chest and hip gone. Their surviving comrades of the 8th formally escorted the remains to the cemetery, marching solemnly in full uniform while the regimental band played a dirge. They then stood at attention as the service was conducted and the coffins were lowered into the ground. William Willis, the third man felled by the Blakely shell, was in the regimental hospital. His right foot had been amputated just above the ankle, but he would live.[70]

The 1st South was summoned to action this day but gained nothing except another memorable episode to add to the regiment's treasury of oft-told tales. A scout had recently spotted a small Rebel army campsite four miles north of town—he counted twenty-two tents—and returned to Jacksonville without being noticed by the enemy. Colonel Rust gave Higginson permission to take four companies of the 1st and try to bag these Rebels. Higginson and Major Strong led the men out of town, cautioning them to move as soundlessly as possible. When the tents came into view, the companies moved in stealthily. The trap was sprung, and only then was the true nature of this "Rebel camp" revealed: It was some family's sheets and underwear and other laundry hung out to dry near their farmhouse. Higginson led his wryly amused soldiers back to town and promptly dubbed the episode the "Battle of the Clothes Lines."[71]

Even more frustrating was the return this day of Corporal Thomas Long with the report that his daring mission into the interior had failed. Of his skill and bravery, however, there could be no doubt. He had made his way by moonlight eight miles westward without being detected, had crept close enough to the Confederate encampment to observe it well, and had then proceeded as planned to the railroad trestle four miles beyond. But to his great disappointment he found the trestle well guarded by enemy soldiers. He could not get near enough to put his turpentine and matches to work. Dr. Rogers recounted this bitter anticlimax in a letter home but added that his respect for Long was undiminished: "I look at that man with a deep feeling of reverence."[72]

Higginson was by now contemplating the future of the expedition in light of the expected departure in a few days of the 8th Maine, whose rations were dwindling with no prospect of resupply. Colonel Rust would of course go with his regiment, leaving Higginson again in command. If the 1st South was to be free to operate farther up the river as Higginson desired, he must ensure that Jacksonville could be securely held by the white troops who remained. He decided to try again to get reinforcements from Colonel Hawley in Fernandina—infantry, if possible, but at the very least one or more pieces of field artillery with their crews.[73]

Because Lyman Stickney had had such success in getting reinforcements earlier, Higginson asked him to undertake this mission. The tax commissioner readily agreed. The army transport *John Adams* was preparing to sail for Fernandina to load up with coal and other supplies at the naval depot there; Commander Steedman had authorized this, with the understanding that his gunboats would get a share. Stickney boarded the *John Adams* on the morning of the twenty-sixth, a few hours before Higginson and his men set out to capture the "Rebel camp." At eight-thirty it pulled away from the wharf, then steamed downriver and disappeared around the bend.[74]

For Stickney this mission was a godsend. He had needed an excuse to return to Fernandina to secure more goods for his Jacksonville store, the prospects of which were now quite bright. Business was picking up in town, for citizens were starting to come in from the countryside to trade. If Stickney could fully stock the shelves of his establishment, he and his partner, Calvin Robinson, could make a killing. Of course he did not mention to Higginson that he would be bringing back personal goods at government expense; the colonel was still blithely unaware even of Stickney's interest in the store. If anybody raised a question, Stickney would swear that the stuff was for the use of the Tax Commission whose work he was so diligently carrying on or for the welfare of the contrabands he was so selflessly tending.[75]

If Calvin Robinson was as unscrupulous as Stickney, there might be even more malfeasance in Jacksonville. Before returning to the town with Stickney to take charge of the store, Robinson had secured from the military authorities an appointment as deputy civil provost marshal. Put in his charge was all abandoned property in Jacksonville not needed by the occupation force, including the enormous amount of furniture, clothing, kitchen utensils, dishware, and other things left in their homes by the citizens who had gone to the Rebel lines on March 19 and others who had refugeed out before the expedition arrived. Robinson was required to inventory this property and see to its safekeeping. To all appearances he did just that, but the temptation to stock his store with some of these articles must have been great. Perhaps the fox had been set to guard the henhouse, or perhaps Robinson was determined to do his duty with strict propriety. In either event, he would feel no pressure from his business partner to stay on the path of rectitude.[76]

Sunrise on Friday, the twenty-seventh, found Montgomery and his men stirring about busily on the east bank of the St. John's across from Palatka. Today they would load aboard the General Meigs all the booty not yet stowed away and then set forth on another adventure somewhere along the river. Montgomery's first order of business, however, was a quick visit to Palatka. He did not intend to tie down his little strike force by occupying the town; the purpose of this excursion was to rescue John Quincy's family from slavery and to gather up any other slaves who might be found.[77]

Montgomery designated fifteen of his men to go on this errand and then rowed out to the steamer with them, leaving the rest onshore prepar-

ing breakfast. Also aboard were Quincy, Chaplain Fowler, and Lieutenant Colonel Billings. Around six the *General Meigs* weighed anchor and
headed across the river.[78]

Palatka was a pretty place, with whitewashed houses and lush flora.
Trees of the most enchanting sort lined the streets and shaded the yards
and gardens: magnolia, live oak, orange, lemon, banana, pomegranate, fig.
Spanish moss adorned some of them, and flowers of many colors bloomed
around the houses. Before the war the town had had a population of six
hundred and a thriving economy. Situated at the head of navigation for
large vessels, it had been a lively entrepôt, its wharves crowded with small
steamers from upriver and big ones from below. It had also been a resort
town, boasting no fewer than four hotels that catered especially to Yankee
invalids. But of course the war had changed everything.[79]

Although Commander Steedman had seen no sign of enemy troops
when the *Paul Jones* stopped here four days ago, it was known that a small
Rebel force camped not far away. Montgomery therefore approached the
town warily. He planned to dock at one of the wharves, send someone
ashore to scout around, and then, if it seemed safe, let Private Quincy
lead a squad of armed men to the house of his family's master. Chaplain
Fowler volunteered to serve as scout.[80]

The *General Meigs* chugged across the river and eased up to a wharf
owned by the mercantile firm of Teasdale & Reid, whose warehouse sat
close by. The ship's crew tied up, then lowered a ladder over the side.
Fowler climbed down onto the wharf and followed one of the streets into
the little town, proceeding cautiously. He encountered no enemy troops;
in fact he saw no one at all. The streets were deserted, and the town was
silent. He looked around a little, satisfied himself that no Rebel troops
were lying in wait, and then returned to the ship and advised Montgomery that it was safe to send Quincy on his rescue mission.[81]

Quincy and seven or eight of the 2nd South Carolina men debarked,
gathered on the wharf, and prepared to set out. Liberty Billings, who was
going with them, also climbed over the ship's side and down the ladder.
He had not yet set foot on the wharf when a voice rang out. It originated
about a hundred yards away where a stout plank fence was visible. The
voice was followed instantly by a volley of gunfire that shattered the still-
ness. White smoke billowed from behind the plank fence. Bullets from at
least fifty rifles zipped through the air toward the wharf. One smashed

through both of Billings's hands as he gripped the ladder, penetrating the fleshy parts between thumb and forefinger. He climbed back onto the boat, awkwardly and in pain. Before he could reach cover, another bullet struck him in the hip. Others smacked into the *General Meigs*, one barely missing the vessel's captain, who was standing near the pilothouse. On the wharf a soldier was down. It was John Quincy, his ankle shattered by a lead ball. The men around him, panic evident on every face, scrambled to get back onto the ship. They dragged Quincy along with them and man-handled him aboard. At the spot where he had fallen lay a pool of blood and fragments of bone.[82]

The gunfire continued as the crew frantically cut the vessel loose from the wharf. It backed hurriedly away and out into the river. As it retreated, Montgomery ordered the crew to shell the town with their two deck guns. The Rebel musketry soon stopped, and the *General Meigs*'s cannoneers ceased fire. In his fury Montgomery considered returning to the town with his whole force and burning it to the ground, every house and hotel and store and church. Only because he thought that Union army authori-ties might want to occupy and fortify it as a satellite post did he refrain from doing so. Reluctantly he decided to concede this round to the enemy and seek retribution elsewhere.[83]

The *General Meigs* returned to the east bank and signaled to the troops ashore. This was, by prearrangement, the command for them to break camp, gather their spoils, and march back to the wharf at Orange Mills, where the steamer would be waiting and everything could be loaded aboard. All this was accomplished in a few hours, and the vessel then set out downriver again, now with the whole force aboard. John Quincy and Liberty Billings lay below deck, having received whatever medical atten-tion could be provided.[84]

Montgomery's intention now was to pay another visit to the Dupont place at Federal Point, where yesterday morning he had seized horses but no slaves. He was convinced that Dupont had carried his blacks off into hiding as the troops approached. Perhaps this time he could catch the planter unaware and strike a blow for freedom. The *General Meigs* docked at Dupont's wharf, and a detachment of troops went ashore. No slave was to be seen, nor was Cornelius Dupont, but the soldiers did find Mrs. Dupont at home. They told her that if she did not reveal where her hus-band had sequestered his black people, they would burn her house down.

The woman was too terrified to lie. She confessed that the slaves had been hidden and told where. When the *General Meigs* continued its downriver voyage that afternoon, the Dupont blacks were aboard. They were no longer slaves, and Cornelius Dupont was no longer a slaveowner.[85]

Quiet reigned in and around Jacksonville this day. Higginson had time to write letters to his wife and mother and to do some more thinking about the expedition's future. His force had occupied the St. John's region for seventeen days now, but the results were considerably short of spectacular. It was apparent that the post of Jacksonville, while essential as a base for the expedition, would not be the great magnet drawing runaway slaves from the interior that he and Rufus Saxton had envisioned. The nearby presence of Finegan's Rebel force undoubtedly deterred seekers of freedom and also prevented the expeditionary force from moving very far inland to free those who could not free themselves. Furthermore, each day that passed without important accomplishments by the expedition bolstered the Northern opponents of emancipation and black enlistment, who might yet succeed in reversing the momentum of those causes. Dr. Rogers had expressed the problem pithily in a letter three days earlier: "Every day of waiting here is a day of strength to our fortifications, but a day of weakness to our purpose." If the Emancipation Proclamation "is ever to be anything more than a dead letter," he continued, "it must be made so before many weeks." Success in Florida would help keep the "traitors at home" from gaining the upper hand.[86]

Higginson agreed. It was time for bold action. He settled on a plan: He would take the 1st South up the river, occupy Palatka or some other point, and then, along with Montgomery, carry out raids into the interior that would truly inaugurate the destruction of slavery in Florida, swell the ranks of the black Union regiments, and tap rich sources of supply. This would, moreover, allow his troops once again to act independently of the white troops. He had been pleased to see them in action side by side, but the cause of black enlistment would be better served if the laurels his soldiers won were theirs alone.[87]

He would set forth on Monday, the thirtieth, three days from now. The 8th Maine would presumably be gone by then, but he was confident that the 6th Connecticut could hold the town and keep Finegan's force pinned down, whether or not Lyman Stickney brought back any reinforcements.[88]

With this decision made, Higginson grew more hopeful than at any time since the expedition arrived in Jacksonville. Although he would soon have to take up once again the agonizing burden of commanding the expedition, he was cheered by the prospect of moving deeper into Florida. The audacious adventure on which he and his men had embarked would be entering a new and perhaps decisive stage. He envisioned triumph and glory for the 1st South.[89]

At three that afternoon, about the time Montgomery's men were liberating the Dupont slaves forty miles upriver, two army transports rounded the bend below Jacksonville and approached the town. There was hope that one might be the *John Adams* with reinforcements from Fernandina, but that turned out not to be the case. One was the *Boston*, which had left Jacksonville four days earlier carrying mail to Port Royal. The other was the *Convoy* from Port Royal, which no one expected. Curiously too, both were empty, bearing no supplies of any sort.[90]

After the vessels docked, someone aboard delivered a dispatch to Colonel Rust, who read it and then forwarded it to Higginson. It conveyed a terse order from General Hunter's headquarters at Hilton Head, dated March 26. Higginson read it with utter astonishment: "All the troops at Jacksonville will immediately be withdrawn."[91]

He could hardly believe his eyes, but the order was clear and peremptory. The expedition was being recalled. This grand and promising adventure was suddenly at an end.

Chapter Seven

JACKSONVILLE AND
THE WEST BANK

MARCH 27–29

S OON AFTER RECEIVING GENERAL HUNTER'S ORDER recalling the expedition, Colonel Rust convened a meeting of army and navy officers to discuss it. The mood at this conference was a mixture of shock, disbelief, and outrage. The order gave no reason for the recall, and the assembled officers were at a loss to understand it. The simplest answer—that Hunter needed every available unit in the department for his imminent campaign against Charleston—satisfied none of them, for they all knew that he had been planning that campaign ever since he returned to departmental command in January. Why authorize the black regiments to undertake the St. John's expedition and subsequently send reinforcements if those troops could not be spared? Higginson ascribed the recall to Hunter's impulsiveness and cited it as yet another instance of the lack of direction in the Union high command that had long impeded the war effort. Others wondered seriously if Hunter was mentally unbalanced.[1]

While this meeting was going on or very soon after, the *John Adams* returned from Fernandina. Aboard were not only Lyman Stickney, coal and other supplies for the expeditionary force, and merchandise for Stickney's store but also some reinforcements that the tax commissioner had wheedled from Colonel Hawley, a field piece with its crew and twenty-five infantrymen of the 7th Connecticut. Informed of the recall order, Stickney was aghast. He urged that its execution be postponed while someone went to Hilton Head to plead with Hunter to revoke it; he would gladly go himself, he said. Some of the officers liked this idea, but in the end it was decided that Hunter's commandment was peremptory and admitted of no delay.[2]

Stickney was distraught at this turn of events, which so abruptly ended his dream of striking it rich in Florida. Higginson too was sickened by Hunter's order. "Just as our defences are complete & all in order for the transfer of part of our forces up river," he wrote in his journal, ". . . we are ordered away. . . . The possession of this place gives the key to Florida, & the present garrison can hold it & spare us to go up river and yet we must go [back]. . . . It is the first time I have been thoroughly subjected to that uncertainty of counsel which has been the bane of the war; it [has] defeated us in this case, just in the hour of success."[3]

That success included not just the manifest achievements and potential triumphs of the black troops in Florida but also the news of the expedition that was spreading throughout the country. As Higginson surely knew, the invasion of the south Atlantic mainland by black regiments had by now grabbed the attention not only of the South but also of the North. Rufus Saxton had proved an energetic publicist. He had followed up his initial message to the secretary of war, sent on March 6 as the expeditionary force was leaving Port Royal, with another eight days later, likewise radiant with optimism: "It gives me pleasure to report that so far the objects of the expedition have been fully accomplished. The town [of Jacksonville] is completely in our possession. . . . There has been constant skirmishing going on for several days, and in every action the negro troops have behaved with the utmost bravery." Somewhat misinformed (his informant being no doubt Lyman Stickney, who had come seeking reinforcements for Higginson) or perhaps exaggerating for effect, Saxton added that the expedition had already captured "many prisoners" and that runaway slaves were "collecting at Jacksonville from all quarters." This communication was eventually released to the Northern press, but well before that, Yankee newspapers had announced the invasion on the basis of dispatches from correspondents at Hilton Head. By March 18 reports had appeared in Washington, Baltimore, Philadelphia, New York, and Boston papers. These made it clear that the expedition was commanded by abolitionists and was intended as an assault on slavery (facts known around the Department of the South long before the expeditionary force even set sail, thanks to leaks from Hunter's headquarters). A Boston *Journal* correspondent, for example, wrote that Higginson and Montgomery had led their black troops to the Main "to set one section of [the Confederacy] on fire" by "a general commotion among the plantation hands." This dramatic revelation, along with the lack of interesting news from other fronts, put the Florida expedition in the national spotlight. Other newspapers across the country quickly picked up the story, while those that had reported it early soon amplified their accounts on the basis of later dispatches from the Department of the South.[4]

The triumphs that Higginson had anticipated, once he took his regiment upriver and unleashed it, would thus have had a large and attentive public audience. Knowing this surely magnified his frustration at the expedition's recall. Every army officer in Jacksonville felt the same crushing sense of disappointment. "[T]he order . . . depresses me," wrote surgeon Rogers; like Higginson, he saw Hunter's contradictory decisions as more evidence of "that fatal vacillation which has thus far cursed us in this war." The naval officers were no less disappointed. Commander Steedman, himself a Southern Unionist, was especially distressed at having to leave the citizens of Jacksonville in the lurch, fearing that those who had embraced the occupiers warmly would suffer reprisals once the town had been evacuated. Some of Steedman's officers had other reasons to regret the recall order. "We are all disgusted at Genl Hunters folly," wrote Benjamin McPherson aboard the *Norwich*, and "are all sorry to leave the place." He was among those who had enjoyed the hospitality of the ladies on Adams Street. "I could of layed her[e] the balance of this cruis[e] pl[e]asantly [but] now we have to return to our old place at the mouth of the rive[r] and swe[a]t it out."[5]

Higginson would quickly cast off his despondency, he was sure, "thanks to my natural buoyancy." He worried about his men, however. After the officers' conference he issued a regimental general order informing his troops of the recall but tried to soften the blow by adding words of praise and encouragement: "The honor of having recaptured Jacksonville will always belong to this regiment & to the Second Regiment S.C.V., in connexion with the gunboats. And we shall no doubt find elsewhere new opportunities for serving our country and fighting against Slavery." This was little comfort to the men, however. As the bad news spread among them, morale plummeted. Given as they were to interpreting events biblically, Higginson observed, they "felt that the prophecies were all set at naught, and that they were on the wrong side of the Red Sea." He feared that they might see him "as a sort of reversed Moses."[6]

Gloom, anger, and frustration soon pervaded the ranks. It was surely no coincidence that that very evening, within hours after the recall order arrived, there occurred the first serious instance of insubordination in the 1st South since the expedition sailed. Private Paul Haywood of Company K left his quarters without permission, taking his musket. Accosted by Lieutenant James West of his company and threatened with punishment for being absent without leave and carrying a weapon when off duty, Private Haywood replied, as Lieutenant West reported, "that I had a damned crabbed way with me; that he did not care a damn for the Guard House; that I might send him there, and be damned." Haywood was subsequently disarmed and arrested.[7]

Preparations for departure began immediately. Higginson's regimental order instructed his captains to "reduce their own & their company baggage to the smallest possible limits, and prepare two days' cooked rations." The officers of the white regiments likewise readied their men. The *John Adams* was sent upriver to find Montgomery and communicate Hunter's order. It left Jacksonville around midnight, the cannoneers and infantrymen from Fernandina still aboard because now there was no point in their disembarking.[8]

The evacuation would be a major undertaking. Besides the nearly twenty-six hundred army officers and men and all their equipment, ammunition, and provisions, a number of civilians would be leaving Jacksonville; they included Stickney and his associates, all the contrabands, and any white residents who wanted to go. Fortunately, there would be plenty of transports available, seven in all. In addition to the *John Adams* and *Boston*, which had brought the black troops to Jacksonville (the *Burnside* had returned to Port Royal on March 20), and the *General Meigs* and *Delaware*, which had been on hand since bringing the Maine troops, there would be the *Convoy*, which had just arrived, and two others—the *Tillie* and *Cossack*—that Hunter had also sent and that would arrive soon.[9]

The sun rose on March 28 in a mostly clear sky and quickly spread its warmth. The temperature was seventy-three degrees by ten forty-five that morning. That was when the *John Adams* returned to Jacksonville and docked at one of the wharves, having located Montgomery's raiding force upriver and passed along the recall order. By now matériel of all sorts was accumulating on or near the wharves in preparation for loading. Dr. Rogers supervised the transfer of his sick and wounded from the hotel-hospital to the *John Adams* and then mounted his horse and rode around the town's periphery to take a last look at the barricades, rifle pits, earthworks, and abatis that the troops had so laboriously constructed and that would soon be abandoned to the enemy.[10]

Around noon the *General Meigs*, carrying Montgomery and the 2nd South Carolina, came into view upriver and steamed to one of the wharves. John Quincy and Liberty Billings, hurt in the ambush at Palatka, were taken aboard the *John Adams*. Dr. Rogers deemed Billings's wounds minor. Quincy's wound was severe, but Rogers decided not to amputate the foot. When he learned that besides suffering this injury, Quincy had failed to rescue his family from slavery, the doctor wondered "how he will harmonize this double affliction with the theory he so often preaches to the men, that when one trusts in God and is not a coward, he will be protected against the bullets of his enemies."[11]

That afternoon or evening Montgomery met with Higginson and related his adventures since setting out from Jacksonville on the twenty-fifth. He and his men had had more excitement after leaving Federal Point yesterday afternoon with Cornelius Dupont's slaves. Several men aboard the *General Meigs* (probably crew members) had formerly been slaves in a community on the west side of the river ten or fifteen miles above Jacksonville and were very familiar with the area; cotton could be found there in abundance, they said, and they were willing to guide a foraging party. Montgomery liked the idea. Before sunset the steamer hove to in an inlet on the west bank known as Doctor's Lake. Montgomery waited until dark and then rowed ashore with his guides and forty of his soldiers. This party then set out on a road west toward the village of Middleburg. The quarter moon provided light.[12]

After trudging six miles inland, they spotted, some distance ahead, the red embers of what appeared to be a campfire. There was no reason to think enemy troops were in this vicinity, but Montgomery, having been taken by surprise at Palatka, was now doubly cautious. Quietly he split his force into several squads and sent them forward to surround the presumed campsite. The men closed in with muskets at the ready.[13]

This resulted in no farce like the 1st South's Battle of the Clothes Line. Lying around the fire, sound asleep, with their rifles stacked nearby, were a Confederate army lieutenant and fourteen of his men. Montgomery shook one of them awake. "What is it?" the man mumbled groggily. "You are prisoners," the colonel told him. "No," came the reply, "we belong to Westcott's company." "Yes," said Montgomery, "*but we don't.*"[14]

The company to which these Rebels belonged was a "partisan ranger" outfit, officially sanctioned by the Confederate War Department but little more than a guerrilla or vigilante band. Such units, most of them ill trained and ill disciplined, were stationed near their home communities and employed by the Rebel army mainly in scouting and hit-and-run attacks on vulnerable Union targets, but along the St. John's they also served as tormentors of suspected Unionists and trappers of runaway slaves. This particular squad, as its lieutenant explained once he was awake, had been assigned to assist some local citizens who were refugeeing into the interior. The rangers had secured two large wagons for this purpose, each pulled by four mules. The lieutenant, whose name was Braddock, cursed aloud as he contemplated the humiliation of being surprised and captured by black troops.[15]

Montgomery's men gathered up the Rebels' rifles and hitched the mules to the wagons. They and their commander then headed back to the river, herding the fifteen prisoners. Somewhere along the way they came across nine and a half bales of long-staple cotton, four thousand pounds of the stuff, and loaded them into the wagons. They also encountered some slaves and brought them along. With those previously taken on the east bank, Montgomery's raiders had now liberated at least thirty blacks. Whether all these freed people were delighted to be abruptly leaving their homes and taking up residence in Jacksonville was uncertain; Montgomery did not ask, and he gave them no choice.[16]

Word of the Rebel rangers' capture spread quickly through the community, and by the time Montgomery's little force reached the landing point at Doctor's Lake a group of women had gathered, anxious about the fate of their menfolk. Among them was the wife of Braddock, the Rebel lieutenant. Braddock asked permission to say good-bye to her, which was granted. Before Montgomery and his men realized what was happening, Braddock slipped through the assemblage of women and ran for the woods beyond. Montgomery spotted him and drew his revolver. An expert marksman, he could easily have brought the fleeing Rebel down but could not bring himself to do so with the man's wife looking on. Braddock disappeared into the woods and was gone.[17]

The other prisoners were rowed out to the *General Meigs* and put aboard, as were the freed slaves, the cotton bales, and the captured rifles, good new English-made Enfields. The lack of a wharf here made it impossible to bring off the other things, so Montgomery let the mules go and had the wagons and harnesses burned. By now it was well past daybreak. The *John Adams* appeared and relayed the message that Montgomery's raid must be terminated immediately. Once all the 2nd South Carolina troops were back aboard, the *General Meigs* steamed downriver to Jacksonville. There the freed blacks were turned over to Lyman Stickney's custody.[18]

By now the mood of anger and frustration over the expedition's recall had spread to the white troops in Jacksonville. Around midday, about the time the *General Meigs* arrived, some men of the 8th Maine entered the town's Catholic church bent on mayhem. Many of the Maine soldiers had long been itching to punish the Southern rebels by warring on their property. Jacksonville offered more to gratify their desire than any other place they had so far been posted, and the Catholic church on Duval Street seemed particularly inviting. Four days before, a number of them had broken into this church and the adjoining parsonage of the parish priest, the only local cleric remaining in the town, and pillaged both, carrying off furniture, paintings, ornaments, and other valuables to their quarters. Calvin Robinson, responsible for the safekeeping of civilian property, had had to secure a squad of soldiers from the provost marshal to round up the stolen property and return it to the priest. Today, however, the avenging Yankees of the 8th were not satisfied with mere looting. As they stripped the church of everything movable that caught their fancy, they set fires, using parish records as kindling. By the time they exited with their plunder, both the church, built not of brick or stone but unfortunately of wood, and the parsonage were being consumed by flames. An alarm was quickly raised, and soldiers and civilians rushed to the scene. Among them was Calvin Robinson, who was appalled to see the plunderers cavorting in the street as the flames rose and the smoke billowed. They had "the pipes of the old church organ in their hands," Robinson wrote, "blowing them and making the day hideous with their discordant noises." The fires were eventually extinguished, but not before the church and parsonage were ruined.[19]

At five-thirty that afternoon the steamer *Tillie* arrived from Port Royal to assist in the evacuation. It carried a dispatch for Colonel Rust from department headquarters, which turned out to be a second order for the recall of the expedition. Like the first, it was dated March 26, but it was more detailed:

Immediately on the reception of this communication you will embark all the US Troops at Jacksonville without exception including the Colored Regiments, and will return to the Stations previously occupied at Beaufort SC.

Of course all the supplies that have been sent to Jacksonville will also be embarked. A complete withdrawal of all the forces from Jacksonville is intended and hereby ordered.

The necessary transportation will be sent immediately.

Promptitude is expected in this movement. And this order will be communicated to the commander of the Colored troops by you, and will govern him.

By order of Maj. Gen. Hunter.[20]

Higginson was shown this order, and that night he pondered it. It was even more peremptory than the first, snuffing out any lingering hope that Hunter might be persuaded to change his mind. Clearly, rejecting Stickney's advice to delay the evacuation and seek an audience with Hunter had been wise. Furthermore, this new order specified what the troops were to do after withdrawing from the Florida mainland: They were to return to their previous posts, which for the Maine and Connecticut regiments meant Beaufort and for the black regiments Camp Saxton. This might mean, although it was hardly conclusive proof, that these four regiments would not take part in the assault on Charleston but instead would be held back to guard the occupied South Carolina Sea Islands.[21]

The new order was as silent as the first about the reason for the recall, but after reading it closely, Higginson was struck by a thought he had not until then considered. It was written and signed not by the department's assistant adjutant general, as was the first, but by Hunter's chief of staff, Brigadier General Truman Seymour. Higginson knew Seymour to be among the conservative regular army officers, opposed to emancipation and the enlistment of black troops. This fact, together with the order's repeated emphasis on withdrawing the black regiments in particular, set Higginson to wondering if there might be a sinister, hidden political motive at work here. Could it be that Hunter had been influenced by Seymour and that Seymour's intention was to deprive the black troops of this grand opportunity to distinguish themselves, gain recruits, and help destroy slavery?[22]

It was easy to imagine Hunter's being thus swayed. Although firm on certain general principles, including black freedom and recruitment, he was suggestible and impulsive. At the urging of Saxton, Higginson, and Stickney, he had abruptly reversed two of his standing policies—using black units for defensive duty only and keeping them apart from white units for fear the whites would object—by authorizing the black troops to invade th e mainland and subsequently sending white troops to fight by their side. Might he not just as abruptly reverse those decisions if someone with influence pointed out the contradictions or argued forcefully against the expedition on strategic grounds? Seymour was unquestionably a man with influence. Although junior to Hunter in rank and length of service and a generation younger, he had a far more distinguished record in this war. Hailed as one of the heroic defenders of Fort Sumter in April 1861, he had gone on to win acclaim as a brigade and division commander in the bloody 1862 campaigns in Virginia and Maryland. He had, moreover, taken part in the army's final subjugation of the Seminoles in the 1850s, giving him a claim to expertise on the subject of Florida as a military objective.[23]

Daybreak came a little before six on the twenty-ninth, illuminating seven transports tied up along Jacksonville's waterfront and piles of maté- riel on the wharves awaiting loading. As soon as there was enough light to work by, the scene came alive with sights and sounds: soldiers and ships' crewmen heaving and grunting and sweating as officers shouted orders; horse-drawn wagons coming and going; gangplanks creaking; pulleys squealing; crates and casks and other objects of all sorts thud- ding into place as they were lowered into holds or onto decks. A sense of urgency prevailed, for it had been decided that the expeditionary force should evacuate the town today, and there was still much to do. Besides all the military equipment and supplies yet to be brought aboard the ves- sels, there were the white and black civilians and their possessions and thousands of soldiers with their muskets and accoutrements.[24]

Lieutenant Luther Bingham, the 1st South's quartermaster, busied him- self on the wharf alongside the *John Adams* and *Convoy*, which were to transport his regiment and its stores. Today was Palm Sunday. Until word of the recall came, he had been eagerly anticipating the second meeting of his Sabbath school for the children of the town; now he must abandon that cherished mission. This was but a small disappointment among the great ones resulting from Hunter's unexpected order, but the devout and earnest young Bingham felt it keenly.[25]

The day was appropriately gloomy, with an overcast sky that blocked much of the sun's light and all its cheer. A southwesterly wind blew, gaining strength as the morning went on, and the instruments aboard the naval gunboats showed the temperature in the upper sixties well before noon and the barometric pressure low. It took no special knowledge of weather to sense that a storm was coming. The gunboats—only the *Norwich* and *Uncas* now, for the *Paul Jones* had steamed away yesterday morning to another blockade post—lay anchored in the river, their guns ready, crews on the alert, and lookouts active, for there was fear that the Rebels might learn of the evacuation and attack when the expeditionary force was in no position to defend itself. Additional security was provided by several companies of the 6th Connecticut, which marched out at sunrise to do picket duty beyond the town.[26]

Higginson sent six of his own companies to the west end of town to remove the cannons from the fortifications. Montgomery's two companies remained aboard the *General Meigs* with their glum Confederate prisoners. Likewise, the artillery crew and small infantry force recently arrived from Fernandina remained on the *John Adams*. Sick and wounded soldiers, at least those of the 1st South, had been taken aboard the transports yesterday. Company D of the 8th Maine, which had been serving as provost guard since the 8th arrived in Jacksonville, was reinforced this morning by small detachments from the 6th Connecticut and other Maine companies. Provost Marshal Henry Boynton thus had about a hundred men available to him for police duty; he would need them all for the challenging job of preserving order in town during the evacuation. Troops not assigned to provost, fatigue, or picket duty or already on the transports were supposed to stay in their quarters until time to embark.[27]

Around eight, before any of the off-duty troops had been summoned from their quarters, a number of fires broke out more or less simultaneously in the upper part of town, where the 8th Maine was billeted. Captain Boynton dispatched his provost guards to put out the fires and apprehend the perpetrators, but they had little success. Many of the fires had been started in the interiors of abandoned buildings and were well under way by the time they were noticed and the alarm was raised, and those who set them were long gone.[28]

The stiff wind soon spread the fires to adjacent buildings. The structures in this section of town were all made of wood, mostly longleaf pine,

which generated thick black smoke as it burned. As Boynton and his provost guards rushed to their work amid the bright flames and dark fumes,
now obliged to serve as firemen as well as policemen, Colonel Rust issued
an order instructing them to shoot on sight anyone caught in the act of
arson.[29]

By now civilians were crowding the wharves in preparation for boarding. Most of them, ninety or more, were contrabands. Some of these people
had been in Jacksonville with their masters when the expedition arrived,
but the majority had come in since. A few had liberated themselves and
fled to the invaders; most had been gathered up by the black troops during
the upriver raids. None of these freed men, women, and children would
be left behind in Jacksonville, although some might have preferred to stay.
All were to be transported to Fernandina or Port Royal, where they would
join those working for the army or cultivating the free-labor plantations.
In addition to these, there were eleven blacks gathered at the Jacksonville
waterfront who had likewise gained their freedom since the expedition
arrived. These eleven would not be taking up residence on the Sea Islands
as laborers, however. They were young men who had enlisted in the 2nd
South Carolina, and they were now huddled with their comrades aboard
the *General Meigs*.[30]

The white residents of Jacksonville, unlike the contrabands, could
choose whether to go or stay. Neither Saxton's formal order launching
the expedition nor Hunter's recalling it had specifically authorized the
removal of whites from the mainland at army expense, but Rust and
the other officers regarded it as only just and honorable. In asserting the
authority of the U.S. government over these citizens, the occupiers had
assumed the obligation of protecting them; to sail away abruptly and
abandon them to their fate was unconscionable.[31]

Fifty of the three hundred or so whites remaining in town, all but four
of them women or children, decided to leave. The motive of some was
desperation: They were penniless, and since the expedition arrived, they
had become dependent for survival on rations doled out by the provost
marshal. Others were impelled by fear of retribution: They had frater-
nized with the invaders and expected the worst should they again come
under Rebel rule. Like the contrabands, these white evacuees would be
transported to Fernandina or Port Royal, but what they would do there
was uncertain.[32]

The civilians who were leaving had been told they could take necessary belongings. The blacks had few possessions, but many of the whites
had a lot. Among them were the ladies of Spanish descent and secessionist sympathy who had regularly entertained the young army and navy
officers in their home and who now concluded that departing with the
expeditionary force was in their best interest. By imploring their officer
friends, they managed to get the use of three army wagons and teams
on Sunday morning to haul their belongings. Back and forth the wagons
went between their house on Adams Street and the waterfront, ultimately
depositing on the wharf five loads of stuff that they insisted they could
not live without.[33]

There were only a few army wagons in the town, and between the needs
of the Adams Street women and those of the military they were in constant use all morning. Other civilians were left to get their possessions to
the transports as best they could. A widow named Cowles and her two
daughters had a particularly trying experience. Laboriously gathering up
what they could, including furniture, bedding, and clothes, and carrying it out to the front porch of their house, they then waited helplessly,
hoping for assistance in getting it all to the wharf. When several soldiers
of the 8th Maine came by, the Cowleses thought their prayers had been
answered. But the soldiers merely informed them that their house was
going to be torched and they had better get out fast. Mrs. Cowles begged
them to help haul her belongings away; they replied brusquely that they
had no time for that. They then entered her house and began pillaging it.
Fearing that they were about to set it afire, the Cowleses grabbed what few
things they could from the porch and dragged them away, leaving all the
rest. They arrived at the wharf with a couple of packed trunks, two chairs,
and a small divan. With these, and the clothes they were wearing, they
would have to begin their lives over somewhere as refugees.[34]

Other civilians were at the wharf with their own possessions gathered
around them: tables, chairs, bedsteads, mattresses, trunks, carpetbags,
baskets, bundles, and other objects of every sort. They sat or stood waiting
amid the military stores yet to be loaded. The army matériel piled beside
the transports or already stowed away in holds or on decks included not
only items of government issue—wooden crates full of ammunition and
medical supplies, barrels of hardtack and salt pork, company cooking kettles, and the like—but also goods that had been seized by the expedition-

ary force since its arrival on the Florida Main, including fourteen bales of cotton, forty-three barrels of pine resin, dozens of horses, and a good deal of cornmeal and other provisions.[35]

Dr. Rogers, already aboard the *Convoy*, gazed from its deck at the scene along the waterfront; all was "hurry and excitement," he wrote. By mid-morning the mood might also have been described as near frantic. Smoke could be seen rising from the upper part of town; the civilians, anxious to get themselves and their belongings aboard the transports and move on to wherever they were going, were distraught and restless; much military matériel and thousands of troops were yet to be embarked; the weather was getting more threatening; and the provost guard was distracted by the fires. Higginson grew concerned. Colonel Rust, he feared, was not equal to the task of managing this evacuation efficiently. It could easily degenerate into chaos.[36]

Ignored by the military in all the commotion were the civilians who had accompanied the expedition. Calvin Robinson was wondering what to do about the abandoned property of Jacksonville citizens that he was responsible for and had meticulously inventoried. Some of it was ware-housed in the brick commercial buildings on Bay Street, but most had not been removed from the houses whose owners had refugeed out and left it behind. In either case, considerable labor would be required to get it aboard a transport—provided the army would allow it to be loaded. Finding that there was simply no labor to be had, Robinson reluctantly concluded that it all would have to be left behind.[37]

The goods in his store were another matter. This problem he left to his secret partner, the ever-resourceful Lyman Stickney. Stickney had no intention of abandoning this valuable merchandise and was prepared to employ all his wiles to save it. He went straight to Rust and informed him that thousands of dollars' worth of property in his charge stood to be lost unless he could get help removing it to the transports. Whether by insinuation or barefaced lying, he led the colonel to believe that this was government property, supplies procured for the Tax Commission or the contrabands. Rust obliged, ordering a large detail of soldiers to the store. They carried all the goods down to the wharf and put them aboard the *John Adams*. Stickney left to his fellow tax commissioner John Sammis the task of packing up the commission's records and office supplies and getting them onto a transport. The contrabands he likewise ignored.[38]

By midmorning the fires in the upper part of town were threatening the buildings where the 8th Maine was quartered. The officers ordered the men to gather their arms and equipment in a hurry and assemble outside, then led them down streets filled with smoke and windblown cinders toward the wharves. Along the way some of the men apparently fell out of the column, ducked into buildings, and set more fires. Perhaps the officers winked at this; perhaps it was done behind their backs. In any event, few of the Maine soldiers were disturbed about it. Even those who took no part in torching the town, such as Andrew Newman of Company G, generally applauded it. Jacksonville was nothing but "a dam secesh hole," in Newman's opinion, and it deserved no better. Besides, he reasoned, if the Yankees did not burn the town now, the Rebels would no doubt do so later. Many of his comrades likewise regarded this mayhem as the Jacksonville secessionists' just deserts. Moreover, they argued, why should we show these enemy civilians any consideration when their own troops had so callously lobbed artillery shells among them? Many also justified the burning as retribution for the horrific, bloody deaths of two of their comrades and the maiming of a third in the reconnaissance of March 25. Unable to avenge themselves on Finegan's Rebels or the lethal Blakely cannon, the men of the 8th turned their wrath on Jacksonville.[39]

Meanwhile the men of the 6th Connecticut not on picket or provost duty were being summoned from their quarters in preparation for boarding. For one of the Connecticut soldiers, a member of Company I who had enjoyed "sparking" since the regiment arrived, this was a memorable day for reasons aside from the evacuation. In a ceremony this morning, probably conducted by the regiment's chaplain and no doubt very rushed and informal, he married a young Jacksonville woman. The two could not have known each other more than nine days. She was among the civilians now crowding onto the transports.[40]

Some of the Connecticut men were now seized by the same vengeful spirit at work in the 8th Maine. Using as kindling the straw and dried moss on which they made their beds, they set fire to the abandoned house where they had been billeted. As the smoke and flames roiled skyward, they and their comrades formed into column in the street under their officer's direction, put their muskets to their shoulders, and proceeded down to the wharf where the *Boston* waited to take them aboard. On one street they passed a house where an elderly woman stood on the porch, wringing her hands and sobbing pitifully. She did not speak to them; why she cried they could only guess. Some thought she must be distraught at their departure.[41]

The four companies of the 1st South Carolina not dispatched to remove the cannons from the forts were at this time still in their quarters in the brick business houses on Bay Street, but before long their officers too gave the order to gather muskets and accoutrements and form up in the street. These companies were to board the *John Adams*. Up to this point no black troops had taken part in the burning of the town, but now, just before abandoning their second-floor billet, some of the men of the 1st, with the explicit approval of a lieutenant, piled up straw and moss as the Connecticut troops had done and set it ablaze. In the street, black soldiers watched gleefully as smoke poured from the building. One of the Maine men saw them as he made his way to the wharf; "from their songs and shouting," he wrote later in his diary, "they appeared to be having a good time."[42]

This fire spread inexorably from one building to the next along Bay. In one of these were most of the 1st South's hospital supplies. They were hurriedly carried out and loaded aboard the *Convoy* only minutes before the building went up in flames.[43]

The Bay Street fire added urgency to the already hectic situation on the nearby wharves. The southwesterly wind kept the fire from moving toward the transports for now, but a shift in wind direction could be utterly disastrous. Besides being crammed with people and horses and provisions and equipment, all the transports carried stores of ammunition.[44]

By now the other six companies of the 1st had finished their work at the forts. Higginson led them down to the wharf where the *Convoy* was tied up. This was one of the smaller transports, only 466 tons, and it was already occupied by the white civilians and their possessions, fifty horses, and the 1st South's commissary and hospital stores. But by Higginson's calculations there should still be room for these six companies, and that was where he intended to put them. As he prepared to get them aboard, however, the captain of the vessel stopped him. The *Convoy* could not safely take on all six companies, he told Higginson. It was too crowded. No more than three companies could board.[45]

Higginson looked around the transport's deck and peered into the hold, then exploded with anger. The civilians' stuff was taking up space everywhere, much of it "aged and valueless trumpery," in his opinion. He ordered his troops to remove it immediately from the vessel and dump it on the wharf: tables, chairs, bedsteads, mattresses, bric-a-brac, everything except trunks and baggage. The civilians pleaded for mercy, but he was unmoved; back down the gangplank it all went. Even then there was barely space for Higginson's six companies. Grumbling black soldiers and crying white women and children jostled for room on the deck and in the hold as the *Convoy* prepared to depart.[46]

By noon pretty much everyone and everything that was leaving Jacksonville was aboard the transports, except for the Connecticut companies out on the picket line and the provost guard trying to keep order and fight fires in town. The transports began raising steam. On one of the gunboats, cannons fired three blank charges in rapid succession, the signal for the companies on picket to pull back to town and embark. This whetted the anxiety felt by all those waiting to depart, for there was fear that Rebel troops might move in on the heels of the withdrawing pickets and fire on the transports before they could get away downstream, as had happened during the evacuation of Jacksonville a few months ago.[47]

The wind grew more blustery but held its course. Gazing around from the upper deck of the *Boston* was a correspondent of the New York *Tribune*, who had come from Hilton Head after news of the recall order leaked from Hunter's headquarters. He found the scene before him eerie and frightening. From where he stood not a living thing was visible on the streets of Jacksonville save one woman, a horse tied to a fence, and a starved-looking dog. He took up pen and paper and began writing the dispatch that he was to send to his newspaper once he was back at Hilton Head: "[T]he scene . . . is one of the most fearful magnificence. On every side, from every quarter of the city, dense clouds of black smoke and flame are bursting through the mansions and warehouses. A fine south wind is blowing immense blazing cinders right into the heart of the city. The beautiful Spanish moss, drooping so gracefully from the long avenues of splendid old oaks has caught fire, and as far as the eye can reach through these once pleasant streets, nothing but sheets of flame can be seen, running up with the rapidity of lightning to the tops of the trees and then darting off to the smallest branches. . . . Is this not war, vindictive, un[r]elenting war?"[48]

With all of his own men now embarked, but with the transports still waiting for the pickets and provost guards, Higginson walked up Ocean

Street to the intersection with Forsythe, wondering about the fate of the Sanderson house, where he had made his headquarters. The beautiful mansion was yet untouched by fire, he saw, although many nearby buildings were aflame. He passed through the front gate and into the garden, which was still prolific despite long neglect. He saw buds emerging on a tea rose bush and picked one. He was less anxious now than pensive, seized by melancholy. This was the first time since leaving civilian life that he had felt close to tears: "To think that this was the end of our brilliant enterprise & the destruction of my beautiful city was a sadder thing than wounds or death,—as for defeat I have not yet known it—and knowing the triumphant hopes felt by all the loyal Floridians & the corresponding depths of their disappointment—and the apparent aimlessness of the evacuation, it was doubly hard." He was comforted, however, by the knowledge that his soldiers had behaved superbly on the expedition; they had won laurels that could never be taken from them. After a time he walked back to the wharf and boarded the *John Adams*.[49]

His friend Seth Rogers was still aboard the *Convoy*, as depressed as Higginson about this sorrowful culmination of a "brilliant enterprise." It was a blow, the doctor feared, from which the cause of black freedom might never fully recover. He compared his profound sense of loss and gloom to that which one feels at the funeral of a friend. His spirit was perhaps weighed down too by the death just this morning of one of his patients, Private Robert Polite of Company G, who had succumbed to "congestive fever" in the temporary infirmary aboard the *John Adams*. Poor Polite had, in a sense, come home to die, for he had been born a slave twenty-one years earlier in northeastern Florida. As Rogers gazed morosely from the transport, his thoughts no doubt turned also to his beloved Charlotte Forten. The expedition's return to Port Royal meant that he would soon see her again, but it would not be the reunion he had been so anxiously anticipating since they last met.[50]

The Connecticut companies came in from the picket line and trooped up the *Boston*'s gangplank. When they were all aboard, Captain Boynton of the 8th Maine gathered his provost guards, led them to the waterfront, and got them embarked. He then boarded the *Delaware*. There were now no Union troops on the Florida Main—save for Private Polite and the others, black and white, who lay beneath the soil.[51]

Flames and smoke were now rising from dozens of buildings. A third of the town's blocks were wholly or partially afire. The pungent smell of burning pine, at once acrid and sweet, was pervasive, inescapable. The smoke was blindingly thick in some places, and everywhere it stung eyes and nostrils. Inescapable too were the sounds of fiery destruction, crackling, hissing, roaring. Higginson was enthralled even as he was sickened. "[T]he streets were full of tongues of fire creeping from house to house," he wrote; "the air was dense with lurid smoke." From the decks and portholes of the *John Adams* and *Convoy*, his men likewise watched in awe. This, they thought, was what the Day of Judgment would be like. "[T]hose who were not too much depressed by disappointment were excited by the spectacle," their colonel recorded. They "sang and shouted without ceasing. I never saw a wilder scene." The ever-strengthening wind shoved the smoke northeastward as it mounted into the sky, where it formed a great black cloud beneath the gray overcast.[52]

It was a little before one when the first transport cast off, pulled away from the wharf, and moved out into the river. The others followed one by one, forming up in single file. All seven sat low in the water, heavy with tightly packed cargo and nervous animals and sweating humanity. The two naval gunboats weighed anchor and took position at the rear of the line. There was no sign of enemy troops.[53]

The nine vessels set out downriver, cautiously following the channel. The sky grew darker, the wind fiercer. The river's surface, normally like glass, was agitated now, rippling with wavelets. Rain began to fall, lightly at first, then heavily. The ships steamed on toward the river's mouth. Jacksonville was soon out of sight, but the great black cloud that rose above it remained visible for a long time.[54]

Chapter Eight

THE AFTERMATH

T HE RAIN FELL IN A WIND-DRIVEN TORRENT as the army transports and navy gunboats continued down the St. John's. But the lookouts were alert, and along one stretch of the river they spotted, through
the gloom, someone onshore waving a white flag. A ship hove to; a few
men were sent by rowboat to investigate. The signaler proved to be a black
woman, a runaway slave. The boat brought her back to the ship. She was
the last person liberated by the expeditionary force, bringing the total to a
little over a hundred.[1]

The nine vessels reached the river's mouth between about five and five-
thirty that afternoon, and there they anchored. The tide was too low to
allow crossing the bar, but even if it had been high, the transports would
have been thwarted by the strong wind, which by now had shifted to the
east. It was too tricky a bar to be dared in choppy water and contrary
wind, especially by heavily laden vessels.[2]

As darkness fell, some of the Maine troops boarded boats and were
rowed to the river's south bank to relieve the crowding on their ship. They
settled in for the night in the decaying buildings of the abandoned town
of Mayport Mills. Sometime later that evening a hundred or so of the
1st South troops on the *Convoy* were put ashore at Pilot Town, on the
little island that hugged the north bank; they found quarters in some
abandoned fishermen's huts and other buildings. This reduced the nearly
unbearable crowding on the *Convoy*, but not by much.[3]

The rain and wind continued through the night, accompanied by occasional salvos of lightning and thunder. The morning of March 30 brought
no cessation of the storm. It was obvious that the transports would be
stuck here for some time, awaiting the convergence of good weather and

high tide. Colonel Higginson ordered that the remaining troops on the *Convoy* and some on the *John Adams* be moved to Pilot Town. He himself stayed aboard the *John Adams*, with little to do but chat with his officers and men, write in his journal, and ponder the expedition's profoundly disappointing outcome. He joked with the men to cheer them up, telling them that "it is just as well to go somewhere else as to stay at Jacksonville, where there was . . . nothing to shoot at but *rebel heels*." He noted wistfully that twenty-one days ago most of the black troops had been anchored at this very spot, anxiously awaiting the arrival of the *John Adams* so that the great adventure might begin. He speculated further about why the expedition had been recalled, hoping that Hunter had done it for some sound military reason but fearing that he had succumbed to impulsiveness or conservative influence. He dreamed that the general might yet reverse his decision and send the black regiments back to Florida to resume their war on slavery.[4]

The storm passed that day but too late to allow the transports to cross the bar. Dawn on March 31 found the ships still sheltering at the river's mouth. Before the sun was very high, Dr. Rogers, whose quarters were on the *Convoy*, requisitioned a boat and paid a visit to the regimental infirmary on the *John Adams*. Among the soldiers being cared for there by an assistant surgeon were Lieutenant Colonel Billings and Private Quincy, both wounded at Pilatka. Billings was healing nicely, but Quincy had taken a turn for the worse. Rogers had decided three days ago not to amputate Quincy's shattered lower leg; perhaps he now regretted that decision, as well as his decision to sail aboard the *Convoy* rather than the *John Adams*, for he found that the leg was badly infected. He immediately performed the amputation but feared for his suffering patient. "His chances for life are only about one in three," Rogers wrote later that day, "owing to old age and impaired constitution."[5]

That afternoon boats were dispatched to Pilot Town and Mayport Mills to begin shuttling the troops onshore back to their transports in preparation for departure. As the men of the 1st South climbed onto the *Convoy*, Rogers observed that they looked generally healthy, certainly healthier than if they had remained crammed aboard the vessel all yesterday and today. They had built fires in their quarters on the island and dried themselves out thoroughly. "Sending the men ashore," the doctor decided, "was a great hit."[6]

By late afternoon, with high tide approaching, the *Convoy* and all but one of the other transports were ready to depart. Their engine tenders raised steam. For some reason it was decided that the *John Adams* would remain here until tomorrow; perhaps there were too few boats available to bring all its disembarked troops back aboard before the tide went out again. Higginson was now aboard the *Convoy*. At five the six transports that were prepared to leave hoisted anchors and steamed eastward. On the lead vessel was a navy pilot. He guided the transports safely across the bar, then got on a boat that took him back to his own vessel.[7]

The transports now turned northward. Those on board able to look back to the west saw not only the *John Adams* and the navy gunboats *Norwich* and *Uncas* at anchor but also two columns of smoke rising from the river's south bank. The Maine soldiers who had been ashore at Mayport Mills had performed a last act of vengeance just before returning to their ship, setting fire to a house and a mill in that rotting little ghost town.[8]

The sun set an hour or so after the transports' departure; but the sky was clear, and a nearly full moon ascended. The ships steamed on through the night. Before the *Convoy* had proceeded twenty miles, however, there occurred on board an ugly and worrisome incident, sparked undoubtedly by the black troops' irritation at being once again jammed into the hold with white refugees and contrabands and perhaps by their lingering frustration over the expedition's abrupt end. It happened that the captain of the ship, perhaps sensing that it was listing a bit, asked the army officers to redistribute the men below deck. The officers complied. One soldier, however—Private Ogaff Williams of Company G—ignored the order to move. An officer of a different company noticed him and demanded his name. Williams refused to answer and then refused to obey an order to report to Colonel Higginson to explain himself. The officer confronting Williams ordered that he be moved by force. Williams responded by trying to draw his bayonet on the officer. The insubordinate private was restrained, disarmed, and arrested. At the very least he would face a charge of disobedience; the incident could be deemed mutiny.[9]

At the entrance to Cumberland Sound the *Convoy* turned west, entered the sound, and then headed southward on the channel to Fernandina, reaching the harbor well before morning. The other five transports, bearing the 2nd South Carolina, the white troops, and most of the expedition's supplies, continued northward to Port Royal.[10]

Higginson had ordered the *Convoy* to Fernandina so that the white refugees aboard and their baggage could be put ashore. This would make the journey to Port Royal that much more comfortable for the contrabands and the six companies of the 1st South remaining on the ship. The refugees disembarked at Fernandina on the morning of April 1; the post commandant was notified that they were now his responsibility. The matter was referred to the post provost marshal, O. S. Sanford, who found himself in a quandary. The little town was already crammed with soldiers and contrabands. Scrambling around, Sanford found a few vacant buildings in which to house the refugees temporarily; but he was dismayed to learn that his new charges, while they had some extra clothes and little personal items with them, were utterly destitute of household furnishings. What they had managed to haul from their homes to the Jacksonville wharf and onto the *Convoy* just before the expedition departed had not, it turned out, been left there after it was dumped back onto the wharf at Higginson's angry insistence. It had been taken aboard the *Boston*, but that ship was now on its way directly to Port Royal, its captain apparently unaware that the things were needed at Fernandina. The ladies of Spanish descent who had managed to get five wagon loads of stuff safely away from Jacksonville now found themselves no better off than the other refugees; all were packed into abandoned buildings in a strange town without so much as a mattress or pillow to sleep on and no idea of what would become of them.[11]

Another who disembarked from the *Convoy* at Fernandina was the tax commissioner and storekeeper Lyman Stickney. He no doubt visited the store in which he was a covert partner with Calvin Robinson; he almost certainly did not visit the Tax Commission office, whose business he disdained. In any event, he had no intention of lingering in Fernandina one minute longer than he had to. After the refugees and their baggage were put ashore, the transport's crew readied it for departure, and Stickney reboarded. But before the ship cast off, tax commissioner Harrison Reed, who had remained in the Fernandina office while Stickney and John Sammis were in Jacksonville, came aboard. He pleaded with Stickney to stay in town long enough to take care of some pressing business that was suffering from his extended inattention. Stickney refused but assured Reed that he was going only to Beaufort and would be back in a week. Frustrated, Reed left. The *Convoy* steamed out of the harbor before noon on April 1.[12]

Northern tip of Port Royal Island, looking north toward
Confederate-held territory, c. 1862; in this area the 1st South
Carolina took up picket duty after the Florida expedition.
(COURTESY OF LIBRARY OF CONGRESS)

Stickney's associates Sammis and Robinson may have returned with
him from Jacksonville on the *Convoy*; more likely, however, both were
aboard the *John Adams*, Sammis with his Tax Commission records and
office supplies, Robinson with the merchandise that had been rescued
from the ill-fated Jacksonville store thanks to Stickney's artful persuasion. Whatever the case, both men returned to Fernandina to stay. The
John Adams remained anchored at the mouth of the St. John's until the
late afternoon of April 1, when it passed the bar under the guidance of a
navy pilot. Its voyage to Fernandina was untroubled, a matter of a few
hours. At daybreak on April 2 it sailed for Port Royal.[13]

The four companies of the 1st South aboard the *John Adams* disembarked at Camp Saxton on April 3, joining the six already delivered by the
Convoy. By this time the other transports had put ashore the 8th Maine
at Hilton Head and the 6th Connecticut and 2nd South Carolina at Beau-

fort. The storm that had delayed the expedition's return had thrashed the Port Royal area too, but by now it had passed, and the sky was clear. The troops began settling back into the familiar routine of camp life in this sleepy theater of war.[14]

The officers and men of the 1st South stayed only a few days at their old campground, however, before their colonel led them off to a new post nine miles north. Here they were assigned to picket duty along Port Royal Island's northern shore, a task previously entrusted to white troops. This part of the island nearly touched the South Carolina mainland, only a narrow channel separating them. Rebel pickets could be seen on the opposite shore. Higginson made his headquarters in the abandoned plantation home of a family named Milne. "Here commenceth a new chapter in this strange life," he announced in his journal on April 6. "No more Camp Saxton—no more forays with the Steamboats—no more . . . garrison life & daily skirmishing at Jacksonville."[15]

As Higginson and his men took up their new assignment, General Saxton in Beaufort brooded over the expedition's fate. No one was more disappointed than he. In the days following his enthusiastic message of March 14 to the War Department he had received further reports of success from the expeditionary force, which encouraged him to plan a visit to the St. John's to see the situation for himself. On the morning of March 26 he was preparing to board a transport headed to Jacksonville when he got word that General Hunter was recalling the expedition. Within minutes he was on his way to Hilton Head aboard his personal steamer to plead with Hunter to reconsider. The commanding general was unmoved, however, and Saxton returned to Beaufort later that day a devastated man. On April 4 he sent the secretary of war another dispatch, its military formality scarcely concealing his anguish and anger: "I have the honor to report the return of the First and Second Regiments of South Carolina Volunteers from Florida. The expedition was in every way successful. . . . We had complete and undisputed possession of Jacksonville and Palatka, and Colonel Montgomery was moving into the interior. . . . [T]he moral effect of the presence of these colored soldiers under arms was very great, and caused a perfect panic among the rebels throughout the State. . . . Had the expedition been allowed to remain in Florida I am confident that its success would have fully equaled your expectations."[16]

Another who mulled over the expedition's disappointing end in these early days of April was Lyman Stickney. The *Convoy* had deposited him at Beaufort by April 2, along with the Florida contrabands nominally under his care. Presumably he turned the blacks over to Saxton; in any event, he gave them no further thought. At this point they had no say in their fate. They would be put to work on the free-labor plantations.[17]

Stickney spent a week or so in Beaufort, then took a steamer to Washington, blithely breaking his promise to return to Fernandina and attend to Tax Commission business. He had bigger fish to fry. Arriving in the capital on April 16, he immediately sent to Treasury Secretary Salmon P. Chase an ingratiating report on his "several months [of] active duty in Florida." He had much information and advice for the secretary. "I am acquainted with the topography of Florida," he boasted, "its people, climate, resources & capabilities." If federal military forces were returned to the Florida Main, Stickney insisted, they could readily conquer the state and prepare the way for its political redemption. That redemption would be assured if the right person were put in charge: "There should be selected as general director . . . a man of sound discretion, firmness and uncalculating patriotism." He stopped short of nominating himself for the position, but his point was hard to miss. Before closing, he used this opportunity to take another swipe at Higginson. The men of the 1st South Carolina were fine soldiers, he wrote, but the regiment "is not properly officered, [and] that alone drags it down." Stickney remained in the North for the next four months, currying favor with the powerful, plotting his future, collecting his salary, and ignoring the work of the Tax Commission.[18]

Three days after Higginson and his troops began their new assignment at the picket post, a female visitor appeared at the regiment's headquarters at the Milne plantation. She was welcomed by the colonel and welcomed even more by Seth Rogers. She was Charlotte Forten, the doctor's lover.[19]

In late March Forten had said good-bye to her students on St. Helena Island and prepared to depart for Florida to fulfill her promise to serve as a teacher there for Higginson's regiment. Rogers had by then written her from Jacksonville, saying it was safe enough for her to come. On March 26 she was in Beaufort with packed trunks, waiting to board the same transport that was to take General Saxton. Deeply disappointed by the expedition's recall, she went back to her free-labor plantation school and waited for the 1st South's return and for news of her beloved. "How I long to see Dr. R.," she wrote in her journal on April 2, "and hear all from his eloquent lips." By the next morning she knew he was back, for a messenger came with a note from him. "He says he will see me soon and tell me *all*. I hope it will be very soon, indeed. I do so long to see him." His duties kept him at headquarters for now, however, so at his beckoning she went to him. She arrived at the Milne plantation on April 9 and stayed until the twelfth, sharing quarters with an officer's wife. She and Rogers took long rides on horseback together during those days. That part of Port Royal Island was especially picturesque, and the weather was splendid and the air fragrant with blossoms. "I think I never enjoyed anything so perfectly," she said; "I *luxuriated* in it." They spent the evenings together too in company with the others at headquarters. One night Rogers read to her from *The Faerie Queene*.[20]

The men of the 1st South settled quickly into their new duties on the picket line. There were occasional alarms, sparked by reports of imminent Confederate raids across the channel. None of these raids materialized, but the sporadic excitement kept the routine of picket duty from becoming boring. Things were quiet enough overall that Higginson could turn his attention to long-delayed matters, among them disciplinary proceedings against some of his men. On April 15 he presided over the regimental courts-martial of the two soldiers arrested during the expedition. Private Paul Haywood of Company K, who had improperly left his quarters in Jacksonville on March 27 with gun in hand and had cursed the lieutenant who accosted him, would pay for his offenses with ten days of imprisonment at hard labor. Private Ogaff Williams of Company G, who had attempted to threaten an officer with his bayonet on the *Convoy*'s return voyage, was found guilty of disobedience and mutiny; he would forfeit one month's pay and spend a month in confinement at hard labor.[21]

The great St. John's "expeditious" had by now become part of the 1st South's lore, its memorable episodes recounted again and again around the campfires. On April 16 a sad postscript was added to the story. Three days earlier Dr. Rogers had visited John Quincy in the Beaufort contraband hospital (where he had sent Quincy as soon as the expeditionary force returned) and was surprised to find him recovering, for he had thought that the foot amputation would probably not save him. The aging soldier was in good spirits; he never complained about being wounded and crippled, and he comforted the other patients with religious exhor-

Contraband hospital, Beaufort, c. 1864; here John Quincy died.
(COURTESY OF NATIONAL ARCHIVES AND RECORDS ADMINISTRATION)

tation. But then lockjaw set in, and death quickly followed. On the six-teenth poor Quincy was buried, never again to see his wife and children in Palatka, never again to lead his fellow soldiers in prayer.[22]

During these weeks following the return to Port Royal, Higginson pon-dered the expedition's recall. He never got a fully satisfying explanation of it, although he heard a lot of rumors and speculation. The most com-mon story was that Hunter had simply decided to concentrate all available troops in South Carolina for the campaign against Charleston. But it was also said that he had received reports that the Rebel general Finegan was to be heavily reinforced and would try to attack and destroy the expedi-tionary force. On April 12 Hunter visited Higginson's headquarters; but he did not mention the recall, and Higginson did not bring it up. The colo-nel continued to wonder, however, if a sinister motive had been at work. He still suspected that one or more of Hunter's conservative staff officers, taking advantage of the general's suggestibility and impulsiveness, had engineered the recall to deny the 1st and 2nd South Carolina a military triumph and to try to derail the movement for full-scale recruitment of black troops.[23]

Higginson's suspicion was almost certainly baseless. There is no sound evidence that Hunter had been manipulated by subversive proslavery advisers, if indeed there really were any on his staff, as is highly doubtful. All the facts suggest that he acted on his own.

A key factor in the general's decision to recall the expedition was the unanticipated strength of Rebel military resistance in Florida. Although he had never (contrary to rumor) received any report that Finegan was to be reinforced, he had been advised by Higginson himself (through Lyman Stickney, on March 14) that the black troops alone could not both hold Jacksonville and move deeper into Florida, given the stubborn opposition that Finegan put up beginning the day after the expeditionary force landed. Hunter had responded—impulsively, it could be argued—by authorizing the 6th Connecticut and 8th Maine to reinforce the black troops, thus freeing them to move upriver and strike inland. But as the date for launching the Charleston campaign neared, he became convinced that he must bring those white regiments back to South Carolina to help ensure the success of the campaign. (He simultaneously stripped away a portion of the garrison forces at Fernandina and St. Augustine for the same reason.) The black regiments would not be taking part in the movement against Charleston—Hunter had decided that long ago—but he now concluded that it was pointless to leave them unsupported on the Florida Main, where they could do little more than man the defenses of Jacksonville, pinned down and unable to accomplish the expedition's greater objectives, all the while tying up supply vessels needed in South Carolina. It was even possible that they would be overwhelmed and destroyed by Finegan's force. And so the commanding general brought the expedition to an abrupt end.[24]

Hunter's ambition, patriotism, and soldierly sense of duty surely played a role here too. He was still under pressure to prove himself worthy of departmental command by some bold, successful exploit. The St. John's expedition had seemed to promise such a result, and he had undoubtedly approved it in part for that reason. But the expedition achieved no immediate, obvious triumphs striking enough to boost Hunter's sagging reputation. In the meantime the navy had readied itself for the assault on Charleston, which, if properly supported by Hunter's forces, might achieve the quick, spectacular success he needed. Charleston was not only a major Confederate port but also the symbolic heart of secession, the city where the Southern rebellion had begun. Its capture would be a staggering blow to the Rebels and would elevate Hunter to the pantheon of Union heroes. He therefore shifted all his attention and every available resource toward that grand objective.[25]

Sadly for Hunter and the Union cause, the subsequent campaign was an inglorious failure. By April 3 the general had moved thousands of troops into position near the city, and there they waited for Admiral Du Pont's naval forces to do their part. The plan was for seven monitors— mighty warships, regarded by some as invincible—and two other powerful ironclads to steam into Charleston Harbor and blast away at the Rebel defensive fortifications until they were destroyed or abandoned, thus allowing Hunter's troops to seize the city. It was modeled on the stunningly successful joint army-navy operation that had captured Port Royal in 1861. On the afternoon of April 7 the Union squadron entered the harbor and opened fire. But it quickly became apparent that the strength of the monitors had been greatly overestimated and the strength of the Confederate defenses greatly underestimated. One by one Du Pont's vaunted ironclads were disabled by enemy cannon fire, while inflicting little damage in return. The battle ended less than three hours after it began. The ships retreated from the harbor, and the great assault on Charleston was over.[26]

This abortive operation came at a time when the Northern public was still digesting news of the St. John's expedition. Press reports on the daring invasion of Florida by black troops bent on emancipating slaves had spread westward after the eastern newspapers broke the story in mid-March. On the twenty-first Cincinnati and St. Louis newspapers announced the invasion; two days later Chicago and Milwaukee newspapers did so. Remarkably, thanks to the miracle of coast to coast telegraphy, a San Francisco newspaper carried the story on March 24.[27]

By that time the expedition was attracting not just the press's notice but also its commentary. Opinion divided along predictably partisan lines. Republican newspapers, including the New York *Tribune*, the New York *Times*, the Philadelphia *Evening Bulletin*, the Philadelphia *Press*, the Boston *Commonwealth*, the Boston *Daily Advertiser*, and the Chicago *Tribune*, spoke favorably of the mission and praised the behavior of the black troops. A *Times* editorial on March 22 commended the soldiers for their restraint in dealing with the citizens of Jacksonville: "The people were in great fear of an indiscriminate massacre [when the troops first appeared]; but the negroes behaved with propriety, and no one was harmed." The editor of the *Daily Advertiser* echoed that compliment on March 31, adding that the troops' "enthusiastic colonel [Higginson] did not go too far when he staked his life upon their courage and discipline." Perhaps the most fervent endorsement came from the *Christian Recorder*, published in Philadelphia by the African Methodist Episcopal Church. "Our colored soldiers prove themselves to be men," proclaimed the editor on March 28. "The expedition into Florida, up to the latest accounts, has proved a complete success. They have already captured Jacksonville, a place from which the rebels drove the Federal troops some time since. From this it will be easily perceived that the colored people are doing more and better for their country than their white fellow-citizens."[28]

Democratic organs professed outrage. An editorial in the Hartford, Connecticut, *Daily Times* on March 21 informed readers that the expedition "was expressly designed *to foment a servile insurrection*. . . . [T]he scheme was aimed to strike a *defenceless* region, in which the wives and children of the rebels only remained, with the slaves on their plantations, in the absence of fathers and brothers who had gone to the war." If the expedition succeeded, the editor went on, Florida would witness "scenes of horror . . . nameless outrages, worse than death, committed on defenceless women by an infuriated and brutal negro horde . . . [and] acts of inconceivable barbarity in the murder of defenceless old men and helpless children." That such a mission could be conceived and applauded was evidence of "both the *fanatical delusion*, and the now unhidden, *fiend like spirit of Hell* that burns in the hearts of some of the Abolition leaders." On March 19 the New York *World* gave its readers a garbled account of the "great negro abolition raid upon southern women and children" and used the opportunity to denounce the Lincoln administration for countenancing the "wretched business of negro soldiering."[29]

The news of the St. John's expedition, received with horror and revulsion by many, was at the same time welcomed joyfully by many others. Among the latter was Abraham Lincoln. On April 1, as yet unaware that General Hunter had recalled the expedition, the president took time to send him a personal note of congratulation. Although he had long regarded Hunter as somewhat rash and had felt obliged to overrule his precipitate emancipation proclamation back in May 1862, he admired the general's noble sympathies and counted him as a friend. Hunter had been one of his personal escorts during the perilous journey that brought him to Washington for his inauguration in the late winter of 1861, when threats of assassination were rife. "I am glad to see the accounts of your colored force at Jacksonville, Florida," Lincoln now wrote. "I see the enemy are driving at them fiercely, as is to be expected. It is important to the enemy that such a force shall *not* take shape, and grow, and thrive, in the South; and in precisely the same proportion, it is important to us that it *shall*. Hence the utmost caution and vigilance is necessary on our part. The enemy will make extra efforts to destroy them; and we should do the same to preserve and increase them."[30]

News of the expedition's recall and the fiery evacuation of Jacksonville provoked a second wave of public reaction. Hunter came under attack by much of the Republican press for his seemingly senseless decision to terminate abruptly a mission he had previously approved and that was by all accounts succeeding. The expeditionary force had "occupied Jacksonville under the most auspicious circumstances for the speedy acquisition of the entire state of Florida," declared the New York *Evening Post* on April 8. "[T]he time had come when a small force could be made effective in opening [the state] to the occupation of loyal citizens and in creating an avenue of escape for the . . . negroes herded in the interior and watched with such malignant vigilance by the rebels. . . . It presented a most promising field for the experiment (as it is still regarded by some) of testing the character and capacity of the negro troops. . . . If General Hunter had desired to do the state of Florida and the cause of freedom and Union in the South the greatest injury . . . he could not have adopted a course more certain of success than the one he has adopted." The Boston *Daily Advertiser* of April 10 claimed that there was no good reason for the expedition's recall; altered circumstances might justify it, "[b]ut has any such necessity arisen which did not exist, or which could not be easily foreseen, . . . when Jacksonville was [first] occupied? . . . Nowhere . . . does there appear to have occurred anything which should not have been taken into account in the first place." The Philadelphia *Evening Bulletin* of April 9 made the same point, adding: "The Government owes it to itself and to the country to have this matter investigated." Perhaps the most deplorable aspect of this sad culmination, some of these newspapers insisted, was leaving the loyal Unionists of northeastern Florida in the lurch after having promised them liberation and protection, the third such abandonment by federal forces in the past year.[31]

The burning of Jacksonville was condemned by newspaper correspondents and editors everywhere, Republican and Democratic alike. "This is the most outrageous act committed by Union troops since the war began," declared the Philadelphia *Evening Bulletin*, a pillar of Republicanism. The Boston *Daily Advertiser* concurred, branding the deed "entirely wanton." The New York *Tribune* published a vivid eyewitness account of the fire that was widely reprinted in other papers. It was penned by a reporter as he watched from a steamer at the Jacksonville wharf on March 29. "Jacksonville is in ruins," it began. "That beautiful city . . . has to-day been burned to the ground, and, what is sad to record, by the soldiers of the National army." Nearly all the Republican papers, however, absolved the black soldiers of guilt. "[T]he negro troops took no part whatever in the perpetration of this vandalism," the *Tribune* correspondent insisted. "They had nothing whatever to do with it, and were simply silent spectators. . . . The 6th Connecticut charge it upon the 8th Maine, and the 8th Maine hurl it back upon the 6th Connecticut." Most other Republican sheets likewise blamed the white troops, while the New York *Times*, taking its cue from Colonel Rust's official report of the expedition, pointed a finger at the most unlikely of suspects, the citizens of Jacksonville.[32]

In the weeks following the expedition Higginson read many of these reports and editorials, including an eyewitness account in the New York *Evening Post* that accused him of "injustice and cruelty" for having the white refugees' belongings dumped back onto the Jacksonville wharf as the expeditionary force departed. He smoldered with resentment over this attack but made no public response, consoling himself with the favorable publicity that his men had won.[33]

In the wake of the Charleston fiasco, General Hunter turned his attention once again to a slave-liberating invasion of the Main. His enthusiasm for such an expedition still burned brightly; indeed, he now envisioned multiple, simultaneous invasions up the rivers of the south Atlantic coast. On April 30 he wrote the secretary of war requesting reinforcements in order "to carry out my plans (already fully matured) of coastwise expeditions of mixed [i.e., black and white] troops to penetrate those regions where slaves are densest, and therein establish posts to which all fugitives may flock, assured of welcome, protection, and employment. . . . [T]he whole slave population of the South is thoroughly alive to the President's proclamation of the 1st of January, and . . . thousands of anxious 'chattels' are feverishly longing for . . . [such] expeditions." Saxton too argued insistently for a return to the Main.[34]

No reinforcements were forthcoming, however. Hunter, who was now under orders to keep troops ready to support the navy in future operations against Charleston and who had sent away a whole brigade of infantry in mid-April to aid a Union commander on the North Carolina coast, could not spare any regiments for even one mainland invasion. But he continued to plan and lobby fervently for such expeditions. In late May he argued his case directly to President Lincoln. At the end of August he again importuned the secretary of war, this time with a truly grandiose proposal: "Let me take the men you can spare . . . , land at Brunswick, Ga., [and] march through the heart of Georgia, Alabama, and Mississippi to New Orleans, arming all the negroes and burning the house and other property of every slaveholder. A passage of this kind would create such a commotion among the negroes that they themselves could be left to do the rest of the work [of destroying slavery in the Confederacy]." He concluded this letter with a wry inversion of Supreme Court Justice Roger B. Taney's infamous dictum in the *Dred Scott* decision: "I am a firm believer in the maxim that 'Slaveholders have no rights a negro is bound to respect.'"[35]

Hunter and Saxton's dream of sending more missions of liberation deep into Rebeldom was never realized. The 1st and 2nd South Carolina regiments carried out several brief operations on the Georgia and South Carolina coasts in June and July, gathering in nearly a thousand slaves in the process, but these were mere raids, not penetrating far inland and not intended to establish permanent posts. By the time Hunter wrote the secretary of war in August, he was in fact living in the North and out of a job, having been relieved of command by order of the president on June 12. Lincoln and his advisers had by then concluded that Hunter would never achieve a decisive victory in the Department of the South with the troops available and that a more vigorous commander was needed.[36]

Hunter's successor, Brigadier General Quincy A. Gillmore, had no enthusiasm for the sort of emancipative missions championed by Hunter and Saxton. Although another (and much larger) St. John's River expedition that was launched in February 1864 succeeded in holding Jacksonville through the end of the war, its purpose was very different from that of March 1863, being mainly intended to seize cotton and other valuable resources for the U.S. government and to deprive the Rebel armies of supplies. Nor were any expeditions of liberation undertaken in other theaters of war. (The invasion up the Red River in Louisiana in 1864, for example, like the 1864 St. John's expedition, did not aim primarily at emancipating slaves.) By 1864 the Union army high command was discouraging operations that promised no immediate and important military benefits.[37]

The Florida expedition of 1863 thus stands as unique in the annals of the Civil War and perhaps in the annals of all military history. Conceived and commanded by radical abolitionists in uniform, in a shining moment of optimism inspired by the Emancipation Proclamation, it was intended first and foremost to ignite the destruction of slavery within the world's most powerful slaveholding society and to establish and defend a homeland for the freed people.

These were lofty and ambitious objectives, to be sure; they were certainly not achieved and were probably beyond the realm of the possible. But it is not unrealistic to speculate that the expedition, had it been given more time to prove itself, might have markedly altered the course of the Civil War.

If Hunter had allowed the black regiments to remain in Florida through the spring of 1863, adequately supported by white troops, Higginson and his men would have occupied Palatka and then joined Montgomery's companies in raids deep into the interior, where there were hardly any Confederate troops to oppose them. The white units in Jacksonville would have kept the great bulk of Finegan's force tied down in that vicinity, protecting the key railroad junction at Baldwin, eighteen miles to the west. (Finegan had fewer than nineteen hundred troops to defend all of Florida east and south of the Suwannee River.) Between the glowing dispatches of Saxton and the laudatory reports of friendly Northern newspaper correspondents in the Department of the South, there would have been no shortage of favorable publicity about whatever successes the black units achieved in liberating slaves, adding men to their own ranks, and discomfiting the Rebels. (Higginson and Montgomery, who were in the best position to know, both declared firmly at the end of March that such successes would have been substantial had the mission been allowed to proceed, and of course the black troops had already scored some notable accomplishments in the several upriver raids carried out before the recall.)[38]

Provided that no disaster befell the expeditionary force through the spring, the Union high command might well have been inspired to encourage more such missions; Abraham Lincoln himself, it should be kept in mind, applauded the idea solely on the basis of reports of the expedition's achievements in March. The Atlantic coast, the Gulf coast, and the Mississippi River valley offered any number of riverine highways into the Confederate interior. Amphibious forces sent up those rivers to establish posts as colonies for runaway slaves and bases for Union raids would have added a dramatic new aspect to the war, with a potential impact on the conflict's outcome and the course of postwar reconstruction. That such a strategy was never adopted by the Union army does not mean that it was unthinkable or unworkable. It must be reckoned one of the viable paths not taken in the American Civil War.

The expedition's significance does not, however, lie solely in what might have been, for it had tangible results that are well worth contemplating. For one thing, it contributed mightily to a shift in sentiment among the white soldiers in the Department of the South in favor of black troops. The newspaper reports of the exploits of the 1st and 2nd South Carolina on the Florida Main, along with the eyewitness accounts of the white troops that had been there, were widely read and heard and discussed in the department. Most were strongly favorable. On April 4 Dr. Rogers talked with an officer's wife who had just come from the camp of the 6th Connecticut at Beaufort. "Mrs. Lander told me," he recorded proudly, "that the sixth Connecticut boys were full of praises of the bravery of our regiment." A soldier of the 8th Maine made this observation the day after his regiment returned to Port Royal from Jacksonville: "I have thought that the negroes would not make good soldiers and so did most of the men in this regt, but in the several skirmishes they have had with the rebels they have won the pra[i]ses of all and the rebels are as afraid of them as they would be of so many tigers." Colonel Montgomery noted with satisfaction the reaction of a group of white soldiers who were present when his men debarked from the *General Meigs* at Beaufort on April 2 with the fourteen Rebels they had captured asleep around a campfire. "Damn 'em," growled the white soldiers when they spotted the uniformed blacks. But then one looked more closely and asked, "What have they got with 'em?" Another answered, "Why, some Secesh prisoners." With this revelation, the whole group spontaneously exclaimed, "Bully for the negroes!"[39]

The shifting mood in the department was noticed by a number of observers in the weeks following the return of the expeditionary force. "[T]he hatred and jealousy of the white soldiers towards the colored," wrote one of the Gideonites in late April, "is dying away." That same month a New York *Tribune* correspondent at Hilton Head remarked: "It is quite amusing to hear officers who were bitterly opposed to arming the negroes a few months since say that if we had but three or four more negro brigades we might accomplish something in this department." Hunter echoed these observations; so did Saxton, who furthermore insisted that all the white troops would now serve willingly alongside the blacks.[40]

The expedition's impact reached far beyond the Department of the South, however. In the North, friends of black recruitment seized on it as proof that Negroes could serve effectively in the Union ranks and should be given every chance to do so. Such evidence was very scarce before March 1863; except for the regiment recruited in Kansas, which had fought one skirmish, no black unit besides the 1st South Carolina had engaged the Rebels. And until the St. John's expedition, no black unit at all had taken part in a sustained combat operation against Confederate forces; nor had any captured and held an important Southern town; nor (as far as evidence shows) had any taken enemy prisoners; nor had any gone into action side by side with white troops.[41]

The editor of the Philadelphia *Evening Bulletin* was one of the champions of black recruitment who recognized the expedition's significance for that cause. "Colors that will not run are what are chiefly wanted in an army," he quipped in an editorial of March 23, "and it matters little whether they be white, brown, or black. . . . The expedition in Florida, up to the last accounts, was advancing prosperously, and had already captured Jacksonville, from which a force of white soldiers was driven by the rebels some time ago. So the blacks seem to be doing better in Florida, at least, than the whites did. Moreover they behaved well and committed fewer acts of pillage than the whites are in the habit of committing. In choosing horses for military service, we have never heard it urged that white horses are better than black horses. Why, then, in a question of fighting should we refuse black men and confine ourselves to white men?"[42]

The news of the expedition not only heartened the believers in black recruitment and justified their faith but also converted some of the skeptics. The moderate Republican editor of the Washington *Evening Star* was among those who experienced an epiphany of sorts. In an editorial of March 24 he confessed that he had heretofore thought that black troops "would do more harm than good" to the Union cause. But the reports from Florida had now convinced him "of the success of the experiment." Speaking specifically of Higginson's regiment, he informed his readers: "So far, their first expedition into the interior has been a complete success, for they had, when last heard from, accomplished everything hoped for up to that time from them; and, besides, had so conducted themselves in the rebel country as to prove that . . . the apprehensions entertained by many that wherever they penetrated, indiscriminate rapine, arson, and murder of defenceless non-combatants would attend their footsteps, were entirely groundless. On the contrary, it turns out that the United States has no more orderly and well-conducted troops in the service than this same negro regiment. It is due to the truth and the cause that these facts should be promptly realized by the country at large." The "experiment," he suggested, if pushed forward, would "be of great importance in weakening the rebels and strengthening the Union cause."[43]

On that same day, in that same city, a momentous meeting was held in the War Department. Secretary of War Edwin Stanton summoned to his office Lorenzo Thomas, adjutant general of the army, and told him that the decision had been made to proceed with full-scale enlistment of black troops. Thomas was to take charge of it for now and move forward with all possible speed.[44]

The adjutant general was taken aback by the abruptness of this announcement. As he well knew, black recruitment up to this point had been a very limited and ad hoc affair. The War Department had simply permitted a handful of interested military and civil officials here and there to organize a few Negro infantry regiments; it had not taken the lead itself. There were now only eight such regiments on duty (one in Kansas, five in Louisiana, two in the Department of the South) and perhaps three or four others being formed. This slow progress reflected not bureaucratic inefficiency but the Lincoln administration's hesitancy to press forward. Although the Emancipation Proclamation had removed all administrative and legal impediments to black recruitment by authorizing the War

Department to enlist Negroes as needed, that policy remained militarily and politically risky. President Lincoln, always sensitive to the importance of timing, was determined not to move too fast. He and his advisers wanted good evidence that black troops would truly benefit the Union army and that a majority of the public in the loyal states would accept them.[45]

When the 1st and 2nd South Carolina sailed up the St. John's to Jacksonville on March 10, the Lincoln administration was still hesitating. When they sailed back down the river on March 29, full-scale recruitment of black troops for the Union army was under way. There can be no question that the expedition, and the editorial response to it, played a crucial role in this pivotal event of the Civil War. (There was no significant news regarding black units in other theaters of war that month.) It is not farfetched to suppose that the *Evening Star* column of March 24, presumably seen that day by the president and his advisers, tipped the balance in their minds; after all, that paper's moderate Republican stance represented the vital center of public opinion that Lincoln was particularly attentive to (see Appendix). In any event, Higginson himself eventually received confirmation indirectly that the Florida expedition had precipitated the administration's fateful decision. In May he had a conversation with a well-connected army officer who had recently spoken with the secretary of the treasury. "Secretary Chase told him," Higginson recorded in his journal, "[that] the Cabinet at Washington kept their whole action in regard to enlisting colored troops *waiting* to hear from us in Florida, & when the capture of Jacksonville was known, the whole question was regarded as settled, the policy avowed, and Adj. Gen. Thomas sent out on his mission. This is, I think, the best expression of the importance of our action that has yet occurred."[46]

The mission that Lorenzo Thomas undertook was defined in a War Department order issued on March 25, the day after he and Stanton met. He was to proceed immediately to the Mississippi River valley, where great numbers of contrabands were in army custody, and begin organizing military units composed of black men—"to the utmost extent to which they can be obtained"—officered by whites. (The Stevens bill, which would have granted formal legislative sanction to such massive recruitment, had been abandoned by Congress in February, but the War Department already had sufficient authorization under previous legislation and the Emancipation Proclamation.) Stanton also dispatched some other military officers, of lesser rank than Thomas, to other theaters of war with similar instructions. President Lincoln personally helped prepare the way for Thomas. On March 26 he wrote to Andrew Johnson, military governor of occupied Tennessee, urging him to assist in the great work. "The colored population is the great available, and yet unavailed of, force for restoring the Union," he told Johnson. "The bare sight of 50,000 armed and drilled black soldiers upon the banks of the Mississippi would end the rebellion at once. And who doubts that we can present that sight if we but take hold in earnest?"[47]

Thus dawned a new day for the cause of black recruitment. From that time forward the War Department raised black units systematically and aggressively, restrained only by the number of able-bodied men who could be enrolled and equipped. In May, Stanton created a Bureau of Colored Troops to oversee the program. Recruiting agents spread throughout the Union states and the occupied parts of the Confederacy. By late October more than 37,000 black men in fifty-eight regiments were wearing Yankee blue. By the war's end in 1865 some 179,000 were serving, or had served, in 120 infantry regiments, 7 cavalry regiments, 12 heavy artillery regiments, and 10 light artillery companies. They constituted a crucial addition of manpower, without which the Union army might have been unable to subdue the Rebel nation.[48]

The widely celebrated exploits of the men of 1st and 2nd South Carolina on the Florida Main were overshadowed before long by the gallantry of other black soldiers in a number of bloody, pitched battles that won national attention. But had the St. John's expedition of 1863 taken a different course, those other men might not have had the chance to prove themselves at Port Hudson and Milliken's Bend, Louisiana, Fort Wagner, South Carolina, Nashville, Tennessee, and elsewhere. Higginson mused on this point in his journal in May 1863. Thinking not just of the expedition but of the entire period of the 1st South's existence up to the time the government inaugurated full-scale black enlistment, he wrote, "There is no doubt that for many months the fate of the whole movement for colored soldiers rested on the behavior of this one regiment," for none of the other Negro units then in service had garnered nearly as much public notice as his. "A mutiny, an extensive desertion, an act of severe discipline, a Bull Run panic, a simple defeat, might have blasted the whole movement for arming the blacks—& through it the prospects of the war & of a race."

It was on the St. John's River, of course, that the regiment faced its severest test during those critical months and where the worst was most likely to have happened. A decisive defeat at the hands of General Finegan, abuse of the civilian population, racial conflict with the white troops sent as reinforcements: Any of these could have constituted the kind of disaster Higginson feared.[49]

The soldiers of the 1st South, no less than their colonel, sensed the meaning of their achievements during the regiment's first months. On Sunday, March 27, 1864, the anniversary, as it happened, of the day the order recalling the expedition was received in Jacksonville, one of the men preached a notable sermon to his comrades. He was Corporal Thomas Long of Company G, who had distinguished himself on the expedition by his daring attempt to sneak behind the Rebel lines and burn down a railroad trestle. Long's message on this Sabbath moved Higginson so deeply that he transcribed a good part of the sermon in his journal, doing his best to capture the corporal's riveting oratorical style:

> We can remember, when we first enlisted, it was hardly safe for we to pass by de camps to Beaufort & back, 'lest (unless) we went in a mob & carried our side arms. But we whipped down all dat. Not by going into de white camps for whip um; we didn't tote our bayonets for whip um; *but we lived it down by our naturally manhood*; and now de white sojers take us by de hand & say Broder Sojer. Dat's what dis regiment did for de Epiopian (Ethiopian) race[.]
>
> If we hadn't become sojers, all might have gone back as it was before; our freedom might have slipped through de two houses of Congress & President Linkum's four years might have passed by & notin been done for we. But now tings can never go back, because we have showed our energy & our courage & our naturally manhood.
>
> Anoder ting is, suppose you had kept your freedom widout enlisting in dis army; your chilen might have grown up free, & been *well cultivated* so as to be equal to any business, but it would have been always flung in dere faces— "Your fader never fought for he own freedom"—and what could dey answer? *Neber can say that to dis African race any more*, (bringing down his hand with the greatest emphasis on the table.) Tanks to dis regiment, never can say dat any more, because we first showed dem we could fight by dere side.[50]

The 1st South Carolina served honorably in the Department of the South through the war's end and for many months beyond, mainly on

picket and garrison duty. In 1864 it was deprived of its original designa-
tion by War Department decree, becoming instead the 33rd United States
Colored Infantry Regiment. But the men continued to call it the 1st South.
They also continued to recount proudly around the evening campfires
their martial deeds, especially their great adventure of March 1863, when
they journeyed deep into the enemy's country to make war on slavery.[51]

EPILOGUE

I N THE EARLY PART OF 1878 Thomas Wentworth Higginson made a tour of the south Atlantic states, his first visit to the South since the war. One of his stops was Jacksonville. He barely recognized the place. Now populous and prosperous, it bustled with life and commerce. Except for the police, no uniformed men were to be seen, nor any scars of war. The burned districts had been rebuilt. The earthworks on the west end of town had been leveled. A bridge now stood where the soldiers of the 1st South had once guarded a ford. The railroad track that led to the Confederate camp and beyond and that had been the site of memorable encounters with Finegan's Rebels had been torn up and replaced by another that went in a different direction. Everything was so changed that Higginson had trouble even visualizing the scene fifteen years earlier—until suddenly some cannons boomed in honor of Washington's Birthday, and he saw in his mind the gunboats that had protected his men while they held the town.[1]

Some of those men had settled in Jacksonville after the war, and Higginson met with them on this visit. They seemed to be doing well, he was pleased to note. He had last seen them in May 1864, a year before the war ended, when he left the Department of the South to go home to New England on medical leave. He was by then physically unable to perform his duties. An injury he suffered in a skirmish on the South Carolina coast in July 1863 had never fully healed, and a later bout with malaria weakened him badly. In the fall of 1864 he tendered his resignation from the army and was honorably discharged.[2]

By that time the officer corps of his regiment had changed dramatically. He had managed to get rid of his vain, incompetent lieutenant colonel Liberty Billings in the summer of 1863 by requesting a fitness examination by a military board; grossly ignorant of his formal duties, Billings failed the test miserably, as Higginson knew he would, and he was discharged from the army. Major John D. Strong succeeded to the vacant lieutenant colonelcy, but he resigned in August 1864 after having been accused by a junior officer of misbehavior during an encounter with the enemy (a charge that a court-martial found him innocent of), and he died in a shipwreck on his way back to the North. Charles T. Trowbridge, the tough Brooklynite and senior company commander, was promoted to major and then lieutenant colonel as Strong moved up and out. An officer from outside the regiment was named its colonel after Higginson departed, but he soon took command of a brigade in the absence of its brigadier general. Trowbridge was the regiment's acting commander from August 1864 until it mustered out in early 1866.[3]

Another loss to the officer corps occurred about the time Billings left, this one deeply mourned in the regiment. Lieutenant Luther Bingham, the ardent young evangelical whose Sunday school for the children of Jacksonville had been abruptly terminated by the expedition's recall, died in Beaufort on July 20, 1863. He never had the chance to test his bravery under enemy fire, a matter he had agonized over as the regiment approached Jacksonville. His death was ascribed to sunstroke and exhaustion suffered while supervising the loading and unloading of transports under the blistering South Carolina summer sun. A few months after he died, Bingham's grieving father published a little book titled *The Young Quartermaster*, a moving tribute to his son's life, work, and faith.[4]

It was about that time that surgeon Seth Rogers resigned from the army, bade farewell to the 1st South, and returned home to Massachusetts, his body wracked by a six-month spell of intermittent illness that he attributed to the semitropical climate. His passionate relationship with Charlotte Forten ended with his departure. By then she had become such a familiar figure around the 1st South's headquarters that Higginson dubbed her the "daughter of the regiment." She continued to teach in her free-labor plantation school until May 1864, when she resigned in ill health and went back to the North. In the succeeding years she supported herself by secretarial work for a missionary society, clerking for the federal government, teaching, and writing. Whether she and Rogers ever met again is uncertain. In 1878, age forty-one, she married a highly educated black man twelve years her junior who until 1865 had been a slave. Although her plan to join the 1st South in Jacksonville as a teacher had been frustrated by the expedition's recall, she ultimately did see the town, living there for four years in the 1880s while her husband served as pastor of a Presbyterian church.[5]

Lyman Stickney returned to the Department of the South in August 1863 but stayed only a few days before heading back to the North. Between December of that year and March 1864 he was in the department again, busily working to boost his political and financial prospects while pretty much ignoring his responsibilities as a member of the Florida Tax Commission. By that time, however, rumors of his malfeasance had stirred the government to investigate. In July 1864, a Treasury Department agent rendered a report, subsequently turned over to the House of Representatives, that blamed the commission's egregious inactivity on "the almost constant absence of commissioner Stickney from his post of duty." The investigator also found evidence that Stickney had diverted to his own use items purchased on the commission's account, had had personal property shipped at government expense, "was deeply engaged in schemes of private speculation and political preferment for his friends, and gave very little attention to the actual duties of his office." Within a year he was under indictment for fraud. However, slippery and smooth-talking as always, he apparently managed not only to avoid punishment but also, until late 1866, to continue collecting his salary. Simultaneously, and for sometime thereafter, he worked as a lawyer and newspaper editor, but his dream of riches and power in a reconstructed Florida never became a reality.[6]

James Montgomery's 2nd South Carolina regiment was eventually brought up to full strength and redesignated the 34th U.S. Colored Infantry. It remained on duty in the Department of the South, but it and Higginson's regiment were brigaded separately. That suited Higginson, for in the months following the Florida expedition he came to dislike Montgomery and to loathe the idea of serving alongside him. In a series of coastal raids in 1863 the Kansan distinguished himself by his undisciplined style and his ruthless pillaging and burning of the property of Rebel civilians, who he believed deserved everything they got. In Higginson's view, he was more a "brigand" than a soldier and his regiment was little better than a gang of rowdies. Even General Hunter, no friend of the secessionist citizenry, felt obliged to caution Montgomery to obey "the laws and usages of civilized warfare." In one sense, however, Montgomery was ultimately vindicated. His few-holds-barred brand of war making was a harbinger of the "hard war" policy that such Union generals as

William T. Sherman and Philip H. Sheridan made famous, or infamous, beginning in late 1864. By that time, however, Montgomery was no longer in the service. Chronic illness compelled his resignation in September 1864, and he returned to civilian life in Kansas.[7]

David Hunter's departure from the Department of the South in the summer of 1863 was regretted by few, except perhaps on the Confederate side. Higginson, for one, never altered his initial judgment that the general was too unenergetic and unfocused to succeed. His subsequent career was undistinguished. He led a large raiding force into western Virginia in 1864, perhaps envisioning the sort of grand expedition of liberation that he had proposed to the secretary of war the year before, but after the Confederates had repulsed him in a small engagement, he withdrew ignominiously. Thereafter his duties were off the battlefield. As he had escorted President Lincoln to Washington for his inauguration in 1861, so he escorted his body to its resting place back in Illinois after Lincoln's assassination in April 1865. Immediately thereafter he presided over the trial by military commission of the assassination conspirators.[8]

Rufus Saxton, on the other hand, remained in the Department of the South and continued to command the respect of most, if not all, who knew him—particularly Higginson, who thought him "noble" and insisted that he had "done the Administration a greater service . . . than any man in America, by his practical vindication of . . . Emancipation." Although longing for a field command, Saxton dutifully stayed at his administrative post, battling tirelessly to see that the black troops and contrabands in the department got a fair shake. His work on their behalf did not end with the war; he afterward served as an assistant commissioner of the Freedmen's Bureau, a War Department agency created to aid in the transition from slavery to freedom. Higginson included a heartfelt tribute to Saxton in a volume of essays he published in 1909.[9]

One of the inequities Saxton battled against was the matter of the black troops' pay. The War Department order of 1862 authorizing him to recruit Negro soldiers stipulated that they were to receive the same pay as white soldiers, and so they did, until a bureaucratic decision in June 1863 reduced their pay, and that of black troops everywhere, on a technical point. Higginson, Montgomery, and many other officers of black regiments joined in protesting the gross unfairness of this policy, as did many of their men. Higginson fired off at least five furious letters to the editors of major Northern newspapers and one to a congressman, carrying on the fight even after he had resigned from the army. Not until March 1865 did Congress pass legislation to rectify the injustice.[10]

On February 9, 1866, the men and officers of the 33rd Colored Infantry assembled in formal ranks on a sandy stretch of Morris Island, South Carolina, within sight of Fort Sumter and the city of Charleston. It was the occasion of the regiment's mustering out. The soldiers listened as Lieutenant Colonel Trowbridge's final order was read. It was more a farewell and a benediction than a formal military order. "Comrades:" it began. "The hour is at hand when we must separate forever, and nothing can ever take from us the pride we feel when we look back upon the history of the 1st South Carolina Volunteers—the first black regiment that ever bore arms in defence of freedom on the Continent of America." It went on to speak of the regiment's origin, its triumphs, and its flag, which "has never been disgraced by a cowardly faltering in the hour of danger" and which would "now . . . be rolled up forever." It adjured the men to prove themselves worthy, as civilians, of "the privileges of freemen."[11]

The men dispersed after their discharge, but in the years that followed most stayed close to their old homes, carving out livelihoods and raising families in South Carolina, Georgia, or Florida, and struggling, against bitter opposition from Southern whites, to make the most of the freedom and rights they gained in the war and Reconstruction. Of those Higginson met or heard about on his 1878 tour, one was a carpenter, two were preachers, one owned a livery stable, and another hunted wild game on the Sea Islands. Several had entered politics. Thomas Long served in the Florida Senate from 1873 to 1881 and sponsored the bill that created a public school system in that state. Prince Rivers became a local magistrate in South Carolina, a delegate to that state's constitutional convention of 1868, a member of the state House of Representatives from that year until 1874, and a major general of the state militia, this last appointment validating Higginson's high opinion of his military abilities.[12]

Another member of the 1st South who achieved a modest measure of distinction in later life was Susie King Taylor, the young laundress and teacher who had married a soldier of Company E and followed the regiment wherever it went, including Jacksonville. For a time after the war she taught black children and adults in Savannah; later she moved to Boston, where she worked as a servant for wealthy white families and helped organize a chapter of the Women's Relief Corps, an auxiliary of the Grand Army of the Republic, a Union veterans' organization. In 1902 she published *Reminiscences of My Life in Camp*, one of the very few firsthand accounts of the Civil War written by a Southern freedwoman.[13]

Many of the black veterans of the 1st South stayed in touch with one another in the postwar years, but they undoubtedly saw few of their former officers again. Higginson was one they did see, of course. So was Trowbridge, who in his handwritten memoir recorded a notable encounter in 1884, when on his return to the North from a Florida vacation, his steamer docked at Port Royal. Casting his gaze on a gang of stevedores loading cotton, he recognized Fred Brown, a former sergeant of Company D. He was delighted to see him; Brown had saved his life once in a perilous situation, and Trowbridge regarded him as a hero. "I hastened on shore," Trowbridge recounted, ". . . he threw his arms around me, and the reunion was such as only old comrades can understand who have braved danger together." The meeting was a hurried one. The steamer soon cast off. From the upper deck Trowbridge waved good-bye to his old comrade. At that moment, "Two young ladies . . . strolled past where I stood." One said, loudly enough for him and other passengers to hear, "Did you see that old white man kiss that nigger?"[14]

Thomas Wentworth Higginson outlived many, perhaps most, of his officers and men and towered above them all in renown. Long before his death in 1911 he was hailed as one of the grand old men of American letters. Only two of his innumerable literary works, however, would be widely remembered after he was gone. One was the first edition of Emily Dickinson's collected poems, which he coedited after her death. The other was his memoir of service with the 1st South, published in 1870 and titled *Army Life in a Black Regiment*, the fourth chapter of which tells the story of the Florida expedition of 1863. The book ends with these words: "Till the blacks were armed, there was no guaranty of their freedom. It was their demeanor under arms that shamed the nation into recognizing them as men."[15]

APPENDIX

Historians and the Lincoln Administration's Decision for Full-Scale Black Recruitment

ALL THE MAJOR STUDIES DEALING with blacks in the Union army (including those by George W. Williams, Bell Irvin Wiley, Benjamin Quarles, Dudley Taylor Cornish, James M. McPherson, Ira Berlin, Hondon B. Hargrove, Joseph T. Glatthaar, and Noah Trudeau) point to the orders given to Lorenzo Thomas by the secretary of war in March 1863 as a watershed event. But none of these studies connects those orders to the Florida expedition; in fact, none offers any explanation at all for this sudden departure in Union army policy. The reason, undoubtedly, is that the standard primary sources on the inner workings of the Lincoln administration shed no light on the decision to go forward with full-scale recruitment of blacks. The diaries of Treasury Secretary Salmon P. Chase, Navy Secretary Gideon Welles, Attorney General Edward Bates, and Lincoln's private secretary John Hay all are silent on this matter. But their silence does not mean that the connection I have made here is false.

For one reason or another, none of the diarists made any entry on or around 24 March 1863. Welles was ill during that time and wrote nothing in his diary between 17 and 31 March. Bates made no entry between 17 and 26 March. Chase did not keep his diary at all between October 1862 and August 1863. Hay made no entry between late September 1862 and early April 1863. Secretary of State William H. Seward, the cabinet member whom Lincoln consulted and confided in far more than any other, did not keep a diary; nor did Secretary of War Edwin Stanton; nor did Lincoln himself. The official letters of these men from the period around 24 March do not discuss the reasoning behind the change in policy, but that is to be expected of official correspondence. The standard source on Lincoln's daily activities as president mentions no meetings on 24 March, but it relies heavily on the cabinet and secretarial diaries and official correspondence; in fact, it records nothing on that day except two notes or endorsements that Lincoln wrote about minor matters unrelated to black recruitment, found in his presidential papers.

The available evidence persuades me that this is most likely what happened: Lincoln or someone close to him saw the editorial in the Washington *Evening Star* on the day of publication, 24 March; in any event, it was brought to his attention that day. This, together with the favorable newspaper editorials and reports on the St. John's expedition already published and Rufus Saxton's 14 March dispatch to the War Department, was enough to make up the president's mind that black recruitment should go forward with no more hesitation. He probably met with Seward and Stanton on the twenty-fourth, either together or separately, to discuss the matter, but the meeting or meetings went unrecorded (it is unlikely that he assembled the full cabinet). Stanton was instructed to begin immediately, and he met with Lorenzo Thomas that very day. By the time the diarists resumed their diary entries the decision was no longer such current news as to be worthy of comment. (Clearly, however, as Higginson's journal entry of 25 May makes clear, the reason for the decision was eventually known to Chase, even if he did not have a part in it.) Thus the explanation for the sudden shift in policy on 24 March fell through the historiographical cracks.

The relevant secondary sources on Thomas's orders as a turning point include Williams, *History of the Negro Troops in the War*, 106–12; Bell Irvin Wiley, *Southern Negroes, 1861–1865* (New Haven, Conn., 1938; reprint, New Haven, Conn., and London, 1965), 305; Quarles, *Negro in the Civil War*, 194; Cornish, *Sable Arm*, 110–15; Benjamin Quarles, *Lincoln and the Negro* (New York, 1962), 158–59; McPherson, *Negro's Civil War*, 170; Berlin, *Black Military Experience*, 9–10; Hargrove, *Black Union Soldiers*, 88–91; Glatthaar, *Forged in Battle*, 37; Trudeau, *Like Men of War*, 47–48; and Michael T. Meier, "Lorenzo Thomas and the Recruitment of Blacks in the Mississippi Valley, 1863–1865," in John David Smith, ed., *Black Soldiers in Blue: African American Troops in the Civil War Era* (Chapel Hill and London, 2002), 249–75. For the diaries, see Beale, *Diary of Gideon Welles*, 1:249–50; Howard K. Beale, ed., *The Diary of Edward Bates, 1859–1866* (Washington, 1933), 285–86; Donald, *Inside Lincoln's Cabinet*, 174; Tyler Dennett, ed., *Lincoln and the Civil War in the Diaries and Letters of John Hay* (New

York, 1939), 49–55; and Michael Burlingame and John R. Turner Ettlinger, eds., *Inside Lincoln's White House: The Complete Civil War Diary of John Hay* (Carbondale and Edwardsville, Ill., 1997), 41–42; On Lincoln's closeness to Seward and dependence on his advice, see Doris Kearns Goodwin, *Team of Rivals: The Political Genius of Abraham Lincoln* (New York, 2005), passim. On Lincoln's activities on 24 March, see Earl Schenck Miers, ed., *Lincoln Day by Day: A Chronology, 1809–1865* (Washington, 1960), 175.

NOTES

ABBREVIATIONS USED IN NOTES

CMSR   Compiled Military Service Records
RAGO   Records of the Adjutant General's Office
RBNP   Records of the Bureau of Naval Personnel
RUSACC   Records of the U.S. Army Continental Commands

Prologue

1. Tilden G. Edelstein, *Strange Enthusiasm: A Life of Thomas Wentworth Higginson* (New Haven, Conn., 1968; reprint, New York, 1970), 211.
2. Among the best of the many works on slavery and the slave experience are Eugene D. Genovese, *Roll, Jordan, Roll: The World the Slaves Made* (New York, 1976), and Kenneth M. Stampp, *The Peculiar Institution: Slavery in the Ante-Bellum South* (New York, 1956).
3. James Brewer Stewart, *Holy Warriors: The Abolitionists and American Slavery*, 2d ed. (New York, 1996) provides an excellent survey of the abolitionist movement.
4. On Northern opposition to the westward expansion of slavery, see Eric Foner, *Free Soil, Free Labor, Free Men: The Ideology of the Republican Party Before the Civil War* (New York, 1970), and Michael A. Morrison, *Slavery and the American West: The Eclipse of Manifest Destiny and the Coming of the Civil War* (Chapel Hill, N.C., and London, 1997).
5. David M. Potter, *The Impending Crisis, 1848–1861* (New York, 1976); Leonard L. Richards, *The Slave Power: The Free North and Southern Domination* (Baton Rouge, 2000).
6. The background information on Higginson here and elsewhere in this Prologue is drawn from Edelstein, *Strange Enthusiasm*; Howard N. Meyer, *Colonel of the Black Regiment: The Life of Thomas Wentworth Higginson* (New York, 1967); Anna Mary Wells, *Dear Preceptor: The Life and Times of Thomas Wentworth Higginson* (Boston, 1963); and Mary Thatcher Higginson, *Thomas Wentworth Higginson: The Story of His Life* (Boston and New York, 1914; reprint, New York, 1971).

7. Edelstein, *Strange Enthusiasm*, 88.

8. On the various abolitionist strategies, see Stewart, *Holy Warriors*.

9. Edelstein, *Strange Enthusiasm*, 25–26, 89, 101, 151, 162, 166, 189, 199, 205. See also Jeffery Rossbach, *Ambivalent Conspirators: John Brown, the Secret Six, and a Theory of Slave Violence* (Philadelphia, 1982).

10. Edelstein, *Strange Enthusiasm*, 162.

11. Stephen B. Oates, *To Purge This Land with Blood: A Biography of John Brown* (New York, 1970), 61; Rossbach, *Ambivalent Conspirators, passim*.

12. Edelstein, *Strange Enthusiasm*, 211.

13. Oates, *To Purge This Land with Blood*, 290–352.

14. Among the many excellent studies of the motives behind secession, see especially Steven A. Channing, *Crisis of Fear: Secession in South Carolina* (New York, 1970).

15. Charles B. Dew, *Apostles of Disunion: Southern Secession Commissioners and the Causes of the Civil War* (Charlottesville, Va., and London, 2001) offers compelling evidence of the white South's fear for the survival of slavery in the wake of Lincoln's election.

16. Edelstein, *Strange Enthusiasm*, 154. On Lincoln's wartime policy regarding slavery, see Allen C. Guelzo, *Lincoln's Emancipation Proclamation: The End of Slavery in America* (New York, 2004).

17. Ira Berlin et al., eds., *The Destruction of Slavery* (Cambridge, U.K., and other cities, 1985), 12–31, 36; Guelzo, *Lincoln's Emancipation Proclamation, passim*.

18. Edelstein, *Strange Enthusiasm*, 243; Thomas Wentworth Higginson, "The Ordeal by Battle," *Atlantic Monthly*, 8 (1861): 88–95; Boston *Commonwealth*, 14 February 1863.

19. Guelzo, *Lincoln's Emancipation Proclamation, passim*.

20. Berlin, *Destruction of Slavery*, 2–3, 11–12, 17–18.

Chapter One **PORT ROYAL ISLAND, SOUTH CAROLINA, JANUARY 1, 1863**

1. New York *Daily Tribune*, 14 January 1863; New York *Herald*, 7 January 1863; New York *Times*, 9 January 1863; Charlotte Forten, "Life on the Sea Islands," *Atlantic Monthly*, 13 (1864): 668; Christopher Looby, ed., *The Complete Civil War Journal and Selected Letters of Thomas Wentworth Higginson* (Chicago and London, 2000), 75; Thomas Wentworth Higginson, *Army Life in a Black Regiment* (Boston, 1870; reprint, New York and London, 1984), 59.

2. New York *Daily Tribune*, 14 January 1863; New York *Herald*, 7 January 1863; New York *Times*, 9 January 1863; Forten, "Life on the Sea Islands," 668; Looby, *Journal and Letters*, 90; Elizabeth Ware Pearson, ed., *Letters from Port Royal, 1862–1868* (Boston, 1906; reprint, New York, 1969), 128; Brenda Stevenson, ed., *The Journals of Charlotte Forten Grimké* (New York and Oxford, 1988), 428; Luther Goodyear Bingham, *The Young Quartermaster: The Life and Death of Lieut. L. M. Bingham, of the First South Carolina Volunteers* (New York, 1863), 180–81; Higginson, *Army Life*, 107.

3. *Frank Leslie's Illustrated Newspaper*, 24 January 1863; *The Liberator* (Boston), 16 January 1863; New York *Herald*, 7 January 1863; New York *Times*, 9 January 1863; Pearson, *Letters from Port Royal*, 128–29; General Order No. 10, 1 January 1863, Order

Book, 33rd USCT Infantry, Regimental Records, Records of the Adjutant General's Office, RG 94, National Archives, Washington (hereinafter cited as RAGO).

4. New York *Herald*, 7 January 1863; "Letters of Dr. Seth Rogers, 1862, 1863," *Massachusetts Historical Society Proceedings*, 43 (1910): 340; Looby, *Journal and Letters*, 76; Pearson, *Letters from Port Royal*, 128; Higginson, *Army Life*, 59; Charles Carleton Coffin, *Four Years of Fighting: A Volume of Personal Observation with the Army and Navy, from the First Battle of Bull Run to the Fall of Richmond* (Boston, 1866), 245–46; Edward W. Hooper to Robert W. Hooper, 2 January 1863, Edward William Hooper Papers, Houghton Library, Harvard University.

5. *Liberator*, 16 January 1863; New York *Daily Tribune*, 14 January 1863; New York *Herald*, 7 January 1863; Looby, *Journal and Letters*, 74; Pearson, *Letters from Port Royal*, 128; Gerald Schwartz, ed., *A Woman Doctor's Civil War: Esther Hill Hawks' Diary* (Columbia, S.C., 1984), 42.

6. *Frank Leslie's Illustrated Newspaper*, 24 January 1863; Forten, "Life on the Sea Islands," 668; Pearson, *Letters from Port Royal*, 129.

7. *Liberator*, 19 December 1862; Port Royal (South Carolina) *New South*, 6 December 1862; Stamford (Connecticut) *Advocate*, 2 January 1863; Stevenson, *Journals*, 404–05; New York *Times*, 3 December 1862. Higginson's wartime journal and many of his wartime letters are in the Thomas Wentworth Higginson Papers, bMS Am 784 (20–23, 699–958), Houghton Library, Harvard University; these have been transcribed and annotated in Looby, *Journal and Letters*.

8. Daniel Ammen, "Du Pont and the Port Royal Expedition," in Robert Underwood Johnson and Clarence Clough Buel, eds., *Battles and Leaders of the Civil War*, 4 vols. (New York, 1888; reprint, New York and London, 1956), 1: 671–91; *The War of the Rebellion: A Compilation of the Official Records of the Union and Confederate Armies*, 70 vols. in 128 (Washington, 1880–1901), Series One, 6: 3–4, 14: 389–90; Robert M. Browning, Jr., *Success Is All That Was Expected: The South Atlantic Blockading Squadron During the Civil War* (Washington, 2002), 7–10, 23–42; William M. Fowler, Jr., *Under Two Flags: The American Navy in the Civil War* (New York and London, 1990), 53–59, 65–78; Berlin, *Destruction of Slavery*, 104–07; *Official Records of the Union and Confederate Navies in the War of the Rebellion*, 31 vols. (Washington, 1894–1927), Series One, 13: 465–66; George Linton Hendricks, "Union Army Occupation of the Southern Seaboard, 1861–1865" (Ph.D. diss., Columbia University, 1954).

9. James M. McPherson, *Battle Cry of Freedom: The Civil War Era* (New York and Oxford, 1988), chapter 19; Herman Hattaway and Archer Jones, *How the North Won: A Military History of the Civil War* (Urbana and Chicago, 1991), chapter 11.

10. Browning, *Success Is All That Was Expected*, chapters 3–5; Hendricks, "Union Army Occupation," passim.

11. *War of the Rebellion*, Series One, 6: 6; Willie Lee Rose, *Rehearsal for Reconstruction: The Port Royal Experiment* (Indianapolis, 1964; reprint, Athens, Ga., and London, 1999), 11–12, 15–16; Berlin, *Destruction of Slavery*, 18–19, 103–05, 119, 125–26; Forten, "Life on the Sea Islands," 593; Clarence L. Mohr, *On the Threshold of Freedom: Masters and Slaves in Civil War Georgia* (Athens, Ga., and London, 1986), 68–75; Boston *Commonwealth*, 3 January 1863; *Liberator*, 10 October, 12 December 1862; New York *Evening Post*, 13 February, 26 March, 15, 16 April 1863; Peter H. Buckingham, ed., *All's for the Best: The Civil War Reminiscences and Letters of Daniel W. Sawtelle, Eighth*

Maine Volunteer Infantry (Knoxville, Tenn., 2001), 34–35; Stevenson, *Journals*, 420, 425–26; Hartford (Connecticut) *Daily Courant*, 13 February 1863.

12. Boston *Commonwealth*, 24 January 1863; Kate Masur, " 'A Rare Phenomenon of Philological Vegetation': The Word 'Contraband' and the Meanings of Emancipation in the United States," *Journal of American History*, 93 (2007): 1050–84.

13. New York *Daily Tribune*, 14 January 1863; Looby, *Journal and Letters*, 76; Pearson, *Letters from Port Royal*, 129.

14. New York *Daily Tribune*, 14 January 1863; New York *Herald*, 7 January 1863; Looby, *Journal and Letters*, 76; John Niven, ed., *The Salmon P. Chase Papers*, 5 vols. (Kent, Ohio, 1993–98), 3: 352, 354n.; Pearson, *Letters from Port Royal*, 129; Bingham, *Young Quartermaster*, 181; Edward W. Hooper to Robert W. Hooper, 2 January 1863, and to Samuel Hooper, 5 January 1863, Hooper Papers.

15. New York *Times*, 23 September 1862; New York *Daily Tribune*, 14 January 1863; Bingham, *Young Quartermaster*, 181.

16. New York *Daily Tribune*, 14 January 1863; New York *Times*, 9 January 1863; Philadelphia *Inquirer*, 9 January 1863; Forten "Life on the Sea Islands," 669; Bingham, *Young Quartermaster*, 181.

17. *Liberator*, 16 January 1863; New York *Daily Tribune*, 14 January 1863; New York *Herald*, 7 January 1863; Pearson, *Letters from Port Royal*, 130.

18. Ira Berlin et al., eds., *The Wartime Genesis of Free Labor: The Lower South* (Cambridge, U.K., and other cities, 1990), 87–101, 104–06, 253; Berlin, *Destruction of Slavery*, 19–20; Louis S. Gerteis, *From Contraband to Freedman: Federal Policy Toward Southern Blacks, 1861–1865* (Westport, Conn., 1973), 49–55; William Dusinberre, *Them Dark Days: Slavery in the American Rice Swamps* (New York, 1996), passim, especially 180–81, 186; Rose, *Rehearsal for Reconstruction*, 224–28; Julie Saville, *The Work of Reconstruction: From Slave to Wage Laborer in South Carolina, 1860–1870* (Cambridge, U.K., 1994), 5–11, 18, 45–60; Akiko Ochiai, *Harvesting Freedom: African American Agrarianism in Civil War Era South Carolina* (Westport, Conn., 2004), 25–34, 65–75; *The Freedmen of South Carolina: An Address Delivered by J. Miller M'Kim, in Sansom Hall, July 9th, 1862* (Philadelphia, 1862), 5–6; New York *Evening Post*, 16 April 1863; Boston *Commonwealth*, 24 January, 20 March 1863.

19. *Freedmen of South Carolina*, 1–4; *First Annual Report of the National Freedman's Relief Association, New York, February 19th, 1863* (New York, 1863); Rose, *Rehearsal for Reconstruction*, 32–62.

20. *American Missionary*, 7 (1863): 39, 65–66, 88–91, 109–10; *First Annual Report*; Rupert Sargent Holland, ed., *The Letters and Diary of Laura M. Towne; Written from the Sea Islands of South Carolina, 1862–1884* (Cambridge, Mass., 1912; reprint, New York, 1969), 20; *Freedmen of South Carolina*, 7, 14–15, 30; Forten, "Life on the Sea Islands," 591, 593–94, 667; William Channing Gannett and Edward Everett Hale, "The Freedmen at Port Royal," *North American Review*, 101 (1865): 9–11; Rose, *Rehearsal for Reconstruction*, 41, 73–74, 85–86, 90–93, 100–01, 129, 234, 236; Margaret Washington Creel, *"A Peculiar People": Slave Religion and Community Culture Among the Gullahs* (New York, 1988), 276–302.

21. Berlin, *Wartime Genesis of Free Labor*, 88–89, 96–97, 100–01, 266; Rose, *Rehearsal for Reconstruction*, 64–66; *War of the Rebellion*, Series One, 14: 385, Series Three, 4: 1029; Boston *Commonwealth*, 24 January 1863; Hartford (Connecticut) *Daily Times*, 4, 7

February, 31 March 1863; Farmington (Maine) *Franklin Patriot*, 9 January 1863; *Liberator*, 12 September, 12 December 1862; New York *Daily Tribune*, 19 November 1862; New York *Evening Post*, 4 March, 16 April 1863; New York *World*, 14 January 1863; Looby, *Journal and Letters*, 40–41, 40n.; Edward W. Hooper to Robert W. Hooper, 15 February 1863, Hooper Papers.

22. Ira Berlin et al., eds., *The Black Military Experience* (Cambridge, U.K., and other cities, 1982), 46–50; Rose, *Rehearsal for Reconstruction*, 145–48; Pearson, *Letters from Port Royal*, 38–42, 125; Henry Noble Sherwood, ed., "The Journal of Miss Susan Walker, March 3d to June 6th, 1862," *Quarterly Publication of the Historical and Philosophical Society of Ohio*, 7 (1912): 38–40; New York *Times*, 9 January 1863; Looby, *Journal and Letters*, 75; Higginson, *Army Life*, 59; Schwartz, *Woman Doctor's Civil War*, 41.

23. *American Missionary*, 7 (1863): 39, 64, 66, 89–90, 109, 129; *Liberator*, 12, 19, 26 December 1862; Forten, "Life on the Sea Islands," 593; *Freedmen of South Carolina*, 6, 8–9, 10, 27; Stevenson, *Journals*, 395–96, 420; Coffin, *Four Years of Fighting*, 229; Boston *Commonwealth*, 3, 24 January 1863; Buckingham, *All's for the Best*, 36–37, 213, 226; Edward W. Hooper to Robert W. Hooper, 15 February 1863, Hooper Papers.

24. *Liberator*, 16 January 1863; New York *Daily Tribune*, 14 January 1863.

25. New York *Daily Tribune*, 14 January 1863; Forten, "Life on the Sea Islands," 669; "Letters of Dr. Rogers," 340, 341; Looby, *Journal and Letters*, 76–77; Niven, *Chase Papers*, 3: 352; Pearson, *Letters from Port Royal*, 130.

26. New York *Daily Tribune*, 14 January 1863; Forten, "Life on the Sea Islands," 669; "Letters of Dr. Rogers," 340, 341; Looby, *Journal and Letters*, 77; Pearson, *Letters from Port Royal*, 130; Stevenson, *Journals*, 430; Bingham, *Young Quartermaster*, 182; Higginson, *Army Life*, 60.

27. New York *Daily Tribune*, 14 January 1863; Forten, "Life on the Sea Islands," 669; Holland, *Letters and Diary of Laura M. Towne*, 98; "Letters of Dr. Rogers," 340, 341; Looby, *Journal and Letters*, 77; Pearson, *Letters from Port Royal*, 130; Stevenson, *Journals*, 430; Bingham, *Young Quartermaster*, 182.

28. New York *Daily Tribune*, 14 January 1863; Holland, *Letters and Diary of Laura M. Towne*, 98; Looby, *Journal and Letters*, 77; Niven, *Chase Papers*, 3: 352; Pearson, *Letters from Port Royal*, 130–31; Bingham, *Young Quartermaster*, 182–83.

29. *Frank Leslie's Illustrated Newspaper*, 24 January 1863; New York *Daily Tribune*, 14 January 1863; New York *Herald*, 7 January 1863; Philadelphia *Inquirer*, 9 January 1863; Looby, *Journal and Letters*, 77; Niven, *Chase Papers*, 3: 352; Pearson, *Letters from Port Royal*, 131–32; Stevenson, *Journals*, 430.

30. Bingham, *Young Quartermaster*, 183; New York *Daily Tribune*, 14 January 1863; New York *Herald*, 7 January 1863; Forten, "Life on the Sea Islands," 669; Looby, *Journal and Letters*, 77, 79; Pearson, *Letters from Port Royal*, 130.

31. Forten, "Life on the Sea Islands," 669; Stevenson, *Journals*, 430; Thomas Wentworth Higginson, *Carlyle's Laugh: And Other Surprises* (Boston, 1909), 175–82.

32. *Liberator*, 19 December 1862; Forten, "Life on the Sea Islands," 595.

33. New York *Herald*, 7 January 1863; Pearson, *Letters from Port Royal*, 132.

34. New York *Herald*, 7 January 1863; Washington *Daily Morning Chronicle*, 8 January 1863; Looby, *Journal and Letters*, 77; Edward W. Hooper to Robert W. Hooper, 2 January 1863, Hooper Papers.

35. New York *Daily Tribune*, 14 January 1863; Looby, *Journal and Letters*, 78; Schwartz, *Woman Doctor's Civil War*, 42.

36. New York *Daily Tribune*, 14 January 1863; Forten, "Life on the Sea Islands," 669; Looby, *Journal and Letters*, 78; Pearson, *Letters from Port Royal*, 132.

37. New York *Daily Tribune*, 14 January 1863; New York *Herald*, 7 January 1863; New York *Times*, 9 January 1863; "Letters of Dr. Rogers," 341; Looby, *Journal and Letters*, 72, 75.

38. Philadelphia *Inquirer*, 9 January 1863; Forten, "Life on the Sea Islands," 669; Looby, *Journal and Letters*, 78; Pearson, *Letters from Port Royal*, 133–34; Stevenson, *Journals*, 432.

39. Holland, *Letters and Diary of Laura M. Towne*, 99; "Letters of Dr. Rogers," 341; Higginson, *Army Life*, 61.

40. Looby, *Journal and Letters*, 61–62, 251–52, 254; Pearson, *Letters from Port Royal*, 133; Stevenson, *Journals*, 431.

41. Looby, *Journal and Letters*, 78, 255; Meyer, *Colonel of the Black Regiment*, 53, 102–07; Wells, *Dear Preceptor*, 108–21; Higginson, *Thomas Wentworth Higginson*, 403–09; Edelstein, *Strange Enthusiasm*, 22, 81, 91.

42. Higginson, *Carlyle's Laugh*, 249–67.

43. Edelstein, *Strange Enthusiasm*, 25–26, 149–51, 242; Meyer, *Colonel of the Black Regiment*, 108–15, 167–73; Higginson, *Thomas Wentworth Higginson*, 403–09.

44. Forten, "Life on the Sea Islands," 668; "Letters of Dr. Rogers," 340; Looby, *Journal and Letters*, 72, 75–78; Stevenson, *Journals*, 3–49, 428–29, 431, 433, 434; Rose, *Rehearsal for Reconstruction*, 78–79; Russell Duncan, ed., *Blue-Eyed Child of Fortune: The Civil War Letters of Colonel Robert Gould Shaw* (Athens, Ga., and London, 1992), 372.

45. Stamford *Advocate*, 2 January 1863; Stevenson, *Journals*, 429, 430, 433, 456; Looby, *Journal and Letters*, 345; Duncan, *Blue-Eyed Child of Fortune*, 372; Edelstein, *Strange Enthusiasm*, 97.

46. Boston *Commonwealth*, 7 February 1863; Forten, "Life on the Sea Islands," 669; Looby, *Journal and Letters*, 72, 75; Pearson, *Letters from Port Royal*, 128, 133, 134; Stevenson, *Journals*, 434.

47. Looby, *Journal and Letters*, 79; Higginson, *Army Life*, 59.

48. Boston *Commonwealth*, 7 February 1863; Higginson, *Army Life*, 59.

Chapter Two **PORT ROYAL ISLAND AND THE ST. MARY'S RIVER, JANUARY 2–FEBRUARY 15**

1. Boston *Commonwealth*, 7 February 1863; *Liberator*, 10 April 1863; New York *Daily Tribune*, 28 January 1863: Philadelphia *Daily Evening Bulletin*, 30 March 1863; Coffin, *Four Years of Fighting*, 245–47; "Letters of Dr. Rogers," 361; Looby, *Journal and Letters*, 46–47, 54, 251; Camp Inspection Return, 1st South Carolina Infantry, 3 March 1863, United States Sanitary Commission Records, New York Public Library.

2. Boston *Commonwealth*, 7 February 1863; Hartford *Daily Times*, 16 January 1863; *Liberator*, 10 April 1863; New York *Daily Tribune*, 26 December 1862, 28 January 1863; "Under the Palmetto," *Continental Monthly*, 4 (1863): 202; Looby, *Journal and Letters*, 80, 251; Pearson, *Letters from Port Royal*, 133; Keith P. Wilson, *Campfires of Free-*

dom: The Camp Life of Black Soldiers During the Civil War (Kent, Ohio, 2002), 8–9.

3. *Liberator*, 10 April 1863; "Letters of Dr. Rogers," 343; Looby, *Journal and Letters*, 70, 80; Camp Inspection Return, 1st South Carolina Infantry, 3 March 1863, United States Sanitary Commission Records.

4. *Liberator*, 10 April 1863; Stamford *Advocate*, 2 January 1863; Looby, *Journal and Letters*, 65, 80, 251, 261; "Under the Palmetto," 202; Schwartz, *Woman Doctor's Civil War*, 42; Camp Inspection Return, 1st South Carolina Infantry, 3 March 1863, United States Sanitary Commission Records; Susie King Taylor, *Reminiscences of My Life in Camp with the 33rd United States Colored Troops, Late 1st S.C. Volunteers* (Boston, 1902; reprint, Patricia W. Romero, ed., New York, 1988), 52; "Letters of Dr. Rogers," 339; school record of 1st South Carolina Regiment, 1862–63, Esther Hill Hawks Papers, Library of Congress, Washington. On education in the camps of black soldiers, see Wilson, *Campfires of Freedom*, 82–108.

5. Looby, *Journal and Letters*, 70–71, 86, 255–56, 287; Edelstein, *Strange Enthusiasm*, 152, 195, 218, 247, 249, 252.

6. Berlin, *Black Military Experience*, 2–3, 5–6, 37–38; Howard C. Westwood, "Generals David Hunter and Rufus Saxton and Black Soldiers," *South Carolina Historical Magazine*, 86 (1985): 165–68, 174; Gerald Robbins, "The Recruitment and Arming of Negroes in the South Carolina Sea Islands—1862–1865," *Negro History Bulletin*, 28 (1965): 150–51. General studies of the recruitment and employment of black troops in the Civil War include George W. Williams, *A History of the Negro Troops in the War of the Rebellion, 1861–1865* (New York, 1888); Benjamin Quarles, *The Negro in the Civil War* (Boston, 1953; reprint, New York, 1989); Dudley Taylor Cornish, *The Sable Arm: Negro Troops in the Union Army, 1861–1865* (New York, 1956; reprint, New York, 1966); Hondon B. Hargrove, *Black Union Soldiers in the Civil War* (Jefferson, N.C., and London, 1988); Joseph T. Glatthaar, *Forged in Battle: The Civil War Alliance of Black Soldiers and White Officers* (New York, 1990); and Noah Andre Trudeau, *Like Men of War: Black Troops in the Civil War, 1862–1865* (Boston and other cities, 1998). On Hunter, see Edward A. Miller, Jr., *Lincoln's Abolitionist General: The Biography of David Hunter* (Columbia, S.C., 1997).

7. Higginson, *Army Life*, 260–61; Berlin, *Black Military Experience*, 38–39; Westwood, "Generals Hunter and Saxton and Black Soldiers," 167–72; Robbins, "Recruitment and Arming of Negroes," 151.

8. Thomas Wentworth Higginson, "The First Black Regiment," *Outlook*, 59 (1898): 522; Berlin, *Black Military Experience*, 39; Westwood, "Generals Hunter and Saxton and Black Soldiers," 174–76; Robbins, "Recruitment and Arming of Negroes," 151, 163.

9. Higginson, "First Black Regiment," 524; *War of the Rebellion*, Series One, 14: 377–78; Berlin, *Black Military Experience*, 39; Westwood, "Generals Hunter and Saxton and Black Soldiers," 172–73, 176–81; Robbins, "Recruitment and Arming of Negroes," 163–64; Trudeau, *Like Men of War*, 17–18.

10. Robbins, "Recruitment and Arming of Negroes," 164; Stevenson, *Journals*, 406; Pearson, *Letters from Port Royal*, 100, 102; New York *Daily Tribune*, 4, 16, 26 December 1862; Rose, *Rehearsal for Reconstruction*, 191–93; Higginson, *Army Life*, 27–29; Looby, *Journal and Letters*, 42, 44–45, 243–47; Edelstein, *Strange Enthusiasm*, 171, 255–56; James H. Fowler file, 33rd Regiment, Compiled Military Service Records of Volunteer Union Soldiers Who Served with the United States Colored Troops:

Infantry Organizations, 31st Through 35th, M1992, National Archives, Washington (hereinafter cited as CMSR).

11. Looby, *Journal and Letters*, 80, 250; Higginson, *Army Life*, 263–64; *War of the Rebellion*, Series Three, 4: 1027, 5: 660; Cornish, *Sable Arm*, 67, 78, 80, 92–93, 95; Trudeau, *Like Men of War*, 13–16, 24–27; Hargrove, *Black Union Soldiers*, 51–68.

12. Thomas Wentworth Higginson to Thaddeus Stevens, 20 June 1864, Thaddeus Stevens Papers, Library of Congress, Washington; *Supplement to the Official Records of the Union and Confederate Armies*, 83 vols. to date (Wilmington, N.C., 1994–), 77: 740; *The Independent* (New York), 27 November 1862; *Liberator*, 6 February 1863; Schwartz, *Woman Doctor's Civil War*, 37–38; Etrulia P. Dozier, "Black Union Soldiers: Who Were the Civil War Black Soldiers?," typescript, South Caroliniana Library, University of South Carolina; Daniel L. Schafer, "Freedom Was as Close as the River: The Blacks of Northeast Florida and the Civil War," in *Civil War Times in St. Augustine* (Port Salerno, Fla., 1998), 96–97, 105; Stevenson, *Journals*, 425.

13. *Liberator*, 6 February, 10 April 1863; Niven, *Chase Papers*, 4: 4; Gannett and Hale, "Freedmen at Port Royal," 27; Pearson, *Letters from Port Royal*, 96–97, 100–01, 103.

14. Boston *Commonwealth*, 7 February 1863; *Independent*, 27 November 1862; *Liberator*, 12 December 1862; *Zion's Herald and Wesleyan Journal*, 24 June 1863; Berlin, *Black Military Experience*, 777; Looby, *Journal and Letters*, 66; Wilson, *Campfires of Freedom*, 182–83.

15. Herbert G. Gutman, *The Black Family in Slavery and Freedom, 1750–1925* (New York, 1976).

16. *Liberator*, 6 February 1863; Berlin, *Black Military Experience*, 60; *Freedmen of South Carolina*, 19; *War of the Rebellion*, Series Three, 3: 20; Looby, *Journal and Letters*, 54, 59–60, 263.

17. Looby, *Journal and Letters*, 80, 101; *Freedmen of South Carolina*, 13; Taylor, *Reminiscences*, 42; Higginson, "First Black Regiment," 531; Higginson, *Army Life*, 233, 234.

18. Looby, *Journal and Letters*, 55; Robbins, "Recruitment and Arming of Negroes," 164; *Liberator*, 6 February 1863; Berlin, *Black Military Experience*, 60; New York *Evening Post*, 15 April 1863.

19. Higginson, *Army Life*, 235–36; John D. Hayes, ed., *Samuel Francis Du Pont: A Selection from His Civil War Letters*, 3 vols. (Ithaca, N.Y., 1969), 2: 157; "Letters of Dr. Rogers," 345.

20. Looby, *Journal and Letters*, 88, 156; Higginson, *Army Life*, 73–74; Prince Rivers file, 33rd Regiment, CMSR; Descriptive Book of Company A, 33rd USCT Infantry, Regimental Records, RAGO; pension file of Prince Rivers, Company A, 1st South Carolina/33rd USCT Infantry, Civil War Pension Files, RG 15, National Archives, Washington; Edward W. Hooper to Robert W. Hooper, 23 January 1863, Hooper Papers; *Freedmen of South Carolina*, 19; New York *Daily Tribune*, 14 January 1863; Pearson, *Letters from Port Royal*, 104, 131; "Letters of Dr. Rogers," 357.

21. *Independent*, 27 November 1862; Pearson, *Letters from Port Royal*, 104; "Letters of Dr. Rogers," 357; Looby, *Journal and Letters*, 172, 174–75.

22. Looby, *Journal and Letters*, 48–50, 248, 249; Cato Wareing file, 33rd Regiment, CMSR; Descriptive Book of Company F, 33rd USCT Infantry, Regimental Records, RAGO; pension file of Cato Wareing, Company F, 1st South Carolina/33rd USCT Infantry, Civil War Pension Files; "Letters of Dr. Rogers," 362.

23. "Letters of Dr. Rogers," 362–63.

24. Ibid., 363–64.

25. *War of the Rebellion*, Series One, 14: 377–78, Series Three, 4: 1027; Westwood, "Generals Hunter and Saxton and Black Soldiers," 180–81.

26. Boston *Commonwealth*, 7 February 1863; New York *Daily Tribune*, 26 December 1862; Looby, *Journal and Letters*, 47–48.

27. *War of the Rebellion*, Series One, 14: 189–92; Boston *Commonwealth*, 22 November 1862; *Liberator*, 12 December 1862; New York *Daily Tribune*, 17 November 1862; Schwartz, *Woman Doctor's Civil War*, 40–41.

28. *War of the Rebellion*, Series One, 14: 192–94; Boston *Commonwealth*, 27 December 1862; Edward W. Hooper to Samuel Hooper, 5 January 1863, Hooper Papers.

29. *Liberator*, 12 December 1862; Thomas Wentworth Higginson to James Rogers, 24 November 1862, T. W. Higginson Papers, American Antiquarian Society, Worcester, Massachusetts.

30. *Liberator*, 6 February 1863; Thomas Wentworth Higginson to James Rogers, 24 November 1862, Higginson Papers, American Antiquarian Society; Looby, *Journal and Letters*, 151, 245; Higginson, *Army Life*, 237.

31. Washington *Daily Morning Chronicle*, 5 March 1863; Buckingham, *All's for the Best*, 221; Looby, *Journal and Letters*, 151; Higginson, *Army Life*, 237; Berlin, *Black Military Experience*, 567; *War of the Rebellion*, Series One, 15: 906–08; Glatthaar, *Forged in Battle*, 201–02.

32. *War of the Rebellion*, Series Three, 5: 118, 660–61; Cornish, *Sable Arm*, 95–96, 99, 113; Berlin, *Black Military Experience*, 7–9, 10; Trudeau, *Like Men of War*, 18–19; David Herbert Donald, *Lincoln* (New York and other cities, 1995), 366–67, 429–31.

33. *Liberator*, 12, 19 December 1862; *Independent*, 20, 27 November 1862; New York *Daily Tribune*, 17 November 1862; Boston *Commonwealth*, 22 November 1862; Washington *Daily Morning Chronicle*, 8 January 1863.

34. Cornish, *Sable Arm*, 52, 81–82; Trudeau, *Like Men of War*, 18; New York *Times*, 15 August 1862; James M. McPherson, *The Negro's Civil War: How American Negroes Felt and Acted During the War for the Union* (New York, 1967), 163–64; Robbins, "Recruitment and Arming of Negroes," 164; New York *Evening Post*, 28 January 1863; Washington *Evening Star*, 24 March 1863.

35. Pearson, *Letters from Port Royal*, 107–08; Hartford *Daily Times*, 16 January, 14 February 1863; Looby, *Journal and Letters*, 54, 209; New York *Evening Post*, 28 January 1863; Port Royal *New South*, 4 October 1862; William Todd, *The Seventy-ninth Highlanders New York Volunteers in the War of the Rebellion, 1861–1865* (Albany, N.Y., 1886), 170; Bingham, *Young Quartermaster*, 162.

36. McPherson, *Negro's Civil War*, 161–63; Cornish, *Sable Arm*, 94–99; New York *Daily Tribune*, 26 December 1862; New York *Times*, 21 August 1862.

37. Edelstein, *Strange Enthusiasm*, 156–59, 186–91, 252–55; Boston *Commonwealth*, 7 February 1863.

38. Looby, *Journal and Letters*, 82, 89, 241, 252, 287; "Letters of Dr. Rogers," 338; Higginson, *Thomas Wentworth Higginson*, 217.

39. Rossbach, *Ambivalent Conspirators*, passim; W. Scott Poole, "Memory and the Abolitionist Heritage: Thomas Wentworth Higginson and the Uncertain Meaning of the Civil War," *Civil War History*, 51 (2005): 207–08; Looby, *Journal and Letters*, 83, 248,

252, 253; General Order No. 1, 25 November 1862, Order Book, 33rd USCT Infantry, Regimental Records, RAGO; *Liberator*, 6 February 1863; *War of the Rebellion*, Series Three, 3: 435; Duncan, *Blue-Eyed Child of Fortune*, 339; Boston *Commonwealth*, 14 February 1863; Forten, "Life on the Sea Islands," 669; Edward W. Hooper to Samuel Hooper, 5 January 1863, Hooper Papers.

40. Looby, *Journal and Letters*, 145, 176–77, 281.

41. Edelstein, *Strange Enthusiasm*, 122, 141–42, 176–77, 185, 257, 326–28; Rossbach, *Ambivalent Conspirators*, 148, 169, 182–84, 268–69.

42. Higginson, *Army Life*, chapter 12; Looby, *Journal and Letters*, 45, 46, 47, 48, 57, 67, 69, 71, 85, 252, 253; Thomas Wentworth Higginson to James Rogers, 24 November 1862, Higginson Papers, American Antiquarian Society; Edelstein, *Strange Enthusiasm*, 257; Keith Wilson, "In the Shadow of John Brown: The Military Service of Colonels Thomas Higginson, James Montgomery, and Robert Shaw in the Department of the South," in John David Smith, ed., *Black Soldiers in Blue: African-American Troops in the Civil War Era* (Chapel Hill, N.C., and London, 2002), 315.

43. Looby, *Journal and Letters*, 67, 106; Berlin, *Black Military Experience*, 60; Wilson, *Campfires of Freedom*, 17–24.

44. *War of the Rebellion*, Series Three, 3: 439; Boston *Commonwealth*, 7 February 1863; Looby, *Journal and Letters*, 71; Wilson, "In the Shadow of John Brown," 316.

45. Looby, *Journal and Letters*, 65, 143, 277; "Letters of Dr. Rogers," 360; school record of 1st South Carolina Regiment, 1862–63, Hawks Papers; Pearson, *Letters from Port Royal*, 74; Higginson, *Army Life*, 231–32.

46. Looby, *Journal and Letters*, 53, 54.

47. Ibid., 54, 75, 80, 88; Higginson, *Army Life*, 239–40, 242, 244; Higginson, "First Black Regiment," 528; Camp Inspection Return, 1st South Carolina Infantry, 3 March 1863, United States Sanitary Commission Records; Berlin, *Black Military Experience*, 58–60; Pearson, *Letters from Port Royal*, 134; *Liberator*, 6 February 1863; New York *Daily Tribune*, 26 December 1862, 31 January 1863; General Order No. 8, 24 December 1862, General Order No. 11, 1 January 1863, General Order No. 24, 13 February 1863, 33rd USCT Infantry, Regimental Records, RAGO.

48. Edward W. Hooper to Samuel Hooper, 5 January 1863, Hooper Papers; "Letters of Dr. Rogers," 338; Higginson, *Thomas Wentworth Higginson*, 218; Forten, "Life on the Sea Islands," 669; Taylor, *Reminiscences*, 88; Boston *Commonwealth*, 7 February 1863; *Liberator*, 6 February 1863; Camp Inspection Return, 1st South Carolina Infantry, 3 March 1863, United States Sanitary Commission Records.

49. Looby, *Journal and Letters*, 50, 67; Boston *Commonwealth*, 7 February 1863; Augusta (Maine) *Kennebec Journal*, 9 January 1863; Farmington (Maine) *Chronicle*, 22 January 1863; Bangor (Maine) *Daily Whig and Courier*, 20 January 1863; Higginson, "First Black Regiment," 526; Glatthaar, *Forged in Battle*, 11–12, 31–32, 181–87, 228–29.

50. Looby, *Journal and Letters*, 45, 50–51, 68; Thomas Wentworth Higginson to James Rogers, 24 November 1862, Higginson Papers, American Antiquarian Society; Higginson, *Thomas Wentworth Higginson*, 217.

51. Looby, *Journal and Letters*, 50–51, 67, 87; Higginson, *Thomas Wentworth Higginson*, 217–18; Higginson, *Army Life*, 244.

52. Looby, *Journal and Letters*, 45, 45n., 81, 82, 85, 100, 150, 259; Special Order No. 1, 12 January 1863, Special Order No. 2, 26 January 1863, Records of the U.S. Army

Continental Commands, RG 393, National Archives, Washington (hereinafter cited as RUSACC), Pt. 2, E-2456; Thomas Wentworth Higginson to James Rogers, 24 November 1862, Higginson Papers, American Antiquarian Society; *Liberator*, 6 February 1863.

53. Looby, *Journal and Letters*, 147–48, 156, 169, 171, 178, 202; Higginson, *Army Life*, 165, 256, 260, 263; Higginson, "First Black Regiment," 521–24; Charles T. Trowbridge file, 33rd Regiment, CMSR; *Liberator*, 21 November 1862; Hayes, *Du Pont Letters*, 2: 142; Taylor, *Reminiscences*, 41, 111–12; *War of the Rebellion*, Series One, 6: 185, Series Three, 2: 30; Cheryl Trowbridge-Miller, "Charles Tyler Trowbridge," www.lwfaam .net/cwdata/ctt_bio.htm.

54. Looby, *Journal and Letters*, 45, 45n., 50, 51, 81–82, 139, 143–44, 245, 250, 277; Higginson, *Army Life*, 255; Stevenson, *Journals*, 424, 431; *Liberator*, 10 April 1863; Port Royal *New South*, 17 January 1863; *New York World*, 29 January 1863; New York *Daily Tribune*, 29 January 1863; Liberty Billings file, John D. Strong file, 33rd Regiment, CMSR.

55. Looby, *Journal and Letters*, 151; Higginson, *Carlyle's Laugh*, 179; "Letters of Dr. Rogers," 348, 354; Boston *Commonwealth*, 7 February 1863; *War of the Rebellion*, Series One, 15: 908; Glatthaar, *Forged in Battle*, 201–04.

56. Looby, *Journal and Letters*, 81, 82, 257–58; Edward W. Hooper to Marian Adams, 7 January 1863, Hooper Papers; Stamford *Advocate*, 2 January 1863; Schwartz, *Woman Doctor's Civil War*, 33.

57. Beaufort (South Carolina) *Free South*, 17 January 1863; Charleston (South Carolina) *Daily Courier*, 27 February 1863; Philadelphia *Daily Evening Bulletin*, 30 March 1863; W. W. H. Davis, *History of the 104th Pennsylvania Regiment, from August 22nd, 1861, to September 30th, 1864* (Philadelphia, 1866), 183; Forten, "Life on the Sea Islands," 587; Schwartz, *Woman Doctor's Civil War*, 33–34; Farmington *Franklin Patriot*, 9 January 1863; P. J. Staudenraus, ed., "Occupied Beaufort, 1863: A War Correspondent's View," *South Carolina Historical Magazine*, 64 (1963): 136–40; Stevenson, *Journals*, 443; Esther Hill Hawks to Mrs. Secretary, 26 November 1862, J. Milton Hawks to Esther Hill Hawks, 11 September 1862, Hawks Papers.

58. Looby, *Journal and Letters*, 45, 52, 71, 81, 248, 253, 254; Stevenson, *Journals*, 405; Thomas W. Higginson file, 33rd Regiment, CMSR.

59. Ezra J. Warner, *Generals in Blue: Lives of the Union Commanders* (Baton Rouge, 1964), 420–21; Higginson, *Carlyle's Laugh*, 175–76, 179; Higginson, "First Black Regiment," 526; Berlin, *Wartime Genesis of Free Labor*, 88, 98–99, 234–35; Looby, *Journal and Letters*, 52, 99, 99n., 142; *Independent*, 27 November 1862; Bartholomew S. De Forest, *Random Sketches and Wandering Thoughts* (Albany, N.Y., 1866), 42.

60. Looby, *Journal and Letters*, 104, 256, 275, 290; *Liberator*, 24 October 1862; *Independent*, 27 November 1862; Port Royal *New South*, 22 November 1862; *War of the Rebellion*, Series Three, 4: 1027, 1029, 1031; Boston *Commonwealth*, 24 January 1863.

61. Looby, *Journal and Letters*, 45, 81, 248; Pearson, *Letters from Port Royal*, 97–98, 102; Berlin, *Black Military Experience*, 53–54; *War of the Rebellion*, Series Three, 4: 1027–29; J. Milton Hawks to Esther Hill Hawks, 10 July 1862, Hawks Papers.

62. Looby, *Journal and Letters*, 52, 183, 186, 248, 253, 279; Pearson, *Letters from Port Royal*, 84, 107–08; "Letters of Dr. Rogers," 342; Higginson, "First Black Regiment," 526, 528; Higginson, *Carlyle's Laugh*, 179; L. B. Russell to John A. Andrew, 14 November 1862, John A. Andrew Papers, Massachusetts Historical Society, Boston; Bingham, *Young*

Quartermaster, 162; Niven, *Chase Papers*, 3: 353; Berlin, *Wartime Genesis of Free Labor*, 218n.; *Liberator*, 6 February 1863.

63. Looby, *Journal and Letters*, 76, 81, 163, 186, 187, 248; Higginson, "First Black Regiment," 526.

64. Looby, *Journal and Letters*, 81; "Letters of Dr. Rogers," 341; Edelstein, *Strange Enthusiasm*, 149, 183, 259.

65. Looby, *Journal and Letters*, 80, 82, 250, 253, 260; Boston *Commonwealth*, 7 February 1863; Higginson, "First Black Regiment," 526–27; Camp Inspection Return, 1st South Carolina Infantry, 3 March 1863, United States Sanitary Commission Records; *Liberator*, 6 February 1863; New York *Daily Tribune*, 31 January 1863.

66. Looby, *Journal and Letters*, 89, 90, 260 (the date of the event is mistranscribed as 19 January in this source); Boston *Commonwealth*, 14 February 1863; Hartford *Daily Times*, 4 February 1863; New York *Daily Tribune*, 31 January 1863; "Letters of Dr. Rogers," 344; Port Royal *New South*, 17 January 1863.

67. Looby, *Journal and Letters*, 70, 90, 92; Boston *Commonwealth*, 7, 14, February 1863; *War of the Rebellion*, Series One, 6: 264; Taylor, *Reminiscences*, 41–42.

68. Looby, *Journal and Letters*, 89, 90; Boston *Commonwealth*, 14 February 1863; Hartford *Daily Times*, 4 February 1863; New York *Daily Tribune*, 31 January 1863; "Letters of Dr. Rogers," 345, 346; *Liberator*, 6 February 1863.

69. Looby, *Journal and Letters*, 88–89, 90; Boston *Commonwealth*, 14 February 1863; New York *Daily Tribune*, 31 January 1863; "Letters of Dr. Rogers," 345, 346; *Liberator*, 6 February 1863.

70. Looby, *Journal and Letters*, 91; New York *World*, 29 January 1863; Miller, *Lincoln's Abolitionist General*, 97–106, 113–15, 122–23, 128; Berlin, *Black Military Experience*, 51; *War of the Rebellion*, Series One, 14: 599; Berlin, *Destruction of Slavery*, 108–09.

71. Looby, *Journal and Letters*, 91, 92; Hartford *Daily Times*, 30 January 1863; New York *Daily Tribune*, 28 January 1863.

72. Looby, *Journal and Letters*, 91; Miller, *Lincoln's Abolitionist General*, 52, 129; Higginson, *Army Life*, 76; "Letters of Dr. Rogers," 347; New York *Times*, 28 January 1863; *Liberator*, 6 February 1863; New York *Daily Tribune*, 28 January 1863.

73. Looby, *Journal and Letters*, 92; Higginson, *Army Life*, 76–77.

74. Higginson, *Army Life*, 80–81; "Letters of Dr. Rogers," 348; Edward W. Hooper to Robert W. Hooper, 23 January 1863, Hooper Papers; New York *Evening Post*, 10 February 1863; *Supplement to the Official Records*, 77: 734–48, passim; Berlin, *Destruction of Slavery*, 105, 122–23.

75. Higginson, *Army Life*, 79–80; Looby, *Journal and Letters*, 93; Edward W. Hooper to Robert W. Hooper, 23 January 1863, Hooper Papers.

76. Higginson, *Army Life*, 80, 83–84, 85; "Letters of Dr. Rogers," 347, 348–49, 353; *War of the Rebellion*, Series One, 14: 195, 197.

77. Higginson, *Army Life*, 84–85; New York *Evening Post*, 10 February 1863.

78. Higginson, *Army Life*, 84–85, 90–91; "Letters of Dr. Rogers," 349.

79. Higginson, *Army Life*, 85–88, 89; "Letters of Dr. Rogers," 350; *War of the Rebellion*, Series One, 14: 195.

80. Higginson, *Army Life*, 88; *War of the Rebellion*, Series One, 14: 195.

81. Higginson, *Army Life*, 89–91; Looby, *Journal and Letters*, 96; "Letters of Dr. Rogers," 350.

82. Higginson, *Army Life*, 91–92; "Letters of Dr. Rogers," 350.

83. Higginson, *Army Life*, 92–93; Looby, *Journal and Letters*, 93; "Letters of Dr. Rogers," 350–51.

84. Higginson, *Army Life*, 93–94; "Letters of Dr. Rogers," 351; *War of the Rebellion*, Series One, 14: 196.

85. Higginson, *Army Life*, 94–96; Looby, *Journal and Letters*, 93–94, 102; "Letters of Dr. Rogers," 352, 353; *War of the Rebellion*, Series One, 14: 195.

86. Higginson, *Army Life*, 79, 96–97; Looby, *Journal and Letters*, 94–95.

87. Higginson, *Army Life*, 97–98; "Letters of Dr. Rogers," 353; *War of the Rebellion*, Series One, 14: 197.

88. Higginson, *Army Life*, 99–100.

89. Ibid., 100–03; Looby, *Journal and Letters*, 96; "Letters of Dr. Rogers," 353, 357; *War of the Rebellion*, Series One, 14: 195–96.

90. Higginson, *Army Life*, 103; "Letters of Dr. Rogers," 355; *War of the Rebellion*, Series One, 14: 195–98.

91. Higginson, *Army Life*, 103; Looby, *Journal and Letters*, 96–97; "Letters of Dr. Rogers," 356; *War of the Rebellion*, Series One, 14: 194.

92. Higginson, *Army Life*, 90, 96–97, 98–99, 103–04; Looby, *Journal and Letters*, 96, 261; "Letters of Dr. Rogers," 354, 355–56; *War of the Rebellion*, Series One, 14: 195–98; Stevenson, *Journals*, 447; Schwartz, *Woman Doctor's Civil War*, 43; Robert Certain (*sic*) file, 33rd Regiment, CMSR.

93. Higginson, *Army Life*, 86, 88; Looby, *Journal and Letters*, 95, 102.

94. Higginson, *Army Life*, 104; Looby, *Journal and Letters*, 95–96, 101; "Letters of Dr. Rogers," 357; Pearson, *Letters from Port Royal*, 153; Edward L. Pierce, "The Freedmen at Port Royal," *Atlantic Monthly*, 12 (1863): 313; Schwartz, *Woman Doctor's Civil War*, 43; Stevenson, *Journals*, 445; *War of the Rebellion*, Series One, 14: 195–98.

95. Hartford *Daily Times*, 10 February 1863; Baltimore *American and Commercial Advertiser*, 14 February, 2 March 1863; Buckingham, *All's for the Best*, 221–22; Jared A. Abell to Hannah, 8 March 1863, Jared Andrus Abell Letters, South Caroliniana Library, University of South Carolina.

96. Edward W. Hooper to Robert W. Hooper, 23 February 1863, Hooper Papers; Looby, *Journal and Letters*, 98, 258, 262; "Letters of Dr. Rogers," 359, 361; Higginson, *Army Life*, 104–05; Hartford *Daily Times*, 27 February 1863.

97. Looby, *Journal and Letters*, 68–69, 98, 99, 262, 291; George W. Dewhurst file, 33rd Regiment, CMSR; Edward W. Hooper to Marian Adams, 15 February 1863, and to Robert W. Hooper, 23 February 1863, Hooper Papers.

98. Looby, *Journal and Letters*, 99–102, 262; *War of the Rebellion*, Series One, 14: 197–98.

Chapter Three **HILTON HEAD, FEBRUARY 16**

1. Higginson, *Army Life*, 32–33, 106; Looby, *Journal and Letters*, 103, 262; Baltimore *American and Commercial Advertiser*, 2, 18 March 1863; Philadelphia *Inquirer*, 6 September 1862; Hartford *Daily Times*, 27 February 1863; Davis, *History of the 104th Pennsylvania*, 181; Richard Skinner to William Johnson, 27 January 1863, Richard Skinner Letters, Southern Historical Collection, University of North Carolina, Chapel Hill; *Official Records of the Navies*, Series One, 12: xxi, 13: 465–66.

2. Baltimore *American and Commercial Advertiser*, 2, 18 March 1863; Philadelphia *Inquirer*, 6 September 1862; Charleston *Daily Courier*, 27 February 1863; Davis, *History of the 104th Pennsylvania*, 180.

3. Baltimore *American and Commercial Advertiser*, 2, 18 March 1863; Philadelphia *Press*, 2 April 1863; Charleston *Daily Courier*, 27 February 1863; Davis, *History of the 104th Pennsylvania*, 180; *American Missionary*, 7 (1863): 89; *War of the Rebellion*, Series One, 14: 434–35.

4. Higginson, *Army Life*, 106–07; Philadelphia *Press*, 2 April 1863; Hayes, *Du Pont Letters*, 2: 44; Richard Skinner to William Johnson, 27 January, 24 March 1863, Skinner Letters.

5. Higginson, *Army Life*, 107, 131; Looby, *Journal and Letters*, 91, 103, 143, 273, 280–81, 291; Higginson, *Carlyle's Laugh*, 176–77; Hayes, *Du Pont Letters*, 2: 45, 127, 373; Philadelphia *Press*, 2 April 1863; Duncan, *Blue-Eyed Child of Fortune*, 340, 350; Niven, *Chase Papers*, 3: 199.

6. Higginson, *Army Life*, 107; Port Royal *New South*, 6 December 1862; Miller, *Lincoln's Abolitionist General*, 66. On Halpine, see Charles Graham Halpine, *The Life and Adventures, Songs, Services, and Speeches of Private Miles O'Reilly* (New York, 1864) and William Hanchett, *Irish: Charles G. Halpine in Civil War America* (Syracuse, N.Y., 1970).

7. Higginson, *Army Life*, 107; Looby, *Journal and Letters*, 262; Higginson, "First Black Regiment," 530; *War of the Rebellion*, Series One, 14: 434–35.

8. Looby, *Journal and Letters*, 199; *War of the Rebellion*, Series One, 14: 194, 197–98, 423, Series Three, 2: 663, 3: 20; Higginson, *Army Life*, 107, 114; Hayes, *Du Pont Letters*, 2: 326–27; New York *Evening Post*, 8 April 1863; Higginson, "First Black Regiment," 530; James Montgomery to Mrs. George L. Stearns, 25 April 1863, George L. and Mary E. Stearns Papers, Kansas State Historical Society, Topeka.

9. *War of the Rebellion*, Series One, 14: 1020–21.

10. *Liberator*, 6 February 1863; *War of the Rebellion*, Series One, 14: 198; Looby, *Journal and Letters*, 87–88, 105–06; Higginson, *Army Life*, 107.

11. *War of the Rebellion*, Series One, 14: 194–98, Series Three, 3: 20; Looby, *Journal and Letters*, 102; Cornish, *Sable Arm*, 98–99; New York *Times*, 30, 31 January 1863; Philadelphia *Inquirer*, 31 January 1863.

12. *War of the Rebellion*, Series One, 14: 189–91, 192–93, 194–98, Series Three, 3: 20; New York *Daily Tribune*, 31 January, 11 February 1863; New York *Evening Post*, 28 January 1863; New York *Times*, 10 February 1863; Boston *Daily Advertiser*, 13 February 1863; Chicago *Tribune*, 31 January 1863; Baltimore *American and Commercial Advertiser*, 31 January 1863; Hartford *Daily Times*, 16 February 1863; New York *World*, 24 January 1863; Wilson, "In the Shadow of John Brown," 314; Glatthaar, *Forged in Battle*, 123.

13. Boston *Daily Advertiser*, 13 February 1863; New York *Times*, 10 February 1863; Glatthaar, *Forged in Battle*, 123; Cornish, *Sable Arm*, 96–98.

14. Higginson, *Army Life*, 107; George E. Buker, *Jacksonville: Riverport-Seaport* (Columbia, S.C., 1992), chapters 1–6; Arch Fredric Blakey, Ann Smith Lainhart, and Winston Bryant Stephens, Jr., eds., *Rose Cottage Chronicles: Civil War Letters of the Bryant-Stephens Families of North Florida* (Gainesville, Fla., 1998), 4, 11–12; Looby, *Journal and Letters*, 100, 105–06, 199–200; *War of the Rebellion*, Series One, 14: 198, 423; "Letters of Dr. Rogers," 361–62; William Warren Rogers, ed., "Florida on the Eve of the Civil War as Seen by a Southern Reporter," *Florida Historical Quarterly*, 39 (1960–61): 157–58.

15. Buker, *Jacksonville*, 57–72; Browning, *Success Is All That Was Expected*, 104–05, 118, 121–23; *Official Records of the Navies*, Series One, 12: 772–73, 13: 243–44, 327, 387, 427, 436, 466, 470, 477, 521; Augusta (Georgia) *Daily Constitutionalist*, 1 April 1863.

16. Edwin C. Bearss, "Military Operations on the St. Johns, September–October 1862," *Florida Historical Quarterly*, 42 (1963–64): 232–47, 331–50; Richard A. Martin and Daniel L. Schafer, *Jacksonville's Ordeal by Fire: A Civil War History* (Jacksonville, Fla., 1984), 101–13, 115, 116; N. S. Snell to Charles Steedman, 14 October 1862, Charles Steedman Correspondence, File 00/488, Special Collections, University of Florida Library, Gainesville; *War of the Rebellion*, Series One, 35(1): 645; Philadelphia *Inquirer*, 6 September 1862; *Official Records of the Navies*, Series One, 13: 461, 489; Hayes, *Du Pont Letters*, 2: 326–27.

17. Higginson, *Army Life*, 107; *War of the Rebellion*, Series One, 14: 736, 772, 783, 838; William H. Nulty, *Confederate Florida: The Road to Olustee* (Tuscaloosa, Ala., 1990), 20, 22, 37–39; Ed Gleeson, *Erin Go Gray!: An Irish Rebel Trilogy* (Carmel, Ind., 1997), 3–11; *Norwich* log, 9 February 1863, Records of the Bureau of Naval Personnel, RG 24, National Archives, Washington (hereinafter cited as RBNP); Augusta *Daily Constitutionalist*, 1 April 1863; Philadelphia *Inquirer*, 13 February 1863; *Official Records of the Navies*, Series One, 13: 461; New York *Evening Post*, 13 February, 8 April 1863; Looby, *Journal and Letters*, 199.

18. Higginson, *Army Life*, 107; Martin and Schafer, *Jacksonville's Ordeal*, 75–89, 113–16; Bearss, "Military Operations on the St. Johns," 344–45, 347–48; *War of the Rebellion*, Series One, 6: 263.

19. Berlin, *Destruction of Slavery*, 106; *War of the Rebellion*, Series One, 14: 363–64, 394, Series Two, 5: 234; Looby, *Journal and Letters*, 96. On the role of the Department of the South in the Union war effort, see Hendricks, "Union Army Occupation."

20. Larry Eugene Rivers, *Slavery in Florida: Territorial Days to Emancipation* (Gainesville, Fla., 2000), 65, 70, 242–43; Julia Floyd Smith, *Slavery and Plantation Growth in Antebellum Florida, 1821–1860* (Gainesville, Fla., 1973), 10–11, 13, 26; Blakey, Lainhart, and Stephens, *Rose Cottage Chronicles*, 29; University of Virginia Geospatial and Statistical Data Center, *United States Historical Census Data Browser*, www.fisher.lib .virginia.edu/census/ (see 1860 census statistics of agriculture and slaves for the four counties along the St. John's River: Duval, Clay, St. John's, Putnam); Sam Bowers Hilliard, *Atlas of Antebellum Southern Agriculture* (Baton Rouge, 1984), 34, 42, 43; John Broward file, Case Files of Applications from Former Confederates for Presidential Pardons ("Amnesty Papers"), 1865–1867: Florida, M1003, National Archives, Washington; A. M. Reed Diary, 6 October 1862, typescript copy, Duke University Library; Samuel Fairbanks to George Fairbanks, 10, 24 July 1862, file 13, Fairbanks Collection, Special Collections Department, Florida State University Libraries, Tallahassee; *Official Records of the Navies*, Series One, 13: 147; *War of the Rebellion*, Series One: 14: 661, 53: 260; Martin and Schafer, *Jacksonville's Ordeal*, 100–101, 116, 117; Schafer, "Freedom Was as Close as the River," 93, 99, 103, 105; John E. Johns, *Florida During the Civil War* (Gainesville, Fla., 1963), 147.

21. *Official Records of the Navies*, Series One, 13: 83–84; *War of the Rebellion*, Series One, 14: 838, 53: 234; New York *Evening Post*, 12, 13 February 1863; New York *Daily Tribune*, 30 March 1864; Philadelphia *Inquirer*, 24 March 1864; Calvin Shedd to wife, 15 January 1863, Calvin Shedd Papers, Special Collections, University of Miami (available

at www.library.miami.edu/archives/shedd); Berlin, *Destruction of Slavery*, 138–39; Mary Elizabeth Dickison, *Dickison and His Men: Reminiscences of the War in Florida* (Louisville, Ky., 1890), 46–47; Martin and Schafer, *Jacksonville's Ordeal*, 99.

22. *Official Records of the Navies*, Series One, 13: 671; New York *Evening Post*, 16 April 1863; Edward W. Hooper to Robert W. Hooper, 23 January 1863, Hooper Papers; Lewis G. Schmidt, *The Civil War in Florida: A Military History*, 4 vols. (Allentown, Pa., 1991), 1: 493; Taylor, *Reminiscences*, 31–32; Blakey, Lainhart, and Stephens, *Rose Cottage Chronicles*, 163; F. L. Dancy file, Case Files of Applications for Pardons: Florida; "Letters of Dr. Rogers," 394; Berlin, *Destruction of Slavery*, 139; Tracy J. Revels, *Grander in Her Daughters: Florida's Women During the Civil War* (Columbia, S.C., 2004), 104.

23. *Official Records of the Navies*, Series One, 13: 108, 109, 147; Looby, *Journal and Letters*, 199; *War of the Rebellion*, Series One, 14: 387, 423; *Independent*, 6, 27 November 1862; Philadelphia *Inquirer*, 6 September 1862; Reed Diary, 4, 5, 7 October 1862; Samuel Fairbanks to George Fairbanks, 10 July 1862, file 13, Fairbanks Collection; N. S. Snell to Charles Steedman, 14 October 1862, Steedman Correspondence; Hayes, *Du Pont Letters*, 2: 120–21; Bearss, "Military Operations on the St. Johns," 347; Martin and Schafer, *Jacksonville's Ordeal*, 99, 116; Schmidt, *Civil War in Florida*, 1: 405; Schafer, "Freedom Was as Close as the River," 91–116; Rivers, *Slavery in Florida*, 230, 239; Revels, *Grander in Her Daughters*, 102–03.

24. *War of the Rebellion*, Series One, 14: 198–99, 35(2): 492, 53: 260, Series Four, 2: 487; New York *Evening Post*, 30 January, 8 April 1863; Savannah *Daily Morning News*, 10 April 1863; *Official Records of the Navies*, Series One, 13: 110, 437, 490; Looby, *Journal and Letters*, 199; Nulty, *Confederate Florida*, 61–65; George Winston Smith, "Carpetbag Imperialism in Florida, 1862–1868," *Florida Historical Quarterly*, 27 (1948–49): 107–08; John Solomon Otto, *Southern Agriculture During the Civil War Era, 1860–1880* (Westport, Conn., 1994), 16.

25. Higginson, *Army Life*, 107. The most comprehensive study of Lincoln's reconstruction policy is William C. Harris, *With Charity for All: Lincoln and the Restoration of the Union* (Lexington, Ky., 1997).

26. *War of the Rebellion*, Series One, 6: 251–52; New York *Evening Post*, 30 January 1863; Benjamin W. Thompson, "Flight from Florida," *Civil War Times Illustrated*, 12 (1973): 12–17; Anne Robinson Clancy, ed., *A Yankee in a Confederate Town: The Journal of Calvin L. Robinson* (Sarasota, Fla., 2002), 5–50; George H. Gordon, *A War Diary of Events in the War of the Great Rebellion, 1863–1865* (Boston, 1882), 301; Richard A. Martin, "Defeat in Victory: Yankee Experience in Early Civil War Jacksonville," *Florida Historical Quarterly*, 53 (1974–75): 1–17; Martin and Schafer, *Jacksonville's Ordeal*, 22–33, 42–43, 52–53, 68–75; Blakey, Lainhart, and Stephens, *Rose Cottage Chronicles*, 14; Smith, "Carpetbag Imperialism," 109; file of Anne Hurlburt, St. John's County, Florida, Settled Case Files for Claims Approved by the Southern Claims Commission, 1871 to 1880, E732, RG 217, National Archives, College Park, Maryland.

27. *War of the Rebellion*, Series One, 6: 130, 250–52, 53: 233–34, Series Two, 4: 47; *Official Records of the Navies*, Series One, 12: 599–600, 631–32, 698, 749; 13: 163, 245, 477; New York *Evening Post*, 30 January 1863; J. W. Pearson to John Milton, 8 April 1862, John Milton Letterbook, Governor's Office Letterbooks, 1836–1909, RG 101, Series 32, Florida State Archives, Tallahassee; Clancy, *Yankee in a Confederate Town*, 52–72;

Gordon, *War Diary*, 301; Martin, "Defeat in Victory," 17–28; Martin and Schafer, *Jacksonville's Ordeal*, 75–88, 94–95; Buker, *Jacksonville*, 62, 63, 64.

28. New York *Evening Post*, 10 February 1863; Benjamin R. McPherson to Theodore McPherson, 5 January 1863, George E. McPherson to Theodore McPherson, 6 January 1863, Theodore H. N. McPherson Family Papers, Library of Congress, Washington; James M. Hunter to John Milton, 27 April 1862, Milton Letterbook; Andrew Fairbanks to George Fairbanks, 4 February 1862, file 9, Fairbanks Collection; *Official Records of the Navies*, Series One, 13: 64, 220, 428, 436–37, 461, 465, 477, 521; "A Letter of Captain V. Chamberlain, 7th Connecticut Volunteers," *Florida Historical Quarterly*, 15 (1936–37): 93; Schmidt, *Civil War in Florida*, 1: 392, 405–06; Martin and Schafer, *Jacksonville's Ordeal*, 113–14, 118–19, 168, 169; Johns, *Florida During the Civil War*, 159–61, 174–78; William Watson Davis, *The Civil War and Reconstruction in Florida* (New York, 1913; reprint, Gainesville, Fla., 1964), 259–66; Buker, *Jacksonville*, 67–68; New York *World*, 24 March 1863. On hardships on the Confederate home front in general, see Charles W. Ramsdell, *Behind the Lines in the Southern Confederacy* (Baton Rouge, 1944; reprint, Baton Rouge, 1997). The standard study of the draft is Albert Burton Moore, *Conscription and Conflict in the Confederacy* (New York, 1924; reprint, Columbia, S.C., 1996).

29. Richard H. Abbott, *Cotton and Capital: Boston Businessmen and Antislavery Reform, 1854–1868* (Amherst, Mass., 1991), 28–49, 82–83; Robert L. Clarke, "Northern Plans for the Economic Invasion of Florida, 1862–1865," *Florida Historical Quarterly*, 28 (1949–50): 262–63; Eli Thayer to Abraham Lincoln, 12 October, 6, 28 November 1861, Abraham Lincoln Papers, Library of Congress, Washington; Smith, "Carpetbag Imperialism," 113–27; Martin and Schafer, *Jacksonville's Ordeal*, 123–24; New York *Times*, 25 January, 8 February 1863; Hilliard, *Atlas*, 26; New York *Evening Post*, 8 April 1863; Nulty, *Confederate Florida*, 20.

30. New York City citizens to Abraham Lincoln, 8 February 1863, L. D. Stickney to O. M. Browning, 11 June 1862, Florida state citizens to Abraham Lincoln, 5 December 1862, Lincoln Papers; New York *Evening Post*, 30 January, 6 February 1863; New York *Daily Tribune*, 10 February 1863; David Donald, ed., *Inside Lincoln's Cabinet: The Civil War Diaries of Salmon P. Chase* (New York, 1954), 155–56, 157; Howard K. Beale, ed., *Diary of Gideon Welles: Secretary of the Navy Under Lincoln and Johnson*, 3 vols. (New York, 1960), 1: 206; Smith, "Carpetbag Imperialism," 117–27; Martin and Schafer, *Jacksonville's Ordeal*, 122–23, 126–27; Martin, "Defeat in Victory," 30–32.

31. New York *Times*, 24 October 1862; New York *Evening Post*, 16 January, 6 February 1863; Smith, "Carpetbag Imperialism," 124–25; *Douglass' Monthly* (November 1862), 740; Philip S. Foner, ed., *The Life and Writings of Frederick Douglass*, 4 vols. (New York, 1950–55), 3: 41; David W. Blight, *Frederick Douglass' Civil War: Keeping Faith in Jubilee* (Baton Rouge and London, 1989), 122–47.

32. Higginson, *Army Life*, 106, 107; Eighth Census, 1860, Manuscript Returns of Free Inhabitants, Shelby County, Tennessee, p. 29/102, National Archives, Washington.

33. Smith, "Carpetbag Imperialism," 112; Jerrell H. Shofner, "Andrew Johnson and the Fernandina Unionists," *Prologue*, 10 (1978): 211; Berlin, *Wartime Genesis of Free Labor*, 101–04, 222n.; L. D. Stickney to Salmon P. Chase, 17 April 1863, Salmon P. Chase Papers, Library of Congress, Washington, D.C.

34. Higginson, *Army Life*, 107; Hayes, *Du Pont Letters*, 2: 326–27; "Tax Commissioners of Florida," U.S. House of Representatives Exec. Doc. No. 18, 38th Cong., 2d sess.

(Washington, 1865), 3, 71, 99, 100, 101; New York *Times*, 16 October 1862; Ovid L. Futch, "Salmon P. Chase and Civil War Politics in Florida," *Florida Historical Quarterly*, 32 (1953–54): 167–68; Jerrell H. Shofner, *Nor Is It Over Yet: Florida in the Era of Reconstruction, 1863–1877* (Gainesville, Fla., 1974), 5–6; Smith, "Carpetbag Imperialism," 116–17, 119–20.

35. "Tax Commissioners of Florida," 18, 65, 72, 97, 181; Smith, "Carpetbag Imperialism," 110–12; Shofner, *Nor Is It Over Yet*, 4; Futch, "Chase and Civil War Politics," 163–64; L. D. Stickney to Salmon P. Chase, 16 April 1863, Chase Papers; L. D. Stickney to Maunsel White, 18 August 1860, Maunsel White Papers, Southern Historical Collection, University of North Carolina, Chapel Hill; William Marvin to Abraham Lincoln, 24 July 1863, George Brainerd to Abraham Lincoln, 9 March 1864, Theodore Bissell to Harrison Reed, 2 April 1864, L. D. Stickney to O. M. Browning, 11 June 1862, Lincoln Papers; L. D. Stickney to Edward Everett Hale, 30 September 1863, New England Emigrant Aid Company Papers, Kansas State Historical Society, Topeka; Washington *Daily Morning Chronicle*, 8 January 1863; *War of the Rebellion*, Series Two, 2: 977; Edward W. Hooper to Robert W. Hooper, 2 January 1863, Hooper Papers.

36. Smith, "Carpetbag Imperialism," 275; Futch, "Chase and Civil War Politics," 163–66; *War of the Rebellion*, Series Two, 2: 980–81; L. D. Stickney to Abraham Lincoln, 17 May 1862, George Brainerd to Abraham Lincoln, 9 March 1864, Lincoln Papers; L. D. Stickney to Salmon P. Chase, 16 April 1863, Chase Papers; "Tax Commissioners of Florida," 3, 180, 181.

37. "Tax Commissioners of Florida," 3, 4, 7–8, 12, 14, 15, 16, 26, 67, 69, 99–100, 181; Futch, "Chase and Civil War Politics," 166–67; Shofner, *Nor Is It Over Yet*, 6; Smith, "Carpetbag Imperialism," 112–13, 260–62.

38. Futch, "Chase and Civil War Politics," 163; Looby, *Journal and Letters*, 113; Edward Everett Hale to L. D. Stickney, 23 September 1863, New England Emigrant Aid Company Papers; *American Missionary*, 7 (1863): 88; Hayes, *Du Pont Letters*, 2: 326–27; "Letters of Dr. Rogers," 348; Smith, "Carpetbag Imperialism," 262.

39. Higginson, *Army Life*, 107; *War of the Rebellion*, Series One, 14: 348, 447–48; Hayes, *Du Pont Letters*, 2: 45, 120; Miller, *Lincoln's Abolitionist General*, 79, 87.

40. *War of the Rebellion*, Series One, 6: 263, 14: 348, 424, Series Three, 2: 292.

41. Ibid., Series One, 14: 424; Looby, *Journal and Letters*, 263.

42. Washington *Daily National Intelligencer*, 16 March 1863; *War of the Rebellion*, Series One, 14: 377, 1020–21; *Liberator*, 6 February 1863.

43. C. M. Clay to Eli Thayer, 29 September 1862, Lincoln Papers.

44. Looby, *Journal and Letters*, 91; Duncan, *Blue-Eyed Child of Fortune*, 340, 350; Pearson, *Letters from Port Royal*, 154–55; New York *World*, 27 February, 24 March 1863; New York *Evening Post*, 4 March 1863; Washington *Daily National Intelligencer*, 2 March 1863; Hartford *Daily Times*, 27 February 1863.

45. *War of the Rebellion*, Series One, 14: 394; Niven, *Chase Papers*, 3: 381; McPherson, *Battle Cry of Freedom*, 486–90.

46. Higginson, *Army Life*, 107.

47. New York *Times*, 25 March 1863; Milwaukee *Daily Sentinel*, 3 April 1863; *War of the Rebellion*, Series One, 14: 226, 423; Higginson, *Army Life*, 108n.; Hayes, *Du Pont Letters*, 2: 326–27; Pearson, *Letters from Port Royal*, 97; "Letters of Dr. Rogers," 381; Edward W. Hooper to Harry Chapin, 15 March 1863, Hooper Papers.

48. *War of the Rebellion*, Series One, 14: 197–98; "Letters of Dr. Rogers," 356, 381.

49. Rossbach, *Ambivalent Conspirators*, 133, 141–42, 145, 147, 168–69, 184, 186–87, 213, 216–17; Edelstein, *Strange Enthusiasm*, 209, 211, 215–16, 221, 224–25, 238, 240–41, 245–46.

50. Looby, *Journal and Letters*, 83, 102; Higginson, *Army Life*, 237; Rossbach, *Ambivalent Conspirators*, 217; Edelstein, *Strange Enthusiasm*, 221, 238; Ira Berlin, *Many Thousands Gone: The First Two Centuries of Slavery in North America* (Cambridge, Mass., 1998), 67, 87–88, 120–21, 169–70, 328–29.

Chapter Four **FROM PORT ROYAL ISLAND TO JACKSONVILLE, FEBRUARY 17-MARCH 10**

1. New York *Daily Tribune*, 27, 28 February 1863.

2. New York *World*, 17 March 1863; Higginson, *Army Life*, 108; Looby, *Journal and Letters*, 92, 109, 263, 264; "Letters of Dr. Rogers," 366, 369; Stevenson, *Journals*, 455, 460; New York *Evening Post*, 4 March 1863; Boston *Commonwealth*, 27 March 1863; New York *Daily Tribune*, 16, 24 March 1863; New York *Times*, 22, 25 March 1863.

3. Miller, *Lincoln's Abolitionist General*, 137; Baltimore *American and Commercial Advertiser*, 28 February 1863; David Hunter to Edwin Stanton, 17 February 1863, RUSACC, Pt. 1, E-4088, vol. 3; Boston *Daily Advertiser*, 28 February 1863; *Liberator*, 6 March 1863; New York *Daily Tribune*, 27 February 1863; C. C. Coffin to John A. Andrew, 17 February 1863, Andrew Papers; "Letters of Dr. Rogers," 364–65; Looby, *Journal and Letters*, 103; Edward W. Hooper to Robert W. Hooper, 23 February 1863, Hooper Papers.

4. Looby, *Journal and Letters*, 103; *Liberator*, 6 February 1863.

5. General Order No. 1, 25 November 1862, Order Book, 33rd USCT Infantry, Regimental Records, RAGO; Looby, *Journal and Letters*, 104, 108, 263; "Letters of Dr. Rogers," 368; Boston *Commonwealth*, 27 March 1863.

6. Looby, *Journal and Letters*, 56–57, 58–59, 62–63, 64–65, 65–66, 78, 86, 253; Higginson, *Army Life*, 187–213, 240–41; Higginson, "First Black Regiment," 529; "Letters of Dr. Rogers," 341–42, 344; Boston *Commonwealth*, 7 February 1863; *Liberator*, 28 November 1862, 6 February 1863; *Freedmen of South Carolina*, 11–13; *Zion's Herald and Wesleyan Journal*, 24 June 1863; Wilson, *Campfires of Freedom*, chapters 6 and 7.

7. Looby, *Journal and Letters*, 103, 105, 107; "Letters of Dr. Rogers," 366, 368; Holland, *Letters and Diary of Laura M. Towne*, 103; Stevenson, *Journals*, 454–55, 456–58, 460–61.

8. Stevenson, *Journals*, xxxiii–xxxvii, 3–40, 42; "Letters of Dr. Rogers," 366; *Liberator*, 12, 19 December 1862, 23 January 1863.

9. Stevenson, *Journals*, xxxiv–xxxvi, 3, 21, 22, 24–36, 38–41, 43–44, 388–449 passim, 461, 464–65; Looby, *Journal and Letters*, 319; Rose, *Rehearsal for Reconstruction*, 161.

10. Stevenson, *Journals*, 36, 44–47, 428–61 passim; "Letters of Dr. Rogers," 340, 358–59, 366; Seventh Census, 1850, Manuscript Returns of Free Inhabitants, City of Worcester, Worcester County, Massachusetts, p. 304, National Archives, Washington; Looby, *Journal and Letters*, 72, 76, 258 (letter's date transcribed as 9 January, but internal evidence suggests 8 February), 277n.; unpaginated map in Pearson, *Letters from Port Royal* (Forten's plantation was Oaklands).

11. Stevenson, *Journals*, 440, 447, 454–55; "Letters of Dr. Rogers," 358–59, 366.

12. Stevenson, *Journals*, 460–61.

13. Looby, *Journal and Letters*, 99, 104, 258, 263; *War of the Rebellion*, Series Three, 3: 14, 20; New York *Daily Tribune*, 30 January 1863; Special Order No. 3, 28 January 1863, Special Order No. 5, 30 January 1863, RUSACC, Pt. 2, E-2456; Charles Halpine to Colonel Morgan, 7 February 1863, James Montgomery Papers, Kansas State Historical Society, Topeka; James Montgomery to Mrs. George L. Stearns, 25 April 1863, Stearns Papers; Pearson, *Letters from Port Royal*, 167; Boston *Commonwealth*, 27 March 1863; New York *Evening Post*, 13 February 1863; Cornish, *Sable Arm*, 103–04, 138.

14. Holland, *Letters and Diary of Laura M. Towne*, 103–04; Looby, *Journal and Letters*, 104.

15. Looby, *Journal and Letters*, 104, 107, 263, 264; James Montgomery to Mrs. George L. Stearns, 25 April 1863, Stearns Papers; Buckingham, *All's for the Best*, 221; New York *Evening Post*, 31 March 1863; Edward W. Hooper to Robert W. Hooper, 23 February, 2 March, 1863, Hooper Papers; *Bangor Daily Whig and Courier*, 19 March 1863.

16. "Letters of Dr. Rogers," 366–67; Duncan, *Blue-Eyed Child of Fortune*, 339, 342, 348, 356, 357, 363, 369; Thomas Goodrich, *War to the Knife: Bleeding Kansas, 1854–1861* (Mechanicsburg, Pa., 1998), 219; Brian R. Dirck, "By the Hand of God: James Montgomery and Redemptive Violence," *Kansas History*, 27 (2004): 100–15; Stevenson, *Journals*, 473.

17. Dirck, "By the Hand of God," 100–15; Milwaukee *Sentinel*, 21 December 1871; Wilson, "In the Shadow of John Brown," 306–27; Holland, *Letters and Diary of Laura M. Towne*, 103; Goodrich, *War to the Knife*, 213–25; Duncan, *Blue-Eyed Child of Fortune*, 339, 343, 348, 356, 357, 363, 369, 378–79; *War of the Rebellion*, Series One, 14: 861; Edward W. Hooper to Ellen Gurney, 27 January 1863, Hooper Papers.

18. Duncan, *Blue-Eyed Child of Fortune*, 348, 366; James Montgomery to Mrs. George L. Stearns, 25 April 1863, Stearns Papers; Donald Yacovone, ed., *Freedom's Journey: African American Voices of the Civil War* (Chicago, 2004), 133–34, 136–38; Wilson, "In the Shadow of John Brown," 306–27; Staudenraus, "Occupied Beaufort," 142.

19. Edelstein, *Strange Enthusiasm*, 235–36; Looby, *Journal and Letters*, 105, 146, 154, 158–59, 258n., 263, 287, 288, 289; "Letters of Dr. Rogers," 367; Duncan, *Blue-Eyed Child of Fortune*, 339, 356, 370; Cornish, *Sable Arm*, 150; Wilson, "In the Shadow of John Brown," 306–27.

20. *Supplement to the Official Records*, 77: 752; "Letters of Dr. Rogers," 369, 370; Camp Inspection Return, 1st South Carolina Infantry, 3 March 1863, United States Sanitary Commission Records; Schwartz, *Woman Doctor's Civil War*, 43–44; Higginson, *Army Life*, 114; James Montgomery to Mrs. George L. Stearns, 25 April 1863, Stearns Papers.

21. Looby, *Journal and Letters*, 264; Edward W. Hooper to Robert W. Hooper, 7 March 1863, Hooper Papers; New York *Daily Tribune*, 16 March 1863; Camp Inspection Return, 1st South Carolina Infantry, 3 March 1863, United States Sanitary Commission Records; "Letters of Dr. Rogers," 369. On the work of the Sanitary Commission, see William Q. Maxwell, *Lincoln's Fifth Wheel: The Political History of the United States Sanitary Commission* (New York, 1956).

22. "Letters of Dr. Rogers," 369, 370; Higginson, *Army Life*, 107–08, 111–12; *Supplement to*

the Official Records, 77: 753; assistant adjutant general to Rufus Saxton, 2 March 1863, RUSACC, Pt. 1, E-4088, vol. 2; Bingham, *Young Quartermaster*, 163; *Miller's Planters' & Merchants' State Rights Almanac for the Year of Our Lord 1863* (Charleston, S.C., n. d. [c. 1862]).

23. *Supplement to the Official Records*, 77: 750, 752; Farmington *Chronicle*, 9 April 1863; Appointments and Promotions, 2nd South Carolina Regiment, RUSACC, Pt. 2, E-2456; "Letters of Dr. Rogers," 370; Looby, *Journal and Letters*, 109, 265; Buckingham, *All's for the Best*, 221.

24. New York *Daily Tribune*, 16 March 1863; James Montgomery to Mrs. George L. Stearns, 25 April 1863, Stearns Papers; Higginson, *Army Life*, 108n.

25. New York *Times*, 25 March 1863; Milwaukee *Daily Sentinel*, 3 April 1863; Looby, *Journal and Letters*, 122–23, 129; "Letters of Dr. Rogers," 368, 368–69, 370, 382; Schwartz, *Woman Doctor's Civil War*, 45; John Quincy file, 33rd Regiment, CMSR; Descriptive Book of Company G, 33rd USCT Infantry, Regimental Records, RAGO; pension file of John Quincy, Company G, 1st South Carolina/33rd USCT Infantry, Civil War Pension Files; Coffin, *Four Years of Fighting*, 247; "Under the Palmetto," 196; Lowell (Massachusetts) *Daily Citizen and News*, 26 March 1863.

26. Philadelphia *Inquirer*, 1 April 1863; "Tax Commissioners of Florida," 4, 14, 30, 75, 141; assistant adjutant general to Lyman Stickney, 28 February 1863, RUSACC, Pt. 1, E-4088, vol. 2; T. W. Higginson to Charles Halpine, 5 May 1863, RUSACC, Pt. 1, E-4109.

27. Taylor, *Reminiscences*, 25–55; Ned King file, 33rd Regiment, CMSR; Looby, *Journal and Letters*, 219.

28. Stevenson, *Journals*, 460–62.

29. "Letters of Dr. Rogers," 370; Farmington *Chronicle*, 9 April 1863; Looby, *Journal and Letters*, 265; New York *Daily Tribune*, 16 March 1863; *War of the Rebellion*, Series One, 14: 419–20, 421, 1020–21; Pearson, *Letters from Port Royal*, 167, 172–73; Niven, *Chase Papers*, 4: 3–4; Edward W. Hooper to Samuel Hooper, 5 January 1863, and to Robert W. Hooper, 2 (*sic*—probably 7) March 1863, Hooper Papers.

30. Higginson, *Army Life*, 108–09, 109n.; Hayes, *Du Pont Letters*, 2: 497; *Official Records of the Navies*, Series One, 13: 738, 739; Looby, *Journal and Letters*, 265.

31. *War of the Rebellion*, Series One, 14: 423.

32. Edward W. Hooper to Robert W. Hooper, 7 March 1863, and to Harry Chapin, 15 March 1863, Hooper Papers; Looby, *Journal and Letters*, 145, 176–77, 281.

33. Farmington *Chronicle*, 9 April 1863; Baltimore *American and Commercial Advertiser*, 17 March 1863; Hartford *Daily Courant*, 13 February 1863; P. J. Staudenraus, ed., "A War Correspondent's View of St. Augustine and Fernandina: 1863," *Florida Historical Quarterly*, 41 (1962–63): 63; Philadelphia *Inquirer*, 11 March 1862; *Report of the Joint Committee on the Conduct of the War*, 9 vols. (Wilmington, N.C., 1998–2002), 3: 313–15.

34. Craig L. Symonds, ed., *Charleston Blockade: The Journals of John B. Marchand, U.S. Navy, 1861–1862* (Newport, R.I., 1976), 125; William H. Cooley to parents, 16 January 1863, William Henry Cooley Papers, Southern Historical Collection, University of North Carolina, Chapel Hill; New York *Evening Post*, 10, 12 February 1863; John Chipman Gray and John Codman Ropes, *War Letters, 1862–1865* (Boston and New York, 1927), 328–29; Rogers, "Florida on the Eve of the Civil War," 146–47; Gleeson,

Erin Go Gray!, 4–5; Calvin Shedd to wife and children, 29 September 1862, Shedd Papers; Staudenraus, "War Correspondent's View," 63–65; Hartford *Daily Courant*, 13 February 1863; Clancy, *Yankee in a Confederate Town*, 103–06; O. S. Sanford to James F. Hall, 1 April 1863, RUSACC, Pt. 1, E-4277; Fernandina provost marshal to provost marshal general, 3 April 1863, RUSACC, Pt. 4, E-1599; Berlin, *Wartime Genesis of Free Labor*, 225–26, 226n.; Schmidt, *Civil War in Florida*, 1: 596; Philadelphia *Press*, 9 April 1863; Jared A. Abell to Hannah, 8 March 1863, Abell Letters.

35. Farmington *Chronicle*, 9 April 1863; T. W. Higginson to Charles Halpine, 5 May 1863, RUSACC, Pt. 1, E-4109; "Tax Commissioners of Florida," 13–14, 50–52, 54, 65–66, 67; Clancy, *Yankee in a Confederate Town*, 5–87, 133; New York *Evening Post*, 30 January 1863; L. D. Stickney to Abraham Lincoln, 17 May 1862, Florida state citizens to Abraham Lincoln, 5 December 1862, Lincoln Papers.

36. T. W. Higginson to Charles Halpine, 5 May 1863, RUSACC, Pt. 1, E-4109; "Tax Commissioners of Florida," 4, 8, 12, 14–16, 30, 34–35, 41–42, 70, 74, 100, 141; Looby, *Journal and Letters*, 117.

37. T. W. Higginson to Charles Halpine, 5 May 1863, RUSACC, Pt. 1, E-4109.

38. "Letters of Dr. Rogers," 370; Farmington *Chronicle*, 9 April 1863; Higginson, *Army Life*, 80–81, 108; Gray and Ropes, *War Letters*, 328, 330; Otis L. Keene, "Jacksonville, Fifty-three Years Ago: Recollections of a Veteran," *Florida Historical Quarterly*, 1 (1909): 12; Rogers, "Florida on the Eve of the Civil War," 157; *Official Records of the Navies*, Series One, 13: 756; *Norwich* log, 8 March 1863, RBNP.

39. *Norwich* log, 8 March 1863, RBNP; New York *Times*, 25 March 1863; Higginson, *Army Life*, 108–09, 112; *Official Records of the Navies*, Series One, 13: 745; "Letters of Dr. Rogers," 370.

40. James Montgomery to Mrs. George L. Stearns, 25 April 1863, Stearns Papers.

41. George E. McPherson to Theodore McPherson, 31 December 1862, Benjamin R. McPherson to Theodore McPherson, 31 December 1862, McPherson Family Papers; "Letter of Captain Chamberlain," 86; Rogers, "Florida on the Eve of the Civil War," 147; Higginson, *Army Life*, 109–10; "Letters of Dr. Rogers," 370, 374; *Official Records of the Navies*, Series One, 13: 245; Buker, *Jacksonville*, 67.

42. Higginson, *Army Life*, 80–81, 110; Benjamin R. McPherson to Theodore McPherson, 31 December 1862, McPherson Family Papers; *Norwich* log, 9 February 1863, RBNP; "Letters of Dr. Rogers," 370.

43. "Letters of Dr. Rogers," 370, 371; *Norwich* log, 8 March 1863, RBNP.

44. *Miller's Almanac 1863*; *Official Records of the Navies*, Series Two, 1: 162–63, 228; Higginson, *Army Life*, 109, 111; Hayes, *Du Pont Letters*, 2: 480; *Norwich* log, 9 February–8 March 1863, passim, RBNP.

45. *Norwich* log, 9 March 1863, RBNP; Higginson, *Army Life*, 110; "Letters of Dr. Rogers," 371; Farmington *Chronicle*, 9 April 1863.

46. "Letters of Dr. Rogers," 371.

47. Higginson, *Army Life*, 110, 112; Farmington *Chronicle*, 9 April 1863.

48. Higginson, *Army Life*, 109, 110; General Order No. 30, 9 March 1863, Order Book, and Register of Deaths of Company I, both in 33rd USCT Infantry, Regimental Records, RAGO; "Letters of Dr. Rogers," 371.

49. Higginson, *Army Life*, 110–12; "Letters of Dr. Rogers," 371; Farmington *Chronicle*, 9 April 1863; *Norwich* log, 10 March 1863, RBNP; *Official Records of the Navies*, Series

Two, 1: 162–63, 228; *War of the Rebellion*, Series Three, 4: 916; *Miller's Almanac 1863*; Gray and Ropes, *War Letters*, 330.

50. *Official Records of the Navies*, Series One, 12: 620; George E. McPherson to Theodore McPherson, 31 December 1862, McPherson Family Papers; "Letters of Dr. Rogers," 371; Gray and Ropes, *War Letters*, 330; New York *Times*, 25 March 1863; Higginson, *Army Life*, 110–11.

51. Bingham, *Young Quartermaster*, passim, especially 92.

52. Higginson, *Army Life*, 111, 112; *Miller's Almanac 1863*; *Norwich* log, 10 March 1863, RBNP.

53. Higginson, *Army Life*, 112; Looby, *Journal and Letters*, 109; "Letters of Dr. Rogers," 371; Rogers, "Florida on the Eve of the Civil War," 147; George E. McPherson to Theodore McPherson, 31 December 1862, McPherson Family Papers; "Letter of Captain Chamberlain," 93; Henry Boynton to J. D. Rust, 1 April 1863, Civil War Regimental Correspondence, 8th Maine Infantry, Maine State Archives, Augusta.

54. *Official Records of the Navies*, Series One, 12: 620; Higginson, *Army Life*, 112; "Letters of Dr. Rogers," 372; Looby, *Journal and Letters*, 109; Schmidt, *Civil War in Florida*, 1: 553 (map).

55. Augusta *Daily Constitutionalist*, 19 March, 1 April 1863; Higginson, *Army Life*, 112; *Official Records of the Navies*, Series One, 13: 745; Farmington *Chronicle*, 9 April 1863; New York *Times*, 25 March 1863; Looby, *Journal and Letters*, 110; Washington *Daily Morning Chronicle*, 26 March 1863.

56. "Letters of Dr. Rogers," 372; New York *Times*, 25 March 1863; Augusta *Daily Constitutionalist*, 19 March 1863.

57. New York *Times*, 25 March 1863; Augusta *Daily Constitutionalist*, 19 March, 1 April 1863; Farmington *Chronicle*, 9 April 1863; New York *Daily Tribune*, 24 March 1863; Blakey, Lainhart, and Stephens, *Rose Cottage Chronicles*, 213; *War of the Rebellion*, Series One, 14: 227; Edward W. Hooper to Harry Chapin, 15 March 1863, and to Marian Adams, 15 March 1863, Hooper Papers.

58. Higginson, *Army Life*, 112; Washington *Daily Morning Chronicle*, 26 March 1863; Farmington *Chronicle*, 9 April 1863; New York *Times*, 25 March 1863; "Letters of Dr. Rogers," 372; Augusta *Daily Constitutionalist*, 19 March, 1 April 1863.

Chapter Five **JACKSONVILLE, MARCH 10–20**

1. Post General Order No. 1, 10 March 1863, Order Book, 33rd USCT Infantry, Regimental Records, RAGO; *Supplement to the Official Records*, 77: 744.

2. Higginson, *Army Life*, 112–13; *Liberator*, 27 March 1863; New York *Times*, 25 March 1863; Blakey, Lainhart, and Stephens, *Rose Cottage Chronicles*, 214; Washington *Daily Morning Chronicle*, 26 March 1863; "Letters of Dr. Rogers," 372.

3. Charleston *Daily Courier*, 19 March 1863; "Letters of Dr. Rogers," 372; Farmington *Chronicle*, 9 April 1863; James Montgomery to Mrs. George L. Stearns, 25 April 1863, Stearns Papers.

4. Higginson, *Army Life*, 113; Looby, *Journal and Letters*, 109, 111; *Liberator*, 27 March 1863.

5. Looby, *Journal and Letters*, 111; *Norwich* log, 10, 11 March 1863, RBNP; Farmington *Chronicle*, 9 April 1863; Philadelphia *Press*, 25 March 1863; Blakey, Lainhart, and Ste-

phens, *Rose Cottage Chronicles*, 215; *War of the Rebellion*, Series One, 14: 227; Washington *Daily Morning Chronicle*, 26 March 1863.

6. *Norwich* log, 11 March 1863, RBNP; Higginson, *Army Life*, 113; Looby, *Journal and Letters*, 109, 111; Post General Order No. 2, 11 March 1863, Order Book, 33rd USCT Infantry, Regimental Records, RAGO.

7. Martin and Schafer, *Jacksonville's Ordeal*, 13–19; "Letters of Dr. Rogers," 372, 375–76; Keene, "Jacksonville," 9–15; Higginson, *Army Life*, 113, 114; Clancy, *Yankee in a Confederate Town*, 8; Blakey, Lainhart, and Stephens, *Rose Cottage Chronicles*, 10, 11–12; Carl M. Becker and Ritchie Thomas, eds., *Hearth and Knapsack: The Ladley Letters, 1857–1880* (Athens, Ohio, 1988), 166; Looby, *Journal and Letters*, 109, 112, 265–66; George E. McPherson to Theodore McPherson, 31 December 1862, Benjamin R. McPherson to Theodore McPherson, 28 March 1863, McPherson Family Papers; Vaughn D. Bornet, ed., "A Connecticut Yankee Fights at Olustee: Letters from the Front," *Florida Historical Quarterly*, 27 (1948–49): 255; Vaughn D. Bornet, ed., "A Connecticut Yankee After Olustee," *Florida Historical Quarterly*, 27 (1948–49): 395–96; Charles P. Lord to sister, 22 March 1863, Charles Phineas Lord Papers, Duke University Library; "Letter of Captain Chamberlain," 92, 93; Henry Boynton to J. D. Rust, 1 April 1863, Civil War Regimental Correspondence; Amelia M. Murray, *Letters from the United States, Cuba and Canada* (New York, 1856), 236; Rogers, "Florida on the Eve of the Civil War," 148; Martin, "Defeat in Victory," 3; Gray and Ropes, *War Letters*, 330.

8. Rogers, "Florida on the Eve of the Civil War," 148n.; Martin and Schafer, *Jacksonville's Ordeal*, 13–19; Looby, *Journal and Letters*, 109, 265–66; Higginson, *Army Life*, 113, 114, 115; "Letters of Dr. Rogers," 373; T. W. Higginson to J. W. Turner, 19 June 1863, RUSACC, Pt. 1, E-4109; Keene, "Jacksonville," 9–15; Charles K. Cadwell, *The Old Sixth Regiment, Its War Record, 1861–5* (New Haven, Conn., 1875), 57; Andrew Fairbanks to George Fairbanks, 4 February 1862, file 9, Fairbanks Collection; "Letter of Captain Chamberlain," 93.

9. Henry Boynton to J. D. Rust, 1 April 1863, Civil War Regimental Correspondence; Post Special Order No. 1, 12 March 1863, Order Book, 33rd USCT Infantry, Regimental Records, RAGO; New York *Daily Tribune*, 8 April 1863; Higginson, *Army Life*, 114; Clancy, *Yankee in a Confederate Town*, 8; Looby, *Journal and Letters*, 109, 110, 113–14, 266; "Letters of Dr. Rogers," 373; *Norwich* log, 10 March 1863, RBNP; *War of the Rebellion*, Series One, 14: 228, 837–38; Blakey, Lainhart, and Stephens, *Rose Cottage Chronicles*, 213.

10. James Montgomery to Mrs. George L. Stearns, 25 April 1863, Stearns Papers; Farmington *Chronicle*, 9 April 1863; Philadelphia *Press*, 25 March 1863; New York *World*, 24 March 1863; *Norwich* log, 11 March 1863, RBNP; *War of the Rebellion*, Series One, 14: 227; Augusta (Georgia) *Daily Chronicle and Sentinel*, 26 March 1863; Augusta *Daily Constitutionalist*, 19 March 1863; Charleston *Daily Courier*, 19 March 1863; Blakey, Lainhart, and Stephens, *Rose Cottage Chronicles*, 215.

11. Farmington *Chronicle*, 9 April 1863; *War of the Rebellion*, Series One, 14: 227; Philadelphia *Press*, 25 March 1863; Blakey, Lainhart, and Stephens, *Rose Cottage Chronicles*, 213; James Montgomery to Mrs. George L. Stearns, 25 April 1863, Stearns Papers.

12. James Montgomery to Mrs. George L. Stearns, 25 April 1863, Stearns Papers; Farmington *Chronicle*, 9 April 1863; Philadelphia *Press*, 25 March 1863.

13. *War of the Rebellion*, Series One, 14: 227; Benjamin R. McPherson to Theodore

McPherson, 28 March 1863, McPherson Family Papers; Farmington *Chronicle*, 9 April 1863; *Norwich* log, 11 March 1863, RBNP; James Montgomery to Mrs. George L. Stearns, 25 April 1863, Stearns Papers; Augusta *Daily Constitutionalist*, 19 March 1863; *Supplement to the Official Records*, 77: 753.

14. New York *World*, 24 March 1863; Farmington *Chronicle*, 9 April 1863; *Norwich* log, 11 March 1863, RBNP; Philadelphia *Press*, 25 March 1863; Mortuary Record of Deceased Soldiers, 34th USCT Infantry, Regimental Records, RAGO; James Montgomery to Mrs. George L. Stearns, 25 April 1863, Stearns Papers; *Supplement to the Official Records*, 77: 753.

15. Looby, *Journal and Letters*, 112; "Letters of Dr. Rogers," 372, 376.

16. Post General Order No. 2, 11 March 1863, Post Special Order No. 1, 12 March 1863, Post Special Order No. 2, 14 March 1863, Order Book, 33rd USCT Infantry, Regimental Records, RAGO; Looby, *Journal and Letters*, 109, 112; Higginson, *Army Life*, 114–15, 118.

17. Post General Order No. 2, 11 March 1863, Order Book, 33rd USCT Infantry, Regimental Records, RAGO; Looby, *Journal and Letters*, 109, 113; "Letters of Dr. Rogers," 376; Higginson, *Army Life*, 121.

18. Higginson, *Army Life*, 115, 116; Bingham, *Young Quartermaster*, 93; Charleston *Daily Courier*, 1 April 1863; New York *World*, 24 March 1863; Looby, *Journal and Letters*, 109, 112, 136; "Letters of Dr. Rogers," 372, 373, 374, 374–75, 376; Farmington *Chronicle*, 9 April 1863; Edelstein, *Strange Enthusiasm*, 148–50, 249, 372–73; Post General Order No. 3, 12 March 1863, Post General Order No. 4, 14 March 1863, Post Special Order No. 1, 12 March 1863, Order Book, 33rd USCT Infantry, Regimental Records, RAGO; Henry Boynton to J. D. Rust, 1 April 1863, Civil War Regimental Correspondence; Buckingham, *All's for the Best*, 225; Taylor, *Reminiscences*, 56.

19. Higginson, *Army Life*, 115–16; Looby, *Journal and Letters*, 110, 112; "Letters of Dr. Rogers," 372, 374–75; Milwaukee *Daily Sentinel*, 3 April 1863; Farmington *Chronicle*, 9 April 1863; *Liberator*, 10 April 1863; Washington *Daily Morning Chronicle*, 26 March 1863; Taylor, *Reminiscences*, 56; Revels, *Grander in Her Daughters*, 111–12.

20. Post General Order No. 4, 14 March 1863, Order Book, 33rd USCT Infantry, Regimental Records, RAGO; Looby, *Journal and Letters*, 109, 112, 112–13; "Letters of Dr. Rogers," 374–75; Higginson, *Army Life*, 115–16, 236; Milwaukee *Daily Sentinel*, 3 April 1863; *Liberator*, 10 April 1863; Blakey, Lainhart, and Stephens, *Rose Cottage Chronicles*, 215; New York *Evening Post*, 12 February 1863.

21. Post Special Order No. 1, 12 March 1863, Post General Order No. 3, 12 March 1863, Order Book, 33rd USCT Infantry, Regimental Records, RAGO; Augusta *Daily Constitutionalist*, 1 April 1863.

22. Augusta *Daily Constitutionalist*, 1 April 1863; Farmington *Chronicle*, 9 April 1863; Eighth Census, 1860, Free Inhabitants, Duval County, Florida, p. 244.

23. "Letters of Dr. Rogers," 372, 378; Blakey, Lainhart, and Stephens, *Rose Cottage Chronicles*, 213; John Drysdale to John Milton, 31 October 1861, document 7426–1861, Letters Received by the Confederate Secretary of War, 1861–1865, M437, National Archives, Washington; Augusta *Daily Constitutionalist*, 1 April 1863; Charleston *Daily Courier*, 1 April 1863; New York *World*, 24 March, 2 April 1863; Port Royal *New South*, 28 March 1863; *War of the Rebellion*, Series One, 14: 838.

24. Augusta *Daily Chronicle and Sentinel*, 26 March 1863; Augusta *Daily Constitutionalist*, 25, 27 March, 1 April 1863; Tallahassee *Florida Sentinel*, 28 October 1862, 17

March 1863; *War of the Rebellion*, Series One, 14: 228, 838, 845; Charleston *Daily Courier*, 20 January 1863; Savannah *Daily Morning News*, 23 March 1863; Ellen E. Hodges and Stephen Kerber, eds., "'Rogues and Black Hearted Scamps': Civil War Letters of Winston and Octavia Stephens, 1862–1863," *Florida Historical Quarterly*, 57 (1978–79): 76.

25. Looby, *Journal and Letters*, 111, 113, 115; Higginson, *Army Life*, 121.

26. Looby, *Journal and Letters*, 109, 110, 112; Higginson, *Army Life*, 113; Gray and Ropes, *War Letters*, 330–31; "Letters of Dr. Rogers," 372; Martin and Schafer, *Jacksonville's Ordeal*, 28–29, 50, 66–67; Samuel Proctor, "Jacksonville During the Civil War," *Florida Historical Quarterly*, 41 (1962–63): 344; subscription agreement, 26 July 1861, contract, 3 October 1861, Edward McCrady L'Engle Papers, Southern Historical Collection, University of North Carolina, Chapel Hill.

27. Looby, *Journal and Letters*, 109, 110, 112, 265–66; Higginson, *Army Life*, 113; "Letters of Dr. Rogers," 372, 375–76; Thomas Hodges file, 33rd Regiment, CMSR.

28. Boston *Commonwealth*, 17 April 1863.

29. Higginson, *Army Life*, 114; New York *World*, 2 April 1863.

30. Higginson, *Army Life*, 114, 121–22; Looby, *Journal and Letters*, 109; "Letters of Dr. Rogers," 372; *Official Records of the Navies*, Series One, 13: 777.

31. Higginson, *Army Life*, 114; Looby, *Journal and Letters*, 109; *Official Records of the Navies*, Series One, 13: 777.

32. Looby, *Journal and Letters*, 109, 110, 113; Higginson, *Army Life*, 114, 121–22, 124; *Norwich* log, 13 March 1863, RBNP; *Official Records of the Navies*, Series One, 13: 777; "Tax Commissioners of Florida," 4, 14, 177.

33. Farmington *Chronicle*, 9 April 1863; assistant adjutant general to Joseph Hawley, 14 March 1863, RUSACC, Pt. 1, E-4088, vol. 2; Charles Halpine to Rufus Saxton, 4 May 1863, T. W. Higginson to Charles Halpine, 5 May 1863, RUSACC, Pt. 1, E-4109; *Official Records of the Navies*, Series One, 13: 777; "Tax Commissioners of Florida," 16, 57, 67; Clancy, *Yankee in a Confederate Town*, 27.

34. Looby, *Journal and Letters*, 109, 110, 111–12; Higginson, *Army Life*, 118, 121; Post Special Order No. 1, 12 March 1863, Post Special Order No. 2, 14 March 1863, Order Book, 33rd USCT Infantry, Regimental Records, RAGO; "Letters of Dr. Rogers," 373, 376; Henry Boynton to J. D. Rust, 1 April 1863, Civil War Regimental Correspondence; T. W. Higginson to J. W. Turner, 19 June 1863, RUSACC, Pt. 1, E-4109; Augusta *Daily Constitutionalist*, 25 March, 1, 16 April 1863; New York *Daily Tribune*, 8 April 1863; *War of the Rebellion*, Series One, 14: 228, 845; Benjamin R. McPherson to Theodore McPherson, 28 March 1863, McPherson Family Papers; *Norwich* log, 12, 16, 18 March 1863, *Paul Jones* log, 17, 18 March 1863, RBNP; Savannah *Daily Morning News*, 23 March, 6 April 1863; Blakey, Lainhart, and Stephens, *Rose Cottage Chronicles*, 215, 216; Charleston (South Carolina) *Mercury*, 23 March 1863.

35. Higginson, *Army Life*, 119; "Letters of Dr. Rogers," 373; Looby, *Journal and Letters*, 111, 309; Schwartz, *Woman Doctor's Civil War*, 44.

36. "Letters of Dr. Rogers," 373–74; New York *Daily Tribune*, 8 April 1863; Higginson, *Army Life*, 118.

37. "Letters of Dr. Rogers," 374.

38. Looby, *Journal and Letters*, 139; Higginson, *Army Life*, 118–19; *Supplement to the Official Records*, 77: 750.

39. *Norwich* log, 11, 12, 17, 20 March 1863, *Paul Jones* log, 12, 13, 17, 20 March 1863, RBNP;

War of the Rebellion, Series One, 14: 228, 837–38; "Letters of Dr. Rogers," 372; Buckingham, *All's for the Best*, 224; *Official Records of the Navies*, Series One, 13: 742, 777–78, 794, Series Two, 1: 171; Hayes, *Du Pont Letters*, 2: 232; Dean S. Thomas, *Cannons: An Introduction to Civil War Artillery* (Gettysburg, Pa., 1985), 53.

40. Higginson, *Army Life*, 130; Looby, *Journal and Letters*, 112, 301, 303. For Higginson's views on manliness, see Edelstein, *Strange Enthusiasm*, 25–26, 151, 162, 189, 195, 205–06, 225.

41. Charles Steedman to Sally, 20 March 1863, Steedman Correspondence.

42. Looby, *Journal and Letters*, 109, 111, 113–14; Higginson, *Army Life*, 112, 114, 115, 121; Post Special Order No. 1, 12 March 1863, Order Book, 33rd USCT Infantry, Regimental Records, RAGO; Clancy, *Yankee in a Confederate Town*, 8; New York *Daily Tribune*, 8 April 1863; Augusta *Daily Constitutionalist*, 25 March, 1, 16 April 1863; *War of the Rebellion*, Series One, 14: 228, 838; Savannah *Daily Morning News*, 6 April 1863; "Letters of Dr. Rogers," 377; Beaufort *Free South*, 11 April 1863.

43. "Letters of Dr. Rogers," 375.

44. *Norwich* log, 14 March 1863, RBNP; *Miller's Almanac 1863*; "Letters of Dr. Rogers," 373, 375; Higginson, *Army Life*, 120.

45. "Letters of Dr. Rogers," 375; Post Special Order No. 2, 14 March 1863, Order Book, 33rd USCT Infantry, Regimental Records, RAGO; Higginson, *Army Life*, 120; Looby, *Journal and Letters*, 149; William J. Randolph file, 33rd Regiment, CMSR.

46. *Norwich* log, 15–18 March 1863, RBNP; "Letters of Dr. Rogers," 376; Looby, *Journal and Letters*, 112; *Supplement to the Official Records*, 77: 753; New York *World*, 2 April 1863.

47. Martin and Schafer, *Jacksonville's Ordeal*, 142; Schafer, "Freedom Was as Close as the River," 108; Reed Diary, 5 October 1862.

48. Looby, *Journal and Letters*, 114, 116–17, 266; Albert Sammis file, 33rd Regiment, CMSR; Descriptive Book of Company C, 33rd USCT Infantry, Regimental Records, RAGO; Martin and Schafer, *Jacksonville's Ordeal*, 142–43; pension file of Albert Sammis, Company C, 1st South Carolina/33rd USCT Infantry, Civil War Pension Files.

49. Florida State Genealogical Society, *Census, Department of the South, November, 1864: For Jacksonville, Fernandina and St. Augustine, Florida: Ordered by the Department of the South, Hilton Head, South Carolina* (Tallahassee, 2002), 76; Eighth Census, 1860, Free Inhabitants, Duval County, Florida, p. 296; Looby, *Journal and Letters*, 134; "Tax Commissioners of Florida," 180; file of John Sammis, Duval County, Florida, Settled Case Files; Martin and Schafer, *Jacksonville's Ordeal*, 85, 125, 246–47; *War of the Rebellion*, Series One, 6: 250–52; Daniel L. Schafer, *Anna Madgigine Jai Kingsley: African Princess, Florida Slave, Plantation Slaveowner* (Gainesville, Fla., and other cities, 2003), 104, 108, 111.

50. Schafer, *Anna Madgigine Jai Kingsley*, 99, 104, 105–07, 111, 112; subscription agreement, 26 July 1861, L'Engle Papers; *War of the Rebellion*, Series One, 6: 250–52; Martin and Schafer, *Jacksonville's Ordeal*, 81–82, 122, 125–26, 143, 247; L. D. Stickney to Abraham Lincoln, 17 May 1862, L. D. Stickney to O. M. Browning, 11 June 1862, Lincoln Papers; "Tax Commissioners of Florida," 14.

51. Looby, *Journal and Letters*, 67, 134; Schafer, *Anna Madgigine Jai Kingsley*, 112; "Tax Commissioners of Florida," 4, 14, 30, 114, 138, 177, 180–81; Martin and Schafer, *Jacksonville's Ordeal*, 246–47.

52. Looby, *Journal and Letters*, 66–67, 114, 134; "Tax Commissioners of Florida," 14;

Albert Sammis file, 33rd Regiment, CMSR; Descriptive Book of Company C, 33rd USCT Infantry, Regimental Records, RAGO.

53. Schafer, *Anna Madgigine Jai Kingsley*, passim, especially 1–3, 78–79, 98, 104, 107, 108, 109; Martin and Schafer, *Jacksonville's Ordeal*, 143, 246–47; Eighth Census, 1860, Free Inhabitants, Duval County, Florida, p. 296; pension file of Albert Sammis, Company C, 1st South Carolina/33rd USCT Infantry, Civil War Pension Files; Albert Sammis file, 33rd Regiment, CMSR; Looby, *Journal and Letters*, 66–67, 134.

54. "Letters of Dr. Rogers," 376–77; Looby, *Journal and Letters*, 113, 132; *War of the Rebellion*, Series One, 14: 838, 839; Augusta *Daily Constitutionalist*, 1 April 1863; Benjamin R. McPherson to Theodore McPherson, 28 March 1863, McPherson Family Papers; Higginson, *Army Life*, 150.

55. *War of the Rebellion*, Series One, 14: 839; Augusta *Daily Constitutionalist*, 1 April 1863; Post General Order No. 8, 18 March 1863, Order Book, 33rd USCT Infantry, Regimental Records, RAGO; "Letters of Dr. Rogers," 376; T. W. Higginson to J. W. Turner, 19 June 1863, RUSACC, Pt. 1, E-4109.

56. Post General Order No. 8, 18 March 1863, Order Book, 33rd USCT Infantry, Regimental Records, RAGO; "Letters of Dr. Rogers," 377; Looby, *Journal and Letters*, 113; Benjamin R. McPherson to Theodore McPherson, 28 March 1863, McPherson Family Papers; Augusta *Daily Constitutionalist*, 1 April 1863.

57. "Letters of Dr. Rogers," 377; Looby, *Journal and Letters*, 110, 113, 266; Higginson, *Army Life*, 121–22; *Norwich* log, 19 March 1863, RBNP.

58. "Tax Commissioners of Florida," 4, 14, 67, 75, 101; New York *Daily Tribune*, 8 April 1863; assistant adjutant general to Joseph Hawley, 14 March 1863, RUSACC, Pt. 1, E-4088, vol. 2.

59. "Tax Commissioners of Florida," 75, 101, 146; chief of staff to officer commanding 6th Connecticut, 20 March 1863, RUSACC, Pt. 1, E-4088, vol. 2; George A. Staples Diary, 18 March 1863, Connecticut Historical Society, Hartford; Looby, *Journal and Letters*, 113; Edward W. Hooper to Harry Chapin, 15 March 1863, and to Robert W. Hooper, 16 March 1863, Hooper Papers.

60. Staples Diary, 19 March 1863; "Tax Commissioners of Florida," 14; Looby, *Journal and Letters*, 113; *Norwich* log, 19, 20 March 1863, RBNP.

61. "Tax Commissioners of Florida," 16, 57, 67, 101; T. W. Higginson to Charles Halpine, 5 May 1863, RUSACC, Pt. 1, E-4109.

62. Looby, *Journal and Letters*, 113, 266; Higginson, *Army Life*, 121–22; "Letters of Dr. Rogers," 378.

63. Looby, *Journal and Letters*, 113, 266; "Letters of Dr. Rogers," 377; Higginson, *Army Life*, 122–23; *Norwich* log, 20 March 1863, RBNP.

Chapter Six **JACKSONVILLE, THE EAST BANK, AND PALATKA, MARCH 20–27**

1. *Norwich* log, 20 March 1863, RBNP; Staples Diary, 20 March 1863; "Letters of Dr. Rogers," 377; Cadwell, *Old Sixth Regiment*, 56.

2. *Norwich* log, 20, 21 March 1863, RBNP; Staples Diary, 20 March 1863; "Letters of Dr. Rogers," 377.

3. Camp Inspection Return, 6th Connecticut Infantry, 14 March 1863, United States

Sanitary Commission Records; *Supplement to the Official Records*, 3: 645–704; Cadwell, *Old Sixth Regiment*, 9–56; *War of the Rebellion*, Series One, 14: 56, 148, 158–59; Horatio Eaton to friend, 22 June, 11 November 1862, Willis Asa Pomeroy Correspondence, Connecticut Historical Society, Hartford; New Haven (Connecticut) *Morning Journal and Courier*, 3 March 1863.

4. *War of the Rebellion*, Series One, 14: 56, 159; New York *Daily Tribune*, 29 November 1862; Stamford *Advocate*, 6 February 1863; Camp Inspection Return, 6th Connecticut Infantry, 14 March 1863, United States Sanitary Commission Records.

5. Looby, *Journal and Letters*, 116; Camp Inspection Return, 6th Connecticut Infantry, 14 March 1863, United States Sanitary Commission Records; Cadwell, *Old Sixth Regiment*, 51–52, 54; Hartford *Daily Times*, 16 January, 18 March 1863.

6. Hartford *Daily Times*, 16 January 1863; Cadwell, *Old Sixth Regiment*, 52–54; "Letters of Dr. Rogers," 378; Martin Emmons to brother, 3 May 1863, C. Eugene Southworth Papers, Duke University Library; Staples Diary, 24 March 1863.

7. Higginson, *Army Life*, 123; "Letters of Dr. Rogers," 378.

8. Higginson, *Army Life*, 123; Looby, *Journal and Letters*, 113, 115.

9. Mansfield French to wife, 25 March 1863, and to children, 9 April 1863, French Family Papers, Onondaga Historical Association, Syracuse, New York; *Liberator*, 10 April 1863; Looby, *Journal and Letters*, 114; Bingham, *Young Quartermaster*, 96; Rose, *Rehearsal for Reconstruction*, 26; "Letters of Dr. Rogers," 378; Cadwell, *Old Sixth Regiment*, 57–58.

10. Looby, *Journal and Letters*, 76, 81, 114, 216–17, 349; Rose, *Rehearsal for Reconstruction*, 26–27, 89, 218, 236, 276–77, 292–93; Mansfield French to wife, 2 March 1863, French Family Papers; M. French to S. P. Chase, 6 January 1863, Lincoln Papers; *American Missionary*, 7 (1863): 88; Boston *Daily Advertiser*, 8 December 1862; *Liberator*, 26 December 1862; *Freedmen of South Carolina*, 3; Hayes, *Du Pont Letters*, 2: 355–56, 545, 545n.; Niven, *Chase Papers*, 3: 352–53.

11. Bingham, *Young Quartermaster*, 92–93, 96–97, 168; Keene, "Jacksonville," 10; Looby, *Journal and Letters*, 114.

12. Bingham, *Young Quartermaster*, 32–33, 36–37, 57–58, 80–84, 86–87, 92, 94, 97–98, 168; Looby, *Journal and Letters*, 51, 349.

13. Bingham, *Young Quartermaster*, 97.

14. Ibid.; *Norwich* log, 22 March 1863, RBNP; Charles P. Lord to sister, 22 March 1863, Lord Papers; Henry L. Burnell to family, 22 March 1863, Henry L. Burnell Papers, South Caroliniana Library, University of South Carolina; *War of the Rebellion*, Series One, 14: 232, 435; Looby, *Journal and Letters*, 114; Camp Inspection Return, 8th Maine Infantry, 6 March 1863, United States Sanitary Commission Records.

15. Bingham, *Young Quartermaster*, 97; Charles P. Lord to sister, 22 March 1863, Lord Papers; Buckingham, *All's for the Best*, 41–43, 226.

16. Looby, *Journal and Letters*, 114–15; Higginson, *Army Life*, 123; John D. Rust to Charles Halpine, 9 May 1863, RUSACC, Pt. 1, E-4109; New York *Evening Post*, 8 April 1863; Charles P. Lord to sister, 22 March 1863, Lord Papers.

17. Looby, *Journal and Letters*, 116, 361; Bangor *Daily Whig and Courier*, 20 January, 14, 21 February 1863; Farmington *Chronicle*, 8, 22 January 1863; Camp Inspection Return, 8th Maine Infantry, 6 March 1863, United States Sanitary Commission Records; Buckingham, *All's for the Best*, xvi–xviii, xx, xxii, 56; John D. Rust to John L.

Hodsdon, 2 February 1863, Jonathan Twitchell to Abner Coburn, 16 February 1863, Rufus Saxton to David Hunter, 16 April 1863, William Rust to Abner Coburn, 22 May 1863, Civil War Regimental Correspondence; New York *Daily Tribune*, 2 March 1863; Augusta *Kennebec Journal*, 9, 16 January 1863; temperance pledges, 22 September 1861, 5 February 1862, John Emory Bryant Papers, Duke University Library; Higginson, *Army Life*, 127; *Supplement to the Official Records*, 25: 332–51.

18. Farmington *Chronicle*, 22 January 1863; Farmington *Franklin Patriot*, 9 January 1863; New York *Daily Tribune*, 2 March 1863; Augusta *Kennebec Journal*, 16 January 1863; Buckingham, *All's for the Best*, 221–22; Henry L. Burnell to family, 22 March 1863, Burnell Papers; Charles P. Lord to sister, 25 April 1863, Lord Papers.

19. Andrew Newman to father, 23 December 1862, 24 May 1863, George Newman Papers, Duke University Library; Buckingham, *All's for the Best*, 49.

20. *Norwich* log, 23 March 1863, *Paul Jones* log, 23 March 1863, RBNP; Staples Diary, 23 March 1863; Buckingham, *All's for the Best*, 46, 227.

21. *Norwich* log, 23 March 1863, RBNP; Looby, *Journal and Letters*, 115.

22. Buckingham, *All's for the Best*, xvi–xix, 56, 67, 237, 252; Looby, *Journal and Letters*, 82, 115, 116; officers of 8th Maine to Rufus Saxton, 15 April 1863, Rufus Saxton to David Hunter, 16 April 1863, William Rust to Abner Coburn, 22 May 1863, Civil War Regimental Correspondence; Charles P. Lord to sister, 12 September 1862, 25 April 1863, Lord Papers; New York *Daily Tribune*, 2 March, 28 April 1863; Farmington *Franklin Patriot*, 9 January 1863; *Liberator*, 10 April 1863.

23. Looby, *Journal and Letters*, 115–16.

24. Ibid., 115; Higginson, *Army Life*, 124.

25. Looby, *Journal and Letters*, 267; *Official Records of the Navies*, Series One, 13: 785–86; *Paul Jones* log, 24 March 1863, RBNP; L. D. Stickney to Salmon P. Chase, 16 April 1863, Chase Papers.

26. *Official Records of the Navies*, Series One, 13: 777; *Paul Jones* log, 23 March 1863, RBNP; Charles Steedman to Rodgers, 29 March 1863, Steedman Correspondence; Savannah *Daily Morning News*, 15 April 1863; *War of the Rebellion*, Series One, 14: 860; *Miller's Almanac 1863*.

27. *Paul Jones* log, 24 March 1863, RBNP; Savannah *Daily Morning News*, 15 April 1863; *War of the Rebellion*, Series One, 14: 860.

28. "Letters of Dr. Rogers," 378; *Norwich* log, 19, 23 March 1863, *Paul Jones* log, 19, 21 March 1863, RBNP; New York *World*, 2 April 1863.

29. Looby, *Journal and Letters*, 114–15, 267; "Letters of Dr. Rogers," 378.

30. Looby, *Journal and Letters*, 114; Henry Boynton to J. D. Rust, 1 April 1863, Civil War Regimental Correspondence; *War of the Rebellion*, Series One, 14: 233; *Supplement to the Official Records*, 77: 744; Higginson, *Army Life*, 123, 124.

31. Martin Emmons to brother, 3 May 1863, Southworth Papers; Benjamin R. McPherson to Theodore McPherson, 28 March 1863, McPherson Family Papers; Blakey, Lainhart, and Stephens, *Rose Cottage Chronicles*, 10; Looby, *Journal and Letters*, 116, 135.

32. Looby, *Journal and Letters*, 114, 115; *War of the Rebellion*, Series One, 14: 232, 234, 841; Buckingham, *All's for the Best*, 46; *Supplement to the Official Records*, 3: 668, 673.

33. *Norwich* log, 25 March 1863, RBNP; T. Frederick Davis, *History of Jacksonville, Florida, and Vicinity, 1513 to 1924* (Gainesville, Fla., 1925; reprint, Gainesville, 1964), 129;

Higginson, *Army Life*, 129; *War of the Rebellion*, Series One, 14: 234; Clancy, *Yankee in a Confederate Town*, 93–94; "Letters of Dr. Rogers," 379; Buckingham, *All's for the Best*, 45–46, 227; Cadwell, *Old Sixth Regiment*, 59; Looby, *Journal and Letters*, 117; Philadelphia *Press*, 9 April 1863; Staples Diary, 25 March 1863; Benjamin R. McPherson to Theodore McPherson, 28 March 1863, McPherson Family Papers.

34. "Letters of Dr. Rogers," 379; *War of the Rebellion*, Series One, 14: 234; Benjamin R. McPherson to Theodore McPherson, 28 March 1863, McPherson Family Papers; *Norwich* log, 25 March 1863, RBNP; Buckingham, *All's for the Best*, 44–45, 224.

35. "Letters of Dr. Rogers," 377–78, 379.

36. Ibid., 379; Taylor, *Reminiscences*, 57; Higginson, *Army Life*, 129.

37. Looby, *Journal and Letters*, 117; Davis, *History of Jacksonville*, 129; Higginson, *Army Life*, 129; *War of the Rebellion*, Series One, 14: 234; Cadwell, *Old Sixth Regiment*, 59; Buckingham, *All's for the Best*, 227; "Letters of Dr. Rogers," 379; Charles Steedman to Rodgers, 29 March 1863, Steedman Correspondence; Taylor, *Reminiscences*, 57–58.

38. Buckingham, *All's for the Best*, 224; Davis, *History of Jacksonville*, 129; Higginson, *Army Life*, 129; *War of the Rebellion*, Series One, 14: 234, 845; Clancy, *Yankee in a Confederate Town*, 92–93; Benjamin R. McPherson to Theodore McPherson, 28 March 1863, McPherson Family Papers; *Norwich* log, 25 March 1863, RBNP.

39. Higginson, *Army Life*, 126; *War of the Rebellion*, Series One, 14: 233; New York *Daily Tribune*, 8 April 1863; Looby, *Journal and Letters*, 111.

40. Higginson, *Army Life*, 126–27; Looby, *Journal and Letters*, 118; Buckingham, *All's for the Best*, 222, 223, 224; "Letters of Dr. Rogers," 379; Davis, *History of Jacksonville*, 129, 130.

41. Looby, *Journal and Letters*, 118–19; "Letters of Dr. Rogers," 379; Higginson, *Army Life*, 126–27; Buckingham, *All's for the Best*, 223; *War of the Rebellion*, Series One, 14: 234.

42. Higginson, *Army Life*, 126, 127; Buckingham, *All's for the Best*, 46–47, 48, 223; Stamford *Advocate*, 17 April 1863; "Letters of Dr. Rogers," 379; *War of the Rebellion*, Series One, 14: 234.

43. Higginson, *Army Life*, 127; *War of the Rebellion*, Series One, 14: 233, 234, 845; Buckingham, *All's for the Best*, 47, 223; New York *Daily Tribune*, 8 April 1863; "Letters of Dr. Rogers," 379.

44. Higginson, *Army Life*, 127; Looby, *Journal and Letters*, 119; Buckingham, *All's for the Best*, 47, 223; "Letters of Dr. Rogers," 379; *War of the Rebellion*, Series One, 14: 234.

45. Higginson, *Army Life*, 127–28; Looby, *Journal and Letters*, 119; Buckingham, *All's for the Best*, 47, 223; Davis, *History of Jacksonville*, 130.

46. Higginson, *Army Life*, 128; Buckingham, *All's for the Best*, 47, 223; "Letters of Dr. Rogers," 379–80; *War of the Rebellion*, Series One, 14: 233; pension files of William Willis and Thomas G. Hoole, both of Company I, 8th Maine Infantry, Civil War Pension Files; Descriptive Roll of Company I and Register of Deaths of Company I, 8th Maine Infantry, Regimental Records, RAGO; Davis, *History of Jacksonville*, 130.

47. Buckingham, *All's for the Best*, 47, 223.

48. Ibid., 47–48, 224; Davis, *History of Jacksonville*, 130.

49. Higginson, *Army Life*, 128–29; Looby, *Journal and Letters*, 119; Buckingham, *All's for the Best*, 47, 223, 224; New York *Daily Tribune*, 8 April 1863.

50. *Norwich* log, 25 March 1863, RBNP; Looby, *Journal and Letters*, 119; Higginson, *Army Life*, 128, 129; Davis, *History of Jacksonville*, 130; Stamford *Advocate*, 17 April 1863; "Letters of Dr. Rogers," 380; New York *Daily Tribune*, 8 April 1863.

51. Higginson, *Army Life*, 128; Looby, *Journal and Letters*, 119.

52. Higginson, *Army Life*, 129; "Letters of Dr. Rogers," 379, 380; New York *Daily Tribune*, 8 April 1863; Benjamin R. McPherson to Theodore McPherson, 28 March 1863, McPherson Family Papers; Augusta *Daily Constitutionalist*, 27 March 1863; Buckingham, *All's for the Best*, 48; *War of the Rebellion*, Series One, 14: 845.

53. Davis, *History of Jacksonville*, 130; Higginson, *Army Life*, 129; Looby, *Journal and Letters*, 119; "Letters of Dr. Rogers," 380.

54. Looby, *Journal and Letters*, 116; *Norwich* log, 25 March 1863, RBNP; New York *Daily Tribune*, 8 April 1863; New York *Times*, 8 April 1863; Higginson, *Army Life*, 124, 129.

55. Looby, *Journal and Letters*, 116; "Letters of Dr. Rogers," 382; New York *Daily Tribune*, 8 April 1863; *War of the Rebellion*, Series One, 14: 861.

56. Schwartz, *Woman Doctor's Civil War*, 44–45; New York *Daily Tribune*, 8 April 1863; New York *Times*, 8 April 1863; Looby, *Journal and Letters*, 139; "Letters of Dr. Rogers," 382.

57. Coffin, *Four Years of Fighting*, 247; "Letters of Dr. Rogers," 382.

58. "Letters of Dr. Rogers," 380; Thomas Long file, 33rd Regiment, CMSR; Descriptive Book of Company G, 33rd USCT Infantry, Regimental Records, RAGO; pension file of Thomas Long, Company G, 1st South Carolina/33rd USCT Infantry, Civil War Pension Files; New York *Times*, 21 April 1863.

59. "Letters of Dr. Rogers," 380; New York *Times*, 21 April 1863.

60. "Letters of Dr. Rogers," 380; Looby, *Journal and Letters*, 132.

61. Philadelphia *Inquirer*, 24 March 1864; Murray, *Letters from the United States*, 227; Rogers, "Florida on the Eve of the Civil War," 156–57; *Official Records of the Navies*, Series One, 12: 620; *Atlas to Accompany the Official Records of the Union and Confederate Armies* (Washington, 1891–1895), plate 146; Gray and Ropes, *War Letters*, 335; Looby, *Journal and Letters*, 267.

62. New York *Times*, 8 April 1863; Savannah *Daily Morning News*, 15 April 1863; James M. Dancy, "Reminiscences of the Civil War," *Florida Historical Quarterly*, 37 (1958–59): 69; *War of the Rebellion*, Series One, 14: 860; James Montgomery to Mrs. George L. Stearns, 25 April 1863, Stearns Papers.

63. Savannah *Daily Morning News*, 15 April 1863; *War of the Rebellion*, Series One, 14: 860; Thompson, "Flight from Florida," 13; Becker and Thomas, *Hearth and Knapsack*, 173; N. S. Snell to Charles Steedman, 14 October 1862, Steedman Correspondence; *Supplement to the Official Records*, 77: 753; James Montgomery to Mrs. George L. Stearns, 25 April 1863, Stearns Papers.

64. Savannah *Daily Morning News*, 15 April 1863; *War of the Rebellion*, Series One, 14: 238, 860–61.

65. Savannah *Daily Morning News*, 15 April 1863; F. L. Dancy file, Case Files of Applications for Pardons: Florida; Eighth Census, 1860, Free Inhabitants, St. John's County, Florida, p. 610; General Order No. 3, adjutant general's office, Tallahassee, 16 October 1861, document 7426–1861, Letters Received by the Confederate Secretary of War; Dancy, "Reminiscences of the Civil War," 66, 69–70, 71, 72; *War of the Rebellion*, Series One, 6: 303, 14: 860, 53: 277.

66. Savannah *Daily Morning News*, 15 April 1863; Dancy, "Reminiscences of the Civil War," 66, 69; Thompson, "Flight from Florida," 13; F. L. Dancy file, Case Files of Applications for Pardons: Florida; *War of the Rebellion*, Series One, 14: 860–61; Eighth Census, 1860, Free Inhabitants, St. John's County, Florida, p. 608; Berlin, *Destruction of Slavery*, 136.

67. *War of the Rebellion*, Series One, 14: 228; Augusta *Daily Chronicle and Sentinel*, 25, 26 March 1863; Augusta *Daily Constitutionalist*, 25, 27 March 1863; Charleston *Daily Courier*, 19 March 1863; Charleston *Mercury*, 21, 23 March 1863; Tallahassee *Florida Sentinel*, 17 March 1863; Savannah *Daily Morning News*, 11, 20, 21, 23, 27 March 1863; Richmond *Daily Dispatch*, 25, 27 March 1863; Richmond *Whig and Public Advertiser*, 27 March 1863; Jackson (Mississippi) *Daily Southern Crisis*, 30 March 1863; John Milton to Florida state senators and representatives, 23 March 1863, Milton Letterbook.

68. Dancy, "Reminiscences of the Civil War," 70; James Montgomery to Mrs. George L. Stearns, 25 April 1863, Stearns Papers; Savannah *Daily Morning News*, 15 April 1863; *War of the Rebellion*, Series One, 14: 238, 860–61; *Miller's Almanac 1863*.

69. James Montgomery to Mrs. George L. Stearns, 25 April 1863, Stearns Papers; Savannah *Daily Morning News*, 15 April 1863; Looby, *Journal and Letters*, 146, 154, 158, 185, 287, 288, 289.

70. Buckingham, *All's for the Best*, 48, 48–49; Register of Deaths of Company I and Descriptive Roll of Company I, 8th Maine Infantry, Regimental Records, RAGO; Davis, *History of Jacksonville*, 130; Looby, *Journal and Letters*, 116; pension file of William Willis, Company I, 8th Maine Infantry, Civil War Pension Files.

71. Looby, *Journal and Letters*, 118; Higginson, *Army Life*, 124–26; "Letters of Dr. Rogers," 380–81.

72. "Letters of Dr. Rogers," 382.

73. Looby, *Journal and Letters*, 267, 268; "Tax Commissioners of Florida," 75, 101, 177; Schmidt, *Civil War in Florida*, 1: 572.

74. "Tax Commissioners of Florida," 75, 101, 177; *Official Records of the Navies*, Series One, 13: 794; *Norwich* log, 26, 27 March 1863, RBNP.

75. "Tax Commissioners of Florida," 4, 8, 12, 14, 16, 57, 67, 101, 177; Looby, *Journal and Letters*, 116; T. W. Higginson to Charles Halpine, 5 May 1863, RUSACC, Pt. 1, E-4109.

76. Clancy, *Yankee in a Confederate Town*, 90–91; Post General Order No. 9, 21 March 1863, Order Book, 33rd USCT Infantry, Regimental Records, RAGO; T. W. Higginson to Charles Halpine, 5 May 1863, RUSACC, Pt. 1, E-4109.

77. *War of the Rebellion*, Series One, 14: 238; James Montgomery to Mrs. George L. Stearns, 25 April 1863, Stearns Papers; *Supplement to the Official Records*, 77: 753; Schwartz, *Woman Doctor's Civil War*, 45; "Letters of Dr. Rogers," 382.

78. *Supplement to the Official Records*, 77: 753; James Montgomery to Mrs. George L. Stearns, 25 April 1863, Stearns Papers; Savannah *Daily Morning News*, 15 April 1863; Looby, *Journal and Letters*, 117, 122; Dancy, "Reminiscences of the Civil War," 70; Schwartz, *Woman Doctor's Civil War*, 45; *War of the Rebellion*, Series One, 14: 238.

79. Bornet, "Connecticut Yankee After Olustee," 400–01; Philadelphia *Inquirer*, 24 March 1864; New York *Daily Tribune*, 25, 30 March 1864; Blakey, Lainhart, and Stephens, *Rose Cottage Chronicles*, 4; Rogers, "Florida on the Eve of the Civil War," 157; Looby, *Journal and Letters*, 267.

80. *Paul Jones* log, 23 March 1863, RBNP; Dancy, "Reminiscences of the Civil War," 69; New York *Times*, 26 April 1863; Savannah *Daily Morning News*, 6, 15 April 1863; *War of the Rebellion*, Series One, 14: 238, 861; Schwartz, *Woman Doctor's Civil War*, 45.

81. *War of the Rebellion*, Series One, 14: 238; *Supplement to the Official Records*, 77: 753; Dancy, "Reminiscences of the Civil War," 69, 70; New York *Times*, 26 April

1863; Savannah *Daily Morning News*, 6 April 1863; Looby, *Journal and Letters*, 122; Schwartz, *Woman Doctor's Civil War*, 44–45; Dickison, *Dickison and His Men*, 179; James Montgomery to Mrs. George L. Stearns, 25 April 1863, Stearns Papers.

82. James Montgomery to Mrs. George L. Stearns, 25 April 1863, Stearns Papers; *Supplement to the Official Records*, 77: 753; Schwartz, *Woman Doctor's Civil War*, 45; New York *Times*, 8, 26 April 1863; "Letters of Dr. Rogers," 382; Charleston *Mercury*, 11 April 1863; Savannah *Daily Morning News*, 6, 10, 15 April 1863; New York *Daily Tribune*, 8 April 1863; Dickison, *Dickison and His Men*, 179; *War of the Rebellion*, Series One, 14: 237–39, 861; Looby, *Journal and Letters*, 117, 122; Dancy, "Reminiscences of the Civil War," 70.

83. Dancy, "Reminiscences of the Civil War," 70–71; *War of the Rebellion*, Series One, 14: 238, 861; *Supplement to the Official Records*, 77: 753; James Montgomery to Mrs. George L. Stearns, 25 April 1863, Stearns Papers; Charleston *Mercury*, 11 April 1863; New York *Daily Tribune*, 8 April 1863; New York *Times*, 8, 26 April 1863; Savannah *Daily Morning News*, 6, 10, 15 April 1863; Philadelphia *Inquirer*, 24 March 1864.

84. *War of the Rebellion*, Series One, 14: 239, 861; Charleston *Mercury*, 11 April 1863; Savannah *Daily Morning News*, 10, 15 April 1863; *Supplement to the Official Records*, 77: 753.

85. Savannah *Daily Morning News*, 15 April 1863; *War of the Rebellion*, Series One, 14: 861.

86. *Norwich* log, 27 March 1863, RBNP; Higginson, *Army Life*, 129–30; Looby, *Journal and Letters*, 117, 267, 268; New York *World*, 2 April 1863; "Letters of Dr. Rogers," 378, 381.

87. Higginson, *Army Life*, 129–30; Looby, *Journal and Letters*, 114–15, 116, 117, 120, 199, 267, 268; "Letters of Dr. Rogers," 381; James Montgomery to Mrs. George L. Stearns, 25 April 1863, Stearns Papers; *Supplement to the Official Records*, 77: 753.

88. Higginson, *Army Life*, 129–30; "Letters of Dr. Rogers," 381; Looby, *Journal and Letters*, 114–15, 117, 267, 268.

89. Higginson, *Army Life*, 129–30; Looby, *Journal and Letters*, 114–15, 117, 120, 267.

90. *Norwich* log, 23, 27 March 1863, RBNP; "Letters of Dr. Rogers," 381.

91. *War of the Rebellion*, Series One, 53: 86; New York *Daily Tribune*, 8 April 1863; "Letters of Dr. Rogers," 381; Looby, *Journal and Letters*, 117, 120.

Chapter Seven **JACKSONVILLE AND THE WEST BANK,**
MARCH 27–29

1. Higginson, *Army Life*, 130, 131; Looby, *Journal and Letters*, 96, 117, 120, 122, 191, 268; New York *Evening Post*, 8 April 1863; New York *Daily Tribune*, 8 April 1863; Charles Steedman to Rodgers, 29 March 1863, Steedman Correspondence; "Letters of Dr. Rogers," 381; Benjamin R. McPherson to Theodore McPherson, 28 March 1863, McPherson Family Papers.

2. *Norwich* log, 27 March 1863, RBNP; "Tax Commissioners of Florida," 4, 14, 16, 57, 75, 101, 177; Schmidt, *Civil War in Florida*, 1: 572; "Letters of Dr. Rogers," 382; New York *Evening Post*, 8 April 1863.

3. "Letters of Dr. Rogers," 382; Looby, *Journal and Letters*, 117, 120, 268.

4. *War of the Rebellion*, Series One, 14: 226, 423; Philadelphia *Inquirer*, 16 March 1863; New York *Daily Tribune*, 16 March 1863; Baltimore *American and Commercial Adver-tiser*, 17 March 1863; Washington *Daily National Intelligencer*, 18 (quoting Boston *Journal*), 31 March 1863. For later newspaper reports, see Chapter Eight.

5. Looby, *Journal and Letters*, 117; New York *Daily Tribune*, 8 April 1863; New York *Evening Post*, 8 April 1863; "Letters of Dr. Rogers," 381, 383; Higginson, *Army Life*, 130; Charles Steedman to Rodgers, 29 March 1863, Steedman Correspondence; Benjamin R. McPherson to Theodore McPherson, 28 March 1863, McPherson Family Papers.

6. Looby, *Journal and Letters*, 117; General Order No. 32, 27 March 1863, Order Book, 33rd USCT Infantry, Regimental Records, RAGO; Higginson, *Army Life*, 133.

7. Higginson, *Army Life*, 133; New York *Evening Post*, 8 April 1863; General Order No. 38, 15 April 1863, Order Book, 33rd USCT Infantry, Regimental Records, RAGO.

8. General Order No. 32, 27 March 1863, Order Book, 33rd USCT Infantry, Regimental Records, RAGO; "Letters of Dr. Rogers," 381; *Norwich* log, 27 March 1863, RBNP; New York *Daily Tribune*, 8 April 1863; New York *Times*, 8 April 1863; Schmidt, *Civil War in Florida*, 1: 572.

9. O. S. Sanford to James F. Hall, 1 April 1863, RUSACC, Pt. 1, E-4277; Higginson, *Army Life*, 130; New York *Evening Post*, 8 April 1863; Benjamin R. McPherson to Theodore McPherson, 28 March 1863, McPherson Family Papers; *Norwich* log, 20, 22, 23, 27, 31 March 1863, *Paul Jones* log, 28 March 1863, RBNP; New York *Daily Tribune*, 8 April 1863; *War of the Rebellion*, Series Three, 4: 915–16.

10. *Norwich* log, 28 March 1863, RBNP; "Letters of Dr. Rogers," 382, 383; Benjamin R. McPherson to Theodore McPherson, 28 March 1863, McPherson Family Papers.

11. *Norwich* log, 28 March 1863, RBNP; "Letters of Dr. Rogers," 382.

12. Looby, *Journal and Letters*, 117; New York *Daily Tribune*, 8 April 1863; *Supplement to the Official Records*, 77: 753–54; James Montgomery to Mrs. George L. Stearns, 25 April 1863, Stearns Papers; *Atlas to Accompany the Official Records*, plate 146; *Miller's Almanac 1863*.

13. *Supplement to the Official Records*, 77: 754; New York *Daily Tribune*, 8 April 1863.

14. New York *Daily Tribune*, 8 April 1863; *Supplement to the Official Records*, 77: 754; "Letters of Dr. Rogers," 382; Looby, *Journal and Letters*, 117; James Montgomery to Mrs. George L. Stearns, 25 April 1863, Stearns Papers.

15. *War of the Rebellion*, Series One, 14: 235–36, 825, 838, 53: 233–34, Series Two, 4: 47; Robert R. Mackey, *The Uncivil War: Irregular Warfare in the Upper South, 1861–1865* (Norman, Okla., 2004), passim, especially 7, 12, 205–06; New York *Evening Post*, 13 February 1863; *Official Records of the Navies*, Series One, 13: 245; *Supplement to the Official Records*, 77: 754; James Montgomery to Mrs. George L. Stearns, 25 April 1863, Stearns Papers; New York *Daily Tribune*, 8 April 1863.

16. *Supplement to the Official Records*, 77: 754; Looby, *Journal and Letters*, 117; New York *Daily Tribune*, 8 April 1863; James Montgomery to Mrs. George L. Stearns, 25 April 1863, Stearns Papers; *War of the Rebellion*, Series One, 14: 860–61.

17. "Letters of Dr. Rogers," 382; Looby, *Journal and Letters*, 121.

18. "Letters of Dr. Rogers," 382; Looby, *Journal and Letters*, 117; James Montgomery to Mrs. George L. Stearns, 25 April 1863, Stearns Papers; New York *Daily Tribune*, 8 April 1863; Benjamin R. McPherson to Theodore McPherson, 28 March 1863, McPherson Family Papers; *Supplement to the Official Records*, 77: 754; *War of the Rebellion*, Series One, 14: 236.

19. Clancy, *Yankee in a Confederate Town*, 91–92; New York *Daily Tribune*, 8 April 1863; Blakey, Lainhart, and Stephens, *Rose Cottage Chronicles*, 10 (map); Andrew Newman to father, 23 December 1862, 24 May 1863, Newman Papers; Buckingham, *All's for the Best*, 46, 49; L. D. Stickney to Salmon P. Chase, 16 April 1863, Chase Papers; Looby, *Journal and Letters*, 112; Augusta *Daily Constitutionalist*, 29 April 1863; Savannah *Daily Morning News*, 27 April 1863; Keene, "Jacksonville," 10.

20. *Norwich* log, 28 March 1863, RBNP; Looby, *Journal and Letters*, 117; "Letters of Dr. Rogers," 382; chief of staff to officer commanding at Jacksonville, 26 March 1863, RUSACC, Pt. 1, E-4088, vol. 3; *War of the Rebellion*, Series One, 53: 86.

21. Looby, *Journal and Letters*, 117–18, 268; "Letters of Dr. Rogers," 382.

22. Looby, *Journal and Letters*, 117–18, 122, 269; Higginson, *Army Life*, 131–32; chief of staff to officer commanding at Jacksonville, 26 March 1863, RUSACC, Pt. 1, E-4088, vol. 3; *War of the Rebellion*, Series One, 53: 86.

23. Higginson, *Army Life*, 131–32; Higginson, *Carlyle's Laugh*, 176–77; Warner, *Generals in Blue*, 432–33.

24. *Miller's Almanac 1863*; Benjamin R. McPherson to Theodore McPherson, 28, 29 March 1863, McPherson Family Papers; New York *Daily Tribune*, 8 April 1863.

25. Bingham, *Young Quartermaster*, 168; *Miller's Almanac 1863*.

26. *Norwich* log, 29 March 1863, *Paul Jones* log, 28 March 1863, RBNP; Charles Steedman to Rodgers, 29 March 1863, Steedman Correspondence; Clancy, *Yankee in a Confederate Town*, 98; New York *Daily Tribune*, 8 April 1863.

27. Looby, *Journal and Letters*, 134–35; Henry Boynton to J. D. Rust, 1 April 1863, Civil War Regimental Correspondence; Philadelphia *Press*, 9 April 1863.

28. New York *Daily Tribune*, 8 April 1863; Henry Boynton to J. D. Rust, 1 April 1863, Civil War Regimental Correspondence; New York *Evening Post*, 8 April 1863; Clancy, *Yankee in a Confederate Town*, 98; "Letters of Dr. Rogers," 383; Davis, *History of Jacksonville*, 132.

29. New York *Daily Tribune*, 8 April 1863; Henry Boynton to J. D. Rust, 1 April 1863, Civil War Regimental Correspondence; Benjamin R. McPherson to Theodore McPherson, 29 March 1863, McPherson Family Papers; Buckingham, *All's for the Best*, 49.

30. New York *Daily Tribune*, 8 April 1863; O. S. Sanford to James F. Hall, 1 April 1863, RUSACC, Pt. 1, E-4277; Looby, *Journal and Letters*, 114, 119; Regimental Descriptive Book, 34th USCT Infantry, Regimental Records, RAGO.

31. Benjamin R. McPherson to Theodore McPherson, 28 March 1863, McPherson Family Papers; New York *Daily Tribune*, 8 April 1863; New York *Evening Post*, 8 April 1863; Higginson, *Army Life*, 130; *War of the Rebellion*, Series One, 14: 233.

32. O. S. Sanford to James F. Hall, 1 April 1863, RUSACC, Pt. 1, E-4277; New York *Daily Tribune*, 8 April 1863; Benjamin R. McPherson to Theodore McPherson, 28 March 1863, McPherson Family Papers; New York *Evening Post*, 8 April 1863; Cadwell, *Old Sixth Regiment*, 60; Looby, *Journal and Letters*, 119.

33. Higginson, *Army Life*, 130; New York *Evening Post*, 8 April 1863; Fernandina provost marshal to provost marshal general, 3 April 1863, RUSACC, Pt. 4, E-1599; New York *Daily Tribune*, 8 April 1863; Looby, *Journal and Letters*, 135.

34. Looby, *Journal and Letters*, 135; Fernandina provost marshal to provost marshal general, 3 April 1863, RUSACC, Pt. 4, E-1599.

35. Benjamin R. McPherson to Theodore McPherson, 29 March 1863, McPherson Family Papers; Cadwell, *Old Sixth Regiment*, 60; Clancy, *Yankee in a Confederate Town*,

99; Fernandina provost marshal to provost marshal general, 13 April 1863, RUSACC, Pt. 4, E-1599.

36. "Letters of Dr. Rogers," 383; Higginson, *Army Life*, 131; Benjamin R. McPherson to Theodore McPherson, 28, 29 March 1863, McPherson Family Papers; Looby, *Journal and Letters*, 135.

37. Clancy, *Yankee in a Confederate Town*, 99; Henry Boynton to J. D. Rust, 1 April 1863, Civil War Regimental Correspondence.

38. John D. Rust to Charles Halpine, 9 May 1863, RUSACC, Pt. 1, E-4109; "Tax Commissioners of Florida," 57.

39. Augusta *Daily Constitutionalist*, 16 April 1863; Charles P. Lord to sister, 25 April 1863, Lord Papers; New York *Daily Tribune*, 8 April 1863; New York *Evening Post*, 8 April 1863; "Letters of Dr. Rogers," 383; Looby, *Journal and Letters*, 135; Davis, *History of Jacksonville*, 132; Andrew Newman to father, 24 May 1863, Newman Papers; Buckingham, *All's for the Best*, 49; L. D. Stickney to Salmon P. Chase, 16 April 1863, Chase Papers.

40. Martin Emmons to brother, 3 May 1863, Southworth Papers.

41. Charles P. Lord to sister, 25 April 1863, Lord Papers; Clancy, *Yankee in a Confederate Town*, 98; *Supplement to the Official Records*, 3: 673; Cadwell, *Old Sixth Regiment*, 60.

42. Charles P. Lord to sister, 25 April 1863, Lord Papers; L. D. Stickney to Salmon P. Chase, 16 April 1863, Chase Papers; Clancy, *Yankee in a Confederate Town*, 98; New York *Evening Post*, 8 April 1863; Davis, *History of Jacksonville*, 132; Bangor *Daily Whig and Courier*, 14 May 1863.

43. Henry Boynton to J. D. Rust, 1 April 1863, Civil War Regimental Correspondence; Augusta *Daily Constitutionalist*, 16 April 1863; Philadelphia *Inquirer*, 27 April 1863; Clancy, *Yankee in a Confederate Town*, 98; "Letters of Dr. Rogers," 383.

44. Higginson, *Army Life*, 131; Clancy, *Yankee in a Confederate Town*, 98; Looby, *Journal and Letters*, 135.

45. Looby, *Journal and Letters*, 134–35; New York *Evening Post*, 8 April 1863; "Letters of Dr. Rogers," 383; *War of the Rebellion*, Series Three, 4: 916.

46. Looby, *Journal and Letters*, 134–35; Higginson, *Army Life*, 130; New York *Evening Post*, 8 April 1863; "Letters of Dr. Rogers," 383; "Tax Commissioners of Florida," 101.

47. *Norwich* log, 29 March 1863, RBNP; New York *Daily Tribune*, 8 April 1863; Higginson, *Army Life*, 131.

48. New York *Daily Tribune*, 8 April 1863; Looby, *Journal and Letters*, 269.

49. Looby, *Journal and Letters*, 119, 120; Blakey, Lainhart, and Stephens, *Rose Cottage Chronicles*, 10; New York *Daily Tribune*, 8 April 1863.

50. "Letters of Dr. Rogers," 383; Robert Polite file, 33rd Regiment, CMSR; Descriptive Book of Company G and Casualties Book, 33rd USCT Infantry, Regimental Records, RAGO.

51. Henry Boynton to J. D. Rust, 1 April 1863, Civil War Regimental Correspondence.

52. Martin and Schafer, *Jacksonville's Ordeal*, 163–64; Blakey, Lainhart, and Stephens, *Rose Cottage Chronicles*, 10; Henry Boynton to J. D. Rust, 1 April 1863, Civil War Regimental Correspondence; Benjamin R. McPherson to Theodore McPherson, 29 March 1863, McPherson Family Papers; *Norwich* log, 29 March 1863, RBNP; Augusta *Daily Constitutionalist*, 16 April 1863; New York *Daily Tribune*, 8 April 1863; Phila-

delphia *Inquirer*, 27 April 1863; Savannah *Daily Morning News*, 6 April 1863; Buckingham, *All's for the Best*, 49; Clancy, *Yankee in a Confederate Town*, 98; Thomas Wentworth Higginson, "Some War Scenes Revisited," *Atlantic Monthly*, 42 (1878): 1; Higginson, *Army Life*, 131.

53. Benjamin R. McPherson to Theodore McPherson, 29 March 1863, McPherson Family Papers; *Norwich* log, 29 March 1863, RBNP; Higginson, *Army Life*, 130; Cadwell, *Old Sixth Regiment*, 61; Higginson, "Some War Scenes Revisited," 1; "Letters of Dr. Rogers," 383; Looby, *Journal and Letters*, 119, 120.

54. New York *Daily Tribune*, 8 April 1863; Benjamin R. McPherson to Theodore McPherson, 29 March 1863, McPherson Family Papers; Cadwell, *Old Sixth Regiment*, 61; Buckingham, *All's for the Best*, 49; "Letters of Dr. Rogers," 383.

Chapter Eight **THE AFTERMATH**

1. Benjamin R. McPherson to Theodore McPherson, 29 March 1863, McPherson Family Papers; New York *Daily Tribune*, 8 April 1863; Buckingham, *All's for the Best*, 226; "Letters of Dr. Rogers," 383.

2. Benjamin R. McPherson to Theodore McPherson, 29 March 1863, McPherson Family Papers; *Norwich* log, 29 March 1863, RBNP; New York *Daily Tribune*, 8 April 1863; "Letters of Dr. Rogers," 383; L. D. Stickney to Salmon P. Chase, 16 April 1863, Chase Papers; Looby, *Journal and Letters*, 119; Cadwell, *Old Sixth Regiment*, 61.

3. New York *Daily Tribune*, 8 April 1863; Buckingham, *All's for the Best*, 49; L. D. Stickney to Salmon P. Chase, 16 April 1863, Chase Papers; *Norwich* log, 29 March 1863, RBNP; "Letters of Dr. Rogers," 383; Looby, *Journal and Letters*, 123, 135.

4. Benjamin R. McPherson to Theodore McPherson, 29 March 1863, McPherson Family Papers; "Letters of Dr. Rogers," 383–84; Looby, *Journal and Letters*, 119, 120, 121–22, 123, 135; Buckingham, *All's for the Best*, 49; *Official Records of the Navies*, Series One, 13: 794.

5. Looby, *Journal and Letters*, 120, 139, 273; "Letters of Dr. Rogers," 383, 383, 384; Berlin, *Black Military Experience*, 57–58.

6. Buckingham, *All's for the Best*, 50; "Letters of Dr. Rogers," 384; Looby, *Journal and Letters*, 123.

7. *Norwich* log, 31 March, 1 April 1863, RBNP; *Supplement to the Official Records*, 3: 668, 77: 754; Looby, *Journal and Letters*, 123, 269; General Order No. 38, 15 April 1863, Order Book, 33rd USCT Infantry, Regimental Records, RAGO; George Gardiner to O. S. Sanford, 1 April 1863, RUSACC, Pt. 4, E-1599.

8. L. D. Stickney to Salmon P. Chase, 16 April 1863, Chase Papers; New York *Daily Tribune*, 8 April 1863.

9. *Miller's Almanac 1863*; General Order No. 38, 15 April 1863, Order Book, 33rd USCT Infantry, Regimental Records, RAGO.

10. O. S. Sanford to James F. Hall, 1 April 1863, RUSACC, Pt. 1, E-4277; *Supplement to the Official Records*, 3: 668, 673; Philadelphia *Press*, 9 April 1863; Looby, *Journal and Letters*, 269; New York *Daily Tribune*, 8 April 1863; Buckingham, *All's for the Best*, 50; Cadwell, *Old Sixth Regiment*, 61; "Tax Commissioners of Florida," 14.

11. Looby, *Journal and Letters*, 121, 135; "Letters of Dr. Rogers," 384; O. S. Sanford to

James F. Hall, 1 April 1863, RUSACC, Pt. 1, E-4277; George Gardiner to O. S. Sanford, 1 April 1863, RUSACC, Pt. 4, E-1599; Schmidt, *Civil War in Florida*, 1: 591; "Tax Commissioners of Florida," 101.

12. "Tax Commissioners of Florida," 4, 14, 25, 30–31, 75, 101; "Letters of Dr. Rogers," 384.

13. "Tax Commissioners of Florida," 14, 57; Clancy, *Yankee in a Confederate Town*, 99; *Norwich* log, 1 April 1863, RBNP; Fernandina provost marshal to provost marshal general, 3 April 1863, RUSACC, Pt. 4, E-1599.

14. *Supplement to the Official Records*, 3: 668, 673, 77: 741, 744, 749, 754; "Letters of Dr. Rogers," 384; Philadelphia *Press*, 9 April 1863; Buckingham, *All's for the Best*, 50; Cadwell, *Old Sixth Regiment*, 61; New York *Daily Tribune*, 8 April 1863; Catherine S. Craven Diary, 29 March–3 April 1863, John Joseph Craven Papers, Library of Congress, Washington; Higginson, *Army Life*, 133.

15. Looby, *Journal and Letters*, 123–24, 140, 269; "Letters of Dr. Rogers," 386; Higginson, *Army Life*, 133–37; Taylor, *Reminiscences*, 58; Stevenson, *Journals*, 473.

16. *War of the Rebellion*, Series Three, 3: 116–17; Stevenson, *Journals*, 464, 465–66; Hays, *Du Pont Letters*, 2: 521; "Letters of Dr. Rogers," 384; Looby, *Journal and Letters*, 122; Edward W. Hooper to Robert W. Hooper, 25 March 1863, Hooper Papers.

17. "Letters of Dr. Rogers," 384; "Tax Commissioners of Florida," 75–76, 101; O. S. Sanford to James F. Hall, 1 April 1863, RUSACC, Pt. 1, E-4277.

18. "Tax Commissioners of Florida," 4, 14, 30–31, 75–76; L. D. Stickney to Salmon P. Chase, 16 April 1863, Chase Papers.

19. Stevenson, *Journals*, 471–72; Looby, *Journal and Letters*, 126.

20. Stevenson, *Journals*, 464–77; Looby, *Journal and Letters*, 124, 126; "Letters of Dr. Rogers," 386.

21. Higginson, *Army Life*, 137–50; Looby, *Journal and Letters*, 124–53, 269–83; "Letters of Dr. Rogers," 386–94; General Order No. 38, 15 April 1863, Order Book, 33rd USCT Infantry, Regimental Records, RAGO; Ogaff Williams file, 33rd Regiment, CMSR.

22. Looby, *Journal and Letters*, 129; Higginson, *Army Life*, 133; "Letters of Dr. Rogers," 384, 385, 388, 389; Descriptive Book of Company G, 33rd USCT Infantry, Regimental Records, RAGO; John Quincy file, 33rd Regiment, CMSR.

23. Looby, *Journal and Letters*, 122, 127, 134, 151–52, 269; Higginson, *Army Life*, 131–32; "Letters of Dr. Rogers," 381, 382, 385.

24. Stevenson, *Journals*, 466; *War of the Rebellion*, Series One, 14: 424, 431, 432, Series Three, 3: 117; Looby, *Journal and Letters*, 122, 134.

25. New York *World*, 24 March 1863; New York *Evening Post*, 4 March 1863; *War of the Rebellion*, Series One, 14: 424–25.

26. *War of the Rebellion*, Series One, 14: 240–43, 436–42; Stephen R. Wise, *Gate of Hell: Campaign for Charleston Harbor, 1863* (Columbia, S.C., 1994), 28–32; Miller, *Lincoln's Abolitionist General*, 138–41.

27. Cincinnati *Daily Enquirer*, 21 March 1863; St. Louis *Daily Missouri Democrat*, 21 March 1863; Chicago *Tribune*, 23 March 1863; Milwaukee *Daily Sentinel*, 23 March 1863; San Francisco *Daily Evening Bulletin*, 24 March 1863.

28. Boston *Commonwealth*, 27 March 1863; Boston *Daily Advertiser*, 31 March 1863; Chicago *Tribune*, 25 March 1863; Montpelier *Vermont Watchman and State Journal*, 27 March 1863; New York *Daily Tribune*, 24 March 1863; New York *Times*, 22, 25

March 1863; Philadelphia *Daily Evening Bulletin*, 23 March 1863; Philadelphia *Press*, 25 March 1863; Washington *Daily Morning Chronicle*, 26 March 1863; *Christian Recorder* (Philadelphia), 28 March 1863.

29. Hartford *Daily Times*, 21 March 1863; *New York World*, 19 March 1863.

30. Roy P. Basler, ed., *The Collected Works of Abraham Lincoln*, 8 vols. (New Brunswick, N.J., 1953), 6: 158; *War of the Rebellion*, Series One, 14: 435–36; Miller, *Lincoln's Abolitionist General*, 50–52, 102–03.

31. Milwaukee *Daily Sentinel*, 21 April 1863; New York *Evening Post*, 8 April 1863; Boston *Daily Advertiser*, 10 April 1863; Philadelphia *Daily Evening Bulletin*, 9 April 1863.

32. Philadelphia *Daily Evening Bulletin*, 9 April 1863; Boston *Daily Advertiser*, 9, 10 April 1863; New York *Daily Tribune*, 8 April 1863; Higginson, *Army Life*, 130–31; New York *Times*, 17 April 1863; New York *Evening Post*, 8 April 1863; Bangor *Daily Whig and Courier*, 14 May 1863; Cleveland (Ohio) *Daily Cleveland Herald*, 11 April 1863; Milwaukee *Daily Sentinel*, 21 April 1863.

33. Looby, *Journal and Letters*, 134–37, 270; Higginson, *Army Life*, 131; New York *Evening Post*, 8 April 1863.

34. *War of the Rebellion*, Series Three, 3: 117, 177–78, 191; Looby, *Journal and Letters*, 134; Stevenson, *Journals*, 466.

35. *War of the Rebellion*, Series One, 14: 441–42, 443, 452, 456–57, 461, Series Three, 3: 191, 740.

36. Ibid., Series One, 14: 318–19, 462–63, 28(1): 194–95, 28(2): 3, 5; Higginson, *Army Life*, 163–76; E. Merton Coulter, "Robert Gould Shaw and the Burning of Darien, Georgia," *Civil War History*, 5 (1959): 363–73; Miller, *Lincoln's Abolitionist General*, 145–46, 153–56.

37. *War of the Rebellion*, Series One, 35(1): 276–77, 279, 35(2): 16; McPherson, *Battle Cry of Freedom*, 722.

38. Looby, *Journal and Letters*, 114–15, 116, 117, 120, 199–200, 267, 268; James Montgomery to Mrs. George L. Stearns, 25 April 1863, Stearns Papers; *War of the Rebellion*, Series One, 14: 838, 840, 860, Series Three, 3: 116–17; New York *Daily Tribune*, 8 April 1863; Hayes, *Du Pont Letters*, 2: 521; Stevenson, *Journals*, 473.

39. Port Royal *New South*, 28 March 1863; "Letters of Dr. Rogers," 386; Buckingham, *All's for the Best*, 225–26; Pierce, "Freedmen at Port Royal," 314; Cornish, *Sable Arm*, 93.

40. New York *Times*, 21 April 1863; *Zion's Herald and Wesleyan Journal*, 24 June 1863; Pierce, "Freedmen at Port Royal," 313–14; *American Missionary*, 7 (1863): 140; New York *Daily Tribune*, 20 April 1863; *War of the Rebellion*, Series Three, 3: 117, 177, 191.

41. Trudeau, *Like Men of War*, 3–7, 27–31; New York *Times*, 19 November 1862; Mansfield French to wife, 25 March 1863, French Family Papers.

42. Philadelphia *Daily Evening Bulletin*, 23, 26 March 1863; *Christian Recorder*, 28 March 1863; New York *Evening Post*, 8 April 1863; New York *Times*, 21 April 1863; Chicago *Tribune*, 25 March 1863; Mansfield French to wife, 25 March 1863, French Family Papers.

43. Washington *Evening Star*, 24 March 1863; New York *Daily Tribune*, 25 March 1863; Philadelphia *Daily Evening Bulletin*, 26 March 1863; Boston *Daily Advertiser*, 31 March 1863.

44. *War of the Rebellion*, Series Three, 5: 118; Cornish, *Sable Arm*, 114–15, 124.

45. *War of the Rebellion*, Series Three, 5: 118, 660–61; Cornish, *Sable Arm*, 95–96, 99, 113;

Berlin, *Black Military Experience*, 7–9, 10; Trudeau, *Like Men of War*, 18–19; Donald, *Lincoln*, 366–67, 429–31.

46. Looby, *Journal and Letters*, 145. The connection between the Florida expedition and the administration's decision is also noted in *Zion's Herald and Wesleyan Journal*, 24 June 1863.

47. *War of the Rebellion*, Series Three, 3: 99–103, 122, 5: 118; Cornish, *Sable Arm*, 99, 110–11, 113–14, 124, 129–30; Quarles, *Negro in the Civil War*, 194; Berlin, *Black Military Experience*, 9–10; Basler, *Collected Works of Lincoln*, 6: 149–50.

48. Cornish, *Sable Arm*, 94–95, 111, 113–14, 124, 129–31; Berlin, *Black Military Experience*, 10; Quarles, *Negro in the Civil War*, 194–95, 197–99; *War of the Rebellion*, Series Three, 3: 438, 1111–15, 5: 118–24, 660–61.

49. *War of the Rebellion*, Series Three, 4: 1027; Looby, *Journal and Letters*, 145, 176–77; Higginson, *Army Life*, 123.

50. Looby, *Journal and Letters*, 209–10.

51. Frederick H. Dyer, *A Compendium of the War of the Rebellion*, 3 vols. (New York and London, 1959), 3: 1636, 1729; Higginson, *Army Life*, 133–76, 214–30, 248–51; Higginson, "First Black Regiment," 531.

Epilogue

1. Higginson, "Some War Scenes Revisited," 1–2, 6.

2. Ibid., 2, 3; Edelstein, *Strange Enthusiasm*, 288–95; Higginson, *Army Life*, 173–74, 248; Looby, *Journal and Letters*, 375; Thomas W. Higginson file, 33rd Regiment, CMSR.

3. Looby, *Journal and Letters*, 139, 144, 162, 162n., 303, 304, 344; Stevenson, *Journals*, 431; Higginson, *Army Life*, 174–75, 249, 255, 256; Liberty Billings file, John D. Strong file, Charles T. Trowbridge file, 33rd Regiment, CMSR.

4. Bingham, *Young Quartermaster*, 9–14, 113–25; Higginson, *Army Life*, 170, 257; Looby, *Journal and Letters*, 349, 349n.; Luther M. Bingham file, 33rd Regiment, CMSR.

5. Seth Rogers file, 33rd Regiment, CMSR; Higginson, *Army Life*, 255; "Letters of Dr. Rogers," 396–97; Looby, *Journal and Letters*, 281, 285, 316, 320, 326–27, 338, 339, 341, 343; Stevenson, *Journals*, xxxvii–xl, 48–55.

6. "Tax Commissioners of Florida," 1–12; Donald, *Inside Lincoln's Cabinet*, 190; L. D. Stickney to Edward Everett Hale, 30 September 1863, New England Emigrant Aid Company Papers; Smith, "Carpetbag Imperialism," 112–13, 260–62, 267–95; Futch, "Chase and Civil War Politics," 165–66, 166–67, 169–88; Shofner, *Nor Is It Over Yet*, 5–15; Martin and Schafer, *Jacksonville's Ordeal*, 171–74, 231–32; Shofner, "Andrew Johnson and the Fernandina Unionists," 213–14, 216, 218; Gray and Ropes, *War Letters*, 502; Michael Burlingame, ed., *At Lincoln's Side: John Hay's Civil War Correspondence and Selected Writings* (Carbondale and Edwardsville, Ill., 2000), 243–44.

7. Dyer, *Compendium of the War*, 3: 1636, 1729; Looby, *Journal and Letters*, 146, 154, 158–59, 185, 287, 288, 289, 344–45; Trudeau, *Like Men of War*, 72–73; *War of the Rebellion*, Series One, 14: 466–67; Dirck, "By the Hand of God," 115; Milwaukee *Sentinel*, 21 December 1871. On "hard war," see Mark Grimsley, *The Hard Hand of War: Union Military Policy Toward Southern Civilians, 1861–1865* (Cambridge, U.K., and other cities, 1995); and Stephen V. Ash, *When the Yankees Came: Conflict and Chaos in the Occupied South, 1861–1865* (Chapel Hill, N. C., and London, 1995).

8. Miller, *Lincoln's Abolitionist General*, chapters 6–9; Looby, *Journal and Letters*, 143, 279–80, 286.

9. Warner, *Generals in Blue*, 420–21; Looby, *Journal and Letters*, 183, 185, 186; Higginson, *Carlyle's Laugh*, 175–82.

10. Higginson, *Army Life*, 267–76; Glatthaar, *Forged in Battle*, 169–76; Thomas W. Higginson file, 33rd Regiment, CMSR; Thomas Wentworth Higginson to Thaddeus Stevens, 20 June 1864, Stevens Papers.

11. Charles T. Trowbridge Reminiscences, 25–28, South Carolina Historical Society, Charleston; Higginson, *Army Life*, 277–79; Berlin, *Black Military Experience*, 786–87.

12. Higginson, *Army Life*, 245, 249; Schafer, "Freedom Was as Close as the River," 113–16; Higginson, "Some War Scenes Revisited," 3; Eric Foner, *Freedom's Lawmakers: A Directory of Black Officeholders During Reconstruction* (New York, 1993), 136, 183–84; pension files of Thomas Long, Company G, 1st South Carolina/33rd USCT Infantry, and Prince Rivers, Company A, 1st South Carolina/33rd USCT Infantry, Civil War Pension Files.

13. Taylor, *Reminiscences*, 7–17, 124–29, 133.

14. Higginson, "Some War Scenes Revisited," 3; Taylor, *Reminiscences*, 112; Trowbridge Reminiscences, 15–17, 30–31; Frederick Brown file, 33rd Regiment, CMSR.

15. Edelstein, *Strange Enthusiasm*, chapter 19; Higginson, *Army Life*, 7–8, 11, 20–23, 251.

BIBLIOGRAPHY

Manuscripts

Abell, Jared Andrus, Letters. South Caroliniana Library, University of South Carolina.

Andrew, John A., Papers. Massachusetts Historical Society, Boston.

Bryant, John Emory, Papers. Duke University Library.

Burnell, Henry L., Papers. South Caroliniana Library, University of South Carolina.

Case Files of Applications from Former Confederates for Presidential Pardons ("Amnesty Papers"), 1865–1867: Florida. M1003, National Archives, Washington.

Chase, Salmon P., Papers. Library of Congress, Washington.

Civil War Pension Files. RG 15, National Archives, Washington.

Civil War Regimental Correspondence, 8th Maine Infantry. Maine State Archives, Augusta.

Compiled Military Service Records of Volunteer Union Soldiers Who Served with the United States Colored Troops: Infantry Organizations, 31st Through 35th. M1992, National Archives, Washington.

Cooley, William Henry, Papers. Southern Historical Collection, University of North Carolina, Chapel Hill.

Craven, Catherine S., Diary. John Joseph Craven Papers. Library of Congress, Washington.

Dozier, Etrulia P., "Black Union Soldiers: Who Were the Civil War Black Soldiers?" Typescript, South Caroliniana Library, University of South Carolina.

Eighth Census, 1860, Manuscript Returns of Free Inhabitants. National Archives, Washington.

Fairbanks Collection. Special Collections Department, Florida State University Libraries, Tallahassee.

French Family Papers. Onondaga Historical Association, Syracuse, New York.

Hawks, Esther Hill, Papers. Library of Congress, Washington.

Higginson, T. W., Papers. American Antiquarian Society, Worcester, Massachusetts.

Higginson, Thomas Wentworth, Papers, bMS Am 784 (20–23, 699–958). By permission of the Houghton Library, Harvard University.

Hooper, Edward William, Papers. Houghton Library, Harvard University.

L'Engle, Edward McCrady, Papers. Southern Historical Collection, University of North Carolina, Chapel Hill.

Letters Received by the Confederate Secretary of War, 1861–1865. M437, National Archives, Washington.

Lincoln, Abraham, Papers. Library of Congress, Washington.

Lord, Charles Phineas, Papers. Duke University Library.

McPherson, Theodore H. N., Family Papers. Library of Congress, Washington.

Milton, John, Letterbook. Governor's Office Letterbooks, 1836–1909, RG 101, Series 32, Florida State Archives, Tallahassee.

Montgomery, James, Papers. Kansas State Historical Society, Topeka.

New England Emigrant Aid Company Papers. Kansas State Historical Society, Topeka.

Newman, George, Papers. Duke University Library.

Pomeroy, Willis Asa, Correspondence. Connecticut Historical Society, Hartford.

Records of the Adjutant General's Office. RG 94, National Archives, Washington.

Records of the Bureau of Naval Personnel. RG 24, National Archives, Washington.

Records of the U.S. Army Continental Commands. RG 393, National Archives, Washington.

Reed, A. M., Diary. Typescript copy, Duke University Library.

Settled Case Files for Claims Approved by the Southern Claims Commission, 1871 to 1880. E732, RG 217, National Archives, College Park, Maryland.

Seventh Census, 1850, Manuscript Returns of Free Inhabitants. National Archives, Washington.

Shedd, Calvin, Papers. Special Collections, University of Miami. Available at www.library .miami.edu/archives/shedd.

Skinner, Richard, Letters. Southern Historical Collection, University of North Carolina, Chapel Hill.

Southworth, C. Eugene, Papers. Duke University Library.

Staples, George A., Diary. Connecticut Historical Society, Hartford.

Stearns, George L. and Mary E., Papers. Kansas State Historical Society, Topeka.

Steedman, Charles, Correspondence. File 00/488, Special Collections, University of Florida Library, Gainesville.

Stevens, Thaddeus, Papers. Library of Congress, Washington.

Trowbridge, Charles T., Reminiscences. South Carolina Historical Society, Charleston.

United States Sanitary Commission Records. New York Public Library.

White, Maunsel, Papers. Southern Historical Collection, University of North Carolina, Chapel Hill.

Newspapers and Journals

American Missionary
Augusta (Georgia) *Daily Chronicle and Sentinel*
Augusta (Georgia) *Daily Constitutionalist*
Augusta (Maine) *Kennebec Journal*
Baltimore *American and Commercial Advertiser*
Bangor (Maine) *Daily Whig and Courier*
Beaufort (South Carolina) *Free South*
Boston *Commonwealth*
Boston *Daily Advertiser*

Charleston (South Carolina) *Daily Courier*
Charleston (South Carolina) *Mercury*
Chicago *Tribune*
Christian Recorder (Philadelphia)
Cincinnati *Daily Enquirer*
Cleveland (Ohio) *Daily Cleveland Herald*
Douglass' Monthly
Farmington (Maine) *Chronicle*
Farmington (Maine) *Franklin Patriot*
Frank Leslie's Illustrated Newspaper
Hartford (Connecticut) *Daily Courant*
Hartford (Connecticut) *Daily Times*
The Independent (New York)
Jackson (Mississippi) *Daily Southern Crisis*
The Liberator (Boston)
Lowell (Massachusetts) *Daily Citizen and News*
Milwaukee *Daily Sentinel*
Milwaukee *Sentinel*
Montpelier *Vermont Watchman and State Journal*
New Haven (Connecticut) *Morning Journal and Courier*
New York *Daily Tribune*
New York *Evening Post*
New York *Herald*
New York *Times*
New York *World*
Philadelphia *Daily Evening Bulletin*
Philadelphia *Inquirer*
Philadelphia *Press*
Port Royal (South Carolina) *New South*
Richmond *Daily Dispatch*
Richmond *Whig and Public Advertiser*
St. Louis *Daily Missouri Democrat*
San Francisco *Daily Evening Bulletin*
Savannah *Daily Morning News*
Stamford (Connecticut) *Advocate*
Tallahassee *Florida Sentinel*
Washington *Daily Morning Chronicle*
Washington *Daily National Intelligencer*
Washington *Evening Star*
Zion's Herald and Wesleyan Journal

Published Primary Sources

Ammen, Daniel. "Du Pont and the Port Royal Expedition." In Robert Underwood Johnson and Clarence Clough Buel, eds., *Battles and Leaders of the Civil War*, 4 vols. (New York, 1888; reprint, New York and London, 1956), 1: 671–91.

Atlas to Accompany the Official Records of the Union and Confederate Armies. Washington, 1891–1895.

Basler, Roy P., ed. *The Collected Works of Abraham Lincoln.* 8 vols. New Brunswick, N.J., 1953.

Beale, Howard K., ed. *The Diary of Edward Bates, 1859–1866.* Washington, 1933.

———, ed. *Diary of Gideon Welles: Secretary of the Navy Under Lincoln and Johnson.* 3 vols. New York, 1960.

Becker, Carl M., and Ritchie Thomas, eds. *Hearth and Knapsack: The Ladley Letters, 1857–1880.* Athens, Ohio, 1988.

Berlin, Ira, et al., eds. *The Black Military Experience.* Cambridge, U.K., and other cities, 1982.

———, eds. *The Destruction of Slavery.* Cambridge, U.K., and other cities, 1985.

———, eds. *The Wartime Genesis of Free Labor: The Lower South.* Cambridge, U.K., and other cities, 1990.

Blakey, Arch Fredric, Ann Smith Lainhart, and Winston Bryant Stephens, Jr., eds. *Rose Cottage Chronicles: Civil War Letters of the Bryant-Stephens Families of North Florida.* Gainesville, Fla., 1998.

Bornet, Vaughn D., ed. "A Connecticut Yankee After Olustee." *Florida Historical Quarterly,* 27 (1948–49): 385–403.

———, ed. "A Connecticut Yankee Fights at Olustee: Letters from the Front." *Florida Historical Quarterly,* 27 (1948–49): 237–59.

Buckingham, Peter H., ed. *All's for the Best: The Civil War Reminiscences and Letters of Daniel W. Sawtelle, Eighth Maine Volunteer Infantry.* Knoxville, Tenn., 2001.

Burlingame, Michael, ed. *At Lincoln's Side: John Hay's Civil War Correspondence and Selected Writings.* Carbondale and Edwardsville, Ill., 2000.

———, and John R. Turner Ettlinger, eds. *Inside Lincoln's White House: The Complete Civil War Diary of John Hay.* Carbondale and Edwardsville, Ill., 1997.

Cadwell, Charles K. *The Old Sixth Regiment, Its War Record, 1861–5.* New Haven, Conn., 1875.

Clancy, Anne Robinson, ed. *A Yankee in a Confederate Town: The Journal of Calvin L. Robinson.* Sarasota, Fla., 2002.

Coffin, Charles Carleton. *Four Years of Fighting: A Volume of Personal Observation with the Army and Navy, from the First Battle of Bull Run to the Fall of Richmond.* Boston, 1866.

Dancy, James M. "Reminiscences of the Civil War." *Florida Historical Quarterly,* 37 (1958–59): 66–89.

Davis, W. W. H. *History of the 104th Pennsylvania Regiment, from August 22nd, 1861, to September 30th, 1864.* Philadelphia, 1866.

De Forest, Bartholomew S. *Random Sketches and Wandering Thoughts.* Albany, N.Y., 1866.

Dennett, Tyler, ed. *Lincoln and the Civil War in the Diaries and Letters of John Hay.* New York, 1939.

Dickison, Mary Elizabeth. *Dickison and His Men: Reminiscences of the War in Florida.* Louisville, Ky., 1890.

Donald, David, ed. *Inside Lincoln's Cabinet: The Civil War Diaries of Salmon P. Chase.* New York, 1954.

Duncan, Russell, ed. *Blue-Eyed Child of Fortune: The Civil War Letters of Colonel Robert Gould Shaw.* Athens, Ga., and London, 1992.

First Annual Report of the National Freedman's Relief Association, New York, February 19th, 1863. New York, 1863.

Florida State Genealogical Society. *Census, Department of the South, November, 1864: For Jacksonville, Fernandina and St. Augustine, Florida: Ordered by the Department of the South, Hilton Head, South Carolina.* Tallahassee, 2002.

Foner, Philip S., ed. *The Life and Writings of Frederick Douglass.* 4 vols. New York, 1950–55.

Forten, Charlotte. "Life on the Sea Islands." *Atlantic Monthly*, 13 (1864): 587–96, 666–76.

The Freedmen of South Carolina: An Address Delivered by J. Miller M'Kim, in Sansom Hall, July 9th, 1862. Philadelphia, 1862.

Gannett, William Channing, and Edward Everett Hale. "The Freedmen at Port Royal." *North American Review*, 101 (1865): 1–28.

Gordon, George H. *A War Diary of Events in the War of the Great Rebellion, 1863–1865.* Boston, 1882.

Gray, John Chipman, and John Codman Ropes. *War Letters, 1862–1865.* Boston and New York, 1927.

Halpine, Charles Graham. *The Life and Adventures, Songs, Services, and Speeches of Private Miles O'Reilly.* New York, 1864.

Hayes, John D., ed. *Samuel Francis Du Pont: A Selection from His Civil War Letters.* 3 vols. Ithaca, N.Y., 1969.

Higginson, Thomas Wentworth. *Army Life in a Black Regiment.* Boston, 1870; reprint, New York and London, 1984.

———. *Carlyle's Laugh: And Other Surprises.* Boston, 1909.

———. "The First Black Regiment." *Outlook*, 59 (1898): 521–31.

———. "The Ordeal by Battle." *Atlantic Monthly*, 8 (1861): 88–95.

———. "Some War Scenes Revisited." *Atlantic Monthly*, 42 (1878): 1–9.

Hodges, Ellen E., and Stephen Kerber, eds. "'Rogues and Black Hearted Scamps': Civil War Letters of Winston and Octavia Stephens, 1862–1863." *Florida Historical Quarterly*, 57 (1978–79): 54–82.

Holland, Rupert Sargent, ed. *The Letters and Diary of Laura M. Towne; Written from the Sea Islands of South Carolina, 1862–1884.* Cambridge, Mass., 1912; reprint, New York, 1969.

Keene, Otis L. "Jacksonville, Fifty-three Years Ago: Recollections of a Veteran." *Florida Historical Quarterly*, 1 (1909): 9–15.

"A Letter of Captain V. Chamberlain, 7th Connecticut Volunteers." *Florida Historical Quarterly*, 15 (1936–37): 85–95.

"Letters of Dr. Seth Rogers, 1862, 1863." *Massachusetts Historical Society Proceedings*, 43 (1910): 337–98.

Looby, Christopher, ed. *The Complete Civil War Journal and Selected Letters of Thomas Wentworth Higginson.* Chicago and London, 2000.

Miller's Planters' & Merchants' State Rights Almanac for the Year of Our Lord 1863. Charleston, S.C., n.d. (c. 1862).

Murray, Amelia M. *Letters from the United States, Cuba and Canada.* New York, *1856.*

Niven, John, ed. *The Salmon P. Chase Papers.* 5 vols. Kent, Ohio, 1993–98.

Official Records of the Union and Confederate Navies in the War of the Rebellion. 31 vols. Washington, 1894–1927.

Pearson, Elizabeth Ware, ed. *Letters from Port Royal, 1862–1868.* Boston, 1906; reprint, New York, 1969.

Pierce, Edward L. "The Freedmen at Port Royal." *Atlantic Monthly,* 12 (1863): 291–315.

Report of the Joint Committee on the Conduct of the War. 9 vols. Wilmington, N.C., 1998–2002.

Rogers, William Warren, ed. "Florida on the Eve of the Civil War as Seen by a Southern Reporter." *Florida Historical Quarterly,* 39 (1960–61): 145–58.

Schwartz, Gerald, ed. *A Woman Doctor's Civil War: Esther Hill Hawks' Diary.* Columbia, S.C., 1984.

Sherwood, Henry Noble, ed. "The Journal of Miss Susan Walker, March 3d to June 6th, 1862." *Quarterly Publication of the Historical and Philosophical Society of Ohio,* 7 (1912): 1–48.

Staudenraus, P. J., ed. "Occupied Beaufort, 1863: A War Correspondent's View." *South Carolina Historical Magazine,* 64 (1963): 136–44.

———, ed. "A War Correspondent's View of St. Augustine and Fernandina: 1863." *Florida Historical Quarterly,* 41 (1962–63): 60–65.

Stevenson, Brenda, ed. *The Journals of Charlotte Forten Grimké.* New York and Oxford, 1988.

Supplement to the Official Records of the Union and Confederate Armies. 83 vols. to date. Wilmington, N.C., 1994– .

Symonds, Craig L., ed. *Charleston Blockade: The Journals of John B. Marchand, U.S. Navy, 1861–1862.* Newport, R.I., 1976.

"Tax Commissioners of Florida." U.S. House of Representatives Exec. Doc. No. 18, 38th Cong., 2d sess. Washington, 1865.

Taylor, Susie King. *Reminiscences of My Life in Camp with the 33rd United States Colored Troops, Late 1st S.C. Volunteers.* Boston, 1902; reprint, Patricia W. Romero, ed., New York, 1988.

Thompson, Benjamin W. "Flight from Florida." *Civil War Times Illustrated,* 12 (1973): 12–21.

Todd, William. *The Seventy-ninth Highlanders New York Volunteers in the War of the Rebellion, 1861–1865.* Albany, N.Y., 1886.

"Under the Palmetto." *Continental Monthly,* 4 (1863): 188–203.

University of Virginia Geospatial and Statistical Data Center. *United States Historical Census Data Browser.* At www.fisher.lib.virginia.edu/census/.

The War of the Rebellion: A Compilation of the Official Records of the Union and Confederate Armies. 70 vols. in 128. Washington, 1880–1901.

Yacovone, Donald, ed. *Freedom's Journey: African American Voices of the Civil War.* Chicago, 2004.

Secondary Sources

Abbott, Richard H. *Cotton and Capital: Boston Businessmen and Antislavery Reform, 1854–1868.* Amherst, Mass., 1991.

Ash, Stephen V. *When the Yankees Came: Conflict and Chaos in the Occupied South, 1861–1865.* Chapel Hill, N.C., and London, 1995.

Bearss, Edwin C. "Military Operations on the St. Johns, September–October 1862." *Florida Historical Quarterly*, 42 (1963–64): 232–47, 331–50.

Berlin, Ira. *Many Thousands Gone: The First Two Centuries of Slavery in North America.* Cambridge, Mass., 1998.

Bingham, Luther Goodyear. *The Young Quartermaster: The Life and Death of Lieut. L. M. Bingham, of the First South Carolina Volunteers.* New York, 1863.

Blight, David W. *Frederick Douglass' Civil War: Keeping Faith in Jubilee.* Baton Rouge and London, 1989.

Browning, Robert M., Jr. *Success Is All That Was Expected: The South Atlantic Blockading Squadron During the Civil War.* Washington, 2002.

Buker, George E. *Jacksonville: Riverport-Seaport.* Columbia, S.C., 1992.

Channing, Steven A. *Crisis of Fear: Secession in South Carolina.* New York, 1970.

Clarke, Robert L. "Northern Plans for the Economic Invasion of Florida, 1862–1865." *Florida Historical Quarterly*, 28 (1949–50): 262–70.

Cornish, Dudley Taylor. *The Sable Arm: Negro Troops in the Union Army, 1861–1865.* New York, 1956; reprint, New York, 1966.

Coulter, E. Merton. "Robert Gould Shaw and the Burning of Darien, Georgia." *Civil War History*, 5 (1959): 363–73.

Creel, Margaret Washington. *"A Peculiar People": Slave Religion and Community Culture Among the Gullahs.* New York, 1988.

Davis, T. Frederick. *History of Jacksonville, Florida, and Vicinity, 1513 to 1924.* Gainesville, Fla., 1925; reprint, Gainesville, Fla., 1964.

Davis, William Watson. *The Civil War and Reconstruction in Florida.* New York, 1913; reprint, Gainesville, Fla., 1964.

Dew, Charles B. *Apostles of Disunion: Southern Secession Commissioners and the Causes of the Civil War.* Charlottesville, Va., and London, 2001.

Dirck, Brian R. "By the Hand of God: James Montgomery and Redemptive Violence." *Kansas History*, 27 (2004): 100–15.

Donald, David Herbert. *Lincoln.* New York and other cities, 1995.

Dusinberre, William. *Them Dark Days: Slavery in the American Rice Swamps.* New York, 1996.

Dyer, Frederick H. *A Compendium of the War of the Rebellion.* 3 vols. New York and London, 1959.

Edelstein, Tilden G. *Strange Enthusiasm: A Life of Thomas Wentworth Higginson.* New Haven, Conn., 1968; reprint, New York, 1970.

Foner, Eric. *Freedom's Lawmakers: A Directory of Black Officeholders During Reconstruction.* New York, 1993.

———. *Free Soil, Free Labor, Free Men: The Ideology of the Republican Party Before the Civil War.* New York, 1970.

Fowler, William M., Jr. *Under Two Flags: The American Navy in the Civil War*. New York and London, 1990.

Futch, Ovid L. "Salmon P. Chase and Civil War Politics in Florida." *Florida Historical Quarterly*, 32 (1953–54): 163–88.

Genovese, Eugene D. *Roll, Jordan, Roll: The World the Slaves Made*. New York, 1976.

Gerteis, Louis S. *From Contraband to Freedman: Federal Policy Toward Southern Blacks, 1861–1865*. Westport, Conn., 1973.

Glatthaar, Joseph T. *Forged in Battle: The Civil War Alliance of Black Soldiers and White Officers*. New York, 1990.

Gleeson, Ed. *Erin Go Gray!: An Irish Rebel Trilogy*. Carmel, Ind., 1997.

Goodrich, Thomas. *War to the Knife: Bleeding Kansas, 1854–1861*. Mechanicsburg, Pa., 1998.

Goodwin, Doris Kearns. *Team of Rivals: The Political Genius of Abraham Lincoln*. New York, 2005.

Grimsley, Mark. *The Hard Hand of War: Union Military Policy Toward Southern Civilians, 1861–1865*. Cambridge, U.K., and other cities, 1995.

Guelzo, Allen C. *Lincoln's Emancipation Proclamation: The End of Slavery in America*. New York, 2004.

Gutman, Herbert G. *The Black Family in Slavery and Freedom, 1750–1925*. New York, 1976.

Hanchett, William. *Irish: Charles G. Halpine in Civil War America*. Syracuse, N.Y., 1970.

Hargrove, Hondon B. *Black Union Soldiers in the Civil War*. Jefferson, N.C., and London, 1988.

Harris, William C. *With Charity for All: Lincoln and the Restoration of the Union*. Lexington, Ky., 1997.

Hattaway, Herman, and Archer Jones. *How the North Won: A Military History of the Civil War*. Urbana and Chicago, 1991.

Hendricks, George Linton. "Union Army Occupation of the Southern Seaboard, 1861–1865." Ph.D. diss., Columbia University, 1954.

Higginson, Mary Thatcher. *Thomas Wentworth Higginson: The Story of His Life*. Boston and New York, 1914; reprint, New York, 1971.

Hilliard, Sam Bowers. *Atlas of Antebellum Southern Agriculture*. Baton Rouge, 1984.

Johns, John. *Florida During the Civil War*. Gainesville, Fla., 1963.

Mackey, Robert R. *The Uncivil War: Irregular Warfare in the Upper South, 1861–1865*. Norman, Okla., 2004.

McPherson, James M. *Battle Cry of Freedom: The Civil War Era*. New York and Oxford, 1988.

———. *The Negro's Civil War: How American Negroes Felt and Acted During the War for the Union*. New York, 1967.

Martin, Richard A. "Defeat in Victory: Yankee Experience in Early Civil War Jacksonville." *Florida Historical Quarterly*, 53 (1974–75): 1–32.

———, and Daniel L. Schafer. *Jacksonville's Ordeal by Fire: A Civil War History*. Jacksonville, Fla., 1984.

Masur, Kate. "'A Rare Phenomenon of Philological Vegetation': The Word 'Contraband' and the Meanings of Emancipation in the United States." *Journal of American History*, 93 (2007): 1050–84.

Maxwell, William Q. *Lincoln's Fifth Wheel: The Political History of the United States Sanitary Commission*. New York, 1956.

Meier, Michael T. "Lorenzo Thomas and the Recruitment of Blacks in the Mississippi Valley, 1863–1865." In John David Smith, ed., *Black Soldiers in Blue: African-American Troops in the Civil War Era* (Chapel Hill, N.C., and London, 2002), 249–75.

Meyer, Howard N. *Colonel of the Black Regiment: The Life of Thomas Wentworth Higginson*. New York, 1967.

Miers, Earl Schenck, ed. *Lincoln Day by Day: A Chronology, 1809–1865*. Washington, 1960.

Miller, Edward A., Jr. *Lincoln's Abolitionist General: The Biography of David Hunter*. Columbia, S.C., 1997.

Mohr, Clarence L. *On the Threshold of Freedom: Masters and Slaves in Civil War Georgia*. Athens, Ga., and London, 1986.

Moore, Albert Burton. *Conscription and Conflict in the Confederacy*. New York, 1924; reprint, Columbia, S.C., 1996.

Morrison, Michael A. *Slavery and the American West: The Eclipse of Manifest Destiny and the Coming of the Civil War*. Chapel Hill, N.C., and London, 1997.

Nulty, William H. *Confederate Florida: The Road to Olustee*. Tuscaloosa, Ala., 1990.

Oates, Stephen B. *To Purge This Land with Blood: A Biography of John Brown*. New York, 1970.

Ochiai, Akiko. *Harvesting Freedom: African American Agrarianism in Civil War Era South Carolina*. Westport, Conn., 2004.

Otto, John Solomon. *Southern Agriculture During the Civil War Era, 1860–1880*. Westport, Conn., 1994.

Poole, W. Scott. "Memory and the Abolitionist Heritage: Thomas Wentworth Higginson and the Uncertain Meaning of the Civil War." *Civil War History*, 51 (2005): 202–17.

Potter, David M. *The Impending Crisis, 1848–1861*. New York, 1976.

Proctor, Samuel. "Jacksonville During the Civil War." *Florida Historical Quarterly*, 41 (1962–63): 343–55.

Quarles, Benjamin. *Lincoln and the Negro*. New York, 1962.

———. *The Negro in the Civil War*. Boston, 1953; reprint, New York, 1989.

Ramsdell, Charles W. *Behind the Lines in the Southern Confederacy*. Baton Rouge, 1944; reprint, Baton Rouge, 1997.

Revels, Tracy J. *Grander in Her Daughters: Florida's Women During the Civil War*. Columbia, S.C., 2004.

Richards, Leonard L. *The Slave Power: The Free North and Southern Domination*. Baton Rouge, 2000.

Rivers, Larry Eugene. *Slavery in Florida: Territorial Days to Emancipation*. Gainesville, Fla., 2000.

Robbins, Gerald. "The Recruitment and Arming of Negroes in the South Carolina Sea Islands—1862–1865." *Negro History Bulletin*, 28 (1965): 150–51, 163–67.

Rose, Willie Lee. *Rehearsal for Reconstruction: The Port Royal Experiment*. Indianapolis, 1964; reprint, Athens, Ga., and London, 1999.

Rossbach, Jeffery. *Ambivalent Conspirators: John Brown, the Secret Six, and a Theory of Slave Violence*. Philadelphia, 1982.

Saville, Julie. *The Work of Reconstruction: From Slave to Wage Laborer in South Carolina, 1860–1870*. Cambridge, U.K., 1994.

Schafer, Daniel L. *Anna Madgigine Jai Kingsley: African Princess, Florida Slave, Plantation Slaveowner*. Gainesville, Fla., and other cities, 2003.

———. "Freedom Was as Close as the River: The Blacks of Northeast Florida and the Civil War." In *Civil War Times in St. Augustine* (Port Salerno, Fla., 1998), 91–116.

Schmidt, Lewis G. *The Civil War in Florida: A Military History*. 4 vols. Allentown, Pa., 1991.

Shofner, Jerrell H. "Andrew Johnson and the Fernandina Unionists." *Prologue*, 10 (1978): 211–23.

———. *Nor Is It Over Yet: Florida in the Era of Reconstruction, 1863–1877*. Gainesville, Fla., 1974.

Smith, George Winston. "Carpetbag Imperialism in Florida, 1862–1868." *Florida Historical Quarterly*, 27 (1948–49): 99–130, 260–99.

Smith, Julia Floyd. *Slavery and Plantation Growth in Antebellum Florida, 1821–1860*. Gainesville, Fla., 1973.

Stampp, Kenneth M. *The Peculiar Institution: Slavery in the Ante-Bellum South*. New York, 1956.

Stewart, James Brewer. *Holy Warriors: The Abolitionists and American Slavery*. New York, 1996.

Thomas, Dean S. *Cannons: An Introduction to Civil War Artillery*. Gettysburg, Pa., 1985.

Trowbridge-Miller, Cheryl. "Charles Tyler Trowbridge." www.lwfaam.net/cwdata/ctt_bio .htm.

Trudeau, Noah Andre. *Like Men of War: Black Troops in the Civil War, 1862–1865*. Boston and other cities, 1998.

Warner, Ezra J. *Generals in Blue: Lives of the Union Commanders*. Baton Rouge, 1964.

Wells, Anna Mary. *Dear Preceptor: The Life and Times of Thomas Wentworth Higginson*. Boston, 1963.

Westwood, Howard C. "Generals David Hunter and Rufus Saxton and Black Soldiers." *South Carolina Historical Magazine*, 86 (1985): 16–81.

Wiley, Bell Irvin. *Southern Negroes, 1861–1865*. New Haven, Conn., 1938; reprint, New Haven, Conn., and London, 1965.

Williams, George W. *A History of the Negro Troops in the War of the Rebellion, 1861–1865*. New York, 1888.

Wilson, Keith P. *Campfires of Freedom: The Camp Life of Black Soldiers During the Civil War*. Kent, Ohio, 2002.

———. "In the Shadow of John Brown: The Military Service of Colonels Thomas Higginson, James Montgomery, and Robert Shaw in the Department of the South." In John David Smith, ed., *Black Soldiers in Blue: African-American Troops in the Civil War Era* (Chapel Hill, N.C., and London, 2002), 306–35.

Wise, Stephen R. *Gate of Hell: Campaign for Charleston Harbor, 1863*. Columbia, S.C., 1994.

INDEX

Page numbers in *italics* refer to illustrations.

ABOUT THE AUTHOR

Stephen V. Ash was born in California in 1948 and attended high school and college in Pennsylvania. He earned his M.A. and Ph.D. at the University of Tennessee and since 1995 has been a faculty member in the history department there. His teaching and writing focus on the Civil War, Reconstruction, and Tennessee history. This is his ninth book. He and his wife, Jean, live in Knoxville, Tennessee.